DONT TREAD ON ME

Essays on How the Media and Congress Plan to Destroy our Republic
and Condition our Youth for World Service through Sex Education,
Drug Education, Violent Videos, Religion, Music, and Corporate Wars

DONT TREAD ON ME

Essays on How the Media and Congress Plan to Destroy our Republic and Condition our Youth for World Service through Sex Education, Drug Education, Violent Videos, Religion, Music, and Corporate Wars

JEAN GLADWYN

Mill City Press, Inc.
212 3rd Avenue North, Suite 290
Minneapolis, MN 55401
612.455.2294
www.millcitypublishing.com

ISBN - 978-1-936400-31-7
ISBN - 1-936400-31-6
LCCN - 2010933774

Cover Design and Typeset by James Arneson

Printed in the United States of America

Table Of Contents

INTRODUCTION

Who would have thought that I, the very shyest of young teens, would have become an activist grandmother, so impassioned about the future of America that I was willing to sacrifice three decades of my life collecting data, listening to and calling radio talk shows and C-SPAN, reading, going to township meetings, Harrisburg, Washington, DC, and even to conferences in Utah?

Well, I did, and I hope to convey what I have learned over the years in the very simplest language so that the readers can have a rudimentary knowledge of what is happening around us and why.

I must confess that I had a dad – a wonderful dad – who was the pillar of the community. He had the ability to influence politicians and to make or break a judge, just by his words and works.

Did I listen to the words of wisdom from this man? Sadly, not all of the time, because teens think that everything is going to be okay. Now I wish that he were around so that I could say, "Dad, what a fool I was to listen half-heartedly to your political knowledge." My dad was in a business which had nothing to do with politics, and he liked it that way, because he saw with very perceptive eyes the corruption growing before him. He loved America and was really sickened by what he saw.

When he entered a room, everyone knew that he was a take-charge man, and they expected him to solve their problems. At the same time, his jokes were fall-down funny.

In South Philadelphia, I grew up with mostly poor Italians, Irish, Greeks, Jews, Syrians, Blacks, and Chinese. We were truly a melting pot; we all respected each other and got along, and I remember my dad calling out to a young Italian boy or Black boy, "What are you doing out alone at this hour of the night? Go home." And they went home.

It was the "village" Hillary Clinton wrote about in *It Takes a Village*. The major difference being that at that time, everyone knew everyone else. Today, in that village she refers to, there are child molesters, crack addicts, prostitutes, and some very nice poor people held hostage in their homes because of the crimes. Hillary lives in a mansion, thanks to politics, and has a nice health plan; I dare her to revisit the place in which I grew up. It's no longer a village, Hillary, thanks to corrupt politicians. "Give 'em food stamps and projects, and keep 'em dumb."

When I was ten years old, my parents took me from a South Philadelphia environment to a private Catholic school where they hoped that I would meet other children who spoke without a South Philly accent. I might add that my family spoke well, and so did most of those with whom I grew up. Today, with government meddling in education, I'm sorry to say, the youth have been dumbed down appreciably, in more ways than one.

At this private school, I saw prejudice at its worst. I was one of two Italians in the class, the other girl being much darker than I. Many days she cried because they treated her like a "wop" (without papers).

I was invited to a birthday party, and she was not. My parents said that if she couldn't go, neither could I. Turned out birthday girl's dad was in the same business as ours, and suddenly Yolanda was invited. Funny thing is that Yolanda's father was a butcher who owned his own cattle, and could have bought the whole school and then some. Incidentally, the nuns taunted her as well.

It doesn't end. At thirteen, I was sent to a public school on the mainline. Unfortunately, I missed their seventh and eighth grades, and started in the ninth. No one knew me. I was treated as though I had been dropped from another planet. To top it off, I didn't wear the standard chartreuse tops and navy skirts. And no designer clothes at that.

Oh well, there I was, eating lunch alone in a cafeteria that held 2,000 people. Also, because of the fact that I had come from a Catholic school with straight A's, the head of curriculum decided to place me in Section B, since "Catholics over-rate their pupils." News to me. The other tragedy was that I had never had Latin or lacrosse.

Needless to say, I was bullied by the ditzy cheerleader types, and the fools who go along to get along.

I never succumbed to the green and navy outfits, but my clothing was okay. But oh, how I was ridiculed for not knowing lacrosse, and not answering Latin questions quickly enough. And none of the cowardly teachers who knew all about the bullying, stepped in to help me. The parents, after all, were rich, and many were socialites. Hardly in the same category as South Philadelphians. The judges, the doctors, the builders, the lawyers, the writers, the workers with special talents, the teachers and the nurses we generated meant nothing to these "very special people."

I never told my dad what I went through, but I did confide in an older brother who marched me off to the incomparable Leary's book store and, over the summer, caught me up in Latin so that I received a summa cum laude award. If I had told my dad, he would have made someone at the top know that his daughter's pain was palpable, and that no one in the school had the sense to do anything about it. (Just like today!)

As time went on, I learned that it is very difficult to be "different." Italian was synonymous with Mafia. It didn't matter that one has to be Sicilian to be in the Mafia -- Frank Sinatra, Perry Como, Dean Martin.

The only good thing that happened to me was that the boys liked me, probably because I wasn't a barracuda like the girls who never learned to say "no." At that time, it was very scary for a boy to test his manhood, and I wasn't about to test my womanhood with a strict dad who told all of us that "any disgrace to the family meant a couple of broken legs." None of us had any reason to doubt his word – plus, my mother would have finished us off.

Finally, in my sophomore year, I developed casual friendships and became a very strong-willed teen. I no longer ate alone and I knew how to play lacrosse.

Best of all, our college prep reviews were held with all groups – A, B, and C. When the chemistry teacher asked questions – even though I knew all of the answers – I didn't raise my hand. I couldn't believe that the A group couldn't answer. But it paid off when I was one of two girls who got into the U. of P. Some "socialites" had to attend a Junior College first. And just for the record, I was popular at Penn.

Thirty years later I got a chance to say "I gotcha!" when I attended a meeting on the mainline having to do with politics.

One of the men at the meeting mentioned the name of the cheer-leader – now a respected and rich society matron. Apparently she was on the board of a committee he chaired. "Oh, I know her. She's the girl who just couldn't say no." The gentleman was duly shocked, and I had done something I would never have done had she not tortured me for two years! Revenge is sweet. And the only weapon was my words.

After I was graduated from Penn I married an Iranian surgeon and we learned that his family was as strict as mine. Unlike the lies that you hear daily on TV and radio, the "72 virgins" is merely a description of heaven inherent in all religions. Moslems bleed and cry just as we do, and it's nasty to say that Moslems want to die in order to meet 72 virgins. This propa-ganda is meant to dehumanize a whole group of people, just as the Nazis did to the Jews. Apparently in 2010 in America, it's okay to blaspheme anyone who disagrees with you. The news media is totally and ruthless-ly controlled by a wealthy few who view the rest of us as their lap-dogs, meant to die for anything the corporate fascists deem important.

I lost my husband to pulmonary fibrosis when he was still young. At the time he came to America in the late '50s, the U. of P. had a subsidiary school in Tehran; tens of thousands of Iranians were western-educated. And the Shah, until Kissinger, sold us oil for fifteen dollars a barrel.

Long story short, when it was time for our children to go to school, we chose a private school in Philadelphia – a school at which Latin, French, and lacrosse were taught!

We were satisfied for a while, until the headmistress called for a mothers' meeting. It was at this meeting that we were told that the "Human Devel-opment Program" (sex education) would include "values."

My antennae went up and I asked, "Whose values? I feel that values are the responsibility of parents." One of the parents who dared not speak because she had been involved in this battle in Catholic schools with her older children – came up to me after the meeting and said, "Bless you for catching on." She sent valuable material to me on the plan to "Simo-nize" children and I subsequently learned that parents all across America felt exactly like me. Even Phyllis Schlafly at the Heritage Foundation had written exposés on the goings on in the classroom. The secret was kept well because the media is no longer the investigator of news but the reporter of selective material and controlled opposition.

Time passed, and one day my child came home to tell me that she was told in one of her classes to continually repeat four-letter words written on the blackboard. It was gratuitous cursing, not something I particularly spent hard-earned dollars for classroom consumption. Regular words like "damn" and the rest, to my knowledge were used in anger – not in a classroom of nine-year-olds. Also these words were heard on the street; I didn't need the Human Development teacher to expand this gratuitous cursing into a prolific library of the worst words one can hear. Knowing full well that this lesson was meant to de-sensitize children, I went to the school anyway.

I was told – as the teacher's guide suggests – "You are the only one." As though I would back off after my school experiences with these sorry excuses for teachers. Sheltered windbags like Hillary Clinton.

Not wanting to cause further problems, I went home and called a mom or two who lived near this teacher. I learned that she was married to a prominent Philadelphia attorney and that she was on boards. They didn't say "college boards." And that their young daughter pulled a Britney Spears (no underwear) in the middle of a heavily trafficked street. I mention this to let you know that these sickos have no clue as to the damage their reckless views cause. Their children, too, are helpless victims.

A few weeks later we were invited to see "The Mating Habits of the Herring Gulls" – a video our children were to view. So far, so good.

Except that a few days later, my child came home with, "Oh, you should see the terrible films we saw today." Apparently the films were switched.

When I went to the school this time, I received some help from a wonderful person with a conscience who worked at the school. A guardian angel. An anonymous note naming the films and where I could view them. I was told that "questions involving family life, sexual knowledge and intimate questions were interspersed in exams from the lower grades all the way up to high school." For instance, a biology test would have four questions pertaining to the subject matter, and then – "Do you tell your parents everything?"

I went to Planned Parenthood to get the two films which I told them would be used by my student nurses.

When my husband and I viewed them, we were shocked at the pornography.

I then waited for the next mothers' meeting and asked the headmistress and her assistant, "By the way, did our children see the 'Mating Habits of the Herring Gulls'?" Parents laughed at me, thinking it was a foolish question. But when I looked at "Aggie," the headmistress, she knew that the game was up. At first, she hesitated because she didn't know how much I knew. "Well, actually, no." To that, the parents – some of them on the Board, jumped to their feet in anger. "What?" I asked if we could view the film, and the answer was – as they are told to say in the teacher's guide – "It's in transit."

Subsequently, I asked privately if I might show the films at school. "No."

Later, letters went out to 300 parents and they saw the films in the auditorium after I informed the Board that I would show the films at the local YMCA if necessary.

Needless to say, the Chestnut Hill Newspaper did not think that the meeting was "newsworthy." (Too many big names on the Board?) I learned a lot about freedom of speech. Freedom belongs to the wealthy.

I later learned that a doctor was planted in the meeting to contest my husband's introductory comments about cursing in the operating room not being allowed when he was the surgeon, and that he wanted our children to learn physiology and anatomy, but not in a titillating, cavalier sexual presentation.

The other doctor who stated that he cursed in his operating room just came off as someone who had no respect for the patient.

Three wonderful parents and I worked tirelessly on the research required to inform parents about the status of this program. Some parents, not directly connected with our children's classes, were afraid to speak out fearing repercussions on their children. Well, we thought of that too, but the damage to your child is far greater when you say nothing. The child knows that his parents are impotent, robotic, yes-men.

I knew that I'd have to place my children in another school, and I did. The price we paid was at the college entrance level when I learned that the human development teacher at the private school was on several COLLEGE BOARDS! And she remembered our names.

I will never forget what my husband said: "Don't worry; if we can't get in the front door, we'll get in the back." And we did. For us, the price of drugs and sex and perversion was too great a price to pay for entrance to a university we might have liked. That's the determination each of us has to make. But you pay now or later with children who turn into strangers.

The films were "Achieving Sexual Maturity" and "About Sex."

BEHAVIORAL POISON

There were two programs at my children's school which really raised my suspicion – the social studies, "Man: A Course of Study" (MACOS), and the "Human Development Program" – a nice name for sex education and pornography. It is also called by other names, usually using the title "Family."

Both of these programs were piloted into this so-called prestigious school in the mid-seventies by Jean Harris, the headmistress there, just before we enrolled.

I heard that Harris had already started the situational ethics process: "Do whatever makes you feel good." You know, "parents are out of it; they really don't fit into today's social climate."

With her credentials, no one questioned her ability to turn out well-educated pupils. But the programs were left to the new headmistress whom I will call "Aggie." It was she who spoke to us about the new program, sex ed, but nothing about MACOS.

Meantime, Jean Harris was on her way to another prestigious school where she met Dr. Herman Tarnower of Scarsdale Diet fame. Unfortunately, the good doctor must have agreed with "do whatever makes you feel good," and he cheated on her. Wrong thing to do when the tables are turned! Ms. Harris managed to make the front page when she shot and killed the poor man. Tsk. Tsk. He was only trying to do what pleased him. So much for these women who have mastered the English language and can use impressive phrases like "Kafkaesque", and who then try to wield unspeakable crimes against society – children, no less. Their look is ultra-conservative; their demeanor austere. No one dares question their motivation or sincerity unless you happen to be raised in a poor neighborhood as I was, and then get transferred to a school in the main line where you actually meet these extremely wealthy women – I think that we used to call them the "debu-tramps." And for their information, the poor of my time may not have spoken the king's English, but we had more class than all of these people put together.

First: "Man: A Course of Study." U.S. Representative John Conlan of Arizona introduced Bill 4108 in the House Science and Technology Committee in 1976. "No funds authorized under Section One should be available either directly or indirectly for further development or implementation of 'Man: A Course of Study (MACOS)' or for concepts or activities related thereto." The amendment failed. But this is what Congressman John Rarick of Louisiana added to the introduction:

Financed with tax dollars, the National Science Foundation is pushing the equivalent of cultural heroin; social change education packages exposing 10-year-old minds to adultery, cannibalism, indifference to human life, and One World Government – plus profit for insiders. Sexual social engineering by experts in psychological warfare is being financed at taxpayers' expense by grants from the National Science Foundation.

More than $6.5 million in public money has been paid out over the past ten years to a group of social experimenters to bankroll their work in "re-educating" American grade school children. The program known as 'Man: A Course of Study' (MACOS) was developed and promoted with your money.

Jerome Brunner, godfather of MACOS, developed the radical program with NSF grants totaling $4,797,380 while he was director of the Center for Cognitive Studies at Harvard University in the early 1960s. Brunner, who served as Eisenhower's chief of psychological warfare during WW II, has now directed his considerable talent for mind-manipulation at American 5th-graders in their social studies curriculum.

In studying human civilization through MACOS, school children are exposed to such various 'human characteristics' as adultery, bestiality, cannibalism, incest, infanticide, murder, revenge, robbery, wife-swapping, and sexual promiscuity. Additionally, the 5th graders are taught to 'empathize' with these characteristics as exhibited in the culture of the Netsilik Eskimos.

This small, isolated tribe of Canadian Eskimos, no more than 150 in the entire world, are used as the only example of human development by MACOS instructors.

Studies of lower animal groups, such as baboons and salmon, are also used by teachers to compare with modern human culture.

Brunner's brainchild was turned down by 50 publishers in the early 1960s as 'sub-standard' and 'too costly' before the NSF got into the act. NSF grants were used, not only to develop MACOS, but to persuade school systems to purchase the program and to train teachers to apply the change-agent techniques. NSF grants to assist in an aggressive private promotion and marketing of MACOS have cost taxpayers $2,166,900 since 1969 [to 1975].

Curriculum Development Associates, Inc. of Washington, D.C., whose president was former Secretary of Labor Willard Wirtz, peddled MACOS for profit and a big chunk of that profit came from the government. A 'sweetheart' contract between the government and MACOS peddlers cheated the taxpayers out of 80% of the royalty revenue from commercial sales of the program.

Instead of receiving the full 15% commission the government is entitled to, because MACOS was developed with public money, the taxpayers got only 3% on the dollar. The money instead went into the pockets of Curriculum Development.

Since 1963, 1,700 schools in 470 school districts in 47 states subjected their children to MACOS indoctrination. The expensive program, including 16 sexually explicit and violent films, 26 booklets, filmstrips, records, photomurals and teaching aids, cost schools $3000 for each 30-student classroom. Student materials were $8.95 per set.

In January, NSF officials announced 19 social studies grants to market and implement MACOS at a cost totaling $697,000. Your taxes were used to promote the sale of a private 'educational course of study' across the country.

The State of Louisiana had eleven schools in Baton Rouge teaching MACOS ideology. Teachers were trained for the social engineering mission at all-black Southern University during four-week, closed-door indoctrination sessions. Both the teaching center at Southern and the teacher-training sessions were paid for through two NSF grants to the university.

At the super-secret teacher seminars, local educators were instructed by MACOS operatives to 'draw students out' about their home and family life, arguments between their parents, social habits, etc., using the same techniques employed by professional investigators. The information from the students was used in classroom discussions of home life. Children were encouraged to take notes about their parents' private behavior and to report on them to their teachers.

Efforts by National Science Foundation personnel to block any Congressional investigation of MACOS was described by an NSF insider as 'nothing short of criminal.'

Not only does the whole MACOS rip-off smack heavily of 1984, it smells particularly odorous of inside manipulation of public money for private gain.

National Science Foundation grants were originated to prepare our youth for building a stronger national defense. They have now been subverted and are being used against American nationalism." (Cong. John R. Rarick, 4/75)

The following is Congressman John Conlan's address before the House:

My office and others have been inundated with outraged complaints from parents nationwide about the National Science Foundation (NSF) spending more than $7 million to promote and market a social studies course for 10-year-olds called 'Man: A Course of Study' (MACOS).

I share their indignation. My amendment is designed to re-assert congressional authority over NSF curriculum activities to stop what is shaping up as an insidious attempt to impose particular school courses and approaches to learning on local school districts – using the power and financial resources of the federal government to set up a network of educator lobbyists to control education throughout America

Congress needs to stop this, and to tightly review NSF curriculum implementation activities. This is especially vital in light of the revelation that when the MACOS issue came up in committee last month, as late as March 6 of this year, neither NSF Director Guyford Stever nor any top officials of the education staff there had reviewed any of the MACOS materials or knew what was in the course, despite a 12-year NSF involvement in developing or marketing the course at taxpayers' expense.

Mr. Chairman, MACOS materials are full of references to adultery, cannibalism, killing female babies and old people, trial marriage and wife-swapping, violent murder, and other abhorrent behavior of the virtually extinct Netsilik Eskimo sub-culture the children study.

Communal living, elimination of the weak and elderly in society, sexual permissiveness and promiscuity, violence and other revolting behaviors are recurring MACOS themes.

This is simply not the kind of material Congress or any federal agency should be promoting and marketing with taxpayers' money.

The course was designed by a team of experimental psychologists under Jerome S. Brunner and B. F. Skinner to mold children's social attitudes and beliefs along lines that set them apart and alienate them from the beliefs and moral values of their parents and local communities.

This aim of MACOS is blatantly spelled out in the course's philosophical and behavioral manifesto – a teacher's book of essays called 'Man: A Course of Study Seminars for Teachers.'

In this MACOS book there is a call for a radical break from traditional loyalties from self-avowed French Marxist Claude Levi-Strauss: 'Ours is the only society from which we have to disentangle ourselves.'

There is a justification for using children's lack of awareness and immaturity to shape new values: 'Infant plasticity and prolonged immaturity provide us as humans with the opportunity to shape the development of our offspring, and in this sense "humanness" is a continuous human invention.' (Levi-Strauss)

And there is a call by behavioral psychologist B. F. Skinner to use lower grade classrooms for conditioning to mold a new generation of Americans toward a repudiation of traditional values, behavior, and patriotic beliefs:

Education is the establishing of behavior which will be of advantage to the individual and to others at some future time. . . . Reinforcements are arranged by the educational agency for the purpose of conditioning. (Levi-Strauss)

These revealing paragraphs from the teacher's philosophical introduction to MACOS all come together in a lengthy essay on human aggression – a central theme of this social studies course for 10-year-olds. This is the new world society envisioned by an elite group of scholars who have developed and promoted MACOS and similar school materials with the generous funding from the National Science Foundation.

There are . . . a few societies where men seem to find no pleasure in dominating over, hurting or killing the members of other societies, where all they ask is to be at peace and to be left at peace. These societies are, of course, small, weak, technologically backward, and living in inaccessible counties; only so they could survive the power-seeking of their uninhibited neighbors. . . .

What seems to me the most significant common traits in these peaceful societies are that they all manifest enormous gusto for concrete physical pleasures – eating, drinking, sex, laughter – and that they all make very little distinction between the ideal characters of men and women, particularly that they have no ideal of brave, aggressive masculinity. . . .

It seems possible that the youth international, which has developed nearly the whole world over, in the last generation has inarticulately sensed the necessity to re-define the concepts of a 'real man' and a 'true woman' if we are not to destroy ourselves completely. . . ." (NSF plans for our children. Imagine blaming 'youth international,' the victims of Nazi brain-washing, for sensing the need to re-define the concepts of a 'real man' and a 'real woman'! And to these psycho babblers, a real man is a cannibalistic, murdering, incestuous, wife-swapping, killer-of-females, Netsilik Eskimo!)

Wars and the unconscionable war-profiteers have re-defined youth who serve these corporate robber barons, and now the schools are aiming for younger victims, K-12, in order to re-mold precious children for a hopeless and decadent future so that the few can indulge themselves with six thousand dollar shower curtains because "Johnny Can't Read." (Author's comments).

Curriculum Development Associates (CDA), a small commercial publishing firm in Washington, published MACOS. Deals were made so that MACOS could undercut competition. Remember that 50 professional publishers had turned this material down.

This means that NSF had given millions to a small group of closely related individuals in order to enable them to turn a profit and virtually force an undesirable curriculum on parents and educators across the country.

Mr. Chairman, NSF and Education Development Center are now embarking on a further multi-million dollar effort, unknown to Congress, to establish a larger educator network to implement other jointly developed social studies programs. Congress must stop this insidious invasion of local autonomy in education which it can do with this amendment.

Their prospectus outlined establishment of a network that would initially create and then sustain linkage between existing educational institutions to disseminate certain social studies courses for use from kindergarten through 12th grade (Prospectus PES 75-01635, grant approved by NSF.)

I cannot imagine a more dangerous plan for a federally-backed takeover of American education.

No child should be subjected to situational ethics by a classroom teacher whose job it is to teach skills which will enable them to read, write, and compute. A teacher's job is not to engage a young child in "to steal or not to steal." Nor is it his or her job to go long with a 9th grader's literature text by Ginn Company, imposing crude language on a child's psyche: (Book Three) – "Real coy, boy. She's crazy for it. Just crazy. Real crazy hungry chick, yeah." P. 7: "All right already, Jesus."

It goes on and on until the child is brought down to the lowest common denominator. The point is to neutralize everyone.

In President Clinton's school plan - Goals 2000 – Doug Bandow writes about the historic change in education with "national" rather than state standards. National standards will measure a student's performance in "art" – not just math and reading and English, but "art" and attitudinal questions.

The National Council for Geographic Education circulated this philosophy: "The most obvious purpose to learn geography is practical. But," contends the Council, "there are also existential and ethical reasons for doing so, since geography helps students understand where they are both literally and figuratively" and "gives a sound basis for assessing new technologies and implications of their use for the environment and culture."

Lest you mistakenly think that geography should be limited to, well, geography, the Council observes: "The power and beauty of geography lies in seeing, understanding and appreciating the web of relationships between people, places and environments." The subject is a broadly integrative subject bridging the humanities and the physical and social sciences.

As a result, the council wants to essentially take over the teaching of economics, international relations, military history, political science and sociology. For instance, the council proposes as one of the subject's core elements comparing "maps of voting patterns, ethnicity and congressional districts to make inferences about the distribution of political power in a state." Students should suggest reasons "why many industrial jobs have been exported to other countries."

"Fourth graders tend to ethnocentricity due to an inability to understand and appreciate other cultures," the council warns.

One could easily discern where these councils are taking our children. These faceless, unknown councils hide behind their secret agendas and no one knows who they are or how they got there.

Obviously fourth graders should not be solving international problems before they fully understand their own American culture.

Nothing was broken and nothing had to be fixed. We need parents who insist on civics, geography, phonics, math, and English and science. They're the subjects which made America envied and we don't need secret tribunals dictating what kids should learn.

On 1/24/06 third graders in Evesham, New Jersey had to watch a film showing "two mommies." Of course, we also have an abundance of books for children on this subject.

I say it's too much too soon, and we have to stop assaulting and experimenting with children. And it has nothing to do with homophobia. It's about giving children time to ponder the grass if they so wish.

Jean Smith, representing the Evesham School District, was on a morning talk show – 1/25/06 (Would that we could hear these type of shows instead of hours of media propaganda.)

She admitted that notices were sent out to parents in September informing them that their children would be viewing some films on "Family Life." And "oh, yes, it was an oversight not to mention the fact that they would be seeing a family involved in same sex marriage. But hindsight is 20/20."

Ms. Smith acted very authoritatively – shades of "Aggie" twenty-eight years ago, just before she was fired – telling the audiences that "IT IS A FEDERAL mandate for our Family Life Curriculum, and I don't know what the commotion is all about now. We thought that the film was needed so that children with two same-sex parents would not be bullied." A parent-caller asked whether or not children who are raised in abusive families get coverage – meaning that the video is selective about its choice of problems.

"Director" of the curriculum, Deborah Chesnoff, told the host that the film was actually meant for "kindergarten through third."

I'm happy that parents are awakening to the rape of our children in the name of stopping bullying. Un-mandate the mandate!

I was bullied, and it made me stronger. These films are not about "bullying" or we wouldn't have tragedies like the one in Columbine. It's about creating an atmosphere of confusion about traditional values, destroying God-centered families, and about turning out children who don't know right from wrong.

Any parent who thinks that the school is acting in the interest of the family should think again. It's about seed grants from foundations such as Rockefeller, Ford, Xerox, etc. Then federal funds are used to further the "mandates" from these behind-the scenes enforcers whose hidden agenda is "re-educating" the youth.

It's up to you to get the mandates and these councils out of your children's lives, and spend our local money on physical education and woodshop. No more "federal" mandates for drug education and sex-education. If it can't be done, we have to get rid of the freeloaders in Washington, D.C. and those in our local and state governments.

There are still a lot of good citizens who could fill these positions – many who have lost their jobs to outsourcing.

We're not allowed to hear from concerned people since our airwaves have been taken over.

Computerized databases, compiling information on every child's attitude, also have to be eliminated. Robots for the New World Order are out.

It's a tragedy that no one in Congress, including Ted Kennedy, Arlen Specter, and John McCain – three senators who have warmed their seats for decades – didn't pick up on this rape of our children. Kennedy and Bush were involved with No Child Left Behind; Clinton and Kennedy set forth Goals 2000. They're shameless bureaucrats taking us into the New World Order.

I hope that this chapter in particular reveals to you the pain I feel when I witness politicians who have lived in luxury at the expense of children, still profiting from lobbyists. They've become so powerful that our phone calls don't matter.

On 4/23/09 I watched Charlie Rose on WHYY interviewing two guests: Brent Scowcroft, former national security advisor to Bush, Sr., and Carlos Pascual (Brookings Institute). I felt that this show captured the disdain I feel for men and women who pose as intellectuals and get away with murder. So I had to add this program to this chapter, "Behavioral Poison."

Scowcroft: "We need to develop the ability to cooperate outside our borders and learn their ways. We're the only country that can galvanize the world. Our foreign policy is no longer acceptable to the world. Obama is changing this by talking to our adversaries. China owns our debt. We're the ones who are the recipients of all of China's goods. They own our treasury."

Pascual: "U.S. participation is critical in climate change. But we cannot do it alone; hence the G20 Conference." (paraphrased)

Rose: "Well, do you think that President Obama can handle this?"

Pascual: "Ha, ha, ha. Yes. He's used to Goldman Sachs and the others, and so is Michelle. And Rahm Emanuel, ha, ha, ha. Rahm's comment about 'getting involved in education,' ha, ha, ha, 'because kids are only cursing at a fourth grade level.' Ha, ha, ha."

All laughed. Ugly, ugly, purveyors of evil. And the rest of us are not allowed to speak.

No wonder our framers wanted the Posse Comitatus, a group of able-bodied men to fight for our rights, our borders. No military! And hyphenated American groups have led the charge to slavery and world service for American children and the rest of us.

Please don't let the words of these former courageous congressmen go unheeded. Congressman John Conlan suggested that we assert congressional authority over the National Science Foundation's curriculum activities, which he labeled as an "insidious attempt to impose particular school courses on children." Unfortunately, these congressmen were from the '70s. Today, we see no shining light to defend anything, merely a bunch of festering boils in the halls of the Capitol building, and they must go if we are to bring our country back.

Consequently, the programs being foisted on our children have grown into Charter Schools and other venues created in 'community'-type programs – under the tutelage of people like Rahm Emanuel and other fools in high places. It's not bad enough that foundations like Rockefeller, Xerox, and Ford brought sex and drug education into our schools. Now the Bill Gates' Foundation jumped aboard in an attempt to dumb down America's children with labor-style interaction, preparing students for 'service' jobs. Remember, Gates is the man who asked Congress to take in more foreign graduates because Americans are not qualified.

I watched C-SPAN 2 (4/28/09) air the programs started in 66 states by a bunch of young men – Richard Barth, Jonah Edelman, and Jay Mathews. The schools are called KIP (Knowledge is Power).

Well, I want to know <u>what</u> knowledge? What are they teaching children? Why must uncertified people be trained to teach, by community groups – in Chicago. Who signed off on these so-called schools and at what price? Who is Mike Feinberg? Who gave him the right to sign off on the Education and Innovation Act (Jay Randolph)? Are these students being taught how to be submissive to a New World Order takeover – that the United States is just one of 122 countries? What are the backgrounds of these CEOs? If they are anything like the CEO (organizer) from Chicago whom I heard on NPR, we're sliding into hell. Do they pledge the flag or ever hear about the greatness of America or are they being trained for "youth groups", "volunteers", etc.? Is this why Pennsylvania Governor Rendell wants to 'consolidate' schools so that parents can't address problems in their local areas unless they travel to wherever governors send them? If so, why are we paying $7000 a pupil to educate children in public schools? Why do property taxes get higher and higher? Why can't <u>all</u> schools be good? Why don't we get rid of teachers' unions? Finally, who of these men selects the history books, math and science books, and why is there no public knowledge of what's going on?

As for freedom of speech, why can't ordinary people express opinions on our airwaves? Why do we have to pretend that this is okay? Why should David Duke or a Catholic Bishop be shunned because they're Holocaust deniers? Aren't Americans intimidated into denying the Palestinian Holocaust? Is there legislation jailing Palestinian Holocaust deniers? Why must Americans pretend that we are free when all of us – except for Fox loonies – know that Israel uses our troops in war after war in the Mideast, Central Asia, Africa, etc.? When Dick Morris, Chris Wallace, Geraldo, Huckabee, and a parade of Christian and Jewish Zionists who have taken over the airwaves act as though their opinions are written in stone, why can't this be addressed? When Moslems are called the worst names by creeps like Michael Medved and scores of American-hijackers, why can't Americans say that Hitler did the same thing to the Jews that our media is doing to the Moslems?

Since when must we join the Nazis in the media, in lockstep, whenever they defend what the ruthless CIA does and has done in countries all over the world? Why must we hear from Jews only when talking about foreign policy? The 'untouchables' have taken over schools, culture and our money. When…when does it stop??? So far, only people of Jewish descent are chosen to run the unconstitutional Federal Reserve, the World Bank, and the International Monetary Fund. If they're so good in economics, why the hell is America in such a mess?

It just so happens that I can answer the last question. Bernie Madoff is a perfect example. He "used" people. When these banker types hear that South Africa has diamonds – they're there – and the South African people be damned. They hear that there are three trillion barrels of oil under the Caspian Sea – and they're there – of course with help from alcoholic dufusses like George W. and the masses of corrupt politicians who help and support puppets that we install all over – wherever money can be made. Banks are used to launder drug money or hide accounts or to buy assets of foreign countries. They think they are unconquerable because of wealth. Well, they're wrong. They've messed with religion and education – two things that made America great. These money meisters may have no allegiance to any country except Israel, but in the interim, our youth culture lives with violence, homelessness, working parents, and no skills. I feel that they've underestimated the youth – hence, we hear sad stories from the returning Iraqi vets – against the war. The young vets learned that they've killed people like themselves – out of jobs, hungry, hopeless.

And then what? There will be no place to run or hide, until we start America again – under the Rule of Law, and oust the 'vipers' who have hijacked America.

Should we punish subordinates in the CIA who acted on torture policy of the higher ups? Definitely, yes! If someone told me to waterboard a victim like me, I'd say – wa-wa-wa-wait a minute…I'm taking our country back! Besides, it's against the International Torture Convention. (Article 2: "No one can use the excuse 'I was told to do it.'")

It's insulting and a crime that the media calls "news" Arlen Specter's switch to the Democratic Party. Specter should have retired twenty years ago. He's useless.

We were reminded (CBS, 4/29/09) of the holocaust once again, now that the "treacherous" Iranian Ahmadinejad – who hasn't bombed anyone – said that 57 countries hate America and Israel. All 57 nations know who runs America.

Meantime, there are 27 exceptions to the Posse Comitatus Act, which Congress passed incrementally so that troops (military) could be sent to Alabama after ten people were killed. I wonder just how many Americans are even taught about the Posse Comitatus. But you can bet that they see pictures of the very old man (on a stretcher) accused of being a gas-chamber operator in World War II. John Demjanjuk came to the United States in 1951 and became a U.S. citizen in 1958. Even though this retired autoworker from Cleveland was extradited to Israel and 'cleared' by the Soviets who believed that he was not the man from Treblinka, the torture continues. So for 30 years our Department of Justice's Nazi-hunting Office of Special Investigation (OSI), started in 1979, continues to go after this man. Since the OSI was started, 61 ex-Nazis have been stripped of U.S. citizenship and 49 have been "removed." OSI has 250 persons under watch…probably all Americans who mistakingly believe that this is America and who dare to call talk radio or maybe read a book on World War II.

I'm certain that Mr. Demjanjuk would rather be dead, but he's kept alive as an example. It's tyranny. Madmen have hijacked America, and the only one I can remember who even mentioned Demjanjuk was Pat Buchanan. And he was crucified, like President Carter, for even questioning der leaders!

Mark Levin, one of the pro-Israeli sycophants, criticized Tony Bennett for saying that he admired President Obama – "Tony Bennett and his wig. He's a very, very, stupid man. The glue for his wig must have gone to his brain." (4/29/09) Wow! Levin is still worried that the President may not bomb Iran even though Obama has broadened the war! Levin wants lock-step! Yesterday! Don't keep the new Prime Minister of Israel waiting. Netanyahu needs our military backing. NOW!

Even Mel Gibson is still under fire for his religious film. Imagine, Jon Meacham, editor of Newsweek, took a swipe at Mel Gibson for getting a divorce, 'after claiming strict adherence to the Bible.' I wonder…are any Americans safe from Nazi scrutiny?

Whenever anyone criticizes Israel or Jewish actions, we get the familiar "we were the first to discover polio vaccine, etc." Well, I'd like to give some of their firsts: many Jews who came to this country were the first 'to dress down' at a formal gathering where traditional Americans wore tuxedos. They were the first to wear no jackets when forecasting the weather on TV, at a salary of $750,000 – until the public found it unacceptable. They were the first to curse, talk filth, and thumb their noses in comedy. And how about their World War II songs: "I'm a Yankee Doodle Dandy" (or did they mean 'dooby'?) and "Over Here, Over There – oh, the yanks are comin'." Between their movies, such as "House on 92nd Street" and the jingoistic songs – young Americans were leaving home and ready to fight in a foreign war, which many Americans were against because they didn't wish to get involved in a war they felt was provoked.

By the way, in Webster's New World Dictionary, "a jingo is a person who boasts of his patriotism and favors an aggressive, threatening, warlike foreign policy; a 'chauvinist.' And what is a chauvinist? …a person unreasonably devoted to his own race, sex, etc., and contemptuous of other races….certainly not an American value.

To continue: they were the first to introduce sex education to five-year-olds. Behavioral psychology was thrown in along with drug education. Maury Povitch and Jerry Springer were the first to profit from the exploitation of uneducated, promiscuous men and women. Bouncers and fighting allowed. Let's not forget People's Court with their influence on defendants: Judge Judy, "Want to know when a teenager is lying? His lips are moving." Judge Pirro: "Oh, it's okay to work in an adult bookstore" (when a plaintiff was trying to express the fact that a mother of a small child could seek other work). Both of these women are in a position to influence a lot of people; neither one should be making the obscene salaries they enjoy. Judge Judy insults witnesses beyond decency. Don't be slow on your feet, or she'll slam you with "do you think that you could ever be as smart as me?" It's I, Judy; it's I.

Howard Stern was the first shock jock to change American culture, although others tried it. Now, we have a copycat in Philadelphia who is posing nude for magazines and influencing listeners with his "young" talk – Michael Smerconish. Mr. Smerconish doesn't understand: kids don't become scum because they've reached eighteen; their parents raised them that way. Conversely, 18-year-olds who were raised badly might have had a chance. This invasion by dirt-mongers is the work of the moneymakers who exploit the weak.

I would like the efforts of Messrs. Teller, Oppenheimer and Enrico Fermi to be put into cancer research rather than in hydrogen bombs killing victims of corporate greed all over the world.

Whenever I view the genocide in Gaza, Lebanon, and wherever land and oil take you, I think of the intelligent victims who might have contributed cures for cancer and other wondrous things. And Palestinians were very bright people. Their lives have been changed by Israelis and cruel American Jews and Christians who dare to tell us that they are fighting for democracy and our freedom! Shame on you cowards! I'd rather scrub floors than wear a military uniform with a UN cap and change the souls of millions of people who have seen their fathers, mothers, aunts, uncles and loved ones die before their eyes. They will never, ever be the same. Even now, the hijackers are pushing their surrogates, Hillary and the rest of Obama's appointees, "to place more restrictions on Iran."

Who gives a damn about your polio vaccine; other people would have done it. No group has a monopoly on brains.

The father of an Israeli soldier, Gilad Shalit, who was captured by Hamas during the recent strikes on Gaza, is coming to the United States to talk to President Obama and Hillary, hoping that they will make the release of his son contingent upon the peace process! Imagine! Eleven thousand Palestinian prisoners in Israel, plus thousands bulldozed by the viper, Sharon, are not equal to one Israeli. We all know that there will never be a two-state solution, so why does the Nazi media continue to pretend.

I resent the fact that President Obama thinks that "change" means young, new. Apparently he thinks that the older people are out of the picture…that Americans want new music, new morals, and new laws. He's wrong.

Etta James, as a matter of respect, should have sung <u>her</u> song at the Inauguration – not Beyonce. When the First Lady went to meet the Queen of England, she should not have worn a cardigan. What's next – bathing suits? Remember, these people are <u>representing</u> America, not its owners. Donald Trump always wears a jacket because he respects himself and his audience. America is about class, not showing off the fact that a personal trainer is working on your arms. They don't get it!

Miss California's opinion on gay marriage brought out our congressional geezers, eating at the taxpayers' trough. More hate crimes legislation – not because they feel that Miss California was wrong – but because they want to stifle speech. Race and gay are good dividers. (4/30/09)

Talk show host Michael Smerconish was telling Suzy Welsh, a guest on his show (4/09) that his mother 'was upset' when she heard that he posed nude for Philadelphia Magazine's May '09 issue. I went to Barnes and Noble to take a look at the chutzpah of the photo, which I couldn't believe. He must have mentioned the word "ass" ten times while talking to Mrs. Welsh. Well, I got three reactions from the picture: 'eeeewwww,' 'yuk,' 'what nerve!' With a body like that I would wear monk's clothing. It's nightmare time. Michael Callahan of Philadelphia Magazine called Smerconish 'powerful.' Callahan must be another troubled dude with serious issues – or should I say 'tissues'?

Character is set by age five or six. A mother already knows by then whether or not her child is a bully or a compassionate person with principles. Parents like me and my parents instilled good qualities in our children, as did millions of other parents. And, of course, friends follow suit when their parents are not firm enough. Role models count.

Nobody ever made me do something I knew was wrong. As you have read in the Introduction, I spent a lot of time at school, alone, because I didn't go along. I didn't want popularity at a price of hurting someone's feelings. Nor would I "make out" to impress girls for whom I had no respect. And, I'm oh, so happy that I never succumbed to stupidity.

I hope that those of you who care what happens to America, keep yourselves apprised of current events. Arlen Specter – big in the news – was once the defense attorney for Ira Einhorn, one of the founders of Earth Day (whom the press never mentions). It so happened that Mr. Einhorn killed his girlfriend and put her body in a closet trunk until the odor gave him away. Since his bail was set low, Mr. Einhorn escaped to Europe and was not caught until recently. The murder was committed in 1981. If Mr. Specter had represented the Unabomber, another environmental whacko – who knows – maybe the Unabomber might have killed more victims.

Senator Kit Bond (on Fox News, 5/3/09): "What are we going to do with the Guantanamo detainees? We want to be safe." I'd like to put at least three detainees in each congressman's home to prevent them from ever coming back to the Capitol. Then, I'd like to put the source of <u>all</u> of our problems, the Congress, in Guantanamo, listening to loud music. We just gave $2.1 billion to Pakistan, while Americans are desperate. Congressman Adam Smith wants to send <u>more</u> money. Are you ready to switch the detainees?

Millions of young people feel like Miss California, but they are not allowed to speak. The so-called gay judge, who asked her that loaded question, shouldn't have been on that panel to begin with. The whole farce was created in order to destroy the religious aspect of marriage; civil marriage isn't enough. They'd like a few changes here and there in the Bible in order to bring it up to date. After all, these are different times. Maybe secular humanism or no absolutes would be more appropriate.

If the Iranians want to replace Ahmadinejad, let them do it. Let's not send in CIA from Israel and the United States (partnership) to provoke the Iranians into hating America. When Ahmadinejad made that statement about Israel's cruelty, he must have been mad as hell. The Iranians are the recipients, like the Palestinians, Syrians, Egyptians, etc., of our intervention. The things he says in anger are a result of what his people have endured, and Iran will never be the same.

Anyone who wants to hear <u>real</u> hate should have listened to C-SPAN when AIPAC (Israel Lobby) was on. 5/4/09 Congresswoman Jane Harmon (D-Calif.) is supposedly working for us, except that most of her time is spent on 'what's best for Israel.' She's the one who was caught on tape trying to reduce the sentences of two Israeli espionage agents, if the lobby could get her 'a seat on the House Intelligence Committee.' (Hmmmm. Wonder why? There was no follow-up to this crime.) Attorney General Gonzales put the kibosh on any investigation because she backed his wiretapping of American citizens. (Bush) And now, these hijackers are getting Jeb Bush in line for president in 2012!

At the AIPAC meeting though, she said that she was <u>against</u> wiretapping, probably because she was caught. If she weren't involved in treasonous business, she wouldn't be for wiretapping on grounds that it is <u>illegal</u>.

At any rate, I got to see close up what treasonous ghouls look like: Congresswoman Jane Harmon (D-Calif.), Dan Senor (CFR), James Woolsey (CIA director under Clinton, 1993-95), Major General Ido Nechustan (Israel), Robert Satloff (Mideast Committee).

SUBJECT: IRAN

BRIEFLY

Harmon:	'Our' goal is to have a limited view and to rev up sanctions against Iran. Military option is on the table!"
Senor:	"What is motivating other countries not to side with America?"
Satloff:	"We need to be tough with China; we need to go to Russia. Turn this spigot tight." (Money from Iran cannot be invested in U.S.)
Harmon:	"There are many different populations in Iran; it is good to separate those factions. Religious people would like to get rid of Ahmadinejad."
Woolsey:	"We have to break the economic power and that power is oil. Twenty-two states depend on oil. We need to turn that oil to salt." (Applause from huge audience) "We have to destroy the oil monopoly which funds Hezbollah."
Harmon:	"I totally agree."
Satloff:	"Syria has given no sign to go against Iran. Syria relies on Iran for nuclear technology. Fortunately, some of our friends took care of that a few years ago. Ha Ha!" (Great applause)
Woolsey:	"I'm quite concerned about their education regarding World War I and World War II. They feel that World War I was created to break up the Ottoman Empire and that World War II was about arms." (And your point, Woolsey?)
Harmon:	"I made two trips to Israel. I talked to Netanyahu. There is more that the United States can do."
Satloff:	"If we and the Israelis are not on the same page with Iran, we will be on the biggest disagreement with the United States."
Harmon:	"We want to support America's and Israel's values."
Major Gen. Nechustan:	"We had 61 years of independence. We need a strong air force with the help of the United States."

The above guests also brought in Pakistan as a possible threat to Israel. Equipped with nuclear weapons and a growing influential Taliban, Israel will be threatened. Not to worry. President Obama is already on the case. And Senators Kyl and Lieberman have drafted SB908.

CONSPIRACY

Ah, yes, we've all heard the talk show hosts who know next to nothing about anything, laugh at the conspiracy thinkers – "Whackos", "Nuts"!

Well, you decide for yourselves. I'll present a minimum selection of writings exposing the "conspiracy." Remember that when a conspiracy is exposed, it is dismissed by a person or persons working for the very corporate meisters who would prefer that their dirty linen not be exposed, or they would be doing serious time for treason.

Carroll Quigley who wrote <u>Tragedy and Hope</u>, was one of President Clinton's favorite professors at Georgetown, so he said. The book recalled the existence of an international conspiracy of rich elitists plotting a New World Order:

"Their aim is nothing less than to create a world system of financial control in private hands, able to dominate the political system of each country and the economy of the world as a whole." Quigley stated that he had personal knowledge of the conspirators and their plan because he had associated with them for over 20 years. Quigley said that he had been given access to their most secret records and approved of their aims.

The publisher, Macmillan, was forced to withdraw the book and it may be hard to find.

Notice below, the dates on the earlier references to the NWO. One of those records exists in a book published during the '30s by Stanford University Press which confirmed not only the goal, but described the network of collaborators being created to facilitate development of a population which would support the transition, titled <u>International Understanding</u>. The Preface to this volume states: ". . . few persons have appreciated . . . the forcefulness of the agencies which have long been engaged in educating toward international understanding." (By their own accounts, these internationalists have been constructing their NWO since the 1870s.) In the Foreword to this report on their progress, HOW it was being done is clarified:

"The new world [is] now to be built . . . [and] the builder of this new world must be education. . . . in such a task one would have to 'change human nature' . . . [with] patient and gradual reshaping of the public mind . . . to bring their influence to bear on schools, on churches, on literature, on business, on politics . . . the building of the new world has indeed begun. . . ."

International Understanding reveals many of the strategies intended to be used to promote their dreams. It also lists more than fifty educational institutions which had been created prior to 1931 to further this program to alter the public mind, and over 650 scholarships and fellowships created for the same purpose. One of these programs was the Rhodes Scholarship which underwrote Bill Clinton's entry into this elite society of "intellectuals."

Eleanor Roosevelt voiced approval of this proposition in her little book entitled: <u>This Troubled World</u> (1938) in which she echoed the theme: "Our real ultimate objective must be 'a change in human nature.' . . . When we have achieved a . . . majority of the people of this type, then we can hope for success. . . ."

The London Observer of Sunday, 11/27/38, covered a speech by Lord Lothian, the wartime British Ambassador to the United States. It was entitled, "Wings Over History: A New Civilization": "But though few yet realize, the older anarchy of multitudinous national sovereignties is about to dissolve and quickly at that.

". . . world Unity is, of course, at present entirely out of sight. . . . But that the world is going to fall into four or five main political and economic groups, each in great measure self-supporting, each under the leadership of a great state equipped with modern military and air power, at any rate for a time, seems certain. Nothing that we can do can prevent it."

In <u>The Aquarian Conspiracy</u>, Marilyn Ferguson talked about "the hidden pictures in children's magazines. You look at a sketch that appears to be a tree and a pond. Then someone tells you to look at something you had no reason to believe was there. . . . Suddenly you see camouflaged objects. . . . a fish or a pitchfork or a toothbrush. . . . Once you have seen them, they are plainly there. . . ."

Ms. Ferguson claimed to be one of "them" and called it conspiracy, named names, places and groups involved. No one came forward to deny her thesis, for what she wrote is part of today's world. She also claimed that the conspiracy just happened; that it had no leaders. (As a Chinese scientist said after the landing on the moon, and asked if he thought there was a God: "Yes, it would be as unrealistic as saying that the components of a 707 jet just came together." This conversation, I might add, took place after Americans felt God-like after their mission, and bragged about what they 'could do next' on national TV.)

In her book she pulled back the screen of secrecy which obscured the existence of a subculture dedicated to "destruction and re-beginning" – destruction of the established order through a "peaceful" revolution, and beginning of a totally managed and controlled new world order.

Universities today are working in conjunction with foundations and politicians and programming teachers in social science so that they can re-educate the youth.

They have the PPBS (Planning, Programming and Budgeting System) in place which gives them the money and the tools to accomplish their goals.

In the '50s, this scheme would have come to an abrupt halt if the investigation of foundations were allowed to continue. Congress cowardly backed away.

This crisis we are in today, wherein the "few" like George W and his cohorts think that they are gods, is what happens when men lose their souls and their minds.

I hate to think that we will end up with a third world country's fate – having the military protect the corrupt government instead of those who pay their salaries. The Shah of Iran threw out the owners of homes on the Caspian Sea and replaced them with the generals who protected him. When do we wake up?

The farmers are always the first victims of a takeover because they are the backbone of our country. Poverty and hunger make victims of us all.

H. G. Wells, considered by many the mentor of the men of the New World Order, wrote in his book <u>Experiment in Autobiography</u>, Chapter Nine, "The Idea of a Planned world" (p. 557) . . . "It will appear first, I believe, as a conscious organization of intelligent and quite possibly in some cases wealthy men, as a movement having distinct social and political aims, confessedly ignoring most of these aims. It will be very loosely organized in the earlier stages, a mere movement of a number of people in a certain direction with a sort of surprise the common object toward which they are all moving."

"The consent of all the sovereign powers of the world to world pacification is quite unnecessary. Indeed, as I point out . . . three or four powers alone could impose an enduring World Pax." (p. 592)

And in Wells' book, The New World Order, published in 1940, he writes (p. 135) . . . "We can anticipate a rapid transfiguration of the earth as its population is distributed and redistributed in accordance with the shifting requirements of economic production."

"A sturdy and assertive variety of the new young will be needed for the police work of the world." (p. 138)

"It is not unreasonable to anticipate the development of an Ad Hoc Disarmament Police Force which will have its greatest strength in the air. . . . An Ad Hoc disarmament police force with its main strength in the air would necessarily fall into close cooperation with the various other world police activities. . . . Already we have a worldwide network of competent men fighting the white-slave traffic, the drug traffic, and so forth. The thing begins already." (p. 139)

Wells also quotes from Professor William James' book The Moral Equivalent of War (pp. 140-141) . . . "The young will have to do so much service and take so much risk for the general welfare as the World Commonweal requires."

Cecil Rhodes (Confessions of Faith): "We should have a secret society like the Jesuits and buy up all of the newspapers, because they control everything."

In the Unseen Hand (Ralph Epperson), p. 203: "The connection between the music and the purpose of the music was discussed by Dr. Timothy Leary, a professor, the self-proclaimed king of the drug LSD in the sixties: 'The person who says rock 'n roll music encourages kids to take drugs is absolutely right. It's part of our plot . . . drugs are the most efficient way to revolution'. . . ."

A musician, Frank Zappa, the leader of the rock group called Northern Invention, added this incredible statement: "The loud sounds and bright lights of today are tremendous indoctrination tools. Is it possible to modify the human chemical structure with the right combination of frequencies? If the right kind of beat makes you tap your foot – what kind of beat makes you curl your fist and strike?"

Milton Eisenhower, brother of the president, to a UNESCO group at the UN, in February, 1963: "Force and ideas are necessary to create a New World Order. No international power can keep peace without sanctions. The U.S. must be able to impose military sanctions with sacrifice of individual sovereignty to the group." (UNESCO – Education, Scientific and Cultural Organization).

THE POLITICS OF CHANGE

Maureen Heaton, the author of <u>Impossible Dream</u>, was the direct descendant through her mother of John Hart, who signed the Declaration of Independence, and on her father's side, of a refugee from the potato famine in Ireland.

It was after WW II that Maureen became aware of a concerted effort to undermine the Republic.

The late, great Congressman John T. Wood of Idaho called this movement "the greatest subversive plot in history." The movement, of course, is the Politics of Change.

Maureen was an activist in the resistance since 1947. She worked within a political party for many years, doing precinct work and serving on county and state central committees. She owned and operated a bookstore-library and was a ghost writer and eminent researcher.

When I first read her book, I felt a camaraderie, for the goal of my book is the same as hers: education, religion, politics, and the media corruption – all part of the game.

She received a commendation from Congressman John R. Rarick. Truly, Maureen was a giant among women. It's insulting today to hear men ask, "What are women interested in?" We're interested in the same things – the economy, the pervasive corruption. Any woman who believes that women are exempt from politics should start reading.

Bernadine Smith, Helen Somers, Adeline Dropka, Catherine Palfrey Baldwin – all extraordinary women who tried to warn the republic. Heroines of mine. All traveling lecturers. None around today that I can compare them to except maybe for Phyllis Schlafly of Eagle Forum who continues to do an extraordinary job in exposing education failures in the United States.

Of course, there are many, many women who are behind the scenes like Barbara Morris who exposed Change Agents in the Schools. And, hopefully, there will always be those women around to expose corruption.

To say that Hillary is a woman's candidate is comparable to telling us to vote for another corporate lackey, a Mickey Mouse, with no offense to Mickey.

Maureen, a California resident at the time of President Ronald Reagan's Governorship, had been receiving bulletins from the California Council on Intergovernmental Relations (CCIR) since she wanted to testify against Local Government Reform and Regionalism before the governor's Task Force, and she needed the documentation.

After her testimony, the bulletins stopped coming from the Council on Intergovernmental Relations. She then went to her State Senator who managed to get her reinstated, and told those in the office that she would be right over.

They were moving into a larger office and there were boxes everywhere. The Secretary started to open each box and handed Maureen a copy of its content. There was one box which the secretary did not open. When Maureen asked if she could have the minutes of the last meeting, the secretary had to leave the room to get them. It was then that Maureen opened the untouched box and retrieved a copy of "The Politics of Change in Local Government Reform." Obviously, it would have been better if they had just mailed her the material.

This secrecy goes on, even though we have a right to see all materials.

Long story short, Maureen sent a copy of the TPOC to the Board of Supervisors of El Dorado who, in turn, sent a very formal Resolution of displeasure to Governor Reagan.

I will partially recount this Resolution:

"Whereas it has been brought to the attention of this board that a report has been issued by the Institute for Local Self Government <u>asserting the authority of the Governor's office</u>, the Office of Intergovernmental Management, and the council on Intergovernmental Relations, which presents prima facie evidence of a deliberate calculated attempt to mislead, coerce, and inhibit the rights of citizens to determine the need for, the desirability of, and the method to bring about changes in the structure of their local governments; and

"Whereas the 'Summary of Conclusions' in this report states: 'There must be a Climate for Change in order for the restructuring of local governments to occur, whether this restructuring involves drastic reform, reorganization, modernization, or a minor administrative realignment; while the following does not represent an exclusive list, <u>the factors mentioned here are those which most often create such a climate</u>:

    a. collapse of government's ability to provide such needed services.
    b. a crisis of major magnitude;
    c. a catastrophe that has a physical effect on the community;
    d. the corruption of local officials;
    e. the high cost of government and the desire for higher levels of services.'"

The resolution (447-74) of the Board of Supervisors of the county of El Dorado, goes on to say that in the study done by the Board, it was concluded that the Local Government and Counties were meeting all the Standards of Good Government, and that no consolidation or modernizing needed to be done.

It ended with: "Be It Further Resolved that the board of Supervisors of El Dorado County hereby calls on all responsible citizens and officials to be on guard against any such attempt to usurp their rights and privileges." (Signed by Sandra Matthews, Deputy Clerk)

In these "studies" to change local government, they mention "change agents." I've mentioned this in "education" where one or two teachers know the "plan," and the others may not. This method runs through the State Legislatures where one or two may know the program, and the others just go along.

The Politics of Change was written on July 1, 1972 by John C. Houlihan and paid for during the term of Governor Ronald Reagan with a grant of $300,000. For years, Houlihan advocated that we abolish city and county governments, and eventually, states.

Houlihan, former mayor of Oakland, was on parole at the time for "divesting" a widow of her savings. Ronald Reagan granted him a pardon.

This plan in unabridged form has 195 pages, and is a matter of public record. The plan has been around for decades and runs through all of the states.

Not too long ago, a citizen could go before his local township board and ask for a variance for his property. Citizens were invited, and could protest or sanction the variance. Request finished.

Now, there are no longer township meetings; requests are brought to the county level. Because of the distance many times telephone tag has to suffice. The planners would like to have councils of governments (non-representative members) to replace commissioners. This is not representative government, and I blame all of the elected representatives for not reporting to us the travesty taking place without the consent of the governed.

No longer can a commissioner or legislator feign ignorance. By now, they all know about the corruption and takeover of our constitutional government. Local school problems will be handled by the Mayor (city manager) instead of a superintendent.;

Perhaps Congressman Charles Lindberg (father of the renowned aviator) could lend some clarity to this assault on our government which we face today. In his book, <u>The Economic Pinch</u>, Lindberg said that he had seen an Establishment document which had been distributed to "insiders" before the turn of the 20th Century, in which the long-range plans for this revolution were described. Lindberg stated that the planning included specifically the removal of private rights to property, because, the document pointed out, "people without homes will not quarrel with their leaders. If those 'leaders' have control of all property through central planning, they can decide who shall have homes, and who shall not – and this controls opposition."

All of us can see that our property taxes are now based on the sale price of our homes Who can guarantee that we can get that sale price determined by a board of unaccountable men and women – men and women taking more and more of our money because of wild spending?

There are no more Charles Lindbergs, Senator Malones, Raricks, etc. to look out for us. The dumbed down educational system has left us with the old and corrupt politicians we see teetering out of Congress and the younger know-nothing doofuses we elect because we have no choice. It has got to change, and we can do it. It should be "end times" for the lobbyists and foundations who give to these treasonous rots for their lucrative campaigns.

In the first Occasional Paper of the Rockefeller General Education Board, objectives were given to achieve world domination by the few:

1. Eradication of historical religious concepts; (already happened);
2. A world organization to bring influence to bear universally (U.N.);
3. Elimination of 'artificial' political boundaries; (NAFTA, no borders with Mexico and Canada);
4. Selected – not elected – officials; (we still have a chance to vote the representatives out as a warning to the newly-elected);
5. Amalgamation of races, in a greatly reduced population; (genocide in Africa, Mideast; refugees fleeing to new land so that no affinity remains in the past. The planners want every country neutralized so that loyalty is placed only with the new masters who control employment.);
6. Control of transportation, communication, education, money, and agriculture; (they have already destroyed farms with high personal and death taxes);
7. A management system to control such a massive undertaking. (Planning committees can institute grants to attain zoning changes, urban development profits, etc.). The Office of Management and Budgeting or Planning, Programming, Budgeting System (PPBS) now controls the spending of our tax dollars. Taxpayers have become more or less figureheads, and it happened, step by step. (Fabian Socialism)

The only objective left out was the gun control directive, but they're working on it.

Our Second Amendment gives us the right to bear arms – against a corrupt government. Those who want to confiscate all guns are not doing it to save lives, but to protect an oppressive government.

PEOPLE IN THE NEWS

<u>Senator John McCain</u> (R. Arizona). In case you were thinking of voting for this war hero, let me fill you in on his past record in Congress.

McCain is always in the news, and one would think that having suffered at the hands of the North Vietnamese, he would have some compassion for the rest of us. Not so.

Mr. McCain would like open borders so that his corporate friends could get cheap labor and a fighting force to protect their overseas assets. And since Congress knows from the last election in 2006 that the public is not in favor of the Iraq war – they voted out the hawkish incumbents – he can use the votes of the illegals. Illegals can now get a voter-registration card when they apply for a driver's license – no questions asked. Never mind that illegals are mutilating the cattle and threatening homeowners in his state, you'll never hear the Senator say "patrol the border." He's happy with his illegal constituency.

Also, when Charles Keating, Jr., an Arizona developer and financier admitted in April 1987 that he had spent eleven million dollars to reverse a federal regulation he didn't like, no one in Washington was surprised. But when Keating acknowledged contributing $1.5 million to five U.S. Senators, and then declared that he had bought their loyalty, jaws dropped. Keating was Chairman of American Continental Corporation, parent company of Lincoln Savings and Loan, no longer in operation. The five senators asked the Federal Regulators to overturn the rule which limited investment options Keating could make.

The five Senators were Alan Cranston, Democrat from California; John Glenn, our beloved astronaut, Democrat from Ohio; John McCain,

Republican from Arizona; Donald Riegler, Democrat from Michigan; and Dennis DeConcini, Democrat from Arizona.

Covering depositors' insured losses cost the taxpayers $2.3 billion. (David Hess, Philadelphia Inquirer, Washington Bureau)

<u>Newt Gingrich</u>, former speaker of the House and constant guest on Sean Hannity's radio show and Fox News, also wants to run for President of the U.S. Newt is an avid warhawk whose chief goal for us is to protect our ally, Israel. Could this blind loyalty to Israel be a result of his third wife's appointment as vice president of the Israeli Export Development Co. whose investors include a number of American business people such as CBS president Laurence Tisch, clothing magnate Sy Syms, and real estate developer, Robert V. Tishman?

Marianne Gingrich had no previous experience in trade promotion, but was hired at an undisclosed salary to help recruit businesses for a free-trade zone in Israel.

The company is a private, high-tech business park where companies will be able to operate free of most taxes and government bureaucracies.

Before this, Mrs. Gingrich worked as a County government "planner" and then in the personnel office of the Secret Service in Washington.

Hisham Sharabi, chairman of the Center for Policy Analysis in Palestine, said, "Had she not been the Speaker's wife, it's not very likely she'd be where she is now" (Philadelphia Inquirer, Susan Baer, Baltimore Sun, 2/5/95).

As though the preceding shenanigans were not enough for a wannabe candidate for President of the United States, Mr. Gingrich, President Bill Clinton, Senator Dole, and Secretary of the Treasury Rubin (under Clinton), conspired to use American taxpayer funds to bail out Wall Street bankers on soured loans to Mexico that should never have been made in the first place. We had to borrow $800 billion from foreigners to cover our federal debt at a cost of $50 billion a year in interest costs that we taxpayers must pay. We lost 1,500,000 jobs as of 1995 and over $30 billion in lost tax revenue (4/15/95, Gus Stelzer, retired automobile industry executive, The Herald).

Incidentally, Rubin previously worked for Goldman Sachs, the very same financial institution making the bad investments.

On hearing that President Ford spoke to Bob Woodward on the Iraq war (7/28/04) and stated that "we can't be going hellfire and damnation all over the globe killing people unless it concerns our national security,"

Gingrich responded, "He (Ford) didn't see 9/11. What do you do when jihadists who hate you have nuclear weapons? Besides, a reporter (De Frank) for the New York Daily News had a different view" (Fox News also owns the New York Daily News). Gingrich profits when the war machine thrives, just as Vice President Cheney thrives when his Halliburton friends do well. War also keeps domestic issues off the table.

<u>Oliver North</u>. "Five years ago today (1984) Lt. Col. Oliver North was furiously stuffing top-secret documents into a shredder. The next day, the nation began to learn what North tried to hide.

"The White House was running a highly profitable weapons-smuggling ring. President Reagan was selling arms to Iran, violating his own solemn vows by ransoming U.S. hostages with missiles.

"His national security officers had skimmed millions in profits from the sales. They siphoned some of the swag to the Nicaraguan contras, secretly financing the rebels in defiance of Congress and the Constitution.

"Today, thanks to a pretty successful cover-up and an impenetrable shield of official secrecy, no one knows the full story of the Iran-Contra scandal. No one has been jailed for the crimes – the lies under oath, and the theft of government funds.

"Oliver North was convicted on three felony counts in May 1989. Convictions were overturned in part. The White House and the CIA put as many obstacles in place as they could. The White House made secret pacts with Manuel Antonio Noriega, the head of the drug cartel." (Source: U.S. District Court Records, Philadelphia Iinquirer, Tim Weiner, 11/24/91)

What a joke when the "useful idiots" Lenin talked about admonish the masses: "Conspiracy thinkers actually believe that our government could pull off a 9/11." How stupid can you get?

Oliver North was given the honor of "War Stories" on Fox News. After all, he did draft a plan to impose martial law in the United States (1984). The secret plan called for suspension of the Constitution, turning control of government over to FEMA (The Federal Emergency Management Agency) (Philadelphia Inquirer, 7/5/85). We all know what an excellent job FEMA did recently (2006) in Katrina, where the situation is still in disaster mode.

<u>G. Gordon Liddy</u>. Another neo con rewarded with a talk show after serving time in jail during the Nixon era. His talk is all about war and more war. On trying to bolster the careers of the armed forces: "Don't give up on

armed services. The posse comitatus was formed for different reasons. You are there to kill people and blow things up." (C-SPAN 7/5/99) Also, "how to shoot government agents: the head, the head." (The Book on Bush: Viking www.progressreport.org).

The posse comitatus to which Mr. Liddy referred is the revolutionary right, under the Constitution, to overthrow a corrupt government when it becomes too oppressive. President Lincoln referred to this clause and pointed out that we should throw the rascals out, bodily, who were perverting our Constitution; but not destroy our form of government which was based upon the laws of God. The legal mechanism for accomplishing this was well understood by our forefathers as the Posse Comitatus and was candidly referred to in the Federalist Papers. The energizing power behind the legitimate posse (consisting of all able-bodied citizens of good repute, above the age of 18) is the Grand Jury which directs prosecution, etc. of those allegedly committing wrong deeds. The jury decides the facts of the case and whether the law is lawful. Of course, those who have been interested in perverting our constitution are anxious that we not know our constitutional background so that we might be rendered impotent in stopping their excesses. (See U.S. Codes 18-2381 through 2385, regarding sedition and treason; and U.S. Codes 13-241 and 242, regarding conspiracy against rights of citizens under color of law.) In "The Terror Conspiracy," Jim Marrs details the Posse Comitatus Act of 1878.

This lack of knowledge about the rights of citizens is to blame for the recent property rights incursions. Case in point, a developer in South Carolina threatened a property owner with confiscation of his $800,000 property if he didn't give it over to the developer. Long story short, an attorney, Dina Berliner, from the Institute of Justice, had to intervene on the side of the property owner.

I'd like to know why we pay county engineers and code meisters when they have come to represent the developers. No longer can we go to our local government representatives, because it has been taken out of their jurisdiction.

Bill O'Reilly, the "fair and balanced" talk show host goes after anyone criticizing the corrupt and secretive Bush administration with vengeance. Secret energy meetings. Secret oil meetings. Never talked about.

But just be a Moslem, and you are a target of his wrath. Or you can be an American professor who gives both sides of a story, and look out. Bill and his often-guest, the raging Zionist lunatic, David Horowitz, are going to get you. Both of them act as judge, jury, and executioner. Both have become the arbiters of free speech. O'Reilly and Horowitz went after a Middle-Eastern professor whom they accused of sending donations to the Hamas. Heaven forbid! Only the U.S., Great Britain, and Israel can attack and kill people. How does anyone defend himself or his people! Well, Mr. O'Reilly and friends went after the Virginia professor until his life wasn't worth a dime. Meantime, I'd like to know to which organizations Mr. Horowitz contributes, especially with his undisclosed background. And since when, in America, are students not "allowed" to hear both sides of a story?

But I shouldn't be surprised. Mr. O'Reilly, not the brightest bulb on the tree – or he wouldn't have that job – criticized President Carter for his new book: <u>Palestine: Peace, Not Apartheid</u>. In this book President Carter addresses the injustice we have repeated on the Palestinians with our one-sided dealings.

<u>Michael Savage</u>. 8/3/06. Guest was the Evangelical looney making mega bucks for selling out his country, John Hagee. Hagee is the pastor of the Cornerstone Church in San Antonio, Texas, who has become the voice for the warhawks. Ranting about the "end days" and the building of Solomon's Temple, he draws quite a crowd.

Believe it or not, there are over twenty million followers who believe this contrived folklore. By their adherence to this belief, they are allowing a major genocide to take place in Palestine, Lebanon, and Iraq. And I know that the churches who teach this "end times" garbage tell their audiences not to get involved in politics because God is taking care of things. It must be Satan that they serve, for they have totally forgotten the Commandment "Thou shalt not kill," and "My Kingdom is not of this world." From experience, I can tell you that these well-dressed adults go to church but couldn't tell you whether or not their children are making bombs in the garage. No wonder teens get violent with "stoops" like this for parents. No respect because they don't deserve respect. What kind of God condones slaughter?

Needless to say, Savage treated this evil man royally; Hagee played right into the warhawk-host's hands. One can only guess what Savage really thought about this excuse for a man; or it seems to me that Mr. Savage would join such a holy man's congregation forthwith.

If Hagee had any respect for humanity, he would never appear on a show which daily dehumanizes Moslems: "terrorists should have nukes in their butts and dropped from planes." Or "Kill the vermin. Bomb the Sunni Triangle, and bring the boys home. Senator Durbin should be tried for sedition for comparing Guantanamo to Nazis. Do you think we should call these Islamic cockroaches 'militants'?" (10/8/04)

He said about the sick man from India who shot at a Jewish Center: "This piece of human offal should have his limbs cut off" (7/31/06).

Savage also has said that all gays should get sick and die, and was fired from MSNBC. (Eric Alderman)

After the anti-war protest that took place on Saturday, January 28, 2006, Savage demeaned Tim Robbins for speaking against Bush and characterized a woman there as "jealous because people have more money, better looks, etc., than she. These people come out of their potholes." (1/29/06)

This is the way people like Savage – who think that freedom of speech belongs to the wealthy – feel about us. Their air time permits them to call those who disagree "cockroaches," etc. Worst of all, they use "anti-American" to describe the real patriots.

Could you imagine replacing the word "Moslem" with "Zionist"? How many apologies would be necessary? Retribution after retribution. Endless persecution. Sanctions. Perhaps even reparations!!

These are the people allowed to speak for all of us, because any caller challenging them is subject to the diatribe: "Get off my show, you blah, blah, blah." Any foreigner listening must think that we all feel like this. I resent this terrible injustice. It's tyranny, and Mr. Bush and the sponsors who pay for this endless hate speech are at the center of it.

<u>Lynn Cheney</u>, Vice President's wife. Looks like the pillar of the community, Wonderful mother and grandmother – which I am certain she is; however, on the Wolf Blitzer interview (10/27/06) another side of Mrs. Cheney came through when she was asked about a book she wrote on brothels and lesbian lovers. ("Sisters.")

Admittedly, she was there to talk about Senator Allen of Virginia who made the offensive comment "macaca" when referring to a dark complexioned man. (Of course, Allen lost the election because no one really believed that the Senator "just made it up.")

But, although Mrs. Cheney said that she was not there to discuss herself, it did not stop Wolf from asking her two other personal questions: "In 1988, didn't you write a book about a vice president who died while having sex with a prostitute?" and "Is your husband in favor of torture?"

To say that one can't judge a book by its cover is an understatement. Writing about lesbians and more sex would not be on my list of things to do. But then, I don't approve of Americans going over to fight other people's wars, either.

Former Congressman <u>Jim Greenwood</u>. Mr. Greenwood has been rewarded with a six figure job at the Biotechnology Industry Organization after serving (I love the word "serve") Bucks County in the State legislature and then in the Congress for 24 years.

Back in 1990, Greenwood, a Republican, was one of 32 individuals from across the nation who was "groomed" for leadership in the Council of State Governments, a 1990 Henry Toll Fellowship program, a five-day symposium held in Kentucky. I suppose at this meeting Mr. Greenwood was taught such "difficult" phrases as "sustainable development," "smart growth," "empowerment zones," and "urban renewal" – all subsidy programs for the buddies of the politicians who go along with the program. Subsidized by us, since the politicians have sent all of the good jobs overseas – it's regionalism.

The Council of State Governments (COG) is one of the bellwethers of the 1313 political syndicate which operates as one of the mail order law factories reshaping American legislatures across the country, without our knowledge or consent.

I will discuss 1313 next. For now, I will say that it is a Rockefeller subsidiary which sends "slip bills," pre-written bills, to the legislatures, through the governor's office so that a state legislator could sign his name at the top and propose it as through it were his or her proposal.

The sad thing is that someone like Jim Greenwood, who majored in social work – not rocket science – can determine the future of Americans and brag: "I can make much more money working for companies like Biotech."

Former General <u>Alexander Haig</u>. (Also Secretary of State). Haig was a paid advisor for COSCO (China Oceans Shipping Co.) Formerly an American Naval Base, the new Chinese owners have been accused of smuggling arms to Chinese gangs in the U.S., and smuggling immigrants. This Long Beach property was attained under President Clinton.

Senator <u>Dianne Feinstein</u>, Democrat from California. Dianne's husband, through the Blum Associates firm, is also linked to COSCO. The Senator claims that her husband started the association with COSCO when she was mayor of San Francisco, and made a sister-tie with Shanghai. (Craig Smith, WSJ, 3/26/97).

Michael Smerconish. The Philadelphia talk-show host, who hits listeners on their drive to work with as much pro-war propaganda as he can muster.

Except for host Glenn Beck whom I consider dangerous because of his lack of knowledge on the Mideast, Smerconish has done more to fuel the Iraq war than some others on WPHT. This bully with earphones has called Moslems "dirt-bags" and belittled the torture at Abu Graib. Of course, he's intrigued with Fox's show, "24" with Kiefer Sutherland and an "anti-terror" team: "I wish our government would do that. I love to see torture. I love to see stabbing" (1/15/06)

From the time Rizzo was Mayor of Philadelphia, Smerconish knew how to start his career – following Rizzo's tail as closely as he could without actually being attached. From there he went to HUD and then government-type law.

A Howard Stern wannabe, he uses phrases like "artsy-fartsy," and he was turned down by the Philadelphia Daily News when he asked if he might use the F-bomb in a column he writes – as though it would have added anything to his drivel. Thanks to the Daily News for sparing us.

His other phrase, "dress British; think Yiddish" reveals exactly where this jerk is coming from. His loyalty is to whomever he figures could pay his bills – if it's Israel, so be it. He's done his show from there, and has paid a visit to Germany's death camps so that his audience could relive the holocaust. What gets me is that he has no feeling about sending other Americans out to die for oil – and definitely no feeling about Palestinian families being destroyed by bulldozers.

When? When do these warhawks realize that ALL life is precious? That a Palestinian or Lebanese mother hurts just as deeply as an Israeli or American mother? No one group has a monopoly on grief. Smerconish and the rest of the young talk show hosts are still young enough to enlist, if they feel so strongly as they portend. But I am jaded enough to conclude that their fear-mongering and hype will give them the ticket they need for their children to get nice jobs, at the expense of all. Why else would someone applaud going to a foreign country, killing hundreds of thousands of those people, and then concluding that nothing will happen to America – particularly with our open borders? It's insanity. Our imperialism has cost us the rise of a barrel of oil from fifteen dollars to over 160. War with Iran will raise the cost to two hundred dollars per barrel, with eight dollars per gallon at the tank.

Looks as though no one can stop these little Hitlers from using the same tactics that the Nazis used against the Jews in WW II in order to demean them and make them easier to hate.

The "dirt bags" he refers to, gave us Dr. Avicena, the first Moslem to start the practice of medicine as we know it today. And President Bush should be criticized for doing the things he is doing, charging taxpayers for a secret army of 100,000 men, 20,000 of them in South Carolina being trained. In short, he is outsourcing army jobs to a private contractor, Blackwater, Inc., without advising Congress or the taxpayers. We don't know who these troops are. They could be mercenaries or gang members (CNN, 1/30/06). Obviously, the President thinks that he is King George IV, and the do-nothing Congress looks on.

<u>Franklin Graham</u>. Called Islam "evil." Franklin, who used to shoot at neighbors' bushes, found Jesus when he realized that daddy Billy makes 80 million dollars in the religion racket. Notice that these religious men never try to get their mighty audiences aware of the detriment to their children via school-taught sex education. If they did, they would lose some of the media coverage. So, you just hug the flag, talk about Jesus, forgiveness, sending money over to Africa, sing hallelujah, and RAKE in the dough!

They should read the Koran wherein it says, "Woe to him who hurts children."

<u>Rudy Giuliani</u>. Former Mayor of New York, who went up to a Head of State, Yassir Arafat, and threw him out of a public place – just to please his Jewish constituents. Never mind what it did to America's image. Now he's treated like the second-coming because of his bringing everyone together on 9/11.

He's afraid that if he runs for President of the United States, his former wife Donna Hanover could hurt his chances. How could a woman whose claim to fame was "The Vagina Monologues" hurt him? To me, he's already damaged goods.

<u>Winston Churchill</u>. Hardly a week passes without Churchill's name being mentioned by politicians and the media. They speak of him as a great British statesman. To me he was just another imperialist, like Roosevelt and Stalin, dividing Europe with a cigar and a smile. In his book

<u>The World Crisis</u>, 1911-1914, Winston Churchill wrote: (referring to the fact that Americans would go into war on the side of Great Britain): "It ought to be possible to organize in Canada an American volunteer force amounting to at least a Division (3 regiments and auxiliary groups), which could go into action as such. Nothing will bring American sympathy along with us so much as American blood shed in the field. What is wanted now is that there should be an announcement made that we will accept the services of Americans who come to Canada or England to volunteer; that they will be formed into units in which they can serve together with their friends and comrades; that they will be able to choose their own regimental officers; that the British Government will bear the whole expense of equipment and transportation; and that they shall share in every way the perils and fortunes of our troops.

"I believe there is a source of fighting manhood here of the highest quality, whose very employment would produce beneficial reactions in every direction. The problem is how to set up the rallying flag in Canada and so indicate where those who wish to help us can go to join." (p. 272)

The sinking of the Lusitania in 1915 by a German submarine brought the U.S. into war. But Churchill talked and wrote about American blood being "shed in the field" in 1914. Hence, plans for America were already written in advance.

Roosevelt was right – nothing in politics just happens. It's planned that way.

Churchill got his "rallying flag" – the provocation he needed.

<u>George Will</u>. Sly old codger – for years playing the part of the "conservative" – saying all of the things we like to hear about God and country. In fact, he's a wolf in sheep's clothing whose real self was revealed on the Laura Ingraham show (1/29/06) when talking about war protesters as anti-American:

"Americans are smart; they know that we can't leave Iraq until we finish" (paraphrase). Translation: Americans are stupid, and they'll go along until we've killed more people. We really should kill them all so that we can control the oil and then use our fourteen bases there to control the whole area – Iran, Syria, Lebanon – with our dear ally, Israel. Oh, Israel.

1313

The Public Administration Clearing House (P.A.C.H.) at 1313 E. 60th Street in Chicago was organized under the direction of the Rockefeller family by a socialist named Charles E. Merriam. The purpose of the P.A.C.H. has been to bring all public officials under one system of control.

The Rockefeller family provided 8 million dollars in the thirties to establish this clearing house so that they could control the indoctrination of state-wide public officials, and persuade them as to the direction they ought to pursue, all the while rendering themselves submissive to the consolidated power building up in Washington, D.C.

Merriam authored a book published in 1941 entitled <u>On the Agenda of Democracy</u>. In his book, Merriam defines democracy as communism. He said that revolution was the old way. . . . The new way is education, persuasion, participation, and cooperation. He taught how to achieve communism.

"Fortunately, our Constitution is broad enough in its terms, flexible enough in its spirit, and capable of liberal-enough interpretation by the judiciary to permit the adaptation of democracy to changing conditions without serious difficulty.

"Legislative bodies are incompetent, it may be said, or corrupt or dilatory, or unrepresentative of the general interest of the community.

"The elective process is not favorable to the choice of the leaders in the community." (Charles E. Merriam)

The Advisory Commission on Intergovernmental Relations (A.C.I.R.) was grafted onto the federal government in 1959. Its duty was to draft legislation to be handed to public officials all over the nation. These were called "slip bills." Public officials were thus expected to get whatever was handed to them – passed into law! This made the public officials look like great thinkers to the voters. A.C.I.R. is essentially a law-making factory through which consolidation of all power and control is to be achieved in Washington, D.C.

The governors are also members of the P.A.C.H. and A.C.I.R. Indoctrination and coordination for a "new world order" comes by their attendance at the annual "Governors' Conference." Elections are engineered so that those who cooperate with the desired power and other structured changes being sought to alter American Constitutional government get heavily financed and then moved into key positions of elected office.

During the seventies all local control was moved to the federal level by persuading local and state officials to accept federal revenue sharing funds and to adopt general plans for cities and communities. These must comply with the federal mandates set down for centralized control. Having achieved the objective of acquiring all control over every aspect of American government, including people, land, armed forces, etc., the federal government has devised ways by which it now <u>transfers</u> (what it has formerly consolidated unto itself) to the United Nations through "treaties" which empower the U.N. to have complete control over the NWO government. In the plan is abolishment of states, cities, counties and land ownership. The nation's governors quietly cooperate in the planned arrangement for the dissolution of the very states they were elected to "preserve, protect and defend." State officials are supposed to keep the federal system in check, but they have joined in the subterfuge. (Second Amendment Committee, Hanford, CA 93232)

Mandates require that grants be made initially by the federal government through a foundation, for example. Then, once the "seed" money is planted, the taxpayer gets the full bill. (Ex., drug education and sex education, environmental ed, computer ed. Once Bill Gates places a few computers in the classrooms, we take the indoctrination, maintenance, etc. over).

Apparently, except for the mayor in Hazelton, Pennsylvania, and now one or two others, public officials have not read the Constitution they swear to uphold. Article I, Section 9, says that only the states can regulate immigration. How the ACLU has the chutzpah to get involved in a states' rights action, I do not know.

The dumbed-down electorate is beginning to pay for the corrupt and incompetent legislators we have foolishly re-elected.

As for Merriam's definition of democracy being synonymous with communism, Webster's New World Dictionary defines communism as: ownership of all property by the community; a dictatorship; state planning; suppression of individual liberties; expansionist by military; ruthless suppression of all opposing political parties, and all deviation within the Party.

A republic is government by the people through elected representatives and we have no representatives. The U.S. was a Republic which placed the Supreme Power in the hands of the people, the voters.

Democracy is mob rule and that's what we have in Washington, D.C. right now.

Presidents don't seem to care about what the people want; air waves are controlled; the State is planning our lives and taking over eminent domain.

And read the Communist Manifesto – we have almost completed the list.

If you don't get what's happening now, don't blame the Germans for not knowing.

Just get out your black Mao pajamas and get ready to sweep streets if Hillary, Gore, Gingrich, Romney, Palin and the rest get the nomination for president in 2012.

Just ask yourself what any of them has done for our border to the south? What have any done to stop the secret agenda of regionalism? Nothing on both counts.

REGIONALISM

The Anderson Herald, May 7, 1977, printed a synopsis of regionalism, minus all of the technical information which I believe strikes at the core of the problem facing our country. I will elaborate later, but first this report from Indiana:

"Many people pooh-pooh the idea there is anything sinister about 'regionalism' as it is being established by the federal government.

"Actually, regionalism can become a vehicle that will remove all state and local authority and place our very lives and daily actions under the direction of the federal bureaucrats.

"Today, every state and every part of every state in the Union has been invaded by this monster. The nation has been divided into 10 regions. Indiana is in Region 5 with headquarters in Chicago. Like other states, Indiana is divided into 10 subdivisions.

"The entire apparatus is manned by non-elected officials who say that their task is merely to coordinate federal with state and local programs. That may sound good on the surface, and could even be the original intention. But, as we all know, good intentions combined with certain actions often lead to absolute control by federal authorities.

"Since Federal funding of state and local programs involves state and local compliance with all kinds of federal demands, the power of the regional super-government is far-reaching. So far only a tiny amount of this power has been used – with some staggering effects.

"Such agencies as the Welfare Department are forced to expand under the threat of a federal funds cut-off. Schools, colleges and universities, businesses, police agencies, city councils, state legislatures and many others find themselves dancing to the tune of far-off bureaucrats who were elected by no one, responsible to no one except themselves, and apparently beyond the reach of the President and other elected officials.

"The mighty machinery of regionalism has been used to push land use programs and environmental programs capable of crippling a city's economy. The bureaucrats pull back when local populations and officials fight back. Then, they persistently begin again.

"Regionalism began with U.S. Public Law 90-577, dated Oct. 16., 1968. Critics say that this law destroyed the constitutional principle of separation of powers by yielding to the Executive powers of great scope, involving land use, planning, and transportation. It was supplemented by Executive Order No. 11490 on October 30, 1969, providing for implementation by presidential order, in event of emergency, and of executive orders of previous administrations, by Proclamation No. 4074 and by Executive Order No. 11647 (Nixon's 10 regions).

"Analysts say these edicts have opened the way for dissolution of state and local government and their replacement by centralized rule from Washington through the 10 regions.

"On May 8, 1977, there was a meeting in the House Chambers of Indiana on House Bill 1417. That bill would void federally imposed regional government in Indiana. It would provide for criminal prosecution and permit civil action against any person trying to uphold or enforce federal regional control in Indiana.

"Senate Bill 102, on which Senator Robert Fair refused to call a hearing, was a companion bill in the Senate.

"This transfer of power from elected officials at the local and state level to appointed bureaucrats in Washington must be stopped. The freedoms and rights guaranteed the people by the Constitution must be preserved. It can only be done by the State Legislature. And legislators are reluctant to act unless the voters take action."

Well, since 1977, women like Adeline Dropka, from LaGrange, IL 6025, Maureen Heaton, from Bellingham, Washington, Senator Malone of Nevada and David Horton, legal counsel for Committee to Restore the Constitution have been the town criers for those of us in Pennsylvania who took up the struggle to alert people about regionalism (or Metro-Government).

We used to have town meetings where we could debate; we now have state legislators sending us bulletins on what they are "doing for us." We used to have freedom to talk on radio; now we have talk on just about any trivia you can imagine.

But, the good news is that we still don't have a regional tax in Philadelphia. Legislators were too scared to put their names on a regional tax bill. Others have tried and failed. Pittsburgh has a regional tax and taxpayers have no say over stadium-funding or any other issues. Appointed officials do the thinking for them. They subsidize stadiums with no option to oppose. And this was in 2007. Hopefully, some of you will call your state legislators and tell them what you want. We want meetings! We want changes!

People always want to know how regionalism will affect them. Well, let me give you the "dream of the urban planners," the unelected bureaucrats behind the scenes who are making all of our laws through "clearinghouses" and who supervise us and collect data bases on our children. The following article is by Sue Ellen Christian, Tribune Suburban Affairs Writers, May 8, 1995. Keep in mind that the "planners" have been trying to foist this idea on the public since the 1920s, and have been unsuccessful.:

"Imagine a metropolitan Chicago in which the city and its struggling inner-ring communities got a cut of the tax revenues from new development on the suburban fringes.

"Imagine that all new housing developments in the region had to provide affordable and public housing.

"And imagine that the area's hundreds of political jurisdictions all were subject to statewide regulations aimed at saving open space and redeveloping vacant industrial sites."

Sounds like the Beatles' version of "Imagine there's no heaven. It's easy if you try. No hell below us. Above us only sky. Imagine all the people. Living for today."

If these plans go through, people can live only for today. Savings will be a thing of the past. Workers will work until they drop in order to accommodate all of the people who don't work – illegals, prisoners, families who have one child after another – except that this time the children of welfare recipients will enroll in suburban schools and be supplied with housing, compliments of the taxpayers. This is why the politicians don't have town meetings on real estate taxes. Instead of the property tax break we're promised, there will be an added tax, plus the property tax. The Pennsylvania

State Legislature tried to pass The Homestead Bill, a bill which had seven exceptions, one of them being that "if the population changes and new schools must be built . . . ." Go to your state legislator and ask him to read the bill – many times, he or she hasn't looked at it since its arrival from the 1313 clearinghouse. Fortunately, those of us who read the bill were able to alert the public, but that was in 1999. Today, the public has no access to talk radio or to the content of bills.

Politicians have brought us over-crowding and all of the problems we face today. Now they want to bring their crime-ridden, drug-ridden cities to the suburbs and they have been doing it step-by-step with Section 8 housing. If people don't want to work, subsidize them! Meanwhile, export American jobs to foreign countries like China, who sends us dog food with melamine, killing our pets.

In 1963, regional "visionary" John W. Bodine, also a Rhodes scholar, was quoted: "A massive citizen effort such as we have had in the last twenty-five years in Philadelphia, has two distinct stages, only the second of which brings into play the power elite. They are the indispensable one-hundredth of one percent – they are the public-spirited non-prestigious workers in the civic vineyard, who have the time and patience to study through the vexing questions, to sort out the alternatives to make the solutions they arrive at respectable, and even commonplace, and thus prepare the way to usher in the second stage when the power elite can take over." (Petshek, Kirk R., The Challenge of Urban Reform 1964)

I might add that the "non-prestigious workers" are those politicians (mayors, etc.) who attend classes at the University of Pennsylvania Wharton School in urban planning and regionalism under professors like Ted Hershberg who sells regionalism to those willing to replace our government with a plan destined to cause havoc and destruction. These politicians, many uneducated, are happy to say that they "went to the Wharton School." On their resumes, when one sees Wharton or MIT, it looks good. Actually, they are indoctrinating courses for the mattoids who then go to on to "usher in the second stage when the power elite can take over." Once these lackeys are in office, it's hard to get them out because the power elite needs their loyalty. Example: a Commissioner when voted out moves on to "Director of Transportation."

Article IV, Sect. 3 of the U.S. Constitution: "a state is not to be formed by the junction of two or more states, without the consent of the legislatures of the States concerned and the Congress." Federal regionalism is unconstitutional. Only when two states merge in a compact could the federal government take over, and this is precisely what our elected men and women have done to States Rights. And they took a pledge to uphold the Constitution, which I'm sure they have never read.

President Nixon placed the United States into ten federal regions in 1969, with Executive Order 11647. Through this order, the President became the chief "legislator" of the land. And although the "planners" want us to believe that they are consolidating states in order to save us money and that this idea is new, the concept of the ten regions was laid out in the New York Times Magazine, April 21, 1925.

Governing these ten multi-state regions are ten representatives from major federal agencies, i.e., Department of Transportation, HUD, EPA, Department of Labor, etc. Under this Nixonian policy of "new federalism," these regional offices are given the authority to approve grants and make policy decisions, and add programs for which we taxpayers must pay.

When organized, these tiers of government could employ staffs, establish joint planning agencies for the development of the region – zoning plans, building codes – and submit them to governing bodies to assist local governments. Sixty percent of the members are officials who have been elected to other local offices – mayors, county board members, etc. These federal councils must have local officials on their boards in order to be eligible for state funds. The growth of this "federalism" can be seen by the increase in the number of federal programs for state and local governments. Example: 20 years ago there were less than a few hundred Federal Aid Programs. Today, they have increased to thousands.

The state created the federal government, not the other way around. Under separation of powers, the federal government has its duties; and the states have theirs. The first three articles of the U.S. Constitution spell this out.

As early as 1946 Congress passed the Administrative Procedures Act, PL-79-404. This bill put bureaucracies in business by giving law-making authority to agencies in the executive sector of the federal government. The Federal Register was established. President Clinton, another Rhodes scholar like Bodine, used the Federal Register when he knew that he couldn't get a bill through Congress. The bill is published in the Register; if, in thirty days, no one protests, the bill becomes law. This makes the

President, rather than Congress, a law-maker. Hence, dictator George W. Bush.

Governors can do the same thing. Their counterpart of the Register is the "Pennsylvania Bulletin." And each state has one. Bureaucracies such as the Pennsylvania Department of Community Affairs, get power that was never meant to be in appointed hands. These Regional Councils are created by the Governor.

After a sharp fight, the Senate passed a bill that would, for the first time, set up a <u>nationwide</u> building code aimed at conserving energy in new homes and office buildings. The Department of HUD could now set up codes that were formerly set up by cities and counties, not the federal government.

We all know what the regionalists are doing to property owners. In Ventnor, New Jersey, homeowners were given $22,000 to convert their shore homes into summer rentals, because the houses, 90 years old, were "too old." (These homes were mansions, probably like 200-year-old homes the regionalists own. Except that their homes are not targets of eminent domain.) Bulldozing other homes to make room for assisted-living facilities is another way of getting more taxes. This redevelopment project is good for no one except the politicians who get campaign money from developers and sell voters out for thirty pieces of silver.

The Delaware Valley Regional Planning Commission (DVRPC) was started in Pennsylvania by Governor Shapp in 1965. The boundaries were exactly like those suggested by a regional group, the City Club in 1923. All states have one. (So much for the "new idea" to save us money by consolidating counties and states.)

The Advisory Council on Intergovernmental Relations (ACIR) has a branch in every state. It is a mail-order legislative mill. It prepares legislation to advance policy of the Rockefellers (1313) and others who are financing this "quiet revolution." The local agencies of government, the State Legislatures, then give the programs or statutes a rubber stamp.

Montana and Louisiana have adopted the Newstates Constitution which wipes out the Bill of Rights, no protection of assembly, of press, religion and other guarantees.

Planners are taking away property through the Environmental Protection Agency. They create a panic: losing control of our water, air pollution, polluted rivers. Then developers can exploit the land and pay off politicians.. (They don't mention the fact that corporations are not obliged to reveal dumping policy.)

The next step – "Government must control all property." Hegelian principle of change – Thesis, Antithesis, and Synthesis. Create a problem; arrive at a solution the public would never accept. Then pass a Land Control Bill like the one Senator Udall tried to pass, but was defeated. Last, the former director of the EPA, Russell Train, places the bill in the Federal Register, and after 30 days, the bill becomes the law of the land.

The ACIR is proof of the conspiracy: making laws by unelected planners, which are binding on the public.

These grant-making regional agencies can also subvert local units of government. The LEAA (Law Enforcement Assistance Administration) was involved in using so-called revenue-sharing funds as a means of subverting local police forces because they offer better communications systems or other advantageous purchases with revenue-sharing funds. The LEAA offers special training programs to local police units. These special training programs financed by and for LEAA, have as their objective the merging of the independent police forces of America into a national police force, just as every dictatorship must have a central police force. In America we find the LEAA is being used as a means for bringing together all of the independent police forces under a central control, just as the government is being centralized. As a matter of fact, LEAA funds are also used by local police forces to train as SWAT units. Now, I am sure that you are aware of the real objective of SWAT training. <u>SWAT training is used to put down counter-revolutionaries, that is, people who deplore tyranny and rise against it</u>. SWAT teams don't go into streets with billy clubs, but with armored cars and heavy weapons. This is a counter-revolutionary force. LEAA funds are also used to train the national guard as SWAT units. We are witnessing the transformation of our local police into an instrument of coercion against the people rather than in support of the people.

The question is, are we going to allow the planners to destroy our government and create a dictatorship in the United States under the guise of humanitarianism?

Booklets were sent out in the late sixties and seventies, entitled "Review of Local Government" and "Modernizing Local Government." People in different states elected review committees to discuss how they could "modernize" local government. Without any knowledge of government or of the conspiracy of federal regionalism, citizens met to discuss local government.

Suddenly appearing at these meetings were legal "experts." "Don't worry about your responsibility; I'll help you." The ACIR "helped." The League of Women Voters and State Economy Leagues "helped." The brochure suggested that the best way to improve local government was to merge counties into "planning districts." Surprise! This is how Regional Government planners brought the States into the conspiracy as their own executioners.

The "approved solution" was given to the citizens for their perusal, and their legal counsel-planner told them to sign it. Subsequently, Section 9 of the State Constitutions on Local Government was changed. It became the basis for the State Legislatures to consolidate all of the counties into Planning Districts or Councils of Governments (COGS), which ultimately would destroy our State Legislatures. It made regionalism constitutional.

All of these concepts came from the Advisory Council on Intergovernmental Affairs in Washington, D.C., and were transmitted to the local ACIRs.

Nelson Rockefeller had, in 1966, proposed the organization of the ACIRs. Later, in 1968 or 1969, he persuaded President Nixon to give the ACIR the appearance of law by having Congress give it validity, and it became a quasi-legal organization.

Although the ACIR had many important names on its letterhead – governors, mayors, and even some members of the President's cabinet – most of whom were in jail because of the Watergate Scandal – Lieutenant Col. Archibald Roberts knew that he had to find the origin of real policy behind the ACIR. He found the Brookings Institute, one of seven major policy-making organizations controlled and financed by the Rockefeller dynasty.

In order to get to the origin of the seditious conspiracy, he went to the Library in New York City, one of the largest repositories of reference in the world, and examined the tax-exempt foundations, to determine which of these or combinations of these could create the kind of revolution that we witness happening in America. Proliferation of agency upon agency is effectively destroying local government by creating "change agents" in local government. The apparatus he found was the Rockefeller Foundation.

The Brookings Institution has its apparatus in every major university in the United States. It uses the brains and expertise of the University to condition the students to change the government. The apparatus is a two-way street. First, the injection of socialism and the expression of socialism through the various legislative remedies offered by the ACIR. Then the feedback comes with a question: "How do we change the government of the United States without arousing the people?" Brookings has its feelers into the "think tanks" of the universities, the Rand Corp., and all of the tax-exempt foundations in the United States, who can hire the best brains in the country. Feedback: "The best way to destroy the government of the United States is to <u>use the existing agencies</u> of government to destroy themselves." And of course, that is what we are experiencing.

The agencies helping to destroy the U.S. government are: (aside from the Chamber of Commerce):

1. Social Science Research Council. Conditioning of Americans to accept changes in government.

2. The Russian Institute of Columbia University. Conditions Americans to accept merger of Russia and U.S. The Chase Manhattan Bank (Rockefellers) gave U.S. tax dollars to Russia for the greatest truck factory in the world. Chase Manhattan also funds, with our money, the exploration of gas, oil, potash and other materials, using slave labor, in order to develop these resources for the profit of international bankers.

3. Council on Foreign Relations (CFR). Many have defined this as the secret government of the United States since its more than 1,500 members occupy key positions in the U.S. government. Its membership includes professors, military personalities, industry, banking, mass media.

4. The Public Administration Clearing House of Chicago (1313) brings all public officials into compliance. The 26 agencies are each specifically designed to train particular agents for various levels of government. There is the U.S. Conference of Mayors, and the Governors' Conference. The Governors' Conference meets, not to improve their expertise in dealing with local problems, but to condition State governors for the next step in Federal Regionalism in the new government being prepared for us.

5. Institute of Pacific Relations was investigated by the Senate after WW II. The Senate found that it was a Rockefeller organization, largely responsible for a propaganda climate in America which permitted the creation of a communist government in China. Agrarian reform in China was given publicity in the United States press, due largely to the Institute of Pacific Relations.

Thanks to the Rockefellers and their Institute, we fought a war in Korea against the Chinese communists and lost 45,000 young men.

This is happening in America because we fail to understand the extent of the origin of the conspiracy itself.

Federal Regions:

Region I Capital – Boston: Connecticut, Maine, Mass., New Hampshire, Rhode Island, Vermont.

Region II Capital – New York City: New York, New Jersey, Puerto Rico, Virgin Islands.

Region III Capital – Philadelphia: Delaware, Maryland, Pennsylvania, Virginia, West Virginia, District of Columbia.

Region IV Capital – Atlanta: Alabama, Florida, Georgia, Kentucky, Mississippi, North Carolina, South Carolina, Tennessee.

Region V Capital – Chicago: Illinois, Indiana, Michigan, Minnesota, Ohio, Wisconsin.

Region VI Capital – Dallas-Ft. Worth: Arkansas, Louisiana, New Mexico, Oklahoma, Texas.

Region VII Capital – Kansas City: Iowa, Kansas, Missouri, Nebraska.

Region VIII Capital – Denver: Colorado, Montana, North Dakota, South Dakota, Utah, Wyoming.

Region IX Capital – San Francisco: Arizona, California, Hawaii, Nevada.

Region X Capital – Seattle: Alaska, Oregon, Washington, Idaho.

Sovereign citizens will be reduced to the condition of "human resources"; their lives planned for them by social experimenters; their children molded into "citizens for the 21st Century" through mind-conditioning by "change agents" in the public schools; social values determined by an all-powerful government, under the humanist guidelines of "no absolutes"; business and industry controlled by the "needs of society"; labor under government dictates, with each worker fitted into the slot most beneficial to the "common good" as decided by computers and "manpower development" experts; private property and personal initiative only a dim memory; even the remnant figures of representation managed and controlled by administrative bodies they, themselves, had appointed or approved.

Redevelopment plans are nothing more than plans by city officials to restructure society. Place assisted living homes here and there and, at the same time, the bulldozing of nice properties as took place in Ventnor, New Jersey, to get rid of low-end ethnic groups and replace them with high-end properties for the developers.

In Philadelphia, we have pay-to-play corruption with public land along the waterfront being given to campaign donors – eight acres, no charge – for eleven years. No one disturbs <u>this</u> pay-to-play area.

Then we have the partnership scams. Many investigations; no action.

The Planning, Programming, Budgeting System (PPBS): A student's test scores, expressed in symbols, are computerized to a Regional Data Collection and Processing Center where a student profile is developed. In turn, this information is sent to a multi-state national center (bank) for permanent storage. This process is called different things: Financial Accountability, Management by Objective, Information System, Performance-Based Education. It is a system by which the federal government develops its goals and objectives and re-shapes policies using the power of the purse. In short, the student had better agree that the UN should be maintained, etc. Values had better be "clarified." Computers are at the heart of this system. The Apple Corp. and others are trying to get Congress to grant them tax advantages so that there will be computers in every school. School boards have been used to make the pre-determined goals acceptable to the public.

Wonder why our electric bills keep going up in spite of the Enron scandals, etc.? PECO Energy Co. slipped $17 million dollars into State Senator Fumo's <u>non-profit</u> Fund as part of a deregulation settlement. It still goes on. Fumo, on bank boards, is doing jail time.

I don't believe that the public is apathetic; I believe that the taxpayers are so busy paying higher and higher bills that they don't have the time to investigate all of the corruption in our midst.

And PPBS is used by the planners as an unending fund (our money) to fulfill their objectives. The Soviet Union uses these data bases as well. "Taking down the wall" was another display of Bull. Remember Chechnya, anyone?

Politicians had no money for Katrina, but we can pay for two wars costing us trillions. And we can still have $3 million to give poor Pillsbury for advertising in third world countries. It's about time that we take the pork out of bills and demand that we get a list of each Congressman's spending – spending meant to guarantee the incumbency of the legislators. I am certain that you've heard about bridges that go nowhere.

American workers are losing pensions through no fault of theirs, but rather because of the fact that the corporations have gone offshore, I feel that the Congressmen should lose their pensions if they have perverted the Constitution, as they have. Proponents of regionalism should be tried for treason.

Incidentally, Ronald Reagan, that "paragon of virtue," was called Ronald Region when he was governor of California. He's also the one who brought in PPBS which requires that all planning and budgeting must come out of Washington's Office of Management and Budget (OMB), thereby making the Director of OMB a kind of second President of the United States. (PPBS – Programming, Planning Budgeting System).

President Reagan bombed a little country like Grenada as president, and imposed "sex education" on public schools when he was governor. Nice guy!

Regional planners can also write presidential executive orders. Makes one wonder how many presidents were the water carriers for those who wish to change our government without the consent of the governed.

The ultimate goal of the elite is to live in the cities, control the ports, control our movements by leasing out toll bridges – which is not their right to do, but is already in progress – and to live as parasites on the dumbed-down masses.

Mayor Bloomberg of New York City, testing the waters for a run on the presidency, has already begun the task of finalizing Home Rule Legislation whereby the Mayor – of all people – is also in control of Education (The Nation, 7/9/07).

The people most affected – teachers, parents and communities are kept out of the circle. Instead, a "chancellor" acting like a CEO will be appointed by the Mayor. In New York City that man is Joel Klein who will treat the

1450 schools as independent bank franchises, "headed by branch managers or principals, whose jobs have been reconfigured as CEOs rather than as educators." Principals are expected to outsource every service from testing to professional development. Thomas Sobol, the former New York State Education Commissioner and professor emeritus of Columbia University's Teachers College, said, "The arrogance, my God, of saying if we know how to run K-Mart, we know how to educate children, represents a giant defeat of democracy."

"Klein will have unfettered control of 1.1 million school children and a $15.4 billion budget"

"Mayoral control has already taken hold in Chicago, Boston, Cleveland, and Washington."

In New York City, Bronx parents were kept out of the meeting. "No science. No history. Only tests," one mother bellowed, shaking her finger at the Chancellor.

One of the Chancellor's corporate consultants received $16 million for a busing consultation which failed the students. Children were waiting and never picked up. There were no trial runs.

Klein divided the 32 old school districts into <u>10 regions</u>. No bid contracts. No accountability. The city is charged with huge bills. And, of course, Bill Gates' foundation donated $100 million. What a partnership!

Data collection is part of instruction. The secrecy attending this new corporate takeover of schools should be a matter of great concern.

The corporate state is upon us, and we need to take action. While we have allowed teachers' unions to call the shots on education, and have allowed unknown persons to dictate the content of curriculums, the victims have been the children.

It's time to face the fact that children are being brainwashed and neutralized with our money by unelected and unknown people. And they want more money for education!

America created the best minds in the world until the social planners took over, step-by-step. They are planning our children into slavery with unlimited money from PPBS. (OMB)

Time to go back to the curriculum that created greatness – Bill Gates profited from the <u>old</u> curriculum.

Benjamin Disraeli, in his famous book, "Coningsby," had one of his characters say, "So you see, dear Coningsby, the world is governed by very different personages from what is imagined by those who are not behind the scenes."

Ninety-five percent of the people know nothing about regionalism; now you know.

If foundations like Bill Gates' cared one string bean about America, he would do what Bon Jovi is doing – building homes for families. Foundations must be taxed so that they can't tamper with the minds of children.

At the moment, the only profiteers from education are publisher-friends of the corporate brokers – writing new books – and the testing industry – checking to see if children are coming up with the right answers.

The mayor also gets to create a New Panel for Educational Policy; a 13-member appointed board which replaces the school board. Once again, a problem is created by government, and then solved by government. The solutions are always disastrous.

I hope that the recent crime in Connecticut was not the result of regionalism. A doctor, in a home invasion, was badly beaten by two parolees who raped and killed his family. When I saw "State Police" on the back of the jackets at the scene, I knew that this small town's police force was merged with that of other towns, and placed under the jurisdiction of the State Police, That would account for the half-hour wait after the 911 call was made by the bank teller. The bank was only ten minutes away from the doctor's home.

This is what the planners call consolidation, or saving us money. I'd rather have local police, as we did before, and I would gladly pay their salaries. The same thing is happening to fire stations.

Someone commented: "This would never have happened in Greenwich." I suppose the doctor's town wasn't important enough.

We usually think of El Salvador as a poor country. Yet, our government is taking us in that direction. People in El Salvador are allowed water one or two hours a day because of the fact that their water is "privatized," much like our electric, given to Ken Lay, or any other corporation buying our legislators. (See chapter on electricity). Foreign entities also buy our newly regionalized lines. Hence, the blackouts. Our sovereignty has been sold to any bidder, step-by-step.

When citizens of El Salvador protested in the streets, they were met with brutal police force – rubber bullets and tear gas. Their signs read "Water is a human right." Their right wing government charged the protesters with "terrorism," after our Patriot Bill. The World Bank (recently run by Paul Wolfowitz until his girlfriend was placed on the payroll) paid the first loan granted to El Salvador corporations. Wolfowitz, a neo-con who hawked our useless war in Iraq, is always part of the web. El Salvador signed the Central America Free Trade Agreement (CAFTA) with George W. Bush. Wolfowitz is also the one who suggested the war with Iraq in 1995 in a paper called "Project for a New American Century."

In Stockton, California, 2003, the city council voted that a multi-national corporation could take full control of the water supply, with no referendum from the people. A private consortium from Stockton and Canada took over. There were spills, bacteria, non-union contractors, lack of transparency, and high rates. When the president of the Council, Mr. Giovanetti, was asked, "Don't you think citizens should get a vote?" Mr. Giovanetti answered, "Absolutely not!" But finally, the council had to reverse its decision because the Consortium (regionalism) wasn't making enough money and their work was disastrous. They were able to break a 20-year contract.

Stockton's reason for privatization was "environmental," which is patently illegal.

Atlanta and other cities have tried this, and in one state, the Supreme Court voted against the people!

So this privatization may be coming to a town near you. The politicians are hoping that drugs and poor education will make their nefarious deeds possible.

FOUNDATIONS

After WW I, the Carnegie Endowment trustees took control of education in the United States, and they recruited the Rockefeller Foundation to assist. According to Norman Dodd, a Yale graduate and New York investment banker who was assigned to investigate the foundations for the Reece committee (1953), the minutes of the Carnegie trustees revealed that "war was the best way to alter the life of an entire people. We must control the diplomatic machinery of the United States by first gaining the control of the State Department."

According to Dodd, "They divided the task in parts, giving to the Rockefeller Foundation the responsibility of altering education as it pertains to domestic subjects, but Carnegie retained the task of altering our education in foreign affairs and international relations." The foundations decided that the most effective method of achieving this goal would be by altering American history, so they awarded grants, fellowships and scholarships to those professors and historians who would re-write and promote one worldism, humanism, and socialism ("Lines of Credit: Ropes of Bondage," Robert Henry Goldsborough, Washington Dutchis Publishers, Baltimore 21210, p. 30).

Each war has changed America. Women had to leave the family and work to pay off America's debt to the bankers.

Men never returned home the same after killing and seeing killing.

When our state legislators couldn't get regionalism taxes through, they set up classes at the University of Pennsylvania in regionalism. In this way, they circumvented the problem, and persuaded subjects like Rep. Greenwood to participate in courses which would eventually change our government without the consent of the governed.

Although our great nation started as a representative republic, students call it a democracy. In the Federalist Papers, Madison devoted two papers to the explanation of the preference for a republic over a democracy (10 and 14).

"Democracy" is served by opinion polls, citizens' committees, and a host of other techniques. All are destructive of representation, which in turn impacts liberty.

We used to have town meetings; today, we receive bulletins of "things" that the state representatives are doing for us. And forget the "servants" in Washington, D.C. They're too busy getting gifts from lobbyists.

Well, we threw some of them out in '06; let's throw the rest out in future electioins. Let's not give the rats any more cheese.

Let the foundations pay taxes like the rest of us, and maybe they won't have time to pontificate about changing the laws which made them rich.

"When Mr. Dodd began delving into the role of international high finance in the world revolutionary movement, the investigation was killed on orders from the Eisenhower-occupied White House. According to Mr. Dodd, it is permissible to investigate the radical bomb throwers in the streets, but when you begin to trace their activities back to their origins in the "legitimate world," the political iron curtain comes down." (None Dare Call It Conspiracy, by Gary Allen and Larry Abraham, p. 19)

SECULAR HUMANISM

The Phyllis Schlafly Report, 2/76, gave the briefest, most informative account of secular humanism:

"Humanism is a religion, and has been so declared even by the U.S. Supreme Court. It is a way of life, an all-encompassing ideology. The Humanist Manifesto states that there is no God, every man is his own creator, there is no right or wrong, ethics are situational, there are no absolutes, there must be no feeling of individuality, the individual must be trained to think of himself as part of a group willing to be manipulated for the good of society rather than for individual gain or achievement. Under humanism there must be no patriotism, no feeling of nationalism developed, because all society must eventually be conditioned to accept living in a global collectivist economy under a one-world government."

The first American to use public education to promote humanism was John Dewey who also served as President of the American Humanist Association. Horace Mann, one of the founders of public education, stated: "What the Church has been for medieval man, the public school must become for democratic and rational men. God would be replaced by the concept of the public good." Beginning in the early 1930s, John Dewey and his many disciples of progressive education have continually promoted and increased the impact of humanism on public education. These include Dr. George Counts who initiated Social Studies in the curriculum (instead of the individual subjects of geography, civics, economics, and political science). Dr. Abraham Maslow, whose Third Force Psychology formed the basis for the National Training Laboratories; J. L. Moreno, who developed Psychodrama and sociograms (and who states that through role playing and psychodrama we can rid ourselves of the God-syndrome); Dr. Carl Rogers of the Western Behavioral Sciences Institute, well-known for its many forms of sensitivity training; Dr. Lester Kirkendall and Dr. Mary Calderone, Directors of SIECUS (Sexuality Information and Education Council of the U.S.), well known for many objectionable sex education programs; H. B. Skinner, father of modern Behaviorism, who is also on the Board of Directors of the American Humanist Association and was named Humanist of the Year; Dr. Sidney Simon of the Center for Humanistic Education, author and promoter of Values Clarification Programs in the schools; Dr. William Glasser, whose so-called "educational philosophy" was rapidly placed in many classrooms under the title "Schools Without Failure" and "reality therapy"; and Dr. Robert Carkhuff, who has been making the rounds with teacher-training sessions and his human and educational development series.

"Thus we find this psycho-social philosophy as the basis for the Hawaii Master Plan for Education (which has been reproduced as a blueprint for use across this country), which states that all classrooms must now be considered 'mental health clinics,' all teachers must be looked upon as 'Mental Health Clinicians,' and all students must be regarded as 'patients.' Then, through the use of psychological techniques which produce behavior modification, the students will be conditioned to an acceptance of the religion of humanism, which is basic to a one-world government.

"This same philosophy is the basis for the Michigan State University project sponsored by the U. S. Department of Health, Education and Welfare called BSTEP (Behavioral Science Teacher Education Programs)."

Some specific programs under this open-ended discussion method are issues such as racial equality, poverty, free speech, sexual freedom, academic freedom, war, ecology, women's lib, homosexual liberation, death, abortion, the occult, witchcraft, suicide, the pill, drugs, family planning, friendship, love, and taxes. These moral, emotional or social issues either replace or are added into discussions on basic academic subjects.

During these discussions the teacher is to remain non-judgmental (no right or wrong), and non-directive. Without any absolutes (there are none), without any basic truths (there are none), without any guidance or direction from the non-judgmental teacher, the group of students "solves" all of these relevant issues. They bring uninformed opinions into discussion, keep exchanging them, finally come up with an uninformed answer based on nothing absolute, and feel that they have solved the relevant issue. These open-ended discussions are used in drug education, sex education, health programs, social studies series and many English courses and reading series. Beginning in Kindergarten and continuing through high school, these programs continuously "modify" the children in their attitudes, standards, values, and beliefs. They alienate them from having any opinions or decisions on Christian-Judeo morals or values taught by the homes and church.

The ideas are introduced through stories, group discussions, social studies, visual aids, and reading materials that mothers and fathers are old-fashioned, mothers and fathers have strange ideas or hang-ups about different things, the morals that Mom and Dad and the church preach are not relevant to today's society, everything is moving so quickly today that older people just can't keep up with the changing times, and besides, look at the mess the world is in today, and after all, who got us into all these problems! Older folks obviously don't know very much, but you young children are brighter than any others. Base your thoughts on the "situation" – not on old and outmoded Christian values and morals!

At the private school my children attended, they role-played who would be thrown off of a boat in trouble. Naturally, the old person. In drug education, they were told by a local policeman that marijuana was "safer than heroin." (Never mind that they are all mind-altering drugs. And he was talking to a group of children who had no previous idea of drugs taken to get a "high.") Death education discussions were also used in conjunction with a child's playing dead.

My children were out of that school when death education began. I wouldn't have allowed my family to engage in this garbage.

Aggie C., the head mistress, had sent me a letter which, in essence, said "Since you are so unhappy here, while I won't ask you to leave the school, maybe you should think about it."

Shortly after that, she was fired. With her firing, parents assumed that the "pilot" program of behavior modification also went. Not true. As I just mentioned, drug education and the whole program was in permanently. Just a few years ago the school had to postpone graduation because of drug problems.

Remember, these were wealthy parents; you can only imagine what these change agents have done to children all over America since 1963 when the program was piloted in to many city schools across the country. But this was a private school.

Did they cause Columbine? Are they responsible for the school shootings, the drug problems, the violence?

I lay these problems at the foot of the schools who allow these dangerous experimental games to be played on an immature group of children. School should be an oasis of peace and knowledge where the child can learn the old way – geography, civics, English, history, math. Parents must be involved.

I have heard parents say in the very beginning of our research, "Well, they have to learn about sex from somebody." These parents have no clue about the experimentation on their children. They make no effort to even talk to their children about what they discussed during the day.

Young people in poor neighborhoods were used as guinea pigs early on – I know from families still living in South Philadelphia.

It took a little longer to get the Jean Harris types in the private schools, but it is everywhere now. Girls dress like prostitutes starting early on, and clothing manufacturers are acting in tandem with this new drive to get children interested in sex earlier and earlier. Ditzy moms all over the place don't protest; they accede to what the child wants. "Everybody wears this stuff." Add tattoos and nose piercings, and they'll be ready to swing from trees in a short while.

If you can't take care of children, don't have them. Their lives are too precious to waste on parents who have no clue about what's happening at school or in politics.

Your children are being "Simonized" before your eyes. Sidney B. Simon (Values Clarification) spoke before several thousand Wisconsin teachers on October 31, 1975. By revealing personal values of his life, he encouraged the audience to reveal personal values of their lives. His values:

1. Places socks in a disc for laundering.
2. Refers to chairperson so that "his" is not dominant over "hers."
3. Removes maraschino cherries from fruit because of the red dye.

From there he goes on to talk about how people feel about death and why some people "red pencil." For instance, Mr. Simon spelled pencil "pencel" on the blackboard. No one knew whether or not he planned it that way. When a teacher corrected it, he accused her of "red penciling." Remember, nothing is wrong in his world. That's why children are promoted without knowing how to read or spell.

Prior to this idea that classrooms should be mental health clinics, we sent children who needed help to school counselors – people trained to help youngsters in trouble. Teachers are not equipped to do this. Playing the role of counselor is not why I send a child to school; it's to deal in cognitive (skills), not affective (behavior) education.

John Steinbacher (The Network of Patriotic Letter Writers, P.O. Box 2003D, Pasadena) reports that "this kind of raw information is grist for the mill of the programmers in regard to the PPBS program (Planning, Programming, Budgeting System). Once they get all this raw material, then they can start the testing, recycling, slewing off the undesirable attributes and moving things back and forth until, finally, at the end of the process, they end up with what the chief programmer for the Honeywell Corporation in Kansas City told me would be 'a generation of programmed robots.' Then, turning to his companion, he said, 'My friend here is with the IBM Corporation as a programmer and he agrees with me that this is the general direction they're taking. They want to be able to decide in advance what the goals should be, what ideal behavior is to be, what values people should have. And then program students in every possible way in order to eventually bring out this particular image."

He reminds us that "Hitler of Nazi Germany revealed to the world what could be done in one generation with the government-run school system when he concentrated on it. He showed it very effectively in the young people with Wilhelm Reick and his 'sex pol' experiments. The Nazi youth camps, within one generation, very effectively conditioned the young so that they would point to their parents and say 'Kill them; they're an enemy of the State.' Communist regimes used this as well."

In a survey that went out to high school students, students were asked, "would you kill a fellow American?" (in America).

In an upstate Pennsylvania elementary school, sixth grade girls were given a vaginal exam. Parents were outraged. What did they do? Nothing. It's the new American way: don't get involved – even if it's your own child. If this isn't the result of behavior modification, what is? "WHAT EVER! Like I mean, like – Ya know what ahm sayin'??" And for this we spend $7,000 a student?

FREEDOM OF SPEECH

Cybernetics was a technique used by the Soviets to manipulate and control information. Listeners and readers were told only what the government wanted them to know.

I like Maureen Heston's description of our press: "Instead of doing 'investigative reporting' of events which patently are needing more light and less heat, the termites of the press go into a mass frenzy over trivia, diverting public attention from matters really needing examination."

She spoke about Herb Philbrick ("I Led Three Lives"), who served as an undercover agent for the FBI in the Communist Party, USA (CPUSA) around 1950. Philbrick learned that the Soviets used a space age technology – cybernetics – in mind control. Cybernetics has a legitimate function as a scientific method for improving electronic circuitry (conduits and cables, logic and memory in computers).

The NEA (National Education Association) took a trip to Moscow in 1934 to "see the future" at work. In January, 1951, the NEA Journal carried an article by George S. Counts describing cybernetics: "It is able to attain power and reach heights of efficiency which dwarf the efforts of earlier despotisms. The system embraces all of the organized processes and agencies for the molding of the minds of the young and old."

As you can see, the "planners of the destruction of America's independence have been busy for many years. One can see why educators are told to accept bilingual students before a child has mastered English or why there was a craze about accepting "ebonics." If a child can't express himself, he's kept from taking any steps up the ladder of life.

When Senator Joseph McCarthy of Wisconsin spoke out against the infiltration of subversives at the State Department, he was shouted down with "Give us names!" This was meant to intimidate the average citizens from speaking out, and it worked. Fact is that McCarthy did give names, but the penetration of the internationalists and one-worlders had hit not only the State Department but the press, the Congress, and higher ups. He called them communists when the word was globalists or internationalists. No borders, no sovereignty, no America. Internationalists don't particularly care whether the form of government is fascist, communist, socialist or democratic, so long as they control the leaders.

Interesting that Joe McCarthy died on May 2, 1959, at Bethesda Naval Hospital under mysterious circumstances for a healthy, vibrant man whose best years were ahead. His doctor said, "Joe McCarthy's health was such in the spring of 1957 as to make it incredible that he should die so swiftly of natural causes." (Medford Evans, <u>The Assassination of Joe McCarthy</u>, p. 4) No autopsy.

At Senator McCarthy's funeral, Louis Budenz, a former member of the communist party, said this about the Senator: "The destruction of Joe McCarthy leaves the way open to intimidate any person of consequence who moves against the conspiracy." (James J. Drummey, "McCarthy," American Opinion, p. 9)

Of course, those who don't know what really happened go along with the propaganda, calling the Senator's America-first technique "McCarthyism" – much as the neo cons label antiwar protestors as "anti-American." Anyone who exposes corruption is anti-government. They hope that no one reads the Declaration of Independence!

When I listened to the McCarthy hearings and heard the passion in the Senator's voice, about America, it marked the last time I ever got a lump in my throat. His courage, his angst about America's sovereignty – the last vestige of congressional honor I've witnessed since the powerbrokers have taken over our airwaves, the press, the Congress, and apparently, the cabinet and the presidency.

I remember, too, the role Hollywood played in warmongering. Our servicemen were conned into hating the 'chinks' (World War II), then hating the 'gooks' (Vietnam), and now it's the 'ragheads.' Keep on hating while the warmongers laugh all the way to the bank!

I can't say enough against 'activist' judges who violate the constitutional separation of powers clause by legislating decisions not meant to be legislated by judges. Once the electorate speaks by voting on an issue that is it! No judge should overturn the decision. These activist judges are mainly the product of democrats who use these fraudulent tactics to get votes. Most blacks and whites did not want their children bussed into unknown districts during the civil rights era. But we got it anyway by a judge overturning our vote.

Now, these judges are at it again with pedophiles. Suddenly pedophiles have the right to offer online tips to other pedophiles on where to watch and meet children. Jack McClellan, a pedophile, is suing the Santa Monica police for showing his photo. McClellan has freedom of speech and a defense attorney. We the people have nothing.

I know that the framers weren't talking about pedophiles when they used the term "freedom of speech." Judges who are interpreting – not their job – should be publicly exposed for their sick rulings on children's rights. Where is Congress?

Isn't it about time that we publish the names of these men and women judges who are preying on our children? What are we waiting for?

At this moment in time, Congress is trying to get legislation through which will inhibit reporters from using "unknown sources." Without "unknown sources" there can be no true investigative reporting without placing sources in jeopardy.

It's the same thing with our editorial pages; thousands of people would like to speak out but can't because of repercussions. But, if you notice, people at the newspaper can write editorials without their names attached. It's intimidation and blasphemy. All of us should be able to read diverse opinions without names or phone numbers attached. No one owns liberty.

What better time to get this legislation through than now – a war's going on, corrupt politicians vying for the presidency, a dumbed-down electorate, appointees taking over jobs of the elected (regionalism), and voters addicted to crack asking for more entitlements as the middle class loses millions of jobs through NAFTA and GATT.

TALK SHOW HOSTS

Since 1996, talk shows have become platforms of "organized dissent." I started to call talk radio in the late '70s, when I discovered what the "internationalists" had planned for children through the educational system, and from there, my eyes were opened to the methodology of their plans. Education and regionalism with its plans to destroy representative government through open space, immigration, environment – as though all of us do not hope for clean air and potable water – are the tools used by teachers and politicians to get their plans moving toward the New World Order.

Christian radio is a farce. Hosts like Janet Parshall, Pat Robertson and others have their agendas. Janet, of course, pretends to take "all calls," but what she doesn't say is that an "inquisition" precedes your call, and if your agenda doesn't fit hers, adios.

Like fascist dictators, they have taken over the airwaves, and with the help of compliant Congressmen and women who say nothing about the airwaves which belong to the people, these "useful idiots" (Lenin) rule day and night with no competition.

I've made notes on what the young and old are forced to listen to, and I know that we deserve something better, or society will crumble.

Bob Grant of New York City was always a lackey with an agenda, and his agenda is pleasing his New York listeners. For many years, he's done "whatever it takes."

Mary Mason, a former, popular black talk show host in Philadelphia, has always done her best to push black candidates and has done very well.

She received six figures for pushing "motor-voter registration" in the '90s. Motor-votes allow illegals to get drivers' licenses, and at the same time, register to vote. Acorn-type community group.

I mention this only by way of telling you that no talk radio is free speech. For instance, Mary was substituting for a white talk show host on another station. Topic was "cheating." Her view was that all men cheat. She stuck with that premise throughout her show, so I had to call in and take the opposite position. No one should be able to indict any group of people without a challenge. The fact that I knew many men who do not cheat wasn't the point. Mary's point was to demoralize the audience into feeling that all men are no good. After all, there were no challenges. A steady diet of this garbage can make anyone sick. Particularly the young.

Another talk show host had a sex therapist on in the evening, giving advice to sub-teens as it turned out. Apparently, the students tuned in without their parents' knowledge. Judy Kuriansky then gave advice: "If the boys like it, it's okay to give sex" (a la Monica Lewinsky and President Clinton). Parents who happened to hear this were outraged and wanted to get her off the air. It so happened that a young doctor returning from hospital duty also heard it, and was astounded at the age of the children. Subsequently, Judy was taken off the air, after a protest in front of the station.

Howard Stern. I began listening to Howard in the early '80s when someone told me that he was "funny." Well, he was, and he could be. Instead, he's chosen to blend funny with crude, and manages to tear down any semblance of civility for the young audiences he generates. Again, who knows whether or not he would be popular if there were competition like Sinbad or any comedian who doesn't drop the F-bomb repeatedly. Nothing about the four-letter word is funny. Johnny Carson and the really great comedians never lowered themselves to a point which demeaned the audience. People like Roseanne Barr and Chris Rock make a living out of the F-bomb comedy routine, and the lame-brained audiences laugh at every cue. After a single routine, you're ready to run for the door in disgust.

I consider Howard Stern the forerunner of the "shock jocks," since it is he who created all of these Howard Stern wannabes. Early on, he admitted that his children were not allowed to listen to his show and I give him credit for that.

On one of the days I listened to the Stern show, he and his laugh-a-holic side-kick, Robin, were in a fit of convulsive laughter over a woman who was brutally attacked, beaten, limbs removed, placed in a garbage bag, and left for dead. The woman managed to make her way to the highway and get help.

Only the lowest people would laugh at such a horrendous happening. But then, it doesn't take much for a fool to laugh. Belching and other body sounds can do the trick.

Howard has poked fun at a teenager who said that he attended a game with his dad. I'm certain that Mr. Stern treats his dad with respect, but then he's not the audience.

Lesbians, stutterers, prostitutes – all are targets on his show. When he left for Sirius at a staggering salary, he probably laughed all the way to the bank. On his taped answering machine, "he left sounds of passing gas" (Philadelphia Inquirer 10/11/05). Sooo funny!

Stern engaged in psychological warfare with his young audience, breaking down any traditional values they might have had, incrementally – as the Fabian Socialists do – a little at a time. Shame on this simpleton who walks around like a Christ figure. His objective is right out of Beria ____:

"The first thing to be degraded in (conquering) any nation is the state of man himself. Nations which have high ethical tones are difficult to conquer. Their loyalties are hard to shake … their spiritual integrity cannot be violated…." Lavrenti Beria, "Psychopolitics" – Lenin School, 1934.

Maury Povich and Jerry Springer are another two who exploit people with problems. "Anything for a buck." And they make a lot in their cesspool.

Rush Limbaugh, formerly a disc jockey, is now considered one of our most distinguished "conservative" pundits. God help us! He began his racket in the Clinton nineties by exploiting Bill Clinton's drawl and affair with Monica Lewinsky. But then I noticed that Mr. Limbaugh played both sides of the money ticket. If a caller happened to get past the screener with an opposing view, he was immediately cut off. No one could say anything about Clinton. Limbaugh preferred to characterize the President as an "ahh, gee" type of country boy. And THAT he is NOT!

Limbaugh began pushing for NAFTA (North American Free Trade Agreement) and GATT (General Agreements on Tariffs and Trade) early on and thanks to Rush's sales job, both treaties passed and Americans are out of millions of jobs. But, of course, Clinton "created" new jobs to supplement the injustice. Except that the created jobs paid minimum wage.

Strange – or not so strange – bedfellow Newt Gingrich suggested to the White House that they "enlist talk show bomb-thrower Limbaugh. He has a microphone big enough to turn the tide."

According to <u>Time</u>, "they learned that President Clinton dispatched Lee Iacocca to enlist Limbaugh in the administration's campaign on behalf of NAFTA."

Limbaugh began hours of relentless lecturing on behalf of NAFTA – no phone calls, just a mishmash of baseless reasoning.

And now this callous man is about hawking the war in Iraq and Iran, if possible. He doesn't have children, so what does he care who dies. He compared the torture at Abu Graib to college fraternity hazings. And characterized Moslems as "always in a state of being soiled."

Laura Ingraham: "Let's carpet bomb Iran" (Ingraham talk show 7/28/06).

Don Imus, "Palestinians are animals. Drop the bomb. Kill them all" (MSNBC 12/03/04).

Mayor Koch: "Bosnians deserve what they get because they were on Germany's side in WW II" (6/19/05). I can only imagine what he says about Iraq and Iran.

Mike Gallagher: "The guys that they (Moslems) captured were people trying to do the right thing; what we've captured are nothing but filthy animals."

In August 1999, two talk show hosts in Philadelphia were asked to leave WWDB. Phone lines were a little too free, so that listeners were beginning to wake up to some of the con games in our midst. Tom Leykis from the West Coast was hired to replace them. His first words on the air: "If there is a protest, I hope that they all go down to WWDB in their wheelchairs to pick up their picket signs. I say from the beginning, if you are sixty or older, or even fifty or older, you are probably not going to enjoy listening to this show. This is talk radio for people who have a life. We cater to people 18 to 49. I am not in the political business. I am in the advertising business" (Kevin Carter, Philadelphia Inquirer, 8/06/99).

He didn't last too long in Philadelphia because he underestimated the intelligence of the listeners – at that time. Leykis had nothing to contribute except put-downs of real entertainers such as Steve Allen whom he invited as a guest, and then proceeded to degrade and insult. Steve Allen had taken out a full-page ad in the Philadelphia Inquirer: "TV is leading children down a moral sewer. How you and I can stop it." He talked about "the tragic consequences of filth, sex and violence in our homes, and the rising homicide rate."

The no-talent, no-account Leykis could have learned something from Mr. Allen who was light years away from Leykis in intelligence.

Since Steve Allen's death, the problems have gotten much worse. Curse words are on much earlier. And the filth of a generation of sex ed in our schools has borne fruit: "Girls gone wild," "ultra fighting," and other monstrous themes. Pity the children growing up in this climate of violence.

The good news is that there are few phone calls to these talk shows, so that they have to have a co-host with whom the host can chat.

We don't have to patronize purveyors of garbage. Sponsors have to get the message. This is not free speech; it is license to assault the young and impressionable.

Glenn Beck's fame came in 2003 when he led a series of rallies across the country to "support the troops" in Iraq. I am certain that Clear Channel, owner of 1200 radio stations and with ties to President Bush had nothing to do with the rallies. And if you believe that, what can I say?

Jay Severenson: "Nic Robertson (CNN) interviewed a piece of 'turd' crying 'look what they've done.'" (referring to a Palestinian after an Israeli attack) (7/18/06). This talk from a man who called all Mexicans garbage and said that he sees nothing wrong with sex with animals!!

Michael Savage: (talking about a sick man from India who allegedly shot people at a Jewish center). "This piece of offal should have his limbs cut off" (7/31/06). And they dare to talk about Mideast Madrassah schools teaching hate!

Tucker Carlson, MSNBC 8/7/06: (that nice collegiate-looking man): "I don't care if Iran, Syria, and Lebanon go up in smoke. I'm worried about the effect this will have on Israel," (referring to the recent bombing of Lebanon by Israel because two soldiers were missing. Nothing was said in the media about the fact that a Palestinian and his family were killed on a beach by Israelis the day before. In the early reporting, this was mentioned once, and then forgotten.)

These paragons of virtue are the ones who judge people like Margie Shott, previous owner of the Cincinnati Reds, for her insensitive statements. These are the people for whom there is no moral equivalency. I would like all of them to take responsibility for the present state of affairs.

We're allowing these wolves in the media to use the same technique used by Hitler when he demeaned the Jews. Now it's okay to demean Moslems so that they're easier to hate.

Wake up, America. Stand up for your right to speak out before these wolves devour the last vestiges of civil liberty and civility.

We mustn't forget National Public Radio which we taxpayers help subsidize. Objective speech? Well, Marty Moss Cuane hosted a 'debate' on Public Television (WHYY) in 1995. The subject: regionalism, a hot issue because of letters to the editor and talk radio callers. Even Cardinal Bevilacqua supported it (religion and politics?). It was to be a call-in show with proponents on stage such as Ted Hershberg, professor at Penn. It turned out to be another display of "organized tyranny."

Earlier, at a meeting on the Penn State Campus, Professor Hershberg didn't fare too well because he couldn't handle the challenges in the audience.

This time, they were prepared. No calls in opposition were taken. All of us were told that the "lines were full" and to call another time.

Once again, the audience at home was left thinking that regionalism must be okay because callers stayed away.

This is criminal, and these treasonous rots are selling out the best country in the world to the highest bidders.

What do you have to lose? Everything. Censorship is brutal; it leaves the public misinformed and demoralized.

As for black radio – the hosts and callers are just as racist and mean as their white counterparts. Reparations, "whitey" – it's all about what happened a century and a half ago. The joke is that none of us can take America back alone – all of us have to be a part of this fight. It so happens that blacks have also climbed aboard the gravy train, and they have to get off as well. Condoleezza Rice is at the top of the list.

The black politicians are emulating the Jewish Holocaust Industry, except that they have substituted slavery for holocaust. They have the Black Caucus, reparations, African aid, just as the Jews have the Israeli Lobby, reparations, Israeli aid. A well kept secret is that Italians in America during WW II were kept in internment camps, just as the Japanese. I never hear an Italian politician talk about aid to Italy; I think that all of them are just happy to be here.

Remember, it's the Constitution which made us free, and it's the raping of the Constitution by those in Washington, D.C. which will bring us into bondage.

Prominent leaders like Farrakhan, if he were legitimate, should have had both blacks and whites in his organization. The fact that he did not is highly suspicious. No Moslem I know excludes people on the basis of race.

To young people who listen to talk radio thinking that they may get information, I extend my sympathy. Station 990 in Philadelphia features Bill Bennett, Laura Ingraham, Dennis Prager, Mike Gallagher, Michael Medved, Michael Savage and Hugh Hewitt. Their hearts are in Israel; their paychecks are here in the good old U.S. of America. And they have the NERVE to call anti-war protestors anti-American.

The Federal Communication Act of 1934 stated that "the airwaves belong to the people." It's time to take them back!

Enter Matt Drudge whose popularity came from discovering that Monica Lewinsky, of Clinton fame, had a stained dress. Now he hypes for the Bush Administration, imitating an old broadcaster from the '40s who wore a hat when he reported the news, in a rat-a-tat-tat fashion: Walter Winchell. Except that Walter was smart.

Just don't call him and mention anything against the war or Israel, as one guest did on Sunday evening. The guest quoted something Seymour Hersh said, and Drudge immediately used the technique that Hersh is old. "<u>Please</u>, get me the <u>Geritol</u>!" Again, if you're old and smart, don't call; if you're young and dumb, welcome aboard! Except that the caller was young. The point they're making is the same as that of the New World Order crowd: The Constitution is old. The republic is old. Belief in God is old. Pledge of Allegiance is old. States are old. Absolutes are old. In short, replace these traditions with us! We have no right or wrong. We like "girls gone wild," torture, censorship, raping of the Constitution, drugs, violence, a constant diet of trivia, and nullification of the Declaration of Independence which states that the public has a "duty" to remove corruption in government.

Is Matt Drudge to be the new-newsman? Or Sean Hannity? O'Reilly? Funny how they all use the same talking points. The only reason they were selected is that they fall far short of the experience and brain power of their predecessors. Their nightmares are <u>young</u> smart callers.

We have another midnight-hour show. The topics are ghosts, aliens from another planet, night people, time travelers, howling from cemeteries, haunted houses. It's Halloween 24-7 all year long. Oh, and if you're still listening, they just may ask Alex Jones to give you a round-up of what's happening in the news, once every month – or year!

Alex Jones talks about 911 truth and secret societies, but he knows not to trample on really important stuff.

The Rush Limbaughs are the ones getting 400 million dollar contracts. Perhaps if he had children, he wouldn't censor callers brighter than he. He's shameless.

Talk show hosts, like Susanne LaFrankie, shouldn't have the power to refuse callers who know more than she about critical information. She not only refused my call but wouldn't allow me to leave a telephone number so that the young caller who was having a problem with the sex ed program in Marlton, New Jersey, could contact me. Having gone through her problem in the '70s at my children's school, I could have given her background information. As it turned out, I was unsuccessful in ever reaching that parent, thanks to that skaggy fascist who now plays guest on "It's Your Call" with Lynn Doyle.

Young people shouldn't be listening to outright disinformation from people like Michael Medved and his sidekick guest Victor Mordecai, who breathlessly inflicts one hateful statement after another about Moslems on a large audience. The audience is large only because there is no competition. Everyone doesn't have a computer.

Medved shouldn't be allowed to use character assassination on his targets. For example, "Ron Paul has a picture of Stalin in his office." It's a bit different when that picture also contains Roosevelt and Churchill, isn't it?

He shouldn't be allowed to deny the fact that the North American Union exists, particularly when a highway costing us $187 billion will be built for Canada, Mexico and the United States. This dope actually believes that all of us out here are stupid.

Michael Savage has said that the United States should send gun-happy gangs out to Iraq. He encourages presidents to bomb Iran. I'm not happy that he wasn't tossed off the air for his comments about autistic children. He's a skag.

On March 19, 2009, Savage asked how anyone in his "bright" audience could believe that, after life on this earth, there would be a spiritual world for the good, along with punishment for the bad. After repeating this question a few times, he said that he would skip it. Then the real motivation for his question kicked in – for us dummy Christians who fight wars for his people, in Israel. Paraphrased: "We talk about water boarding being torture. Well, how about 'lips off, tongues sliced, eyes taken out with a screwdriver,'" etc. He went on and on describing horrific details, as only a Dr. Jekyll and Mr. Hyde could. This hate from a man who wants to be called 'Doctor' because he brags about his knowledge of nutrition and his degrees. Just think of how much he hates anyone criticizing Israel, as Iran's Ahmadinejad did. Remember, Iran suffered because of America's embargoes on their country. We were best friends until Israel hijacked our dopey Congress – old coots who won't leave their permanent jobs unless they're carried out in wheelchairs – Kennedy, Dodd, Kay Hutchison, Clintons, Schumer, Lieberman, Barney Frank, McCain, Specter – who gave American jobs to foreign countries. In 1979, when the Iranians held our hostages, the ayatollahs were disgusted because the Shah was another doormat for Israel. I'd be a bit surprised if <u>all</u> of the so-called "missionaries" taken hostage were not CIA working for our Knesset in D.C. I covered this earlier – Iranians knew that the CIA was always meddling in their business, and U.S. newspapers concurred. Remember, we (under Eisenhower) took out Mossadegh, their elected leader who would have created the one democracy in the Mideast. The Shah was our puppet, .like Mubarak in Egypt, and like the two new guys in Germany and France – Merkel and Sarkozy. Notice that nobody in Congress mentioned the fact that "40 billion was given to French and German banks in these bailout packages so that foreigners can buy our assets. Nobody read the bills which they signed, just as they do when in our State Legislatures, under regionalism. The planners propose and the lackeys sign!

Since Glenn Beck has his own cable show on Fox News, it seems that he has gotten even more stupid – if it's possible. He now reports what should be serious news but makes faces and contortions, probably because he thinks it's amusing. It's not amusing; I think that most people like to hear straight news. Between this new show at 5 p.m. and his radio show, it's more than people should take – even right wing kooks who listen to Fox and believe in wars and torture.

He had Michael Scheuer on to discuss public dissatisfaction. Scheuer, who was a former CIA agent working on the Bin Laden Unit, left the agency because of dissatisfaction. ("Marching Toward Hell")

The first words out of Mr. Scheuer were "this government is the cause of our problems." It took Beck less than two seconds to cut Scheuer off with "wa wa wait." No Scheuer. No apologies. Beck went to another guest. And this host continually says "I love my country." LOL

Besides O'Reilly and Hannity, the women anchors are Megyn Kelly, a tough pro-torture, pro-tell children about two mommys, etc., and the sweet-looking but deceiving Kimberly Guilfoyle who is for torture and more torture: "If we investigate (CIA torture), it will undo the good work we did in the Mideast." Yes, like killing and maiming a million people.

As for Smerconish, he now has <u>two</u> syndicated radio shows, because he's been a good little dooby, and Fox gave him O'Reilly's old radio show on WOR.

This dolt still falls to the floor whenever his co-producer, Greg, plays the track with gas sounds, a la Howard Stern, the master creep. Often, Michael throws in phrases about "drug legalization" so that his audience gets the impression that he's cool – savvy! This should give you some idea of audience IQ. Most of his time is spent in reading excerpts from books he enjoys and advertising his own books. Sports and trivia, too, are his talents, as well as a segment by female producer TC, who treats listeners to a reading of some patriotic happening from the past. (Oh, they're so patriotic. Its' touching!) (3/20/09)

Most of his guests agree on the war in Iraq broadening into Pakistan and possibly Iran. The only opposing view I've heard was that of authors Mearsheimer and Walt ("The Israel Lobby"). The segment was brief, of course, and no calls.

He had a guest on discussing torture policies and ever-so-subtly he injected a false fact. With his talent for coup dê grace, Michael said, "I have two syndicated radio shows and I get a 'lot' of callers who don't agree that we should go after a past administration for torture tactics." (paraphrased) (4/24/09) He omits the fact that he and Greg do most of the silly talking and that rarely, if ever, does he take an opposing call – certainly not on the torture subject. He's no dummy; he knows who butters his bread. The listeners are left with a false perception that most Americans want to "move on." But then his listeners watch "24:" and war games, so I suppose it's okay.

Isn't it odd that the two old buddies, Senators McCain and Lieberman, came out <u>against</u> punishing those who formulated torture practices

– particularly when that great hero, McCain, said, during his campaign debates, "I oppose torture." Ugh. Double ugh.

Dom Giordano, WPHT, had David Harris from the American Jewish Committee on and treated him like the Second Coming. What a lackey Giordano is, and he proudly admitted that Mr. Harris monitors radio. Probably caller 'Clark' is from Harris' goon squad. For years, he has tagged me on every show, including Boston. His modus operandi was to change any subject about which I was speaking to sports or some asinine trivia. He couldn't refute facts, so he attacked the person – "she calls," etc. I must say that it never gets easier when bullies attack because I refuse to allow the Clarks to muddy the waters our children will inherit. Sadly, a 'Christian' male host laughed at the hurtful things he said; only Rollye James saw him for what he was and called him a 'moron.' But then, the male host wasn't as smart as Rollye. (The male host, Darryl Berger, was from Bucks County WNPV, and the creep Clark now has his own finance show. Clark Howard on HLN.)

Hosts – black hosts such as Joe Watkins were exceptionally nice – and so was his screener. Sadly for us, the Nazis at WPHT let him go. WPHT wants to hear only the families of servicemen so that they can thank them for the great job they're doing – killing innocent people. Talk shows like Larry King and The View are there to promote degeneracy. Audiences at The View – women my age and much younger – stood up for Beyonce Knowles who demonstrated in her dancing that she is just another saleswoman for porno. (With three ditzy men in heels.)

The first lady, Michelle Obama, remarked on Larry King (4/23/09) that, "I'm glad that my daughters have someone to look up to." Really? Etta James – you look up to; B.B. King – you look up to; But Beyonce? You're kidding, right? She's another Madonna. Money means nothing when you've destroyed America's assets – the children.

So-called Christians, like Janet Parshall, interviewed General Richard Meyers (WFIL, 3/22/09), who predicted that we will be in Iraq for decades. I don't think so; Americans are out of jobs and patience. Spending $365 million a day on a war that we should not have started in the first place is not a popular idea. Janet: "We helped build Iraq's infrastructure. God put the right people in the right place at the right time." God had nothing to do with it. Apparently, this evil woman hasn't heard that Iraq's infrastructure was bombed ruthlessly even taking down their treasured museum, with articles of antiquity stolen. Janet can't believe in God, or she would know that her day is coming when all of us are judged.

Susan Boyle, the singer from England, offered hope to me when I saw rooms full of people crying at the sound of her angelic voice. Americans are ready for a change but not a change to tyranny, as those despicable appointees surrounding Obama would like to bring about. We want those criminals – in whichever administration – who harmed America, brought to justice, not only for us, but so that the world can see that we're not going to take it anymore.

If nothing is done, then I know that it's because all of the politicians are soiled goods, contaminated by regionalism, treaties, education takeovers, and lobbyists. Let's make all of them pay with jail time and pension loss.

Our President – no president – should be visiting Holocaust sites (4/23/09) after our loonies walked out of the meeting in Geneva. Obama probably got his orders from 'above' as lackey Hillary did when she said, "More restrictions on Iran" (because Ahmadinejad called Israel 'cruel' at the Geneva meeting).

I wish that I were wrong, but after years of uncovering what these traitors have done and are still doing to this country, I've broken 'the code.' It's all written in the wills of people like Carnegie and many others who decided long ago to play games with our lives – if we let them. The recent drama about the Mexican flu should be left directly at the doorstep of Congress, which, for 20 years, did nothing about border security because, in the NWO, there are no borders – just billionaires who make their money on the backs of the American people. Wall Street runs our corrupt government.

The flu scare, like the anthrax scare of a few years ago, was created by the monsters we have elected to protect us. The purpose is to keep the politicians in office forever. Witness Fox News inviting yet another dumb Bush – Jeb – as a guest and probably another presidential candidate. Haven't we been insulted enough with the Bush family and the Clinton family, and the Kennedys? These 'planners' never give up, and they use their foundations to start our problems. We are even given a forecast of the next presidential election – Newt Gingrich, Sara Palin, Romney, and good old Jeb Bush. Possibly Caroline Kennedy of 'ya know' fame.

They're passing all kinds of hate crime legislation to keep us from speaking out. They tried to scare residents of New York City with Air Force One flying at a low altitude, with a U.S. fighter jet right behind – at a cost of $330,000. We were told that it was a 'photo op.' Well, we should ask names of the fools who planned this scare tactic and let them pay for their stupidity. Imagine what would happen if you or I pulled such an obvious crime. The whole deal was to tell us "look what could happen unless you give us more power, more authority, to come into your homes and lives. Those bad, bad Moslems could kill you. You need us."

Remember, President Bush used Blackwater mercenaries – with no mercy – to kill Moslems who did nothing to us. The gang in Washington will have no hesitation to use these foreign forces on U.S. citizens who protest.

Already Glenn Beck is claiming ownership of the Tea Party Tax Protestors. Well, Americans are smarter than that. No tax protestor wants our taxes to go to wars in Afghanistan, Pakistan, Syria, Iran – it will never end. My guess is that Glenn Beck rounded up some of his listeners, not tax protestors.

Thomas Jefferson said that when people fear government, it's tyranny; when government fears the people, it's liberty.

Kudos to the author of "Red, White and Muslim" (Asma Hassan, born in America of Pakistan parents). In my opinion, she made Prager look like the Israeli loyalist he is – in a gracious way. (5/5/09)

First, no one ever invites a Moslem on to talk about his religion because they don't want Americans to know how intelligent they are. Knowing Prager he thought that he could beat a woman in a debate.

Of course, the usual question about women and abuse. She was great. Then "Which Moslem country practices the 'beautiful Islam' you talk about?" She mentioned Malaysia and Senegal. Next, the usual: Prager: "The biggest black eye you've received was in not protesting the terrorists." Author: "I get this question a lot from radical talk show hosts, although you are treating me well. We have had public demonstrations, but CNN was the only station that covered it!

"If a tree falls and no one hears it, does that mean that the tree hasn't fallen? I assume that Catholics are against abuse by priests; they don't have to demonstrate. Can't you say that about Moslems?"

I thought that she was brilliant. Of course, I would have added, "Where are the Israelis and American Jews protesting the Holocaust of the Palestinians?"

Just so happens that I know where they are. They're at AIPAC with their hands out for wars on Pakistan and Iran, and asking for grants for higher education, which most, if not all, Americans are not allowed to talk about or know about.

I wish that you could have heard Ms. Hasan. Prager has said in the past that it's wrong to compare any suffering to the suffering of Jews. And that's it in a nutshell. None of us has feelings; they are special people. Damnit, I want my freedom to speak returned to the rest of us!

They've taken our religion away, and that has caused untold suffering all over the world. A world with no absolutes will bring nothing but grief.

MONSIGNOR ADAMO

Monsignor S. J. Adamo used to be a talk-show host on WWDB in Philadelphia. He was given one day per week and was one of the most loyal supporters of Israel, hanging up on anyone he even suspected of mentioning Israel. And this was in 1991 when we had a sort of free speech, until all of the stations were bought up – against anti-trust laws – by corporate take-overs. What we have now is a joke: right wing know-nothings defending corruption, because of a pay check.

Then an epiphany occurred in the priest's life; he went to Israel – not led by right-wing evangelical workers – but by historians, objective travelers.

First, his column changed. He apologized for his stance on the Mideast. Then he wrote an article in the opinion column of the Philadelphia <u>Daily News</u>, 9/19/91.

First he talked about Israel's "demand" for a guaranteed loan of $10 billion, since it was the "U.S. who had pressured the Soviet government into allowing Jewish émigrés into Israel. The billions are now needed to settle them in ….. Israel.

"Does America have to underwrite every good cause it espouses? Is not moral collaboration enough?

"Why, when we won't help our own, are we so willing to help a foreign country that oppresses its inhabitants? More than 1.7 million Palestinians are being dehumanized by the Israeli juggernaut. What about our moral duty to help them, rather than their exploiters?

"The reason is as simple as A.I.P.A.C., initials of the Israeli lobby. The Israeli lobby can hurt politicians in two ways – first, by withdrawing political contributions; second, by funneling money to their opponents.

"In a book by Congressman Paul Findley, <u>They Dare to Speak Out</u> (largely ignored by the American Press), he documents the demise of such politicians as former Senator Charles Percy and J. William Fulbright and Congressman Paul McCloskey – as well as himself – victims of the Israeli lobby's wrath.

"On the basis of George Bush, Sr.'s rejection of the Israeli request (demand), the Israeli lobby went into action.

"More than 1,000 lobbyists began at once to visit members of Congress with their arrogant demands.

"The only problem is: Does Congress have enough spineless members to cave in to Israeli demands?

"Israel boasts it is the only democracy in the Mideast.

"But what kind of democracy keeps thousands of people in prison without charges and without a trial?

"One of their own soldiers recently wrote about the brutal torture of Israeli prisoners. The article was reprinted in the July 18 issue of the <u>New York Review</u>.

"'At the end of the watch you sometimes hear horrible screams . . . and from the other side of the galvanized fence of the interrogation section come hair-raising human screams. Literally hair-raising.'

"'The torture goes on. Thousands upon thousands of political prisoners are questioned by the Sin Bet (the Israeli secret police.)

"'Yes, questioned and tortured.' The author adds, 'This is something without parallel in any part of the world today that is thought to be decent. And you are a partner to it – you comply.'

"And here in America we provide the weapons and the money without demanding an end to the brutal treatment of the Palestinians.

"And the American press conspires to stay silent, lest they be accused of anti-Semitism."

Readers, these are all arguments I have made on Talk Radio when they allowed me to speak at two in the morning when they felt no one was listening.

I remember my husband's talking to one of my children's friends about the Middle East. The conversation got down to the Palestinian problem, and I noticed that only the teenager was talking. Later, I asked Ali why he didn't challenge the young man. His answer: "Apparently he thinks that he knows more than I, so why should I burst his bubble?" Propaganda and misinformation reign happily in the U.S.

It was so nice to read Father Adamo's comments; I thought that there was no hope for this intransigent man.

I'd like to add here another column Father wrote about George Bush, Sr.

"A peace activist named John Schuchardt was dragged out of the church where President Bush, Sr. went to pray, by security agents. The unwelcome worshipper had disturbed the service by shouting out during a time when the minister had asked the worshippers to express their concern for sick friends or relatives.

"'I have a concern,' said Schuchardt. 'Think of the 18 million people of Iraq – half of them are children under 15. We must think what it means to be bombed by more than 2000 planes every day.' Later at the end of the service he exclaimed: 'In the name of God, stop the bombing!' Unfortunately, it was a request the president would consider only if God delivered it in person – maybe.

"Since God did not manifest himself at this point in history, the guardians of the president moved in on John Schuchardt and removed him from the First Congregational Church in Kennebunkport, Maine. But what had he done to endanger the president's security? Are we menacing the president when we demand that he do some deed 'in the name of God'? Maybe it bothers Bush's conscience to hear such appeals. The would-be prophet got thrown out of church and thereby silenced. And Bush departed in security.

"Schuchardt's outburst may have been the last hurrah of the peace movement in America. It is obvious that the militarists are in the ascendancy. Not since WWII has there been such unbridled lust for victory. Jingoism rules the day. This bellicose spirit has been cleverly orchestrated by the president and his top advisers. They have whipped up the war spirit and anointed it with patriotism before the peace activists could get rolling. They have won the propaganda war and convinced most Americans that this is war of the good and the beautiful against the bad and the ugly. They end their speeches with a hearty 'God Bless America.'

"The so-called 'peaceniks' have had their day. Will it ever come back again? Not in this generation. Too much has changed over the nearly

20 years since the Vietnam war ended, not with a bang but a whimper. The first sign of the change was the complacency with which we accepted Reagan's invasion of Grenada and recently Bush's conquest of Panama.

"But is all war evil? No. There comes a time when people must fight to preserve their way of life, to avoid bondage to those who would enslave them. But examine the history of our wars and see how few were fought for freedom and security. Most were carried out on foreign soil to protect or extend our wealth and power. Or do you think we were in jeopardy from North Korea, then Vietnam and now Iraq?

"No war in this century remotely resembles a war of defense!

"And now we have bombed Iraq into senselessness. Our air power has inflicted death and destruction from unreachable heights. The Iraqis are sitting ducks for our smart weapons and technology. There is no heroism in such a war; we have learned to kill from a distance, murdering soldiers and old men and women and children without facing them. Our soldiers are now machines; the blood and gut heroes of the past are gone forever.

"Where is the nobility, the chivalry in such warfare? It is as cold and ruthless as an assassin's knife. This is the ultimate terror and the ultimate cowardice: death from the unseen foe. And when the war is over, let there be ticker-tape parades for our great machines!"

God bless you, Msgr. Adamo, wherever you are! The Monsignor passed not too long ago.

TELECOMMUNICATIONS ACT OF 1996

On President Clinton's watch (and you thought it was about Lewinsky) we suffered the biggest de-regulation of radio stations in the U.S., which overturned the rule limiting to forty the number of radio stations around the country that a single company could own. Clear Channel now owns over 1,200 radio stations, or roughly one in every ten in the country, over 776,000 outdoor advertising displays, such as billboards and street benches, as well as 200 major concert halls across the nation. The company represents the biggest and most profitable bands and stars in the business, ranging from NSync, Tina Turner, and Pearl Jim to sports legends like Michael Jordan and Andre Agassi.

John Hogan, the president of Clear Channel radio, and his rival Joel Hollander, president of Infinity, were recently at a gathering where attendees paid $875 for a special "super session."

Hogan told his audience that the radio multi-national was there to provide consumers with what they wanted. "It is really the audience that is the litmus test. I have certain opinions and political beliefs. It shouldn't be up to me; it is up to this community."

Patrick Clawson, a local reporter, disagreed. "Since Clear Channel came into our community and consolidated the stations there, and began to take up a wide share of revenue from that market, Clear Channel now broadcasts from Baltimore over one hundred miles away, and that centralized news agency has never had a reporter in our community.

"We had an industrial plant accident in our area not long ago where the plant manager called the stations at 3 A.M. because they needed to get the word out to the community about the accident, and also to advise the employees not to come to work, but he was greeted with an employee of Clear Channel who said, 'Sorry, all our programs are delivered by satellite, and we can't put anything on the air until 6 A.M.'

"With the elimination of local programming how does this method of operation serve the public interest?"

Hogan declined to reply. Pete Tridish, founder of Prometheus F.M.: "When you have a company that not only owns one radio station but eight radio stations in one town, plus all the billboards and all the concert venues, etc., etc., you have a level of power that competitors have no way to compete. Once their competitors are out of business, they have a free reign to do just about anything they please, the same as any other monopoly."

Herein lies the problem: Larry Mays, the founder of Clear Channel: "If anyone said we were in the radio business, it wouldn't be someone from our company. We're not in the business of providing news and information. We're not in the business of providing well-researched music. We're simply in the business of selling our customers' products."

Yet when radio began in this country, it was not supposed to be simply a commodity. The Federal Communications Commission (FCC), a government federal agency that was established by the Communications Act of 1934, was charged with allocating spectrum space "to maximize the public interest and to encourage a diversity of voices so as to promote a vibrant democracy."

Norman Soloman, the Executive Director of the Institute for Public Accuracy, said, "The FCC has functioned much more as a lap dog to the media industry than any kind of watch dog on behalf of the public to further deregulate and further hijack the public airwaves for private profit."

Clear Channel has gone beyond just axing news. Many believe that the company fires anyone with political opinions other than their own, such as Davey D., the host of a popular talk radio show on KMEL, a black-owned station in Oakland, California, that launched the careers of rappers such as Tupac Shakur and M.C. Hammer.

In October 2000 when the U.S. was on the verge of launching its invasion of Afghanistan, Davey D broadcasted an interview with Barbara Lee, the only member of the U.S. Congress to vote against the war.

KMEL, which had recently been bought by Clear Channel, heard about the show and promptly fired him.

On the other hand, Clear Channel has not been opposed to all forms of political organizing. In 2003, the company paid for pro-war rallies around the country to support the invasion of Iraq as well as for a 33,000-pound tractor to smash a collection of Dixie Chicks' CDs, tapes and other paraphernalia, at an event in Louisiana because the band had the arrogance to protest the war.

Today, the rules of ownership which spawned Clear Channel have been further loosened. The FCC, which was led by Michael Powell, son of the then-Secretary of State, Colin Powell, voted in June of '03 to allow companies to buy more television stations and own newspapers as well as broadcast outlets in the same city.

Meanwhile, local broadcasters are worried about multinational competition as a result of yet another set of proposed new rules that would allow national satellite radio channels like XM and Sirius to broadcast in local markets by inserting "local" weather reports from their national headquarters. (Dante Toza, correspondent with Free Speech Radio News, Montgomery Cty. Observer, 10/29/03).

We deserve what we have gotten in Philadelphia. It used to be that literate talk show hosts would allow knowledgeable patriots on the radio to warn about impending bills, regionalism, corruption. Irv Homer, a Philadelphia talk show host, would allow guests to discuss subjects, whether or not he agreed with them. But that era has gone, thanks to the incremental taking of our rights to airtime away. A ruthless talk-host group has entered, and they don't care what happens so long as they get paid.

Thank goodness that I don't have to report or listen to the incompetents in Philadelphia now that my job is finished. No one with any sense could call or even listen without getting stressed at the stupidity of the callers and talk show hosts. Radio has degenerated into commercials, Frank Sinatra, health shows, garden talk, carpentry, car talk, and trivia about which song a band leader of the fifties played in a certain movie. Or, as I've heard on Boston's WYZ radio – "how are your snoring habits" – I fell asleep and when I awoke four hours later, the usual dufusses were still discussing their topic of snoring. Needless to say, radio is a depressant, and we have to get our airwave rights back!

Only one Congressman, Dennis Kucinich, is interested in the Fairness Doctrine returning, so that we, the people can have access to the airwaves. Please call the Congressman (202-225-3121). He has also bravely spoken out against the war. I have found that Congressman Kucinich, a Democrat, has a conscience, as did Chuck Hagel, former Senator from Nebraska. I would oppose Congressman Kucinich's stand on national health care, simply because I can't afford health care for illegals. Of course, another good man is Ron Paul of Texas.

The other members of Congress are on a path to destroy this country, and we need our country back!

CULTURE IN AMERICA TODAY

Since the public schools started behavior modification in sex education and drug education in 1963, this is where we are:

"If there were any doubt left in America that popular music isn't what it used to be, along comes a hit album to erase any confusion.

"The first two weeks out, it sold a million copies. The happy and successful musicians who are rolling in dough – rap band NWA (Niggers With Attitude – their title, not mine). Topics: roughing up girlfriends, raping women, killing prostitutes, beating women who don't submit to Lewinsky-type sex, stealing, killing policemen. The sick thing is that people couldn't wait to buy this trash. Eric Schnurer, a Philadelphia attorney specializing in First Amendment laws, says that this garbage is "protected just as the Ku Klux Klan has a right to hold a rally" (Steve Lopez, Philadelphia Inquirer, 8/18/91).

Mr. Schnurer, like all attorneys who take these offensive cases, always uses "it goes to the issue of limits" in a free society. Yet, the same type ACLU attorneys don't see freedom to express opposition to this barbarism, as free speech. When we have a woman battered in America every fifteen seconds, this talk represents license to assault, not free speech.

We have Eminem, another angry young man rolling in dough, only because the record distributors, in my opinion, want to create an atmosphere of decadence and hopelessness. Eminem's money is made from those who want to stereotype white trash.

I really don't care whether or not Eminem had a bad childhood – although I wish that he hadn't. I know lots of young people who had bad childhoods who never chose to take out their hurt on others. The point is, what kind of damage is he now inflicting on other undeserving victims with his angry lyrics? It's sad to think about what tiny tots are exposed to in a world full of violence and hate, unless saner minds take over.

Look at television with hip-hoppers hawking their repetitive sounds, pointing their fingers up, touching their crotches. It's America's blight, an insult to real musicians who went before: Fats Domino, Little Richard, Ray Charles, Luther Vandross, James Brown, Mahalia Jackson, Lena Horne, Ella Fitzgerald, Louis Armstrong, Duke Ellington. These were super-talented class acts who had the ability to make an audience laugh or cry at the sound of their dulcet tones.

Rappers, on the other hand, with their back-up dancers, shaking "booties" better left unmoved, let alone shaken, make one want to run to the nearest exit to heave. But money is made because they are stereotyping themselves as lazy and promiscuous.

We have Britain's rejects like Eric Clapton who came here in the '60s and then proceeded to inject hate speech against women: "I may have to blow your brains out, Baby." If socialism were so wonderful with great health care – and they pay for it – all of London's singers, and now actors, newsmen, etc., wouldn't be here in the United States.

Democrats, with their big hearted giveaways to young mothers who have one child after another with different fathers, and who get food stamps and other subsidies and have no incentive to leave the projects, are nowhere in sight to pick up the pieces when a four-year-old is raped. And the projects are breeding grounds for crime and violence. Rarely does one hear a success story, although there are a few coming out of the projects. Usually it takes a strong mother or grandmother to inspire and discipline teens who everyday are met with challenges from other teens who are not so lucky.

While I realize that a woman can make a mistake, more than one mistake is too many. All Americans have lots of opportunities for job training, day care, transportation, and education. There is no excuse for exposing child after child to crime. With women acting like prostitutes, dating one jobless man after another and exposing children to this hapless life, what chance does a white or black child have? Women who have one child after another with no fathers in sight should be penalized. Society should not pay their bills.

The so-called big-hearted Clintons and Kennedys aren't living anywhere near the projects. They're just hoping that the products of crime will volunteer to protect America's assets in other countries.

That's why I've never voted for a Democrat. They have a vested interest in perpetuating poverty. But now, both parties have joined in the "dumbing down" process. It doesn't bother them that rappers can't speak well. Government will lend them a hand, and you know how they treat veterans. Politicians are busy giving jobs to illegals who will do anything to make a living, or so they say.

Marilyn Manson, another looney-tune who is rich and famous from huckstering his violent music, continues his masquerade. No conscience here.

I wish that there were an island that we could send these misfits to – like the British did with Australia. Pedophiles, sickos who laugh at cock-fights and dog-fights, and those who take part in the new "ultimate fighting" wherein the boxers engage in kicking, gouging and punching each other, can be sent to a place where they could fight to the death if that's what they want.

Sports violence, too, is another curse on our culture, along with fathers and mothers who attend Little League games and take their anger out on a coach who gets nothing for his trouble.

"Students are allowed to go to school with FU on their T-shirts, and anarchist moms call it 'Free Speech'" (Dr. Laura, 8/9/00). These mothers and their children should be tossed out of school, along with bullies and discipline problems. I have no obligation to pay for schools with no standards and principals with no backbones.

We have a gang problem, again emanating from poverty and illegal immigration. We have a justice department which no longer works for the victims and is too busy being active in legislation – not their job.

Though I liked the Beatles, even they who came to this country and made a fortune with their collegiate look had their subtle message about the New World Order:

"Imagine there's no heaven
It's easy if you try;
No hell below us
Above us only sky.

Imagine all the people
Living for today . . .

Imagine there's no countries
It isn't hard to do
Nothing to kill or die for
And no religion too.
Imagine all the people
Living life in peace . . .

You may say I'm a dreamer
But I'm not the only one
I hope someday you'll join us
And the world will be as one . . .

Imagine no possessions
I wonder if you can
No need for greed or hunger
A brotherhood of man.
Imagine all the people
Sharing all the world . . .

You may say I'm a dreamer
But I'm not the only one.
I hope someday you'll join us
And the world will live as one."

Of course, "Lucy in the sky with diamonds" refers to drugs which you'd have to be on if you believe the disgusting rot about no borders, no God. Just peace. And drugs?

I wonder if we could all join Yoko in the Dakota Building. Or Paul, who couldn't part with his "possessions" in a divorce suit, when he realized his judgment was bad.

After all, they did ask us to join them. As for me, I hope that there's a hell for all of the bad people influencing the young.

Black Entertainment Television (BET) was started by Robert Johnson who said that the difference between his music videos and Don Imus' insulting comments about the Rutgers' Women's Basketball Team was "artistic freedom." Freedom? Freedom to spread an image of America that is sickening to any civilized person in the world? MTV, BET, and Nickelodeon (always demeaning Arabs), have no merit. Children who have no direction and whose parents use TV as a babysitter, are being victimized by a group of CEOs and junk-salesmen selling misogynist music videos to an audience trying to be hip. The Federal Communications Commission might as well be defunct for all of the action they take. Why we pay these officials remains a mystery.

I blame Viacom for allowing this trash to hit the airwaves and pollute the minds of the young who already are handling too much too soon, so that they can make inordinate amounts of money. And then the rappers themselves who perpetuate the victimization role so well are making money by belittling women. It makes no difference whether the women are mothers or girlfriends, they despise all women. Disgusting!

Teachers, too, make money from this trash through pension investments. The Chicago teachers' union doesn't seem to care that their profits come at the expense of the students they teach.

Shows like the Sopranos depicting Italians as degenerate killers in undershirts, and "24" are bad enough – we don't need a constant revue of vile dancing and bad language.

How many jets do these CEOs need before we the people say "That's it!"

Where are the parents who should be protesting at schools for better reading and language courses instead of sex and drug education mandates? They're over at Wal-Mart subsidizing Red China or looking for a mate and some junk food.

No one group in this country, religious or ethnic, has a monopoly on grief. No one group deserves endless apologies, except for the children abused by the media and parents who don't give a damn!

School "choice" for parents who never cared about what their children were being taught in the first place is a joke.

China has it right – if you can't afford one child, don't have two! But in America, the middle class supports <u>everybody's</u> children, while promiscuous mothers think giving birth is a right. It's not; it's a privilege.

Not to worry! Congressman Bob Smith of New Jersey, whose mind must be made of mush, has taken in thousands of Chinese women who want more babies they can't afford. When does this travesty against middle class stop? When do we vote out the Bob Smiths who engender votes through this miscarriage of justice?

SECRET SOCIETIES

I remember in the early nineties, when people who knew what was in store for us were allowed to speak out. These were people who prevented Mayor Rendell from reaching his dream of regionalism. This was before President Clinton put the kibosh on free speech with his Telecommunications Act of 1996 and before Mr. Rendell became Governor of Pennsylvania.

In 2009, we are seeing that the things those patriots were warning us about have come to pass. The Mayor and the Governor get inordinate powers through Home Rule Legislation and regionalism. They can control education and just about anything else. Once they get the regional tax, they can control where you live, breathe, and work.

Everyone has heard the ridicule aimed at anyone mentioning "Black-hawk helicopters" or "secret societies," such as the Council on Foreign Relations (CFR), not so-secret anymore. Unfortunately, the intimidation aimed at any caller mentioning the Bilderbergers or the trilateralists prevented free speech. Yet, you'll hear the media contend that the First Amendment protects the speech of those with whom you don't agree. They view pornographers as those with whom we disagree, but Ron Paul callers are cut off or not heard at all. And we fools allow this injustice to continue.

I don't plan to go into the history of the secret societies, but I will give you a brief summary taken from Criminal Politics, October '91. And, I will remind you that newspapers today, in 2009, headline "Black Hawk Down: Five Marines Killed." Now that the masses have been thoroughly brainwashed, and hopefully dumbed down, the media can pull anything on us, and get away with it, including martial law, like any other third world country.

Brief Summary:

"The Trilateral Commission is the private group founded by David Rockefeller in 1973, designed to be a super-sophisticated offshoot of the much older and larger Council on Foreign Relations and of the European Bilderberg Society. These groups are frequently referred to in the independent press by many names, but most frequently as the "Trilateral Combine" or the "Globalists" and their policies are most frequently referred to as "Globalism.""

"The publishers of Criminal Politics view the 'Combine' as a super high-level (and illegal) political party. Their first candidate for president (hand picked) was none other than James Earl Carter in 1974. David Rockefeller managed to dupe the Democratic National Committee in 1972 into believing that Jimmy Carter was a Democrat, when in reality he was a "Trialateralist." Today, the Trilateral Combine controls BOTH the Republican National Committee and the Democratic National Committee from behind the scenes…Michael Dukakis was selected as a fall guy for the preselected winner of the Zionist Trilateral Party – George Bush, Sr.

"The Trilateral Combine's political aspirations broke through strict press censorship back in February, 1980 during the Republican Primary Campaign of George Bush, when he was competing with Ronald Reagan for the presidential nomination. The 1980 Primary Campaign is the only case (that we are aware of) where the established press carried stories of the Trilateral Combine. There are still copies of those clippings available in our files.

"The goals of the 'Combine' are simply worldwide control through world government…. They foster the elimination of nation states, borders, independent currencies, and national governments. They claim to work for "world peace" and the brotherhood of man, when in fact they impose their control over all nations of the world.

"They are working strenuously for the formation of a world currency (the EURO) and a world central bank (which already exists in the form of the IMF (International Monetary Fund and the World Bank)…. The Atheistic Combine is anti-American, anti-Catholic and anti-Protestant. The Combine maintains lock-tight control over the United States through the Republican National Committee (which finances destabilization campaigns against certain conservative organizations).

"Alan Greenspan, former head of Federal Reserve, stood by…to bring on 20% interest rates, if the Combine's policies were not followed by the United States Senate and the House of Representatives. The Combine functions much as does the Communist Party in the Soviet Union and the Combine has its "Politburo" in the form of David Rockefeller, Henry Kissinger and the publishers of the *New York Times* and the *Washington Post*, which are the party's two major mouthpieces."

"One of the most notorious of secret societies was the German Illuminati, founded by Adam Weishaupt in 1776. Weishaupt was a professor of Canon law at the University of Ingolstadt and a former Jesuit. Its aim was to replace Christianity by a religion of reason. It was banned by the Bavarian Government in 1785." (Encyclopedia Britanica, 15th ed., S.V. "Illuminati") "The goal of Weishaupt's new religion would substitute the religious man with the "illuminated' man who could solve his problems through the use of his mind." ("The Unseen Hand" by A. Ralph Epperson, p. 81) He believed that national governments should be replaced by world government.

"The story of modern-day Communism begins with a secret society called the Order of the Illuminati.

"It was about this organization that the 1953 Report of the California Senate Investigating Committee on Education stated: "So-called modern Communism is apparently the same hypocritical world-conspiracy to destroy civilization that was funded by the Illuminati and that raised its head in our colonies here at the critical period before the adoption of our Constitution." ("The Capitalist Conspiracy," G. Edward Griffin, p. 53)

"Communism is never a spontaneous or even willing rising of the downtrodden masses against the bosses who exploit them – but exactly the opposite."

The objective of the Insiders is to change the tenure of the land, to drive out the present owners of the soil and to put an end to ecclesiastical establishments. They do not want constitutional government." ("The Unseen Hand," p. 77)

Nesta Webster, one of the major researchers into the illuminati has summarized their goals as follows:

1. abolition of monarchy and all ordered government;
2. abolition of private property;

3. abolition of inheritance;
4. abolition of patriotism (nationalism);
5. abolition of the family (i.e. of marriage and all morality, and the institution of communal education of children);
6. abolition of religion. (Ibid.)

As you can see, Communism is just another reason for war, for destroying land and lives and ultimately enslaving all who think that the proletariat (or working class) will finally have a say in government. It's the design of the rich who need war to build debt future generations will have to pay.

The Insiders have done a good job, raping the constitution, incrementally, with the help of the headless horsemen in Washington, DC, and our state and local offices.

These unelected policy makers, such as the Bilderbergers and the CFR, the Trilateral Commission and the Illuminati, meet in Davos, Switzerland and other posh spots to discuss our economy, military endeavors, world leaders, environment, education and God knows what. They make decisions for us without our knowledge.

Another society, the Masonry or Freemasons, is the largest and oldest of the secret societies. "One modern source lists seventeen American presidents as having been Masons." (Holy Bible, Masonic Edition, p. 49) Adam Weishaupt, father of the 18th century Illuminati Society, eventually consumed European Masonry, a 5000-year-old entity.

There is also a Christian component to the freemasons. The First Degree of Masonry teaches candidates to follow the precepts of the Holy Bible; however, the candidates are sometimes led into Deism, the forerunner of Unitarianism. Deists believe that God existed merely to create the universe but then withdrew to meddle no more in the affairs of men." (NWO, William T. Still, p. 30)

It is the higher degree mason who is said to have blood rituals and to worship Lucifer. Interesting to me was the number of Luciferian statues I've seen outside of some expensive homes in Florida. It gave me the creeps to say the least.

Of course these societies work in conjunction with the many foundations whose function seems to be disabling the culture of America through education and government. Rhodes scholars – many of whom are in government (President Clinton) – and the Carnegie and Rockefeller Foundations, Ford, Pew and others have played a huge role in educating students for a one world government.

In the late 1800s, multi-millionaire diamond tycoon Cecil Rhodes and some of his wealthy British friends decided to form a secret society loosely based on the legends surrounding King Arthur and his Knights of the Round Table, but based on Masonic principles. The group, formed in 1891, consisted of an inner circle, including Rhodes, Lord Rothschild and others known as the "Circle of Initiates" and an inner circle which came to be known as the Round Table.

Rhodes left much of his fortune to the Rhodes Scholarship, a program he established to bring foreign students to Oxford. In my opinion, they are unquestioning, robotic-type students.

"In the middle 1800s when Marx and Engels wrote the Communist Manifesto, there was only one power in Europe and that was the Rothschilds." ("World Revolution," Nesta Webster, p. 20)

"The question remains to be answered whether the Rothschilds were secret financiers behind the Illuminati, the consequent French Revolution and the Jacobin incursion of citizen Genet into the United States. (Genet was sent from France as an ambassador in 1793 and started the "Democratic Clubs," an offshoot of the Illuminati Masonry Society.) Certainly the Rothschilds' influence upon industrial America was profound, working through the Wall Street firms Kuhn, Loeb and Co. and J.P. Morgan Co., the Rothschilds financed John D. Rockefeller so that he could create the Standard Oil Empire. They also financed the activities of Edward Harriman (railroads) and Andrew Carnegie (steel)." ("Descent into Slavery," Griffin, p. 33)

When Trotsky came to New York in 1917, "he found wealthy Wall Street bankers who were willing to finance a revolution in Russia," wrote journalist William T. Still.

One of these bankers was Jacob Schiff, whose family had lived with the Rothschilds in Frankfurt. Another was Elihu Root, attorney for Paul Warburg's Kuhn, Loeb and Company. According to the New York Journal – American, "It is estimated by Jacob's grandson, John Schiff, that the old man sank about $20 million for the final triumph of Bolshevism in Russia." Root, a CFR member, contributed another $20 million, according to the Congressional Record of September 2, 1919.

To illustrate the interconnectedness of America's wealthy and powerful elite, another grandson, Andrew Schiff, is married to the daughter of former Democratic Vice President, Al Gore.

As you can see, the rich old boys don't wait for provocation for war; they create it.

As Adam Weishaupt said, "One must speak sometimes in one way, sometimes in another, so that the real purpose should remain impenetrable to our inferiors." (Nesta Webster, p. 31)

FEDERAL RESERVE

Larry Abraham (<u>Call It Conspiracy</u>): "In order to understand the conspiracy, it is necessary to have some rudimentary knowledge of banking and, particularly, of international bankers. While it would be an over-simplification to ascribe the entire conspiracy to international bankers, they nevertheless have played a key role. Think of the conspiracy as a hand with one finger labeled 'international banking,' and the others 'foundations,' 'the anti-religious movement,' 'Fabian socialism,' and 'communism.' It was the international bankers about whom Professor Quigley spoke when he said 'their aim was nothing less than control of the world through finance.'

"One major reason for the historical blackout on the role of the international bankers in political history is that the Rothschilds were Jewish. Anti-Semites have played into the hands of the conspiracy by trying to portray the entire conspiracy as Jewish. Nothing would be farther from the truth. The traditionally Anglo-Saxon J. P Morgan and Rockefeller international banking institutions have played a key role in that conspiracy. But there is no denying the importance of the Rothschilds and their satellites. However, it is just as unreasonable to blame all Jews for the crimes of the Rothschilds as it is to hold all Baptists accountable for the crimes of the Rockefellers.

"The Jewish members have used an organization called the Anti-Defamation League as an instrument to try to convince everyone that any mention of the Rothschilds is an attack on all Jews." (Larry Abraham, <u>Call It Conspiracy</u>, p. 45)

According to the U.S. Constitution, (Article 1, Sect. 8): "Congress shall have the power to coin money, and regulate the value thereof."

But President Wilson who gave us the income tax, also gave us the Federal Reserve Act of 1913, and Congress thereby surrendered our sovereignty to a cabal of international bankers who proceeded to swindle Americans ever since.

Congressman Louis T. McFadden of the Banking Committee addressed the House on 6/10/32:

"Some people think that the Federal Reserve Banks are U.S. Government institutions. They are not. They are private credit monopolies which prey upon the people of the United States for the benefit of themselves and their foreign and domestic swindlers, and rich and predatory money-lenders" (75 Congressional Record 12595-12603).

This special act of Congress is in direct violation of the 16th Corpus-Juris Secundum Sect. 141, which states that Congress cannot delegate or sign over its authority to any individual, corporation or foreign nation.

So, in essence, Congress has signed the printing of money over to private corporations, disregarding the Constitution which they swear to uphold.

Today, one lone Congressman, Ron Paul of Texas, dares to speak out against the Federal Reserve. And, of course, right before him, 1994, another Congressman, Henry Gonzales, also of Texas, repeatedly attacked the Federal Reserve. You can read his arguments in the Congressional Record.

Gonzales: "The 'money' which the banks issue is for bookkeeping entries only. It costs them nothing. It is not backed by their wealth, efforts, property, or risk. It is not redeemable except in more debt paper.

"I will repeat for the benefit of my colleagues, so many of whom expressed surprise when I have explained exactly what the Federal Reserve Board is: It is not a government agency. It is a private corporation. And the stocks in that corporation are owned by the private commercial banking system. The Federal Reserve is a federally chartered corporation whose stock is owned by the member banks. As I said yesterday, all through written history of mankind, any individual or group of individuals who, for whatever reason, has power of any kind and no accountability, will find themselves corrupted and working against the best interest of the American people. I think it should be a major concern of everybody to know how the most powerful committee in the United States determines how much we will pay for goods and services we buy, and whether we will have jobs or employment or, more importantly, whether your share, your share of stock in our government is that dollar note you have in your pocket – and that is a Federal Reserve Note. And you have to pay interest to print that note, believe it or not."

Mr. Gonzalez wanted to know:

1. Why it wasn't reported to the Congress that over the last ten years the value of the dollar decreased by 2/3rds in comparison to the Japanese yen and the German Deutsche mark. And why we had to pay more for things we bought.
2. Why the "Fed" loaned $700 million to Mexico without consent of Congress.
3. When the Federal Reserve Bank planned to release complete transcripts of future meetings on foreign disbursements.

"The Fed is upholding the stonewalling tradition to protect its turf, and the immense political power it has built up over the years, by the bankers who lobby the Congress.

"But I will say this to the panjandrums (pompous officials) of power, Mr. Greenspan, and to you, my colleagues and the privileged orders of our country: if we do not get complete accounting, the day will come when the people in full knowledge will rise in wrath and indignation and chase all of these moneylenders that have sold out their inheritance from this temple of democracy."

Bankers print money and then send it to us through their member banks for our homes, cars, etc., at any interest rate they desire, and if we don't pay, they confiscate your property. Congressmen who need pork for their districts borrow the money, and we pay the debt.

They can lend money to foreign countries and if the foreign countries cannot pay, we forgive the debt and pay it ourselves.

After President Roosevelt confiscated citizens' gold, under threat of fines or prison, he declared the gold the property of the federal government, and then sold it to his foreign friends at a handsome profit. They alone could exchange their paper dollars for gold. The money got moving again when we went to war and the bankers could profit from arms and other war-related materials and services.

It was economist Murray Rothbard, the most preeminent student of Austrian economists, Ludwig von Mises and Fredrich von Hayek, who summed up the era in the run-up to WW II:

"During the 1930s, the Rockefellers pushed hard for war against Japan, which they saw as competing with them for oil and rubber resources in Southeast Asia and as endangering the Rockefellers' cherished dreams of a mass China market for petro products. On the other hand, the Rockefellers took a non-interventionist position in Europe where they had close financial ties with German firms. The Morgans, in contrast, were committed to financial ties with Britain and France. WW II might therefore be considered as a coalition war. The Morgans got their war in Europe, the Rockefellers in Asia.

"And thanks to the Fed's pyramid scheme, keeping the United States government afloat requires nothing short of a global monetary hegemony, since any pyramid scheme remains visible only so long as its base continues to expand.

"Hence the International Monetary Fund was created so that the United States could lend money to third world countries, NATO, the U.N. – all of these military schemes to empower the bankers to take not only our taxes but our homes and livelihoods, if they wish. And all they do is print money at a cost of $240."

Three strategies for government shortfalls:

1. Domestic borrowing through sale of Treasury Bonds – leads to higher interest rates.
2. Foreign borrowing through Treasury Bond sales – leads to over-price dollars which discourage imports. This is why Red China keeps the value of their yuan down, enabling us to import inexpensive items. Unfair practice. Good for them; bad for us.
3. Direct increase of money. Too much money and not enough goods – inflation; sudden lessening of money in circulation with a rise in its value, leading to a fall in prices, raise in interest rates – deflation.

"Investment bankers are the first to get printed money for United States Treasury Bonds, so that the investors could pay down government debt. This enables them to print more money and engage in the securities markets abroad as well by "selling" the natural resources of third world countries and underwriting their debt. This is deficit spending – spending more than we produce – but this is how Congressmen get their campaign financing. Pleasing the corporations, not us. Commercial bankers take care of loans on real estate, etc." (Anne Williamson, <u>The Fed</u>, pl. 15 - ©2001, WorldNetDaily.com).

The Fed was also the financier of WW I. By their selling war bonds, we were able to pay the $40 billion it cost. Taxes paid for $15 billion, and the war bonds, $26 billion.

Congressman Charles Lindberg, the father of the aviator, understood what was going on and said, "If you establish this kind of system, you will create the means by which depressions and inflations will be created scientifically. We will have a group of bankers who will sit down together, in complete concealment, and determine whether we shall have inflation or deflation; they'll be more powerful than Congress itself, and they will make the entire American people their slaves and servants.

"From 1913 to 1933, the United States paid interest on the debt with gold which we guarded for the bankers at Fort Knox until we had to declare bankruptcy.

"Jefferson warned us: 'If the American people ever allow private banks to control the issue of currency, the banks will deprive the people of all property until their children will wake up homeless on the continent their fathers conquered.'

"Enough presidents tried to do away with this Federal Reserve scheme which was contrived in a very secretive way.

"At Hoboken, the core group, which was connected principally to J. P. Morgan's, Jacob Schiff's, and David Rockefeller's banking interest, dressed up in disguise and journeyed from Manhattan to the railroad station in Hoboken, New Jersey.

"At Hoboken, they boarded J. P. Morgan's private railway car using assumed names. From Hoboken, the eager team of would-be counterfeiters traveled in a sealed railway carriage to Morgan's vacation home on Jekyll Island, off the coast of Georgia. It was on Jekyll Island that the scheme to swindle the American people out of sound money by establishing the Federal Reserve was accomplished" (Anne Williamson).

Abraham Lincoln tried to issue interest-free Treasury notes (Criminal Politics, p. 7):

"According to the Encyclopedia Britannica, Presidents James Garfield and William McKinley were killed by lone assassins for the same reasons."

Before that, even in 1790, there were attempts to start a central bank, when Alexander Hamilton converted the public debt into interest-bearing bonds payable to the bankers. In 1811, Hamilton's bank charter expired, and by 1812, the international bankers precipitated the War of 1812, between Britain and the United States, in which the White House and other buildings in Washington, D.C. were burned.

The bank charter was extended for twenty years. Andrew Jackson, one of the few great presidents, vetoed the bank charter when it expired in 1836.

In National Geographic: Jackson told Van Buren: "The bank is trying to kill me, but I will kill it." Second, he said, "If the American people only understood the rank injustice of our money and banking system … there would be a revolution before morning. . . ." Finally, Jackson remarked, directing his words to the bankers trying to push for a renewal of their bank charter: "You are a den of vipers. I intend to rout you out…."

Jackson's statements were reported in all grade and high school books until the late 1960s, but the context was never given.

An effort to assassinate President Jackson was attempted, but failed.

President Reagan made a slip in 1980, saying that the "Federal Reserve is accountable to no one."

Benjamin Franklin: "The inability of the colonists to get the power to issue their own money permanently out of the hands of George III and the international bankers was the PRIME reason for the Revolutionary War."

Anne Williamson explained an "ordinary transaction" very well:

"The Central Bank buys, usually, old existing government bonds, though in principle it could buy any public asset, through what are known as the Fed's 'Open Market Operations.' When the Fed makes a purchase, the Fed writes a check on the Federal Reserve System out of thin air. The recipient – let's say a private citizen who sold a warehouse business for $1000 to the Fed – goes to his commercial bank and deposits the Central Bank's check. The commercial bank of the depositor then takes the check to the Central Bank and says, 'Put it into my reserve account,' thereby increasing the bank's required reserves with the Central Bank, which then allows it to pile a multiple of checkable money created out of thin air on top of the actual note value of the original check created out of thin air from the Central Bank.

"So out of $1000 deposit in a bank, $100 goes to the vaults, $200 to the bank's reserve account with the Central Bank, and the remainder is exploded into $10,000 of checkable money the bank can lend."

Chairman David Rockefeller of Chase Manhattan Bank controls all twelve Federal Reserve Banks and, thus, our economy.

"Since the keystone of the international banking empires has been government bonds, it has been in the interest of these international bankers to encourage government debt. The higher the debt the more the interest. Nothing drives government deeply into debt like a war; and it has not been an uncommon practice among international bankers to finance both sides of the bloodiest military conflicts. For example, during our Civil War, the North was financed by the Rothschilds through their American agent, August Belmont; and the American South through the Erlangers, Rothschild relatives.

"But while wars and revolutions have been useful to international bankers in gaining or increasing control over governments, the key to such control has always been control of money. You can control a government if you have it in your debt; a creditor is in a position to demand the privileges of monopoly from the sovereign. Money-seeking governments have granted monopolies in state banking, natural resources, oil concessions, and transportation. However, the monopoly the international financiers most covet is control over a nation's money." (None Dare Call It Conspiracy, Gary Allen and Larry Abraham, p. 41).

ANTI-TRUST LAWS AND CAPITALISM

Laws passed in the U.S., especially between 1890 and 1915, to prevent large business corporations, called Trusts, from combining into monopolies in order to avoid competition were instituted to encourage Free Enterprise.

President Theodore Roosevelt wanted the government to be the arbiter between capital and labor, guaranteeing justice to both, and favor to none. He applauded enormous productivity of factories, and the higher living standards, but knew that abuses could take place in this new industrial combination. In 1903 Congress established a Department of Commerce and Labor which contained a Bureau of Corporations to investigate Trusts.

Roosevelt proposed stronger government regulation of the railroads. At the same time, he insisted that trusts which had a practical monopoly on necessities of life, such as transportation, coal, oil, beef and sugar, must not charge an unreasonably large toll on the public for this monopoly, but must be regulated by the government. (A Complete History of the U.S., Clement Wood).

"One misunderstanding about capitalism is that business is at odds with government and wants to see its reduction. Not hardly. It is entrepreneurs and citizens alone who feel the weight of leviathan (something huge). Successful businesses are always, as day follows night, enthusiasts for (and willing collaborators with) government's involvement in the economy because they rely upon government's minions to provide them with subsidies from the public purse while protecting their markets and industries from the leaner men of free enterprise" (Anne Williamson, World Net, The Fed).

We deploy the military to back up corporations all over the world. We now subsidize factories built in Mexico and abroad, putting American workers out of work – we call it "protecting our interests" – and we import less expensive items for consumers. But we still pay the same price for sneakers. The payoff is to Congress. Even their children get six figure jobs from the corporate powers they protect.

Hillary and Bill had a nice little scheme going on when they were in Arkansas and in Washington, D.C.

"For example, nothing more sophisticated than mutual, back-scratching lies at the bottom of the Clintons' assorted Whitewater scandals. Clinton nailed down the couples' franchise every two years by getting re-elected governor of Arkansas while his spouse handled the paperwork at the Rose law firm.

"Both Clintons manipulated funds under their control to their own and their supporters' interest, at the expense of the public that only one of them was elected to serve. Hillary favored using organizations superficially dedicated to the 'public good,' like the Children's Defense Fund and the Legal Services Corporation.

"While in Arkansas Bill preferred mucking around with state bond funds, teachers' pension funds, and so on, but they both loved doing banks, taking easy government money dedicated to various target groups along with savings and loan institutions. In return, the Clinton 'supporters' returned part of the take in the form of political contributions that enabled Clinton to succeed at the polls. In essence, the Clintons acted as gatekeepers to public funds that – via Bill Clinton's authority through the electoral process – others (Clinton political supporters) could then loot quasi-legally. The 1996 campaign finance scandals and the excessive international lending of both the International Monetary Fund and the World Bank, are merely the result of the Clintons' efforts to internationalize their tried and true Arkansas methodology, which had consistently delivered power to them.

"Theirs is an old and – for citizens – sad story" (Anne Williamson).

The IMF was created in the fading days of WW II – expansion of the Fed's base and the preservation of its pyramid scheme.

Our national debt is over nine trillion dollars, but in excess of $20 trillion when the costs of still unfunded, government-provided pension and medical commitments are taken into account. And the Federal Reserve answers to no one, by design.

And, of course, the "surplus" Clinton allegedly left us with is another scheme perpetrated by Wall Street's raising stock funds, not by the products offered on the market, but by the private investments. The subsequent taxes on the "dot coms," etc. which did extremely well, paid the taxes for the surplus.

Hillary's Defense Fund allows children to sue their parents, compliments of her payments to trial lawyers. A lot of community and faith-based organizations get help from the Clintons and the rest of our sell-outs in Congress. Separation of church and state means nothing in this political racket.

What we have today is not capitalism with its checks and balances, as Theodore Roosevelt wanted with the anti-trust laws. The corporations, over the years, have changed the laws so that they favor the mergers and oligopolies which control production and sales of a product or service by a few companies. Since Vice President Cheney was CEO at Halliburton, Halliburton gets no-bid contracts all over the world from Iraq to Katrina – with no accounting for the loss of billions of dollars. Now, Halliburton wants its base to move to Darfur where they would pay no taxes. And Katrina still doesn't have its trash picked up.

And poor McDonnell Douglas. We had better bomb more countries so that they can manufacture more F16s. They're losing money!

What can we do? Let the foundations pay their fair share of taxes. Get them off of the feeding tubes like the rest of us. And if Kellogg's isn't satisfied with the money they make from cereal, don't let them merge with two or three other corporations, having nothing to do with cereal.

And, when they are greedy and need to grab bananas from poor countries and pay the labor one dollar per day, let them hire their own armies so that when the natives hate the corporations, they don't see American faces in American service suits defending the travesties going on under the name American.

Now that we know that wars create debt for the nasties, let's forgive ourselves the debt as we do with third world countries when we need their support for wars we shouldn't start.

When President Johnson's crew thought up the Gulf of Tonkin fiasco, claiming that North Vietnamese gunboats had attacked the U.S. Sixth

Fleet in the Gulf of Tonkin off the coast of Vietnam, it was a lie. Nevertheless, it created the bogeyman needed for the Vietnam War.

The Iranian standoff with the British sailors was also more provocation for the warmongers to get the U.S. – already present in the Gulf with fleets of personnel – ready to bombard Iran or any country hurting "corporate" interests, not ours. If Chavez could sell oil to the poor at a low price, what is wrong with our greedy Exxon-Mobil and the rest?

Today America has concentration of power in the hands of the few giant corporations. They dominate foreign policy and act as bullies giving American jobs away. They've put our farmers out of work with their Archer Daniel Midland conglomerates, so that we now get most of our produce from foreign countries. We're not even told when our food is radiated because of the e-coli bacteria.

We subsidize their tax dollars and supply their foreign companies and banks with troops, while they store their money somewhere in the Fiji Islands and elsewhere.

Woe to us if we don't challenge this corporate state.

OIL AND THE NWO CONSPIRACY

I felt that an article first published in 1990 by Youth Action News, together with substance, facts and analysis offered by C. B. Baker, would make a most enlightening exposé for those of you who may like a little background into the "oil crisis" in the Mideast.

C. B. Baker starts out with a speech George Bush, Sr. made on September 11, 1990. Notice it is 9/11. Significant? I don't know.

At any rate, George Bush, Sr. (the 41st President of the U.S.) claimed that it was necessary to send hundreds of thousands of troops to Saudi Arabia in order to defend the "New World Order." "Few people who heard that speech understood that this 'NWO' concept meant the transfer of vast amounts of America's wealth (derived from skyrocketing oil prices) to Saudi Arabia which, in turn, deposits that wealth into Chase Manhattan Bank, Citicorp, and other big international banks which are allied with the Trilateral Commission." From these deposits, these international banks can indirectly give foreign aid to Russia or any country deemed an ally of this conspiracy.

"The Trilateralists have long planned to deliberately create a serious political and economic crisis. Iraq, because of its newly discovered oil fields, became a threat to the interest of the bankers and at the same time, the perfect target to set up a so-called 'cause' of the crisis. It was relatively easy for the trilateralists in the Bush Administration and the Soviet KGB (which had a strong influence on all levels of the Iraqi government) to encourage and manipulate Saddam Hussein into invading Kuwait, so that invasion could then be used as an excuse to justify war against Iraq, skyrocketing oil prices and the establishment of a NWO.

The 9/23/90 New York Times carried a detailed transcript of U.S. Ambassador to Iraq, April Glaspie's official meeting with Iraqi President Saddam Hussein. "The meeting was in Baghdad, on July 25, only days before the invasion. Saddam stated: 'We do not want too high prices for oil.' Saddam reminded Ambassador Glaspie that beginning with the big 1974 hikes, Iraq opposed the skyrocketing of oil prices." (And I might add here, so did the Shah of Iran oppose the raising of oil prices until Henry Kissinger paid the Shah a visit and told him to raise prices, as the Shah revealed in his book, Answer to History. Also, keep in mind that Iran and the Arab world sold us oil at $5 per barrel for many, many years – that is until "alliances" with Britain and Israel and trilateralist-imposed dictatorships caused undue suffering among the people of the Middle East and in other countries as well. George Washington very wisely admonished us not to engage in "foreign alliances.")

"Foreign minister Tariq Aziz stated: 'Our policy in OPEC (Organization of Petroleum Producing Countries) opposed sudden jumps in oil prices.' Saddam added: 'Twenty-five dollars per barrel is not a high price.' Ambassador Glaspie's answer showed the conspiratorial motivation in creating the war crisis. She stated: 'We have many Americans who would like to see the price go above $25 per barrel because they come from oil-producing states.'" (That would be President Bush, Sr. and his Secretary of State, James Baker.)

"Ambassador Glaspie then produced Bush's green light for the Iraqi invasion of Kuwait. 'We have no opinion on the Arab-Arab conflicts, like your border disagreement with Kuwait. I was in the American Embassy in Kuwait during the late '60s. The instruction we had during this period was that we should express no opinion on this issue and that the issue is not associated with America. James Baker has directed our officials to emphasize this instruction. We hope that you solve this problem using any suitable method....' April Glaspie's meeting took place five days after the CIA reported to the White House that Iraqi military mobilization on the Kuwait frontier looked like preparation for invasion." (Source: National Public Radio ... All Things Considered 9/17/90).

The 9/23/90 New York Times stated: "Interviews with dozens of administration officials, law-makers and independent 'experts' and a review of public statements . . . show that instead of sending Saddam blunt messages through public and private statements that invasion would be unacceptable, the State Department preferred equivocal statements . . . about the American commitments to Kuwait."

Ambassador Glaspie's boss at the State Department was John H. Kelly, Assistant Secretary of State for Near Eastern and South Asian officials. Two days before the invasion he repeated the same message as Glaspie gave Saddam in open Congressional testimony. Later, at a September 18 hearing before the House Foreign Affairs Subcommittee, Representative Lee Hamilton (D. Ind.) told Kelly: "You left the impression that it was the policy of the United States not to come to the defense of Kuwait . . . I asked you at the earlier hearing, before the invasion, if there was a U.S. commitment to come to Kuwait's defense if it were attacked. Your response over and over was that we have no defense treaty relationship with any Gulf country."

The 9/17/90 Washington Post described another public signal that the Administration made before Iraq's invasion: "In the same week that Glaspie met with Saddam, Secretary of State Baker's top public affairs aide, Margaret Tutwiler, said 'the U.S. was not obligated to come to Kuwait's aid if the emirate were attacked.'

The Washington Post also carried an article by former U.N. Ambassador Jeanne Kirkpatrick who reported that both the Defense Department and CIA had received repeated warnings of Iraq's impending invasion of Kuwait, which were dismissed by the State Department. Kirkpatrick said, "Because these administration officials did not warn Saddam against aggression, but instead repeatedly affirmed that the U.S. had no alliance or commitment to Kuwait, Saddam Hussein had no opportunity to realistically assess the probable consequences of seizing Kuwait."

Despite multiple warnings from intelligence agencies, the Bush Administration took no action to warn the thousands of U.S. citizens in Kuwait and Iraq. Even a few hours advance warning would have allowed Americans in Kuwait sufficient time to flee in their cars to the Saudi border, a short distance away. The White House war conspirators wanted plenty of U.S. hostages to help generate anti-Iraqi propaganda and hysteria.

The 9/9/90 Washington Post reported that a member of the Kuwaiti Sabah family said that he still remembered "how the U.S. Ambassador had repeatedly asked the Kuwaiti foreign ministry for direct access to Kuwaiti facilities in 1987-88" (meaning that the Trilateralists planned to deploy U.S. troops around Iraq before Saddam's second invasion of Kuwait.) (If you look at an old Ottoman Empire map, you will see that this part of Kuwait with its oil belonged to Iraq.)

The 9/9/90 New York Times described the secret war game . . . barely two months ago, "before some of the U.S. Army's top brass assembled at Fort Leavenworth, Kansas." This secret war game involved rehearsals for a U.S.-Iraqi military conflict.

The 9/28/90 issue of the Philadelphia Bulletin stated: "There is no question that the State Department, working together with Israeli (and Soviet) intelligence laid a careful trap for Saddam Hussein, encouraging him to believe that he could seize Kuwait without any serious repercussions. At the same time, the Bush administration was engaged in feverish preparation to use the seizure of Kuwait as the pretext for an American military occupation of Persian Gulf States."

The Bulletin continued: "That, at the same week the U.S. State Department gave the green light to Iraq's territorial claims against Kuwait, the Pentagon's Central Command was conducting Operational Internal Look '90. According to a spokesman for General Schwarzkopf, Supreme Commander in the Middle East, this exercise was based on 'almost exactly the scenario for an Iraqi invasion of Kuwait.' The advanced guard of U.S. troops was able to deploy into Saudi Arabia at previously unheard of speeds because American military forces were preparing for Iraq's invasion of Kuwait long before the event."

The August 6, 1990 Time Magazine reported that a few days before Iraq's invasion, "The U.S. Army in West Germany began moving 100,000 artillery shells loaded with nerve gas chemicals out of NATO storage dumps." These shells were allegedly going to be incinerated on Johnston Island, a U.S. atoll 825 miles southwest of Honolulu, but their real destination was apparently the Persian Gulf, where they could be used against Iraq.

Immediately following Iraq's invasion of Kuwait, the Bush Administration sent falsified intelligence reports to King Fahd of Saudi Arabia in order to convince him that his country was about to be invaded by Iraq. In reality, Iraq never made any threatening moves against Saudi Arabia. President Bush had to exert pressure on Fahd in order to land U.S. troops.

The 10/16/90 New York Times carried an extremely revealing article about Jordan's King Hussein and his repeated efforts to prevent war. Jordan's King Hussein said Saddam Hussein (no relation) told him that he never intended to invade Saudi Arabia. Furthermore, the King said, Prime Minister Margaret Thatcher had told him during a meeting ... that "the U.S. troops were halfway to Saudi Arabia before they were formally requested." King Hussein confirmed this later through his own sources.

The 9/21/90 New York Times reported that President Bush repeatedly turned his back on an Arab solution. Jordan's Crown Prince Hassan stated: "I say in the first weekend an Arab solution was offered and undercut by the U.S. If war comes," he said, "it will be largely because every Arab attempt to resolve that crisis has been thwarted by the American (Bush) intransigence and ignorance of the Arab world. Every time a group of leaders say they have a peace package, the Americans knock it down." But President Bush continued to recognize Soviet dictator Joseph Stalin's conquest of the Baltic Republics.

"President Bush and the media have spread the lie that Iraq was the cause of skyrocketing oil prices. The truth is that Iraq wanted to sell its oil, but that Bush wanted to drive up the price of oil by setting up a blockade around Iraq, preventing that nation from selling oil on the world market."

People like Former Secretary of State Lawrence Eagleburger, saw nothing wrong with placing an embargo on Iraq – who had done nothing to us – preventing medicine and other life's necessities from reaching children and adults who subsequently died. If nerve gas and our carpet bombs didn't get them, this embargo surely would, while Eagleburger enjoys a good steak in his protected home, making a living on the suffering of others.

President Bush's embargo against Iraq prevented that nation from oil exports which would pay for the cost of opening up new, previously undeveloped oil fields. Iraq would have become a serious rival to the economic power of Saudi Arabia and our own oil Mafia.

Following WW I and the break-up of the Ottoman Empire, there had been a long-term conspiracy to suppress the amount of oil that Iraq is able to supply to the world market. Today, we hear this story about ethanol and "alternative" fuels – which would cost another bundle – when all it would take is for the U.S. and England and Israel to keep their blood-stained fingers out of the Mideast and their resources. The sad part is that uninformed servicemen and women are fighting – not to protect America – but to protect the greed of the corporate mafia.

The 8/31/90 Washington Post carried an article about the creation of Iraq and Kuwait by Imperial Britain. In 1922, in a "meeting in a tent in the Arabian desert, a British high commissioner, named Sir Percy Cox, drew what became the Kuwait-Iraq border." The newly created Iraq "lacked access to the sea, something that the British war office deliberately had chosen to deny the new country, limiting its influence in the Persian Gulf and keeping it dependent on Britain." (British Petroleum?)

The British attempt to control Iraq continued down to Margaret Thatcher, Prime Minister, being the first national leader to demand military actions against Iraq after the 8/2/90 invasion of Kuwait. Remember, the Queen gave General Schwarzkopf a "Distinguished Service Medal" for his work in Iraq. It is unconstitutional to accept a medal from a foreign country, but the General did protect her oil interests, after all.

The Washington Post reported that the 1922 British decision to deny Iraq access to the sea "was intentional, not by accident," said a London-based Iraqi political scientist who had studied Britain historical records on the making of Iraq . . . "Iraqi King Ghazi ibn Faisal proposed a union with Kuwait in the 1930s, but was rejected by the Sabahs" (puppet-ruling family of Kuwait installed and maintained by the British and International bankers.)

Kuwait had been part of Iraq under the old Ottoman Empire. After Iraq's monarchy in 1958 there were several more Iraqi attempts to annex Kuwait. Saddam's invasion of Kuwait was the latest of many Iraqi attempts to gain access to a deep sea port. The Iraq-Iran War of the 1980s (in which the U.S. was on Iraq's side) was caused by Iraq's attempt to gain access to the sea by securing absolute control of the Shatt and Arab Waterway.

The Washington Post reported that an anonymous Iraqi politician, though in political exile, who strongly opposed Saddam Hussein, defended Iraq's right to gain access to the sea. The newspaper stated, "Depending on the outcome of the present crisis, the issue of Iraq's access to the sea could go unresolved, making yet another conflict with Kuwait or Iran inevitable. Iraq has to export oil to live, and to export oil, we must have a port," he said.

This continuing action by the international bankers to deny Iraq access to the sea was one of the key reasons for President Bush to send 300,000 troops to the Persian Gulf.

The 9/9/90 Washington Post reported, "Iraq has a long-standing desire for a port at the northern end of the Gulf through which it could import food and export oil. There is little agreement among diplomats and Middle East specialists about how Iraq's maritime ambitions could be reconciled with the interests of the U.S., Iran, and the Arab Gulf States."

Also, "the real reason for the crisis, contrary to all the propaganda about Iraq's military threat to its neighbors, is that Iraq's neighbors and their international banking friends want to severely limit Iraq's ability to export oil."

Saddam Hussein hired a Dutch firm to dredge out a channel to allow big, deep sea tankers and cargo ships to reach Iraq's port of Umm Qasr, located 20 miles inland from the Gulf. Again, the Washington Post reported that the U.S. Government had put great pressure on the Dutch Government to order its citizens to halt the dredging work, so that Iraq could not be serviced by large, ocean-going tankers.

As soon as the Iran-Iraq war ended in 1988, the International Bankers, Saudi Arabia and Kuwait began to wage various forms of economic warfare against Iraq. The 9/3/90 New York Times reported that the big trilateral-allied oil corporations helped Kuwait develop a sideway oil drilling method, which helped that nation extract oil from the Rumalla oil fields (most of which are in Iraqi territory) – in effect, stealing billions of dollars in Iraqi oil. Kuwait also was producing oil in excess of 700,000 barrels a day over its OPEC quota, thus driving petroleum prices down to such a level that Iraq could not earn enough from its own sales to start developing its recently discovered, massive new oil fields. This Kuwaiti action cost Iraq $14 billion per year.

The true economic reasons for the 1990 Mideast war crisis were described on the front page of the 8/26/88 Wall Street Journal, which announced in headlines, "Iraq moves up fast as a petroleum power with huge reserves: It will soon join Saudi Arabia as a key Mideast player; many fields unexplored; prices may be held down."

The article appeared at the end of the Iran-Iraq war. The newspaper stated: "The Saudis may be joined at the pinnacle of the world of oil. Peace in the Persian Gulf, if it sticks, may elevate Iraq as a new petroleum powerhouse, keeping a lid on oil prices in the short term and possible reshaping political alliances in the Arab block over the long term."

The Wall Street Journal reported that after the Iran-Iraq War, the Iraqis resumed plans "to explore reserves that they had begun to tap when the war erupted. Even with many oil fields still presumably undiscovered, Iraq claimed recoverable reserves of 100 billion barrels, second only to Saudi Arabia's 169.5 billion barrels."

Iraq suffered $8 billion in damages to its oil facilities alone and owed as much as $90 billion in war-related debt. Thus, the vast new oil fields could not be developed unless Iraq was able to export from the production of the older (undamaged by the war) oil fields.

Before the war, Iraq was able to export 3.5 million barrels of oil per day. In addition to its 100 billion barrels of proven petro reserves, the Iraqis' oil minister Issam Abdul Al-Chalabi said, "a further 50 billion barrels of reserves might be added."

At the end of the 1988 Iraq-Iran war, Iraq was able to produce 2.8 million barrels a day. The Wall Street Journal reported that Iraq announced plans to open up these new oil fields and build new shipping facilities so that it could export as much as seven million barrels per day, which is large enough to constitute a severe economic threat to the trilateral bankers and their multi-national oil companies and the Soviets as well.

The 8/26/88 Wall Street Journal described the main cause of the Saudi Arabia's new hostility to Iraq is that the glut of oil produced by Iraq would lead to lower prices for years and that no other member of OPEC would be inclined to curb their outputs to make room for the additional oil.

The 10/17/88 Business week: "The Iraqis aim to catch up with the Saudis in production and capacity . . . and eventually OPEC quotas." As soon as the Iran-Iraq war ended, Saudi Arabia and Kuwait suddenly began massive over-production in order to drive down the price of oil. Starting in the fall of 1988, "the Saudis drove the world prices down by pumping nearly one million barrels per day above their OPEC quota of 4.3 million barrels."

In the interim, Saudi Arabia also wiped out small U.S. oil producers. American producers couldn't keep up with $10.00 per barrel, and Iraq, looking for money to develop its new oil fields, couldn't either.

The 10/9/88 New York Times predicted that the results of an excess oil-pumping-war against Iraq and small U.S. companies "would lead to a surge in oil prices in the long run," which is what happened in 1990.

The Savings and Loan crisis had been building for many years from the early 1980s. The 1988-89 Saudi-Kuwaiti action to flood the world with oil and drive down prices to below U.S. production costs triggered the U.S. Savings and Loan collapse.

Hardest hit in the industry were the thousands of oil producers who produced 33% of all domestic oil and 41% of the total, outside Alaska.

"Half the wells in Oklahoma couldn't be operated at $13 per barrel . . . Southwestern banks faced another surge in energy loan defaults."

The truth is that this economic crisis was a direct result of President Bush's close friends in Saudi Arabia and Kuwait. U.S. troops have been sent to defend these enemies of America. President Bush, Sr. belonged to the Carlyle Group of Investors in arms, etc., along with Osama bin Laden's father.

The Saudis and Kuwaitis have a very close relationship with the trilateral-allied oil giants. The 10/3/88 Wall Street Journal: "Despite plunging prices ARCO's profit was surging." So, in fact, "were the profits of Exxon Corp., Mobil Corp., and nearly every multinational oil company. The nation's eighteen biggest oil companies leaped by about one-third." The industry also eliminated excess refining capacity, mothballing in the 1990 decade more than one-third of its refineries. The resulting tight supplies forced the oil industry to import not just crude oil but gasoline. As the big companies cut costs, they also cut prices, sometimes driving independent distributors out of business." Once the independents were driven out of business, the big companies skyrocketed prices.

The 9/5/90 Washington Post: "The U.S. is especially vulnerable (to shortages) because more than one hundred refineries have closed in this country, while no new ones have been built. The refineries that remain open are operating very close – dangerously close to full capacity." In 1981, America had a refinery capacity of eighteen million barrels per day. By 1990, that refinery capacity had been reduced to 15.5 million barrels per day. This shocking reduction is a threat to U.S. national security. Today, we can say that for thirty years, no new refineries have been built. It's all about money. Greed. Six thousand dollar shower curtains.

By June 1990, so many small, independent American oil producers and refineries had been closed down and driven out of business that it was safe for the trilateralist bankers to unleash their long-planned New World Order monopoly conspiracy to close down the output of major oil producing nations (such as Iraq and Kuwait). The Saudis will double their sale – the profits of which go directly to the big trilateral banks in New York.

By June 1990, the U.S. was importing 52.3 percent of our oil consumption. It was at this time that President Bush ordered the near total cut-off of U.S. offshore oil exploration.

President Bush's subsequent embargo on all Kuwait and Iraq oil had driven world oil prices to their highest levels. The 8/6/90 Wall Street Journal reported: "if the embargo (of Kuwait and Iraqi oil) is successful, it will leave the world short of oil within three to six months." Tom Burns, director of economics for Chevron Corp., admitted, "We're creating an oil shortage where one didn't exist."

Gasoline is routinely imported into some major U.S. markets because domestic refineries can't always satisfy demand, which is a direct result of the big oil companies' earlier closures of vast numbers of American refineries.

On 6/26/90, Bush ordered a ban on all offshore drilling for huge areas of the U.S. The 6/26/90 Congressional Quarterly reported that Bush "imposed a moratorium through at least the year 2000 on these areas: almost 99% of California, all of Washington and Oregon, all of New England from Rhode Island north, and Southwest Florida from about Marco Island south to the Keys. The Florida decision involves buying back 73 already-sold leases at a taxpayer cost of up to $200,000,000.

"At a time of severe U.S. budget deficits, the decision also means the loss of substantial lease revenues, which have generated upwards of $80 billion for the U.S. Treasury since 1970."

On 8/18/90, after the oil embargo on Iraqi and Kuwaiti oil, President Bush signed another bill that banned oil and gas exploration of North Carolina's Outer Banks.

At the same time President Bush suppressed American production, he encouraged the big U.S. multinational corporations to help the Soviet Union expand its oil production. The 8/15/90 Washington Times reported that the USSR had already signed agreements with Texaco and Chevron Corporations for "the development and production of vast oil reserves."

In September, the U.S. Secretary of Commerce, Robert Mosbacher, led a large group of American corporate leaders (many of whom were trilateralists) to Moscow. His delegation included representatives from major energy companies who could supply "western know-how and expertise" to bolster Moscow's falling oil production. When the Soviets helped Saddam invade Kuwait, they had a devious economic motivation.

The 9/17/90 Business Week Magazine stated: "What's unfolding is much more than a boost in production for the Saudis (to offset the Iraqi-Kuwaiti production). Protected by American F15s, the Saudis say higher levels are here to stay."

The 8/26/90 Washington Post reported that "were a stalemate to occur in the Middle East, the result could be a world economic realignment similar to that which occurred in the early 1970s." This is what President Bush meant when he said that troops were sent to Saudi Arabia to enforce the NWO.

The main recipients of the outflow of capital are big U.S. banks – Chase Manhattan in New York City and London; Citicorp., Bankers Trust Co, and J. P. Morgan. These deposits are used by the big bankers to make loans to Russia, China, and others to spiral up our debt to even higher levels. When the banks make bad loans, we bail them out with wars, as we did in the Gulf War.

On 9/4/90, Secretary of State James Baker told the U.S. Congress that America and Arab nations should "establish a new regional security structure for the Persian Gulf area to permanently 'contain' Iraq." This proposal would restrict Iraq's access to the sea and limit that nation's ability to export oil. Thus oil prices would stay artificially high. Under this new "security structure," Israel would be able to establish political dominance over (and possible military occupation of) the Persian Gulf area. Israel's part was to be kept secret, but a State Department official accidentally revealed the Israeli involvement in Baker's plan.

The 9/12/90 Washington Post reported: "A senior U.S. official held out the prospect that the new Persian Gulf regional security system could include nations that have not been on good terms with each other in the past and perhaps even those who have been mortal enemies such as Israel and many Arab states." This would give the Soviets, too, a significant political foothold in the Gulf region. Remember that when the Russians were in Afghanistan, they were beaten badly by the Mujahadeen. I think that we should learn from that experience that no occupier is welcome. Obviously, the Middle East wants a chance to solve its own problems without any intervention. But they also want control of their resources which corporate America will not allow.

The 9/18/90 Wall Street Journal: "Arabs would not welcome a long-term U.S. presence," said an Egyptian official privy to foreign policy decision-making, "because they understand the truth about the conspiracy behind the Gulf crisis. The establishment of a permanent U.S. presence would convince many Arabs that the U.S. somehow contrived to create the Kuwaiti controversy to win a toehold in the oil-rich region."

The 9/24/90 Washington Post reported that if the old Kuwaiti government were restored to power, it would invite a permanent American presence. "One senior U.S. official said he believed that Kuwait was ready to discuss granting the U.S. and perhaps other Western countries (probably including Israel) military basing rights in Kuwait as part of a new regional security system if the Iraqi army were driven out." The Kuwaitis and the U.S. government are extremely cautious about concealing Israel's role in this planned new occupation of Arab territory.

The 9/20/90 Wall Street Journal reported: "Senior U.S. military officers are pushing to keep a permanent force of nearly 10,000 American troops in Saudi Arabia and to secure air bases throughout the Persian Gulf. There were longtime plans to stay in the Gulf in force and to leave behind huge stockpiles of U.S. weapons and equipment for future emergency use."

The 9/23/90 New York Times carried an article by James Webb, former Assistant Secretary of Defense and Secretary of the Navy in the Reagan Administration, strongly opposing the Bush Administration's decision to send massive numbers of troops and equipment to the Gulf.

Webb stated, "Bush Administration officials talk in vague terms about the reasons for the huge U.S. military deployment in Saudi Arabia. Defense Secretary Cheney is telling us to prepare for a commitment that may take years. Others (in the White House) have been quoted as saying we may be there for a decade. At the same time, we are being reassured (amidst many loud calls to initiate a war with Iraq) that the U.S. military commitment is 'wholly defensive.'"

Webb added: "The huge build-up of U.S. forces began after it became clear that Iraq had no military design on Saudi Arabia."

A book by Loras Toscano, "Triple Cross: Israel, the Atomic Bomb, and the Man Who Spilled the Secrets" (published by Birch Lane), details how Mordechai Vanunu, the technician at the Israeli nuclear weapons factory defected and gave his story to the London Times. Vanunu revealed that "Israel has one hundred ordinary atomic bombs since 1980, and has been assembling a number of hydrogen and neutron bombs which are not for defense, but are in fact dangerous offensive weapons." To Vanunu, the

"Demona program suggested that Israel might use its bombs to start a war, not defend itself against one."

The 8/30/90 New York Times: "Israelis want the U.S. to attack Saddam Hussein, and the sooner the better."

Mort Zuckerman, another pro-Israel proponent in the American press, stated in 9/24/90 U.S. News and World Report: "Hussein will win unless America is prepared to go to war – with as many allies as will join us. No further provocation is needed. We cannot allow Hussein time to splinter our coalitions and exploit our distaste of force." Richard Perle, one of George W's hawks on the Iraqi invasion, in the 9/23/90 New York Times: "The chilling prospect of a diplomatic or political solution to Iraq's aggression is the reason why it is dangerous for the U.S. to seek one out. . . . A coup could leave Iraq's military power in place. . . .President Bush should ready an attack on Iraq's military." Perle had been a hawk through the two Bush administrations.

The 10/12/90 column of Rowland Evans and Robert Novak: "Israel's publicly announced policy that Saddam must be destroyed can only be accomplished by Americans. 'We Jews are worried sick,' an American Jewish leader told us. 'It cannot be allowed to appear that Israel wants American boys to do its work against Saddam.'"

All of the aforementioned people knew well that Iraq had help from the Soviets. The electronic jamming of U.S. AWACS (Airborne Warning and Control System) flying over Iraq's no-fly zone was a technology given to Iraq by the Soviets. Iraq is a sovereign state. The U.S. had no right to invade their space. (Col. Thomas Beardon wrote a book about this.)

The hate-Mideast campaign has been going on since the early 1980s. In 1981 Israel destroyed Iraq's nuclear reactor, rendering the system useless. Then Israel moved millions of Russian Jews to the occupied West Bank and Gaza, after a deal with President Gorbachev, for which we gave financial aid. This move forced more of the Palestinians into Jordan, already overflowing with Palestinian refugees. Most of the $25 billion needed for the new Israeli settlements were paid by us, and demolished when the Palestinians reclaimed the West Bank.

If one listened to pro-Israel callers on radio and C-Span, there was and is always a concerted effort to say "send the Palestinians to Trans-Jordan; that is where they belong." They forget that Palestinians belong in Palestine and that Israel is the occupier.

The 9/17/90 U.S. News and World Report stated: "In their anger, some Saudi leaders suggest that Jordan might be a building-block for a new Palestinian homeland." The Saudis took over Mecca, the Islamic Holy Site, only after the King of Jordan's grandfather was thrown out as the ruler of Mecca. This is the cause of the Saudi rivalry. They would like the Gulf region to be controlled by the U.S. and Israel. The desire for an Israeli take-over of Jordan fits in with the notion of a Greater Israel.

Zbigniew Brzezinski, the original founding director of David Rock-efeller's Trilateral Commission, wrote in the 10/7/90 New York Times: "One cannot preclude attempts at deliberate provocations, designed to inflame American public opinion and to precipitate a military collision between America and Iraq. . . . In view of reports of Israel's fears that America may opt for a peaceful outcome of the crisis, . . . it is also quite possible that outside parties may set in motion events that derail the peaceful strategy."

And now you know the rest of the story. Keep in mind that this "plotting" took place in the 1990s and that the same gang of war hawks surround George W. Bush – Cheney, Rumsfeld, Wolfowitz, Perle. In fact, in 1995, a report was written, "Project for a New American Century," which called for "American Global Leadership"…that we and our money must impose "democracies" all over the world. America, it suggested, must take care of Iraq, Iran and Syria. And isn't this what the corporate-owned media is pushing today? After the Iraqi quagmire?

We received our orders from this old gang of war hawks: Elliot Abrams, Gary Bauer (the 'born-again Christian' who apparently sanctions slaughter), William Bennett (the former Secretary of Education under President Reagan who promised to eliminate the Department of Education and did nothing except make millions to "gamble" away while writing books about "virtues"). He's rewarded with a propaganda talk show. Also, Dick Cheney, Eliot Cohen, Steve Forbes, Frank Gaffney, Don Rumsfeld, Paul Wolfowitz. Many more.

In my opinion, traitors all; they have sold out this glorious country we inherited, for thirty pieces of silver and turned the world our children face into a violent abyss with no safe havens to which they can run. Pity those "useful idiots" who call those of us who know the old America well – Bush-haters, America haters.

During the Shah's time, we trained the Savak in torture. We brought them American curriculums with sex education and drug education, thanks to our "foundations." Today, Iran – once like the America of sixty years ago with strong family life – resembles the promiscuous, drug-ridden culture we've created in America.

Every country we touch has turned to violence because the "black budget" of our Defense Department has no accountability. They can send American troops anywhere. They can put down any offensive resisting government. They can transfer prisoners to countries to be tortured (rendition) so that Americans don't hear about it. How do they get away with it? By designating these acts "classified," of course. Only the corporate dynasties who pay our most corrupt Congress will profit from these un-American acts.

Finally, CNN, 12/7/06, interviewed Joe Kennedy, son of Robert Kennedy, and John Fund (Wall Street Journal).

John Fund always defends corporate profits and war. Killing. Wipe out any who disagree with Bush and his "war in Iraq." Pretty much this rhetoric is what you'll hear from him, Frank Gaffney, Daniel Pipes, William Kristol. And they are always guests on Fox News, the "ditto" squad for the right wing whackos. No, fascists.

So that I'm not surprised that Joe Kennedy's idea of going to Venezuela in order to encourage Hugo Chavez, a populist from Venezuela, to sell his oil through CITGO, which he owns, to poor Americans, was met with harsh criticism.

John Fund – "Chavez wants cheap propaganda." Listen Mr. Fund, if Americans can cut loose of the oil mafia, it's a good thing. The number may be up for you and your cohorts at the Wall Street Journal.

Joe Kennedy – "Venezuela has been in the business of selling cheap oil for 25 years. They can sell 588 million barrels of oil to the United States. I don't like the idea that Bush ordered a coup on Chavez. It is the only country supporting the U.S. during its revolution. We sold over 500,000 cars to Venezuela.

"The Wall Street Journal uses Venezuelan oil. Are we to cut off all business with Venezuela because of a speech Chavez made at the U.N.? Then we should also take American banks out of Venezuela. Why do we do business with the Kuwaitis when they keep the price of oil high? (By now you should know the answers.)

"Citgo gives $80 million to muscular dystrophy. Why doesn't Exxon? Bush allowed oil prices to go from $25 dollars per barrel to $160 per barrel."

Good for Joe Kennedy. This kind of forgives – in my mind – President Kennedy for refusing to talk to Fidel Castro when he came to us for aid. It was then that Castro went to Russia and the rest is history. Also – but I can't forgive – Senator Ted Kennedy for disallowing Europeans to come to the U.S. and instead welcoming the rest of the world for which there are no limits. Immigration Act, 1964.

At least Joe Kennedy is standing up against the oil companies – not just for the poor – but for all of us.

You can guarantee that Fox News will label Chavez a communist for those who don't read. Meanwhile, the U.S. builds up Russia and China! And if we attack Iran, oil will go to $200 per barrel and cost us eight dollars per gallon. If Chavez can do it, why do we need the oil mafia? We don't. We need the small producers who were stopped from drilling by George Bush, Sr., the son of the war profiteer, Prescott Bush, and the father of the corporate lackey, George W. Enough!

NATO BACKGROUND

In the 1930s it was fashionable to say that we should have kept out of WWI. People felt that we had been duped into entering the war by British propagandists and by unscrupulous industrialists and arms dealers who saw a chance to profit from war. Our bankers had loaned money to England and France. Many Americans believed that this financial involvement had helped drag us into war.

Congress began developing a series of neutrality laws designed to prevent what were then commonly regarded as the fatal mistakes of 1914-1917 (WWI).

Between 1935-1937, measures were taken (neutrality laws) to: (1) forbid loans and the sale of war materials to countries at war; (2) forbid travel by American citizens on the ships of belligerent nations; and (3) to sell supplies only to belligerent nations who could pay cash and carry supplies away in their own ships. President Roosevelt felt that these laws should apply to aggressor nations only, but Congress did not wish to offend any foreign power. Ever since George Washington, the U.S. had neutral trade rights which were abandoned because of the specific language in the neutrality laws. Now, our efforts to remain neutral might have encouraged aggressors such as Hitler and Mussolini to conclude that victims would get no help from the U.S. Plus the fact that the security of the U.S. might be endangered by selecting sides.

The Neutrality Laws were wiped out with the Lend Lease Act of March 11, 1941.

In 1942 we gave aid in the form of planes, munitions, tools, food, and money to foreign countries whose defense was deemed vital to the defense of the U.S., such as England. President Roosevelt and Churchill decided to extend Lend Lease to Russia as well when Hitler unleashed a sudden attack on Russia, hoping to gain the rich oil fields and wheatlands. The Russian winter defeated the Russians. Under Lend Lease, Russia subsequently became the military war machine and threat it is today – with American tax dollars (History of America, p. 617, Ralph Volney).

Along came the North American Security Zone, forerunner of NATO (North Atlantic Treaty Organization), wherein we would protect any U.S. cargo at sea. Thus we secured naval bases in Greenland and Iceland, and President Roosevelt authorized an American naval and air patrol of the North Atlantic security zone. "We will not hesitate to use our armed forces to repel attack." Just two days before, German Admiral Erich Roeder had announced that any American naval help to the British would mean immediate attack by Germany. The President justified this policy because it kept war from our own shores. Sound familiar? President Roosevelt was giving aid to a nation at war: Britain.

Subsequently, Roosevelt and Churchill drew up the Atlantic Charter:

1. No territorial or other gains should result from the war.
2. No territorial changes should be made without the consent of the parties concerned.
3. All parties should have the right to choose the form of government under which they would live, and self-government restored wherever possible.
4. All nations should have access on equal terms to the trade and to the raw materials of the world.
5. Nations should cooperate to provide improved labor conditions, economic advancement, and social security.
6. The Nazi tyranny should be destroyed so that peace may be established.
7. The men of all nations should be free to traverse the high sea and oceans without hindrance.
8. Aggressive nations should be disarmed and provisions made for the organization of a wider, more permanent system of general security. (These resemble Wilson's 14 points).

The Yalta Conference (also called the Crimea Conference) ending WWII, was attended by Churchill, Roosevelt, and Stalin (killer of 45 million people). Decisions made at Yalta were not made public for reasons of military secrecy. When they were disclosed after the war, they became the subject of much controversy.

"Only the communists acquired something from WWII: Eastern Europe, and a foothold in Asia. The war had a commonly overlooked irony. The war began to save Poland from conquest by Germany, yet when it was over, Poland had been acquired anyway – by the Soviets."

President George Washington warned us to keep away from foreign entanglements.

In April 1949 (Truman) the U.S. signed the NATO Pact which made the U.S. a full and direct participant. The movement toward NATO, in essence for mutual military security, began the previous year as Soviet pressure intensified around Berlin and threatened to engulf Czechoslovakia. In March 1948, Great Britain, France, Belgium, the Netherlands, and Luxembourg signed the Treaty of Brussels which provided for common defense in the event that the European territory of anyone of them was attacked.

Iceland, Denmark, Norway, Canada, Italy and Portugal were added. All pledged to go to war should their forces be attacked in Europe, North Africa, or on the Atlantic.

Then, in September 1949, the Soviet Union exploded its first atomic bomb. This ended American monopoly of nuclear weapons. The Cold War began and, under Stalin, the Soviets entrenched themselves in Eastern Europe. So much for the Atlantic Charter which stated "no territorial gains."

Our Lend Lease Aid to Russia, together with the Yalta giveaway, gave us the bogeyman we needed for the Cold War, profiting the arms merchants and the rest of the war machine.

When President Reagan told Gorbachov to "take down that Wall (Berlin)" in 1989, we became allies again with a communist nation which we still aid and abet when they attack their old Soviet Republics of Chechnya, etc. All Moslem regions. Whether we attack Malaysia, Indonesia, Bosnia – our enemies seem to be Moslems.

FDR was correct when he said "In politics, nothing happens by accident. If it happens, it was planned that way." In 1999, the U.S. gave $17 billion to NATO which has done nothing but get us into war after war. As with the UN, we pay one-fourth.

President Clinton placed Russia under the NATO umbrella for "collective security" even though Russia has 20,000 nuclear weapons and continues to attack Georgia, Tajikistan, Azerbaijan and Chechnya – with our financial aid. Nobody checks the "earmarks" placed in bills allowing congressmen to give financial aid to any country or thing they wish. In return, they get jobs for their families, campaign money, trips.

Nowhere in the U.S. Constitution does it say that we have to be the policemen of the world Yet, three Soviet block nations – Hungary, Poland, and the Czech Republic were welcomed into NATO in 1999. There is U.S. military presence in fifteen NATO nations – Belgium, Canada, Denmark, France, Germany, Greece, Iceland, Italy, Luxembourg, Netherlands, Norway, Portugal, Spain, Turkey, and the United Kingdom. There are 23,604 troops in the United Kingdom and tens of thousands in Germany.

We should bring these troops back from Europe, save ourselves tens of billions of dollars it costs to maintain the newer, poorer nations which cannot afford the armaments, etc. needed to police the world. The U.S. hosts 22 nations (1,200 troops) for peacekeeping exercises at Camp Lejune, NC, costing us $8.5 million per year. This, in preparation for the one-world police state.

I'd like to close with a comment by Lord Ismay, the head of the North Atlantic Community at the time of this military alliance: "It is true," said Lord Ismay, "that our first task is to prepare a shield against Soviet aggression, but NATO has a larger, broader purpose – in creation of an Atlantic Community. . . . We start at the bottom slowly, practically, and take time in order to build something more durable. . . . The nations are not giving up their sovereignties in the common venture; they are pooling them" (N.Y. Mirror 9/21/52).

Articles 52-54 of the U.N. Charter authorized the existence of NATO. The NATO treaty begins: "The Parties undertake, as set forth in the Charter of the United Nations . . ."

THE REPORT FROM IRON MOUNTAIN

One Worlders faced the problems of how the world and its people would survive if war were to be done away with and permanent peace maintained. Insiders have been seeking an answer to that question for decades. More than forty years ago, a three-year study was done on the "desirability of peace." Hence the Report from Iron Mountain.

Conclusions:

"War has provided both ancient and modern societies with a dependable system for stabilizing and controlling national economics.

"The war system has provided the machinery through which the motivational forces governing human behavior have been translated into binding social allegiance.

"War has been the principal evolutionary device for maintaining a satisfactory ecological balance between gross human population and supplies available for its survival. War orientation has provided the fundamental motivational force of scientific and technological progress.

"Two possible solutions could be used as 'substitutes for the functions of war' says this Report which is the blueprint for the development of a world-wide environmental war to replace the present war system.

"The first suggests 'uniting mankind against the danger of destruction by "creatures" from other planets or from outer space. . . But to include features associated with science fiction would be a dubious undertaking.' In short, to unite all the people of the world against an enemy from outer space would require proof that there really is an enemy from outer space."

Quote: "It may be, for instance, that gross pollution of the environment can eventually replace the possibility of mass destruction by nuclear weapons as the principal apparent threat to the survival of the species. Poisoning of the air, and of the principal sources of water supply is already well advanced and would seem promising in this respect; it constitutes a threat that can be dealt with only through social organization and political power."

The Report from Iron Mountain, published in 1965, warned that it would take a generation-and-a-half of promotion, publication and propaganda before it could become operable on a world-wide scale.

The London Examiner hailed the Earth Summit as the "First Green Summit." And here was the strategy to lead us to World government. Said the Economist: "What defense has been to the world's leaders for the last fifty years, the environment will be for the next fifty. The Hegelian dialectic calls for the discovery or creation of a problem, publicity and propaganda to increase to proportions of a crisis, then the presentation of a prepared solution to the problem" (Don Bell Reports, 2/7/92).

It's obvious to many that war and destruction have been profitable for the arms merchants and the corporate powers who are now controlling our lives.

I'll mention here, only briefly, HAARP, the High Frequency Active Auroral Research Program, managed jointly by the U.S. Air Force and U.S. Navy (http://www.earthpulse.com/haarp/vandalism/html). An article by Dr. Nick Bigich and Jeanne Manning, "Angels Don't Play This Haarp," is interesting reading.

You will see how the military is using this technology to add mayhem to our environment. I sent for material on this topic and Senator Santorum sent a copy of Senate Bill 517, entitled "A bill to establish Weather Modification Operations and Research Board, and for other purposes." (Dept. of Commerce)

Senator Kay Bailey Hutchison of Texas left a meeting to vote on this bill. "Other purposes?"

WARS

I felt that <u>And Men Wept</u> by Catherine Palfrey Baldwin, an extraordinary researcher, would give you the best understanding of war and the reasons for war. Catherine lived during this time, and was a brilliant, well-read and insightful woman. I see no equals around today, if any, simply because her agenda was America, and only America.

"During the years of 1910-1911 England realized that the situation for her was not good; they realized that a war was in the offing. It was at this time that Lord Asquith offered Winston Churchill the post, Head of the Admiralty. The culmination came in 1914 when World War I broke out; it was a trade and economic war.

"Contrary to the advice of our all-wise Founding Fathers 'not to entangle in foreign affairs,' this country was drawn into the vortex of the intrigue. For a while it was a question of whether we would go on the side of England or Germany. The J.P. Morgan banking house was the fiscal banker for the British and the French. Morgan used not only his own bank's money but called on the bankers around the country. Things were not going so well for the Allies. England had her back to the wall. More help was needed; the bankers around the country were alarmed. They had loaned other people's money, and called J.P. Morgan for the loans, but he couldn't meet them. It was then that Mr. Morgan took a trip to Washington, and President Woodrow Wilson declared war. The U.S. Treasury took over the Morgan loans, which meant that they were transferred to the backs of the American people. They are still our obligation since Britain has never paid a dime. The principal was cancelled and this government required only payment of the interest.

"It was well known that British boats were coming into this country with guns mounted. They were returning with war supplies. This went on for some time before the sinking of the Lusitania. It was the excuse for the declaration of war against Germany by Mr. Wilson, on Good Friday, April 6, 1917. The fact that American citizens were on board made it much easier for Mr. Wilson.

"Perhaps it would be fitting to remind you at this time that at the inquest in Cork, Ireland, the Captain of the Lusitania was asked why he proceeded so slowly and why he did not zigzag in mine-infested waters. His reply was: 'Orders from the Admiralty.'

"Again asked: 'You knew you were going to be bombed?' He refused to answer.

"Our involvement with the Allies was not without a protest. In the U.S. Senate was that great patriot, the Honorable Robert LaFollette. Again and again he rose to his feet on the Senate floor, protesting the U.S. Treasury taking over the Morgan loans and putting them on the backs of the American people. Because he took this stand, he was vilified and crucified and smeared from one end of this country to another.

"One might not agree with this great patriot in all matters, but he must be given credit for the stand he took for this country and the American people. It was about 1924 that this 'crucifixion' was taken up in the U.S. Senate and a bill passed to reimburse this great patriot for the monies he had been forced to spend to defend himself.

"Never will I forget the night the American Legion bestowed their Medal of Honor upon him for his valiant stand. Never will I forget that great patriot as he accepted that medal, with tears streaming down his cheeks. He uttered these momentous words: 'I stood for my country at a time when it was hard to stand'

"At the close of this war, termed WW I, and you might ask yourself why it was called WW I. Was it because to put over their plans of World government, those internationalists knew that there would have to be more wars? Was it on the advice of Andrew Carnegie – 'Not by any one big step but little steps, one by one'?"

Unless you read the <u>Unseen Hand</u> by A. Ralph Epperson (Publius Press, 3100 S. Philomena Pl. (Ste. B) Tucson, AZ 85730 or 520- 886-4380), p. 109, you will remain in the dark about what the bankers and corporate thieves have planned for us and our children.

"While the banking fraternity was financing the Russian Revolution, they were bringing WW I to a close with the signing of the Treaty of Versailles. President Wilson led the American Delegations to the signing of the treaty in Paris."

This war was fought from 1914-1918 between the Allies -- Britain, France, Russia, and Italy, and the Central Powers – Germany, Austria,

Hungary and the Ottoman Empire. (Also known as the Great War.) The leaders were George Clemenceau, Kaiser Wilhelm II of Germany, and Woodrow Wilson of the U.S.

After four years of fighting on land and sea, the Kaiser's great force was beaten. The German, Austrian, Russian and Turkish empires all collapsed. Republics were formed in Germany, Austria and Russia. The Kaiser ran away to Holland and evaded the consequences of his policy.

The peace terms imposed on Germany by the Allies were crushing. Many felt that the terms were a guarantee to start WW II.

German shipping was handed over; the German Navy was scuttled in the North Sea by its own crews to escape the same fate; German fortresses were razed; the army disarmed and reduced; German colonies were divided among the victors; Alsace-Lorraine and other territories Germany had taken in the past were taken back. Germany had to pay a staggering sum – a sum compared with which the reparations she extracted from France in 1871 were a mere trifle. This hard Peace Treaty of Versailles was signed by Germany in the same Hall of Mirrors which had seen the birth of the fallen German Empire. History holds no record of a more complete defeat.

Dreadful times followed in Germany. The new republican government at first had difficulty in maintaining itself. German money decreased vastly in value. The French occupied the rich coal fields of the Ruhr valley, when Germany could not fulfill the peace terms of the latter.

Finally, stability was restored. Richer nations loaned money to Germany and Germany was able to fulfill her obligations. Germans showed remarkable skill and courage in mending their fortunes.

However, it did not last. The peace settlement was so one-sided that no country really gained by it. In 1929, a great business depression settled over the whole world. German reparations finally had to be wiped out. A new party calling itself the National Socialist (Nazi) gained strength. It opposed the republican form of government. In 1933 the leader of this party, Adolf Hitler, was made chancellor with almost supreme power. (Book of Knowledge, 1933)

"Hitler's rise to power was financed by a curious combination of major German, British, and American banks and steel companies, including U.S. Steel. This is well documented in the book I Paid Hitler, published in 1941 and written by Germany's leading industrialist Fritz Thyssen. Thyssen, Chairman of Germany's United Steel Works, was a German nationalist. He saw the Bolsheviks as a threat to Germany and sincerely believed that

Hitler was the answer to their defeat.

"He broke with Hitler and fled from Germany in 1939 after Hitler's pact with Stalin allowed the invasion of Poland that September. It was no surprise to Thyssen that the West wanted Hitler to come to power. He stated in his book:

"'Hitler rearmed Germany to an incredible degree at an unheard of speed. The Great Powers closed their eyes to this fact. Did they really not recognize the danger, or did they wish to ignore it?'

"The German chemical giant, I.G. Farben, received after WW I, a $30 million loan from the Rockefellers' National City Bank. They quietly grew to be the largest chemical concern in the world. After WW II, a U.S. War Department investigation revealed that without I.G. Farben's immense resources, 'Germany's prosecution of the war would have been unthinkable and impossible'." (NWO, Wm. T. Still) (Anthony Sutton, <u>Wall St. and The Rise of Hitler</u>)

Though Hitler lost the war and Russia gobbled up Eastern Europe and half of Germany, and millions of civilians were lost to U.S. and British bombing, the international financiers and industrialists profited greatly. And secret societies like the illuminati kept their dream of One World domination going on.

Larry Abraham summed up the banking interests well in <u>Call It Conspiracy</u>, p. 47:

"Actually, nobody has a right to be more angry at the Rothschild clique than their fellow Jews. The Warburgs, part of the Rothschild empire, helped finance Adolf Hitler. There were few if any Rothschilds or Warburgs in the Nazi prison camps! They sat out the war in luxurious hotels in Paris or emigrated to the U.S. and England. As a group, Jews have suffered most at the hands of these power seekers. A Rothschild has much more in common with a Rockefeller than he does with a tailor from Budapest or the Bronx."

In World War II we sacrificed 700,000 service men and women so that corporations and bankers could do well. And you could say the same thing with the war in Iraq or any war. In my opinion, contractors like Halliburton and Bechtel don't really care if you're Christian or Jewish. It's the bottom line.

Was 9/11 used as an excuse to get us into war? We've never been allowed to investigate. Consider this incident from WW II, and ask yourselves: "Who profits?"

From an article in the Los Angeles Times – 7/91:

"According to a story by Richard Vartabedian, the 'Flying Tigers' of General Claire Chennault were not just U.S. volunteers fighting for Chiang Kai-Shek. Recruited at U.S. bases, offered five times normal pay, they were sent off to fight Japan months before Pearl Harbor, in a covert operation run out of FDR's White House by Lauchlin Currie (later exposed by Courier Elizabeth Bentley as a Soviet spy).

"Here is real history. Robert Schriebman, attorney for the Flying Tigers, has a secret memo dated August 1941, from Army Air Force General Henry 'Hap' Arnold, affirming that creation of the Flying Tigers 'has the approval of the president and the War Department.'

"What the Pentagon has been denying for fifty years, the Pentagon admitted in May: the Flying Tigers, though their planes carried the insignia of the Chinese Army, were on 'active duty' for the U.S.

"None of the above diminishes the heroism of these incredible pilots who lost only four of 294 planes. Their record is legendary. But at the very time these warriors were recruited to go fight Japan, FDR was bound by the Neutrality Act, prohibiting aid to 'belligerent' nations.

"Does not the secret, illegal dispatch of U.S. pilots to fight Japan constitute an impeachable act? Does it not confirm what historians have argued: that FDR deliberately sought to goad Tokyo into war, to embroil the U.S. in the Pacific, as the 'back door' through which to take us into war in Europe, a war FDR and Churchill concluded we had to fight – even the Congress voted, although the people wanted us to stay out?" (Criminal Politics reprint 7/1991)

In Iraq, President Bush, Sr. sent over 40,000 sorties and the CIA to covertly provoke trouble with the Kurds in the north and the Shiites in the south – all as a prelude to attacking a country rich in oil. If it were about people, we wouldn't have killed over 800,000 Iraqis and caused the emigration of two million people from their middle class.

It's amazing that we still hear that President Bush did a good job. No protection at our border. Hospitals closing because they can't handle the influx of illegals. One half trillion dollars thus far has been spent on defense, except that all of our troops are outside of the United States. We're spending more than a trillion dollars on the war -- $12 billion a month – and much of the money is unaccountable. Katrina, a domestic issue is a disaster. Drugs are everywhere. Violence in schools is increasing. Jobs going overseas. President Bush is taking orders from the new president of Mexico, Calderone, to jail members of our border patrol for stopping drug traffickers from entering the United States. And apparently George Bush never read the

Federalist Papers or the Constitution, or he would know that, even though he was "Commander-in-Chief," – no president can have the armed forces under his control for foreign deployment and the U.N. for more than two years. It's absolute power! To top it off, he has engaged the services of private contractors, Blackwater, who have sent 100,000 mercenaries making $680 to $1,000 per day to help fight the Iraq war. No one has an accounting of who they are, except that some are from Chile. No investigation coming from our do-nothing Congress. And 92% of Chileans are against the war.

Jeremy Scahill wrote <u>Blackwater</u> which exposes the dangers of delegating American service jobs to anyone not in our military. These mercenaries are trained on 7,000 acres owned by a wealthy Christian conservative who contributes to James Dobson, etc., in North Carolina. He has a mock high school called "Are you ready, high" (sounds like a crackpot to me). The men wear commando outfits with wrap-around sun glasses. Originally, they were sent to guard Paul Bremer after "Shock and Awe."

Get this! They work for the State Department! No laws govern them. Remember the torture at Abu Graib? Private contractors were not blamed, although involved.

The leader of Blackwater promised President Bush "Osama's head on a platter!" I suppose decapitating people is easier when Henry VIII or we do it.

These rogue operators drive around, shooting at Iraqis. The Freedom of Information Act provides no reference, but U.S. taxpayers pay their salaries. Fred Fielding and Ken Starr defend these out-of-control bullies. I certainly don't want innocent deaths on my conscience. Apparently the Christian Right cares not.

Vice President Cheney and Secretary of Defense Rumsfeld have wanted privatization of the military for a long time. Hence, Halliburton and Bechtel – war profiteers, all. Away from public scrutiny.

Blackwater bankrolls political campaigns while we pay the price.

David Martin of CBS asked author Scahill why he thought President Bush, from "the most powerful country," had to hire mercenaries. Scahill: "He likes the cover it provides."

This is a dangerous undertaking in the United States. We had a president in the White House who didn't care that more than 62% of the people were against the war in Iraq, with control of the U.S. military AND a privatized group of 100,000 men at his disposal. These privatized contractors made 37,000 air strikes. And we talk about the atrocities of Saddam Hussein!

Thank God for the intelligence of another woman, Kristen Breitweiser (<u>Wake Up Call</u>), a widow from 9/11. In an interview on C-SPAN, 3/31/07, Ms. Breitweiser, who voted for George Bush, said that "no one in Washington is looking out for us." She had to work for months to even get a commission involved. The FBI claimed that they had no computer to collect the information on 9/11 and connect the dots; they still don't have the computers. "National security should be a priority. We should not start wars in countries that did nothing. We should spend more on national security – border, mass transit, chemical plants." (While I agree on money for the border, I believe that mass transit and chemical plants belong to private owners.)

We still don't have an investigation on why the president continued reading a goat story to second graders for ten minutes after someone whispered, "We're being attacked."

And we sent Condoleezza Rice and Pelosi to the Middle East. We'd do better sending two heads of broccoli!

Irving Kristol, the father of William Kristol who is a frequent guest on Fox and who is editor of The Weekly Standard, stated:

"With the end of the Cold War, what we really need is an obvious ideological and threatening enemy, one worthy of our nettle, one that can unite us to opposition" (Pat Buchanan, <u>Where the Right Went Wrong</u>).

Irving Kristol created thereby the "bogeyman" we needed – the "rag heads," the "Islamo-fascists," the "dirtbags."

Kristol, the "conservative," was a Trotskyite. (One who believes that communism should depend on the proletariats of all nations, not just the Soviet Union. What they leave out is the tyranny which follows.) The proletariat, or working class, to them means "the workers in their fields" – and nothing else!

Like father, like son. William is a neo-con warhawk. His dad and the rest of the Trotskyites and socialists joined the forces of FDR and the Democrats, but later went over to the Republican party where they could do more harm increasing our defense buildup. More wars. More money. More fodder dying on foreign soil for bloody causes.

This is what son William said on C-SPAN on 9/23/06: "The appeasement of Neville Chamberlain (a British Prime Minister who tried to avoid war between Britain and Germany by negotiating the Munich Pact under which Hitler's Germany would be allowed to extend its territory into parts of Czechoslovakia) didn't work." (So from 1938 to this day you'll hear the anti-war people called "Chamberlain Appeasers.") "In the future you may find sympathy for the jihadists. Partly an intellectual problem and partly moral, communism was a utopian scheme which led to tyranny and eventually murder. The combination of Islam and fascism one can trace to France." (Funny how former Trotskyites always denounce communism as though they were never a part of it.)

I remember the 1960s when the Black Panthers such as Huey Newton and Eldridge Cleaver went over to Russia, thinking that socialist countries offered a better life. After an incident wherein black men were arrested for speaking to white Russian girls, they came quietly back to the U.S. Eldridge Cleaver found religion.

In a "report" entitled Project for the New American Century, 1995, neocons like Paul Wolfowitz, suggested to President Clinton, that the U.S. go after Saddam and Iraq in order to gain a strong foothold in the Mideast---long before 9/11. This committee of neo-con militarists also mentioned Syria, Lebanon and Iran. Then, in order to cope with a rising China, they thought that Kim Jong Il should be minimized as a leader of North Korea by broadcasting hostile statements through Radio Free Asia—which was done---provoking Kim into nuclear mode. Wolfowitz, Perle, Bolton, etc. felt that uniting North and South Korea would afford us the base needed in East Asia for our corporate cronies to have "access to rapidly growing economies." Japan, for the first time since WWII would help. As you know, these plans served as a foreign blueprint for George W. Bush who stacked his cabinet with PNAC members. Their real objective was the Middle East oil. As a matter of fact, there was a secret meeting with the vice president about oil deals. Of course, we the people are not privy to such meetings; we are peasants and peasants who apparently can't read. The meeting was in Iraq.

So far, everything predicted in that "report" was carried out by the former puppet in the White House, George W. – except for Iran. Obviously, the "intellectual" neocons didn't count on the outcome of Iraq, so that their plans for Iran are on hold.

People like Jonah Goldberg, unknown until his mother's fame with Monica Lewinsky, wrote in the National Review: "The U.S. must go to war with Iraq."

Michael Ledeen, an ex-pentagon official, said: "Every ten years or so, the U.S. needs to push up some small crappy little country and throw it against the wall, just to show we mean business." These are the monsters who surrounded George Bush. David Frum wrote the president's speech coining the phrase "axis of evil" referring to Iran, Iraq, and North Korea. Imagine! Nothing about Red China or the drugs on our southern border.

David Frum and Richard Perle, the other warmonger, wrote a book together, after their deeds in Iraq were carried through.

Podhoretz, Krauthammer – all agents of war. In my opinion – racists to the max, and they have the gall to talk about hate speech!

Remember, these war advocates are not physics majors but usually English or political science graduates. They know how to say NOTHING very well! They are the same ones who tell us which enemies to hate – forget the fact that we bombed the hell out of Normandy and Dresden and did a nice job on the French. "Rape the women." (WW II vets)

France was opposed to German occupation of Vichy, France. The Nazis were collaborators with Vichy. In 1944, the French rounded up the Jews whom they considered a problem because of their political and economic influence and deported them. Jews were kept from jobs. The Vichy government and DeGaulle were working together. (D.C. Jewish Community Center, 10/4/06. Renee Poznanski. www:d.c./cc.org). So we must hate France in perpetuity.

Sounds like the occupation of Palestine, except that there was no reason to round anyone up, except Moslems. Are we to hate Zionists??

Israel should not be calling the shots in United States' Foreign Policy Decisions. France still helped us gain our sovereignty in the Revolutionary War, or we would still be under England's thumb.

About wars (1848), Abraham Lincoln echoed the sentiments of our Founding Fathers when he wrote: "Kings had always been involving and impoverishing their people in wars, pretending generally, if not always, that the good of the people was the object. This (engagements in war), our (1787) convention understood to be the most oppressive of all kingly oppressions; and they resolved so to frame the Constitution that no one man should have the power of bringing that oppression upon us."

President Bush and his neocon advisers surely feel that they are above the law.

Chris Hedges, author (C-SPAN2, 4/29/07): "This war can be summed up in one word: impeachment. I have friends in Gaza, Lebanon, and Iran, and if we go into war against Iran, I will not pay my taxes. . . . This administration has taken Trotsky's permanent revolution to a new level: permanent wars."

And now, George Tenet, director of the CIA under Presidents Clinton and Bush, tells all in a book – that the entry into war with Iraq wasn't even debated. The neocons and Bush used inconclusive intelligence.

AN OVERVIEW ON THE WAR ON TERRORISM

I feel that this article, by Jim Marrs, a native of Fort Worth, Texas, is invaluable to the young among you who have been indoctrinated in our public schools. Marrs is a distinguished author and investigative journalist who served in Vietnam and worked for the Fort Worth Star Telegram, as a military and aerospace writer.

"What should be thoughtfully considered is the dismal record of United States Foreign Policy since WWII. This policy, as confirmed by the New York Times years ago, has been in the hands of the Council on Foreign Relations elite since at least 1939. This elite and its associates includes former Presidents George H. W. Bush, Bill Clinton, Gerald Ford, Jimmy Carter, Richard Nixon and virtually every CIA Director, as well as a considerable number of familiar past and present government officials such as Dick Cheney, Henry Kissinger, Wesley Clark, Strobe Talbott, Alexander Haig, Alan Greenspan, James A. Baker III, Sandy Berger, Colin Powell, Zbigniew Brzezinski, Frank C. Carlucci, John Deutch, Lawrence Eagleburger, Robert McFarlane and Casper Weinberger.

"The policy is one of neo-colonialism; that is, the subjugation and control of other nations through military dictators or wealthy families supported by, and often placed in power by the U.S. military or intelligence services. The names of nations that have felt the brunt of U.S. CIA and/or military activity as a result of foreign policy include Somalia, Afghanistan, Mexico, Guatemala, Panama, Colombia, Indonesia, Dominican Republic, Iraq, Iran, Libya, Palestinian Territories, Cuba, Vietnam, Korea, Nicaragua, Lebanon, Grenada, Haiti, Serbia, Kosovo, Bosnia, Brazil, Chad, Sudan, etc.

As Dr. Martin Luther King, Jr. stated during the Vietnam War: 'My government is the world's leading purveyor of violence.' He did not say 'my country' or 'my people.' It is the government – or rather, those who control it – that is responsible, although we, the distracted and unaware citizens who claim to live in a democracy, must take our fair share of the blame.

Is there precedence in history for what is happening to America today? So much so, there is not enough space to present it all. Nero burned Rome, blamed it on his enemies and took dictatorial power. But consider what happened just last century.

On February 27, 1933, the German Reichstag or Parliament was destroyed by fire. Hitler and his Nazis blamed it on communist terrorists. They even captured a Dutch youth named Marinus van der Lubbe, who carried a Communist Party card. After some time in custody, the youth confessed to being the arsonist. However, later investigation found that one person could not have started the mammoth blaze, and that incendiaries had been carried into the building through a tunnel which led to the offices of Hitler's closest partner, Hermann Goering.

Less than a month later, on March 24, 1933, a panicky German Parliament voted 441 to 94 to pass an 'Enabling Act' at Hitler's urging, which was the starting point for his dictatorship. As a result of this act, Germany soon saw gun confiscation, national identity cards, racial profiling, a national security chief (Heinrich Himmler) and later, mass murders and incarcerations in concentration camps.

One of the Western leaders who supported Hitler and his policies was Prescott Bush, grandfather of George W. Bush. He must have taken notice of Hitler's method for gaining unwarranted power.

Since the Reichstag fire, the Bush family and their associates in the Council on Foreign Relations, Trilateral Commission and the Bilderbergers, have often mimicked Hitler's tactics of creating a problem, offering a Draconian solution and advancing their agenda through any resulting compromise.

The real enemy is whoever is behind the September 11 terror attacks. Osama bin Laden, so closely connected to the financial interests of the Bush family and the CIA, may be the mastermind, or he may be a convenient scapegoat – yet another provocation to stampede Americans into another war for oil.

We must thoughtfully consider where the real source of terror lies: with one bearded fanatic in an impoverished Middle Eastern country, or with those who would profit while shredding the U.S. Constitution in the name of defending freedom."

Jim Marrs also gave us this excerpt from a speech delivered in 1933 by Major-General Smedley Butler, U.S.M.C., on Interventionism:

"War is just a racket. A racket is best described, I believe, as something that is not what it seems to the majority of people. Only a small inside group knows what it is about. It is conducted for the benefit of the very few at the expense of the masses.

I believe in adequate defense at the coastline and nothing else. If a nation comes over here to fight, then we'll fight. The trouble with America is that when the dollar earns only six percent over here, then it gets restless and goes overseas to get 100 per cent. Then the flag follows the dollar and the soldiers follow the flag.

I wouldn't go to war again, as I have done, to protect some lousy investment of the bankers. There are only two things we should fight for: one is the defense of our homes, and the other is the Bill of Rights. War for any other reason is simply a racket.

There isn't a trick in the racketeering bag that the military gang is blind to. It has its 'finger men' to plan war preparations, and a 'Big Boss': supernationalistic capitalism.

It may seem odd for me, a military man, to adopt such a comparison. Truthfulness compels me to. I spent thirty-three years and four months in active military service as a member of this country's most agile military force, the Marine Corps. I served in all commissioned ranks from Second Lieutenant to Major-General. And during that period, I spent most of my time being a high-class muscle man for Big Business, for Wall street, and for the Bankers.

In short, I was a racketeer, a gangster for capitalism.

I suspected I was just part of a racket at the time. Now I am sure of it. Like all the members of the military profession, I never had a thought of my own until I left the service. My mental faculties remained in suspended animation while I obeyed the orders of higher-ups. This is typical of everyone in the military service.

I helped make Mexico, especially Tampico, safe for American oil interests in 1914. I helped make Haiti and Cuba a decent place for the National City Bank boys to collect revenues in. I helped in the raping of half a dozen Central American republics for the benefit of Wall Street. The record of racketeering is long. I helped purify Nicaragua for the international banking house of Brown Brothers in 1909-1912. I bought light in the Dominican Republic for American sugar interests in 1916. In China I helped see to it that Standard Oil went its way unmolested.

During these years, I had – as the boys in the back room would say – a swell racket. Looking back on it, I feel that I could have given Al Capone a few hints. The best he could do was to operate his racket in three districts. I operated on three continents.

U.S. SCHOOL OF THE AMERICAS

The U.N. Truth Commission, in 1999, released a report on the 34-year-long Guatemalan civil war during which time 200,000 Guatemalan civilians (most of them Mayan and other indigenous people) were put to death by the Guatemalan military and police forces. Those murders – not at all the acts of "rogue" soldiers, but part of deliberate policy – were committed by officers trained in counter-insurgency by the U.S. Military, primarily at the School of the Americas at Fort Benning, Georgia.

Sadly, for decades many Americans have accepted the fact that our government has co-opted the leadership of the military in several third world countries.

The terrible truth here is that the killing of these people is something our government, not those of Guatemala, El Salvador, Honduras, Haiti, Colombia and Mexico, desired. It has been our policy to crush any incipient challenge to dominant U.S. interests. Our government has been in the business of protecting U.S. multi-national corporations for decades. This policy was summarized by George Kennan in 1948 in a secret internal State Department memorandum.

Kennan wrote: "We have about 50% of the world's wealth, but only 6.3% of its population. . . . We should cease to talk about vague and . . . unreal objectives such as human rights, the raising of living standards, and democratization.

Covertly, that philosophy has ruled U.S. foreign policy ever since 1948. Meanwhile, a series of spin doctors have perpetuated the tale that our government is the leading defender of democracy in the world."

Russ Christenson, Philadelphia Inquirer 3/8/99, went to Central America, also believing that the U.S. was defending democracy. He taught history in Costa Rica, ran a large aid program, and defended refugees trying to gain asylum here in the U.S. He conducted seminars on the role of the U.S. in "death squads" of Central America.

His e-mail address is: rustyc@exploremaine.com.

Incidentally, President Clinton was asked to close the school at Fort Benning and refused. The school has trained "notables" such as Noriega, drug czar, and Iran's Savak, their secret service torture team.

STATE DEPARTMENT AND LOBBYISTS

Senator Joe McCarthy of Wisconsin surely has been smeared over the years, since the late '50s. And it was always that he was hunting out "communists."

Isn't communism the reason given for our going into Vietnam?

I hope that even the least political savvy among you has concluded that communism has never been an impediment for the financiers. Through trade, we have built up Red China to a point which may threaten us. American arms dealers gave the Chinese what they needed in missile information. And we, by patronizing Wal-Mart, have been the conduit for the Chinese to build a strong army and navy. We built up Russia during Lend Lease. So let's not talk about "communism" as an ideology we hold in disdain. When money's involved, American banks go anywhere, and our troops go there to protect them. Never mind that leaders like Stalin killed forty-five million people. All McCarthy said was that our State Department was infiltrated.

Congressman Paul Findley of Illinois wrote <u>They Dare to Speak Out</u> (Lawrence Hill Books), in which he warned about the harm lobbyists were doing. I thought that his dedication was most appropriate: "To our grandsons – may they always be able to speak without fear."

Unfortunately, anyone who speaks out against our foreign policy is punished by AIPAC, the American Israel Public Affairs Committee. Their victims are many – Adlai Stevenson III, George Ball, Wm. Fulbright, Georgie Anne Geyer, Paul McCloskey, Cynthia McKinney and many others.

Israel is no longer considered a foreign lobby, thanks to our paid-for Congress.

During President Carter's administration, Congressman Stephen Solarz demanded that Secretary of State Cyrus Vance "get Ambassador Seelye of Syria out of the embassy." Vance was furious, not with Solarz, but with Seelye. Seelye's crime was in not allowing Syrian Jews out of Syria. The reasons could be many: Moslems are sometimes not allowed to leave either. Could be due to brain drain, or they were afraid to lose their people to another country.

President Carter's administration had an office for the Jewish Community in the State Department as well as in the White House.

Diplomats confirmed the fears of having a Jewish Liaison Office in the State Department. The seventh floor of the State Department is home to the office of senior State Department officials. Staff members brought in by political appointees – and every administration has them – are usually responsible for leaks. They get access to policy planning and sensitive material.

A former Defense Department official recalled: "There were individuals on Capitol Hill that the Pentagon viewed as conduits to Israel. A number of times we would get requests from Congressmen or Senators for intelligence materials. We knew damn well that these materials were not for their own edification. The information would be passed to Israel."

"In the opinion of all these sources, Israeli penetration of State and Defense had reached an all-time high during the Reagan administration. In 1984 people known to have intimate links with Israel were employed in offices throughout the bureaucracy and particularly in the Defense Department, where top secret weapons technology and other sensitive matters are routinely handled.

"The three personalities of greatest importance in this area were: Richard Perle, Stephen Bryer, and Noel Koch, principal deputy to Richard Armitage, Assistant Secretary for International Affairs. Koch was formerly employed by the Zionist Organization of America" (<u>They Dare To Speak Out</u>).

Today the State Department actually influences legislation. "Iran's comments fall short of OUR expectations" (CNN 8/23/05).

What may be good for Israel may not be good for America. Congress is responsible for selling out our once-loved country.

So McCarthy was right; our State Department is a mess. Nobody's watching the store.

LOBBYISTS

The fact that the corporations have already chosen the nominees for president is a joke. It's not so funny that we have to listen to their mindless chatter for a year, but we also have to be reminded of the money nominees have gotten from the lobbyists whom they will serve.

John Kerry (D-Mass.) listed 300 meetings with lobbyists since 1989. The Bush Administration went to court to avoid disclosing meetings of Vice President Cheney and others, held during the planning of our energy policy.

We have lots of Political Action Committees (PACS) who give generously to politicians who favor their causes – teachers' unions, labor groups, trial lawyers who represent illegal aliens. Even a teacher who is derelict in his or her duty can't get fired. Nor can a disciplinary problem be expelled without the help of a trial lawyer whose salary we pay.

We also have foreign lobbyists. Cuban exiles have advanced legislation stating that anyone from Cuba who reaches our shores can stay here and get all of the freebies he needs. If he's a criminal, he'll get representation from a slug in the trial lawyers' association.

Since 1979, leaders of the Cuban-American National Foundation – even they have a foundation – contributed $3.2million to political campaigns. They created the Miami Radio and TV station Marti which has cost us $280,000,000.

The 1996 Helms-Burton Act stripped the president of authority to lift the embargo against Cuba because of pressure from Cuban exiles in this country. Congressmen Helms and Burton were paid by us to be the lackeys of a foreign entity.

When Fidel Castro came to President Kennedy and asked him for financial help, he should have given it to him and saved us a lot of angst. Instead, he refused and Castro went to Russia. The rest is history.

Representative Ileana Ros-Lehtinen (R-Fla.) is one of the recipients of foreign gratitude. She and now deceased Representative Lantos of California were always on C-SPAN hawking for the Israeli lobby.

"With expert American advisors and millions to spend, nations from Australia to Zaire know how to get what they want from Uncle Sam" (U.S. News and World Report, 3/29/82).

Once a politician learns the ropes of the game, he can leave his job as a "servant" to America and go to a foreign country and represent their best interests against us. William Colby, former Director of the CIA, represents a foreign country. Former Vice President Mondale, under President Carter, represents Japan. Clark Clifford, former Secretary of Defense, represents Australia. On and on it goes. Even former Congressman Tauzin, now makes two million dollars per year backing Medicare Chief Tom Scully so that congress can't negotiate lower prices for Lipitor.

AIPAC is a very powerful lobby. The American Israeli Public Affairs lobby managed to side-step the Foreign Agents Registration Act, and is now considered non-foreign, thanks to our "Israeli-occupied Congress" (Buchanan).

I know that millions of people are unable to watch C-SPAN. Too bad, for it is there that one can learn a lot about the corruption going on under our noses.

For example: on 2/25/02, C-SPAN carried the following program:

CAFE (The Corporate Average Fuel Economy) Bill set the average miles per gallon at 27.5 for new passenger cars and at 20.7 m.p.g. for light trucks. The Democrats wanted higher requirements because of the growing concern about air pollution. LOL

With this issue in mind, enter the Jewish Community Council for Public Relations. Discussing the CAFE Bill, again before Congress, the Council added its concerns:

1. They wanted the 27.5 m.p.g. raised to 40 m.p.g.; SUVs, 20.7 to 30 m.p.g.

2. Higher gas taxes.
3. Support of block grants for Jewish Communities, adding $2.8 million to the $1.7 million.
4. They want to "fit into Peace Corp., Americorp," etc. "The President has allocated $30 billion" (Chris Shays with Connie Morella, Security of Virginia).
5. Grants for non-profits - $200 million.
6. Pass Middle East Commitments Act which holds the Palestinian Authority responsible for actions of Hamas.

Now, what does CAFE have to do with Palestine or pork giveaways? This goes on and on with Congressmen who are giving America away, bit by bit, and then insert money for bridges which don't exist, in order to keep people in their districts temporarily happy.

May I call myself the Catholic Community Council for Public Relations and get a few million dollars? I don't think so!

More recently on C-SPAN, always in the evening, are "short speeches," during which time a Congressman or Congresswoman can address any subject he or she wishes. One can always count on Tom Lantos of California to be there with his regular group.

On September 20, 2006, Tom Lantos was asking for a yes or no vote on resolutions he had introduced (HR 415 about HR 942).

The first resolution concerned the fact that Iran (Persia) was the first country in that region to elect a monarchy with a parliament. "This is an opportunity for Americans to send them notice of a Centennial Congratulatory Note since the democratic move took place in 1906. We can call on Iranians to develop a democratic constitution. Iran is becoming an autocratic society. We can say 'expel your dictators,' and the world should join us. Second, let's condemn the treatment of the religious sect, Bahai." (Bahai membership is almost exclusively Jewish, mainly due to issues of anti-Semitism.) "Third, President Bush after 911 should declare a day without violence, a Global Family Day."

It is clear to me that this type of rhetoric provokes violence; it assumes that the readers of the "Congratulatory Note" are stupid; hence, this resolution is arrogant and insulting. Not worthy of America!

This insulting rhetoric was on C-SPAN when President of Iran Ahmadinejad was visiting the United States during the UN Meeting.

Thankfully, Representative Dennis Kucinich of Ohio stepped into the meeting. Essentially, he said, "Wait a minute. This legislation is making a case for war, and we have to be very careful about that. The IAEA (International Atomic Energy Agency) disputes the report sent out to Congress which states that Iran was ready to build a nuclear weapon" (Washington Post).

At this point, Rep. Ileana Ros Lehtinen (R-Fla.) spoke up (Ros Lehtinen represents Cubans, many of them Jewish as well): "All financial assets of Iran should be frozen. We should bring the fight to their door. Non-profits should be frozen. A Palestinian anti-terrorism bill disallowing extremists to get money from U.S. should be passed, cutting off life line funds as weapons, and should include Lebanon, Syria and Iran. Stop aggression toward Israel and the U.S." Needless to say, her diatribe went on for twenty minutes.

Rep. Kucinich: "They (Iran) enjoyed a democratic government as they did in 1906, but in WW II, Britain and Russia invaded Iran to get oil. In 1951, Mossadegh was elected as the first Prime Minister and wanted to nationalize oil. Britain placed an embargo on Iran. (British Petro) We can't praise a democracy overthrown because of oil. And we do not care about human rights."

"Yes, Virginia, there is a Santa Clause!"

Thank God that courageous Congressman Kucinich knows history. Would that even five members of Congress would speak out against this hate speech, provoking wars. And I'll bet that Lantos and his group were the first to speak out for the disaster at Walter Reed, so long as their tails are covered.

Also, Congressman William Delahunt (D-Mass.) spoke up: "There is no accountability for hundreds of billions of dollars. Five years later, we are losing the war in Afghanistan. In contrast to what was said earlier on the floor, drug money finances terrorism; violence reigns."

These two courageous Congressmen spoke as America-firsters, and I applaud their knowledge. Article I, Sect. I – "Congress has the right to investigate."

John Mearsheimer from the University of Chicago, and Stephen Walt, Harvard, co-authored <u>Israeli Lobby</u>. "We define the lobby as a group of interests. They put pressure on universities and institutions to stop criticism. Iraq was conceived by the neo-cons. We rewarded Iran, after they helped us, by calling them the 'evil empire.' The recent attack in Lebanon was pre-planned The support of Israel does not make sense in American policy. Not in America's interest. We need debate. The fact that Israel has a right to defend itself, no one denies, but the collective punishment campaign on civilians by destroying roads, bridges, is wrong. After four weeks of bombing, Lebanon is reduced to rubble. Entire families killed, and the Red Cross was prevented from getting in.

"Unfortunately, the legal scam does not end here. There are hundreds, some say thousands, of PAC groups representing Zionist requests, without the tag of religion."

The American Enterprise Institute sponsors one-world themes. I don't know who appointed this questionable group – in my opinion – as the arbiter of childhood education, but on C-SPAN 2, 10/6/06, Charles Pennington said, "Childhood education for nuclear energy support is essential. Public acceptance depends on early childhood education. If the public understands, the politics will be right." Like sex and drug education, Mr. Pennington?

Esther Aguilera (Congressional Hispanic Census Institute) and Raquel Egusquize (Ford Motor co.) can get on and talk about "partnerships" formed so that young Latinos could get safety training for their children, better health care, along with educational training for "leadership positions." Partnership is a nice word for "you pay, we play." Reminds me of a County Commissioner in Montgomery County, Pennsylvania. He purchased a ski resort at Spring Mountain. We paid half and he paid half. Who owns it?

Lobbying is bleeding us dry!

IMMIGRATION

In 1965, Ted Kennedy passed the 1965 Immigration Act which replaced a policy based on quotas for various countries with one that allowed relatives of recent immigrants from Third World countries easier entry into the U.S.

Article I, Section 9 of the U.S. Constitution states that only the States shall have the right to decide immigration flows. The Supreme Court, in Cramer, quoted a definition of treason as "an act which weakens or tends to weaken the power of the U.S."

We were always able to designate how many immigrants could enter this country. Sometimes it was 153,000. But these entries had to have health tests and a place to go and a waiting job. Since we were an industrial nation, there were plenty of jobs and willing applicants. These applicants had to show that they had no criminal backgrounds, and were willing to assimilate. And assimilate they did. They had no welfare backups, no food stamps, no language teachers. They learned English any way they could.

Today, because of all of these mandates by the federal government, and the tight-fisted corporate thugs who give peanuts to those desperate Mexicans who work in fruit groves, we are forced to subsidize labor with housing, education, food stamps, lawyers, SSI, and health care.

We are forced to overlook the fact that many forest fires in the U.S. are caused by illegals coming to this country in droves – 20 million unaccounted for – and when a child is born, they've hit the lottery as a free-loading family. We have overtaken Mexico's poverty problems.

America can't take in as many Germans, Irish, Italians and Poles, etc., because Ted Kennedy wants mostly Third World immigrants.

Twenty-five percent of our jails are filled with unregistered aliens. Gangs, many undocumented, walk the streets threatening anybody and everybody.

Supplemental Security Income has robbed poor Americans from getting their fair share because they now must wait for those who don't belong here to get theirs first.

One case – the Rivera family in Boston – illustrates why Americans are angry. Eulalia Rivera, her 18 children and their 89 progeny collect $750,000 to $1,000,000 a year in government benefits. Their main form of support, however, is not Aid to Families with Dependent Children (AFDC), the program for single mothers and children, but disability payments from SSDI. Most of the family members collect benefits for their "nerves."

As you can see, "they all come to America to work."

Illegals cost us billions of dollars a year, particularly since they can use emergency rooms as a doctor's office.

The diseases brought over to America haven't been seen here for decades: tuberculosis, hepatitis, and even food contamination. Children in school have to be inoculated and re-inoculated since anyone is allowed in any school. No questions asked.

Our city hall is packed with Hispanic-workers with accents, who treat poor Americans like trash, and who deny the applicants payments. But, if an Hispanic walks in, mountains are moved. I've witnessed this travesty.

Let's stop the welfare payments. Stop giving payouts to illegals who have babies here, and can apply for licenses, etc. They would soon leave.

In 1982 the Supreme Court ruled that schools cannot deny education to illegals. In other words, property taxes go up to support people who should not be here. Congress won't act because they're getting illegal votes, and the Supreme Court has no right to legislate! Remember what Lincoln said: "Judicial power is not legislative power; it is merely a right to apply, not to interpret."

If we the people don't straighten this mess out, Congress won't do it. But some knowledge of the Constitution is needed, and I hope that I've done that. Schools are not doing the job.

Recently Ted Kennedy and John McCain tried to pass an amnesty bill for the twenty million illegals here. When President Reagan granted amnesty, we were told that it would deter illegal immigration. Wrong!

Figures pertaining to the number of illegals in this country range from 12 million to 20 million. I feel that no one really knows because no laws are being followed.

When right-wing radio recently took credit for the demise of the Kennedy-McCain Amnesty Bill, they were justified. The people spoke and it worked.

But, when Patrick Buchanan and the rest of us spoke out on immigration more than 15 years ago, when the problems were easier to solve – some of these same right wing talk show hosts were the ones who wouldn't let us speak without calling us names. They had no clue about the problem, but they controlled the microphones.

At present, the problem will take a King Solomon to solve. And where is the do-nothing Congress who created this problem? Why they're still haggling over a fence, or "national guard with no weapons." Term limits would do it for our corporate toadies in Congress.

If it weren't for the fact that the Democrats were looking for illegal votes – remember, talk show hosts were given money for advising their listeners that they could "apply for a driver's license and register to vote" – a nice flow of Europeans and people from all countries could have been assimilating and enjoying life in the United States. But no – corporate lackeys like Kennedy who should have been thrown out of Congress after his Chappaquiddick scandal, decided that he could stay in office indefinitely if only he could impress the illegals that he had a "big heart." Just so long, that is, as they keep away from his compound and stockade fence, and his Fiji Island money.

So, Mayor Dinkins of New York City, another "big-hearted" guy with our hard-earned money, took in 500,000 poor people from the Dominican Republic. What these politicians are doing is making us inherit every country's poor, plus the drugs and the inevitable crime that follows, to say nothing about impoverishing the rest of us. They really don't care about people – so long as those people serve in the U.S. Army – for which we pay – and are there to carry their water and shine their shoes.

Nothing in the Constitution says that States have to accept these edicts coming from the federal government. And please, save us all from the "kind sentiment" of the uninformed callers who say, "My father was an immigrant."

Bill Gates, who made his billions in this country and enjoys "foundation" status, thanks us by requesting that we take in more technically-trained foreigners each year – maybe 250,000, Mr. Gates? – so that he could choose from the "best and the brightest." (CNN, 7/8/07). Of course, he's referring to the H-1B visas. This man has no loyalty to this country or any other county. He's inhumane.

When Senator Barack Obama was a presidential candidate he declared it a "victory for race" when U.S. District Court Judge James Munley decreed that the Mayor of Hazelton, PA had no right to keep illegals out of Hazelton. Again, a judge is "legislating."

Imagine, a poor mining town, with average workers making the same amount of money they earned five years ago, have no right to say, "We can't handle the social services required for people who should not be here." This is Barack Obama. I wonder where in the world he would get more respect or more lucrative a salary and standing than he does in America. Poor whites don't matter to this guy! It's "his people," his voting bloc that matters.

The One World dreamers have neutralized millions of people through wars and immigration so that, in fifty years, no one will remember America, Germany, or any other country that had a republic. At the moment, we are a balkanized mess with loyalty to the country we left. And that's the way the "masters" like it.

REDISTRICTING IS <u>NOT</u> REAPPORTIONMENT

Reapportionment is mentioned in the first section of the Constitution and clearly stated to assure equal "representation." Redistricting, on the other hand, is a "changing" of districts in order to maintain the "turf" of the incumbents. This process is used to ferret out dissent, to prevent opposition, and to assure the re-election of those in office.

Three conservative districts can be fused into one, thereby losing two conservative representatives, or two conservative districts could unite with one liberal district and be neutralized.

The intent of redistricting is also to get rid of a Congressman who didn't "go along."

California is always the testing ground for "planning" our lives with "hidden" agendas such as sex education, United Nations' advocacy, environmental issues, etc. Anything, which is taken to a vote, would fail.

California courts extended a constitutional provision which would deny citizens the "equal representation" clause in the 9th Amendment and the "states rights" clause of the 10th Amendment.

Of course, the courts have become judicial "activists," legislating rather than applying the law. So that when parents voted not to have their children bused twenty miles away, the courts remanded the order and forced busing anyway. This is in violation of separation of powers.

Those whom we have elected conspired to divide up constituencies for political gain and used public funds to do it. Both the courts and the legislators consult "systems specialists" (planners) rather than taxpayers to make their decisions. For instance, planners use different companies such as Andrew Young (before he was involved in the Savings and Loan scandal in California) to study voting patterns, census data, and files on individual citizens, to determine whether or not an incumbent is desirable. The candidate who best fits the planners' goals is elected. These employees looking into citizens' records are not screened.

Unless citizens become aware of what the legislators are doing, these professional wheeler-dealers will continue the Soviet-type elections we now have and may portend the future of what was once the land of the free.

Prima facie evidence of "a deliberate, calculated attempt to bring about changes, which are not wanted by the citizens, through creating a 'climate for change' was uncovered in California in 1974." (Referenced in the following chapter.)

Existence of the intent to usher in a New World Order by disenfranchising every living soul who is not a participant, collaborator or cooperator in the nefarious scheme has created an army of alarmed people, nationwide. Many Americans are seeing the threat hanging over the future of their country for the first time. The problem is that conditions were designed to produce that climate for change, and those to whom the newly alarmed unwittingly turn for help are often willing agents of the cabal behind it all.

"An area that needs immediate attention is the voting booth. With redistricting replacing reapportionment, combined with the removal from office of every incumbent constitutionalist, no term limits and controlled financing of campaigns, the end of any semblance of 'representation' is in sight." (Maureen Heaton, <u>Impossible Dream</u>)

When we see a city legislator representing a suburban constituency, as we see in Pennsylvania, a red flag should go up.

And Pennsylvania is now voting on redistricting. No word from my state legislator; I heard about it by accident.

Voting districts must be clustered, not fragmented, in order to represent the people in that district. It's constitutional.

DAMNIT, IT'S MY BOOK

Damnit, it's my book, and I'll tell it like it is! By now, my readers know that I do a lot of note taking and taping on topics meaningful to the youth who are not being told the truth. The youth will inherit the mistakes of the corrupt brutes we have empowered to run our government. Needless to say, I'm mad as hell with those hijackers who have conspired to "change" America since before World War I. Their ruthlessness and lust for money and power continues to this day, with no hope of mercy.

While I'd like not to mention the name of Michael Medved, nevertheless, this man is extremely dangerous to our freedoms because of his affinity to Israel, internationalism, and propaganda. On (1-22-09), he characterized a brave woman in the White House Press Corps, Helen Thomas, as a cackling witch. It just so happens that Helen Thomas dares to ask questions affecting you and me – unlike the rest of the go-along press corps. This 'religious' man went on and on, cackling and laughing, because of her age – but mostly because of the fact that she struck a nerve.

These neo-con talk show hosts get away with murder when they discuss "censorship." No caller – unless he tricks the complicit screener by not admitting to 'everything' he plans to say – gets through. Rush and the Zionist lineup on 990 – Prager, Bennett, Savage, "Dennis the Menace" Miller, Medved, Hewitt (ugh), and Mike Gallagher are obviously all against the Fairness Doctrine, proposed by Congress, in order that we might hear both sides of an issue. I'm not holding my breath on the Fairness Doctrine's effecting change since I don't trust either party, particularly since I've heard

Air America and MSNBC, etc. Everything can be discussed – as all of us know – except Israel.

I won't go into all of the odd things that have happened to me since I decided to write about the impending fall of our country unless we act. One of those things happened at 6 a.m. Saturday (1-31-09) when I was awakened out of a deep sleep and couldn't go back. So, I decided to listen to the radio. But NPR had nothing interesting so I went over to 990. I'm a glutton for punishment. It so happened that Michael Medved was interviewing a guest, George Friedman, who wrote "The Next One Hundred Years." The interview was a playback of his Monday (1-26-09) show which I missed. On Monday 55,000 Americans lost their jobs – Home Depot, Boeing, Pfizer, Caterpillar, Staples, etc.

Surely this was an answer from heaven, for I could not have gotten a better climax to my research than your hearing the plan for our future, from the 'horse's mouth.' Everything I've spoken about is spelled out in the final plan of this treacherous author who is an advisor to business-es, governments, and politicians. "Security and the future" are his strong points. God help us!

This is the plan for America in the 21st Century if we allow madmen to lead our way. Friedman reveals, in a simplistic way, just what Clin-ton's professor at Georgetown said that he agreed with – the "conspiracy." (Professor Quigley)

Following is the dialogue between Medved and the guest.

Medved: "Who will be the next dominant Moslem power in the Mideast? Iran?"

Friedman: "No. It will be Turkey, the 17th largest economy in the world – next to Israel. Turkish power is expanding into the Baltics, etc. Turkey is Moslem but has no tolerance for fundamentalists. The "war on terror" will be won by the United States. Turkey is Moslem, but its military is secular.

"We're worth hundreds of trillions in assets."

(My comment: Two Minnesota legislators recently suggested selling prisons and airports, along with bridges, but we dopes aren't supposed to know this. (1-31-09) And, these assets belong to the Public!)

Medved: "Thoughts on Federal Reserve?"

Friedman: "We've managed to muddle through with this institution for 100 years." (Sure, keep on printing and building debt.)

Medved: "There's a country which people look down upon as a troubled, dysfunctional nation, but you say that it will rise as a world power in 2100 and will be America's chief rival. You say that we will face a very difficult and unpleasant challenge from a New World Power – Mexico."

Friedman: "Yes. It has the 13th largest economy in the world; its GDP is one trillion dollars; it has 110 million people and Free Access to the U.S. economy. Mexico receives $25-40 billion a year from the United States in drug money, in dollar transfers which finance their economy. In the next 70-80 years, they will grow not only in size and be in the top ten economies, but will have a population transfer. Americans are aging. At the moment we want the Mexicans out, but in 20 years we'll want them back because we won't be able to run the economy without them."

Medved: "People who talk about rumors of America's decline and irrelevance, losing influence – you say are greatly exaggerated."

Friedman: "We will dominate the 21st Century in ways that even Rome didn't do. China has some limitations. Twenty years ago, we talked about Japan's dominating; in the '50s, it was Russia, after the Sputnik. China has huge problems. Although it has developed greatly in the last 30 years, it has 1.3 billion people whose living standard resembles that of Nigeria. One billion people make less than $2,000 a year. Their coastal area booms. They have to export because their people can't afford to buy their products. If Americans don't buy their products, they're in trouble. Over one-half of the loans made to China have not been paid back. Their financial system is in chaos. We expect it to fall apart in the next 10 years."

Friedman: "In decades to come, the leading European Power will not be France or Germany, but Poland. In the beginning of the 20th Century, if you said that the dominant countries would be Japan or China and that they would be super powers, or that Israel would be the dominant power in the Middle East, people would laugh at you. Poland faces Russia. Poland is an ally of the United States. The United States supplies their F16s and missile defense systems. Just think about those countries which had strategic military relationships with the United States – South Korea, Israel, West Germany, Japan. Poland will be that country in the 21st Century. Polish-American relationship will be critical. Russia will be expanding and coming back big time. Poland will be a dinosaur; it will 'jumpstart' their economy." (More imports; less jobs in U.S.)

Medved: "I resonate with what you're saying. The most exciting trip in my life was to Poland. The population will determine growth or decline. Russia has a declining population, but Poland, being Catholic, is better off than most countries."

Friedman: "One of the myths is the population explosion of the 20th Century, but it has ended."

Medved: "I didn't notice in your book that in 2100 the UN would be in control of the world. Ha Ha!"

Friedman: "That's because it's not going to happen. Ha Ha!"

(My comment: NATO will be the international police force.)

Friedman:"Wars are going to happen all of the time. I didn't disagree with President Bush on the Iraq war, but on the management of it."

Medved: "Will there be a lower standard of living for Americans in ten years? President Carter made this statement saying that Americans don't have a perspective. You, however, have provided that perspective."

From here, Medved went on a diatribe against President Carter – remember, Carter called Israel 'apartheid'? Medved: "I'm saying everything I want about Carter, since I won't be able to do it once he dies."

Friedman: "I was reading President Carter's comment about perspective."

Medved: "Part of perspective is that the worst president was President Carter. You say that the 21st Century will bring more wars, but that they will be 'less bloody.'"

Friedman: "Wars will happen all of the time, but today "we" have weapons much more accurate; if you want to destroy a factory, you don't have to destroy the whole city. In World War II, in order to destroy a factory in Hamburg, basically you had to destroy Hamburg. One of the interesting things in Iraq is that only 4,000 people were killed. In Korea, we lost 30,000; Vietnam, 50,000. It has to do with protective systems. Technology has made war, thank God, a lot less bloody. We're not going to have fewer wars, but it won't be the holocaust of the 20th Century." (Get that! "Thank God.")

Medved: "The coalition of those killed (Iraq) was 160." (He's referring to foreign troops killed.)

Friedman:"Media is a dangerous thing because they can frame this as a disaster."

Medved: "Thank God."

Friedman: "When you consider the casualties inflicted by the Soviets with their weapons and ruthlessness, it won't he pretty, but better."

Medved:"If you were to invest money in some other economy, what would it be?"

Friedman:"Turkey."

These dedicated Zionists – yes, Zionists – have no loyalty to this country or they wouldn't take the liberty of talking over us as though whatever they say is a fait accompli. After all, Americans are never allowed to hear the other side, so they wouldn't know that Turkey, the Unites States and Israel were like blood brothers in their desire to destroy Iraq, especially by making the Kurds a power in the north of Iraq. They're ruthless, and they understand that the Kurds are easy to recruit and to foment trouble in conjunction with the CIA. It's "pay to play" everywhere in politics. The Turks are the ones who committed the genocide on Armenians that Congressman Lantos used in one of his resolutions.

The times may be changing, though, since Americans are losing their jobs. On NPR, 1-30-09, even the Turkish Prime Minister walked out in a huff after shouting at the Israeli Prime Minister who got 25 minutes to speak to the World Delegation, which met in Davos, Switzerland. The Palestinian was allowed to talk for only 12 minutes, with interruptions. When the Prime Minister walked out, he was soundly applauded. Perhaps people are waking up to the fact that – though we have grievances and loss of jobs – there is no forum for airing grievances, either at home or in Davos, Switzerland. Gaza recently had $2 billion in damages to their infrastructure, and the United States volunteered $20 million. Again, we have to borrow for the aid – thanks to the murderers in Israel, our allies, who continue to prod our military to "kill, kill."

Journalists like Tom Friedman, NYT (Meet the Press, 1-25-09) are treated with kid gloves because they expect it. They never face a challenge, and they have the money and power to keep us in the dark. It's our money – U.S. money; hard-earned.

During the conversation with the host, Friedman made a statement which should be familiar to all: "Another 911 and it will be the end of liberty as we know it; there'll be more than checking shoes!" (Another 911?) Seems that Pearl Harbor was a good pretext for war.

Incidentally, I have no respect or sympathy for the 22 Arab countries that we pay to 'play nice' with Israel. When greed exceeds compassion, it's elementary that "what goes around will come around." I have no sympathy for the lackeys like George W. Bush or the generals who march in lock-step because of greed; I blame all of the past presidents for selling us out to Israel at $10 million a day plus what they make on community rackets, nonprofit grants, aid, lobbyists, trade, consulting, security, etc., etc. But "Americans may not have enough for social security." I say put the rascals from Wall Street in jail for stealing from those whose pensions were involved. After Bush's bailout of banks, $20 billion went to CEOs who failed the public. Their bonuses should be frozen and kept for those people who worked hard and lost everything because they thought that the Security Exchange Commission was monitoring the funds.

Obama's give-away stimulus bill to illegals, the State Department, global warming, new cars for government workers, Amtrak, Acorn (the community racketeers), windmills, and other bloodsucking organizations is another means of throwing our money in the street. Obama proves that it isn't about race; it's about common sense, courage, and loyalty to America – only America.

Notice that none of the above-mentioned people, whether Medved, George Friedman or Tom Friedman, are worried about the fact that Mexico makes $25-40 billion a year from drug sales in the United States. They all want immigrants to fight their wars – continual wars which will involve Polish "Catholics." Everything is planned. They already know that Mexico will become a New World Power, compliments of the druggies in the United States, victims of politicians who have done nothing about our borders – like John 'the hero' McCain.

They don't care that China owns our debt; they're more concerned that America builds up the Chinese and Mexican and Polish economies. And I think that George Friedman made a slip when he said that "in the beginning of the 20ᵗʰ Century, people would laugh at you if you said that Israel would be the dominant power in the Mideast." No, we never thought that an "occupier" would rise to such heights as Israel with our billions in aid and U.S. military support. It's a big joke!

Where will we get the trillions for the Zionist wars? Americans will have to compete with many nations. The lives of the youth will be torn by more broken homes, drugs, lack of education, and hopelessness – but, we have to change it. These hijackers have taken God out of our lives and want uneducated Americans – out of jobs – to believe that help is coming when Jesus returns to earth and Jews rule. Well, we've already been there, done that, and it isn't pretty. They count on dumb Catholics to vote for pro-life candidates who believe in annihilating millions of children. They own our jobs and our lives, and it has to change. Every congressman or woman should have all assets earned on our time – speeches in foreign countries as lobbyists working against us – frozen and placed in a repository for those maimed in their stupid wars. Congressmen like Barney Frank, Kennedy, Feinstein, Boxer, Dodd, McCain, Orrin Hatch, Lieberman, Kay Bailey Hutchison and all of those who went along with Trade Treaties that made hardworking Americans lose their good paying jobs, should suffer the consequences.

Obama promised to renegotiate the Trade Treaties (or Traitor Treaties). Now, let's see what he does. So far he has surrounded himself with tax cheats and lobbyists who made money by selling America out. These same politicians, who are against our dropping out of NAFTA and Gatt, are crying 'protectionism." Yes, we should protect our jobs here in America before outsourcing jobs to China, Japan, Mexico, Poland, Israel, Colombia, and so on and so on. It's our country and airports and bridges belong to the people, not to the dummies and traitors in Congress.

We now know that nothing will be done to block drugs coming into the United States because of the fact that Mexico needs that $40 billion coming in from the U.S. to build their economy. The media hype about building fences, etc. is all just a ploy to stop the public from protesting.

Meantime, gangs and single women having 14 children help divert Americans away from jailing the real culprits in government. There is no drug war; it's a scam meant to create addicts among the poor who will be used for violence. Remember what our "insider," George Friedman, predicted: "that the United States will dominate the 21st Century in ways that even Rome didn't do." I 'resonate' with this man who knows to invest his money in Turkey. Surely he must have been advised by the bankers who are part of the insider scheme to bankrupt America and who hold our war debts, along with China and other super rich people. And keep in mind that corporations that go offshore make some sweet deals in order to avoid paying taxes in the United States by placing their profits in the Cayman Islands, Bermuda or even the Fuji Islands – you know, like Ted Kennedy. Senators, like Tom Daschle, who don't report $128,000 in taxes and still have chauffer driven cars as our servants, love to raise our taxes for whatever cause will bring them votes. Then their wives can make six figures by lobbying for pharmaceutical companies so that we pay 60% more for drugs than Canadians do. Mr. Daschle did a lot of influence-peddling for health related issues – hence, President Obama's choice for Health and Human Services. This department rakes in exorbitant amounts of money for bureaucracies that employ tons of unneeded people at insurance companies – while doctors make nothing. Who suffers? You and I. Why? Because we're obligated to pay for illegals who cost us $750 at an emergency room compared to $25-30 at a physician's office. Also, we pay for fatherless children because Congress refuses to believe that raising children requires more than food and a Band-Aid; it requires love and care, or the rest of us pay when victims grow up. Jails are full of them.

Therefore, when someone like George Friedman tells Medved that the "United States will dominate the 21sat Century in a way that even Rome couldn't do," I picture a scene involving a coliseum where the fun and games took place. Friedman was right. We would need to bring back Mexicans at that time, so that their slaves could help our slaves build this huge arena where events of all kinds could be enjoyed by the super rich. The slaves, of course, would get at least $1,000 a year – if they were productive.

I can see it now: boxers kicking other boxers with blood all over the floor while women and men cheer; nude women running around in drug stupors – cursing to make the audience laugh. To top it off – lions chasing people who believe in God! What a wondrous sight – bankers arriving in chariots because of the ethanol crisis. Wow!

For the record (2-1-09) writers for the *New York Times*, like Andrew Rosenthal, are preparing Americans for the treasures to come by calling those who don't wish 20 million illegals in the United States to get blanket amnesty, as President Obama may do – "racists." This divide and conquer scheme works so well even though we have a black president. The sad truth is that neither race nor ethnicity means anything in the New World Order when the paid hit men in NATO step in to pulverize dissidents. That's when the elite take over and the real fun begins.

It's a sad day in America when the sex-slave trade and the drug trade are earning billions for the worst characters in the world – the scum of the earth, and a known bank can launder the money. Victims are children and teens exposed to TV shows with no moral obligation to anyone except their fat wallets – by people who should know better. For instance, in early afternoon, one can watch TMZ, a Fox channel, and see Harvey Levin laughing at someone physically handicapped, a popular little person in Hollywood open-mouth kissing an infant. During an earlier hour, Mr. Levin dons his attorney face on People's Court. I was frankly shocked when I saw Levin turn his other face – pervert.

Another tip about our future in America came from NPR's Terri Gross, who interviewed author P.W. Singer, "Wired for War," 1-23-09. Mr. Singer is a Senior Fellow at the Brookings Institution, 500 members strong.

The hostess and the author had a very spirited dialogue about the new technology of "pilotless" predators and global "warhawks." The United States now has 5,300 Predators and 12,000 ground robots. Singer said that when he talks to "Generals," they say "soon we'll be using tens of thousands of them." Imagine! And the average person has no idea of the plans of these unconscionable psychopaths, to kill innocent people from a distance. At $500 billion a year for defense, these cowards could have black budgets and secret weapons in secret locations such as Area 51 and Nevada – cowards with medals for bravery. The military is being used as hit men for the Wall Street mob. Thank you for your service, dudes!

Singer commented that no code of ethics exists. He recounted the story of a young 18-year-old man who joined the Air Force without getting a high school diploma because he couldn't pass English. But this young man was "fantastic" on videos. "With this new technology one could send out 500 lb. bombs from a computer in Nevada and land them in Iraq."

So the young man, thinking that they had caught "Chemical Ali," dropped two 500 lb. bombs on the suspected home of Chemical Ali. "We cheered when we saw this burnt ragdoll figure bouncing up and down – until we learned that we had wiped out a family, not Chemical Ali. Another time we thought that the Predator wiped out Osama bin Laden…."

Amy Goodman (Democracy Now) is another brave soul who dares to talk about what's happening in Gaza. Two brothers were killed – one an architect and the other a major in commerce. Their brother, living in the United States, said that it took his brothers longer to get their degrees because of the many Israeli checkpoints. And we say nothing about the Israeli use of white phosphorous in their genocidal attempt to wipe out every last Palestinian. My criticism of Amy Goodman: she plays the race card much too much. She can't seem to forget Martin Luther King!

I'd like to close down the $500 billion we give to military "yes men." I am so sick of their camouflage regalia and their AK47s. This is not the military I knew from family, friends and neighbors who believed that they were defending the Constitution.

We need less nukes and more doctors. We need teachers who can speak well. Throwing money at education won't help. New graduates, indoctrinated into globalism and social justice without thought of America, are useless. Brilliant science and math teachers are needed in a hurry. Knowledge of America's beginning along with a study of the Constitution are necessary objectives. We have to fix the two and one-half generations of indoctrinated victims.

The framers must be turning in their graves when they witness this return of the Fall of Rome with all of its depravity and wickedness in America, the once citadel of liberty to all who sought justice.

Today, in America, your name goes on a Zionist list if you defend the wrong people, and the wrong people today are Moslems. I can only imagine how many brilliant Moslems have been killed and tortured under George Bush and Dick Cheney alone. Will they get reparations as the Jews did from the Germans?

KURDS

Once a nomadic group from Southeastern Turkey and the Caucasus, the non-Arab Muslim Kurds are a factious and disparate group. Twenty million people strong, they are spread through Turkey, Iran, Iraq, Lebanon, Syria and some former Soviet Republics.

During the fall of the Ottoman Empire, the Kurds had a chance at statehood, but because of infighting, they were unsuccessful.

The bombing of the Kurds with mustard gas in 1988 by Saddam Hussein is nothing new. During the 1920s, according to Vivian Bird, when Iraq was a British protectorate known as Mesopotamia, the Royal Air Force undertook bombing missions which were intended to subdue rebellious Kurdish tribes in Iraq who were protesting the high taxes of the British puppet King Faisal. Secretary of War, Winston Churchill suggested using mustard gas which was not popular with the Royal Air Force commander; however, "the bombing campaign was carried out with great brutality during which time many Kurdish towns were attacked with incendiary bombs and machine-gun fire." (Vivian Bird is a British Journalist who reports on world events from her base in Cornwall.)

Today Turkey is guilty of human rights violations against the Kurds living there, twelve million strong, and for whom Turkey refuses to grant autonomy. The Kurdish Workers Party (PKK) is guilty of nightly guerilla attacks against the Turks.

Turkey is the U.S. line to the Middle East, the Balkans and the Caspian Basin, and oil. Both Turkey and the Kurds are pro-West and pro-Israel, so the U.S. looks the other way when the Turks act out against the Marxist Kurdish groups within its own borders.

We use the bases in Turkey to facilitate the passage of oil and gas from the Caspian to world markets and to access Iraq and Iran for our bombing missions.

In the Kurds' past there is also the Armenian genocide by the Turks in which the Kurds participated.

Since the Gulf War, Kurds started streaming into parts of Italy and Germany. I do believe that there will be a bloody civil war in Iraq now that the U.S. has made a de-facto Kurdish state in the north of Iraq, granting them revenue rights from oil. When former Congressmen like Senator Biden of Delaware talk about a "three state solution" to the problems in Iraq, it insults the intelligence of those who know history. I'm convinced that the military and the Congress know nothing about the Mideast except what our allies tell them. And heaven knows, they're never right…intentionally.

At the moment, we are using Israel's trained team of Kurds in northern Iraq and the U.S. trained teams of former Iranian exiles in the south to gather intelligence needed for a possible strike against Iran's suspected nuclear sites, according to retired U.S. intelligence officials. In "Patterns of Global Terrorism," the State Department's annual publication, the Mujahadeen-e-Khalq is listed as a "terrorist group'; yet, it is used for intelligence gathering by the Kurds. In this case, they are our terrorists, so it makes it okay.

When we were on Iraq's side in the Iran-Iraq War in the '80s, the Mujahadeen terrorists fought on Saddam's side. That's how we knew that he had chemicals and weapons of mass destruction made in the good old U.S.A. The Mujahadeen were the ones who helped Saddam suppress opposition within Iraq and performed internal security (this according to United Press International 2/05).

When the U.S. invaded Iraq in 2003, the munitions and weapons of the Mujahadeen were seized. But then George W. Bush decided to use them in covert missions against Iran.

Because of the fact that the Kurds sided with the U.S. and the C.I.A. against Saddam, we rewarded them with the de facto state, and this is precisely why the Iranians never trusted the Kurds whom they felt were a wandering group left over from the Soviet fifth column. Turns out they were right; we wouldn't want a group of dissidents in the U.S. to join with a foreign force to take over our country either.

Although the Kurds should have economic and cultural freedom, a state is counter-productive.

So whom did we appoint as president of Iraq? A Kurd, Jalal Talabani, naturally. Sometimes I wonder if the people who represent us are just ruthless and cruel or just plain ignorant. Or both.

As Michael Medned said on his talk show, "Keep killing."

C.I.A.

The budget for this group is $30 billion per year; yet we have no accounting of what they do.

Recently, before the war in Iraq, the CIA played their usual games of inciting trouble in the north of Iraq with the Kurds, and in the South with the Shiites. No self-respecting American would sanction a foreign entity covertly entering our country and fomenting race wars or religious wars. The CIA does exactly that.

"The CIA director has authority to waive a regulation barring attempts to recruit clergy and employees of members of Congress and congressional committees.

"As journalists have argued, when individuals and governments overseas learned that some missionaries worked for the CIA, suspicion immediately fell on all missionaries" (Philadelphia Inquirer, Rothberg, 2/23/96).

When hostages were taken in Iran, 1979, the Iranians felt that the American missionaries they took as hostages were CIA agents, and we gave them great cause to believe it.

The intelligence budget should not be classified. In my three decades of research, I have found that the CIA has done more harm than good – especially in the training of people like Noriega at the School of the Americas in Fort Benning, Georgia.

Secretary of State Warren Christopher, during Clinton's presidency, asked that a Haitian fugitive with CIA links, who was accused of leading a terror campaign against pro-democracy forces in Haiti, be detained in the

U.S. and deported. The fugitive, Emmanuel "Toto" Constant was detained, but set free. Haitian officials believed that his release was predicated on the fact that Constant knew too much about the CIA activities in Haiti. (Philadelphia Inquirer, George Gedda, 6/21/96).

Robert Scheer, a contributing editor to the L. A. Times, put it well in the Philadelphia Inquirer, 11/14/95: "Whenever times get tough, some timely CIA expose would come along to pay the rent. The use of Michigan State professors to train Ngo Dinh Diem's secret police to torture, remains a personal favorite. That and the attempt to restore democracy to Cuba by hiring the Mafia to rub out Castro with poisoned cigars. They had to do something after the failure of the Bay of Pigs.

"Remember the 1954 coup against Jacobo Arbenz, the elected leader of Guatemala, which saved Central America for the free world and United Fruit? (Like oil, corporations control anything they can grab from third world countries.)

"And the more recent revelation that the Guatemalan military officers who allegedly killed a U.S. citizen were on the CIA payroll?"

Perhaps the following article by Russ Christensen, a retired INS hearing officer who lives in Temple, Maine, will best describe the workings of the CIA and now, Israel which has joined our intelligence agency. (e-mail address is: rustyc@exploremaine.com) You decide whether or not they should be in business. And Homeland Security also gets $30 billion. The answer from the previous administration (George W.) was that America hasn't been bombed since 9/11. Of course not. We've killed just about everybody moving. I'd call it genocide.

"The truth is coming out, and despite the pain, I'm glad.

"Late last month, the U.N. Truth Commission released its report on the 34-year-long Guatemalan civil war. More than 200,000 Guatemalan civilians (most of them Mayan and other indigenous people) were put to death by the Guatemalan military and police forces. Those murders – not at all the acts of 'rogue' soldiers but part of a deliberate policy – were committed by forces led by officers trained in counter-insurgency by the U.S. military, primarily at the School of the Americas at Fort Benning, GA.

"Sadly, for decades, many Americans have accepted the fact that our government has co-opted the leadership of the military in several Third World countries.

"The terrible truth here is that the killing of these people is something our government, not those of Guatemala, El Salvador, Honduras, Haiti, Colombia, and Mexico, desired. It has been our policy to crush any incipient challenge to dominant U.S. economic interests. Our government has been in the business of protecting U.S. multinational corporations for decades. This policy was summarized by George Kennan in 1948 in a secret internal State Department memorandum:

"Kennan wrote: 'We have about 50% of the world's wealth, but only 6.3% of its population. In this situation we cannot fail to be the object of envy and resentment. Our real task in the coming period is to devise a pattern of relationships which will permit us to maintain this position of disparity without positive detriment to our national security. To do so, we will have to dispense with all sentimentality and day-dreaming; and our attention will have to concentrate everywhere on our immediate national objectives. We need not deceive ourselves that we can afford today the luxury of altruism and world benefaction. . . . We should cease to talk about vague and . . . unreal objectives such as human rights, the raising of the living standards and democratization.'

"Covertly, that philosophy has ruled U.S. foreign policy ever sine 1948. Meanwhile, a series of spin doctors have perpetuated the tale that our government is the leading defender of democracy in the world.

"When I first went to Central America in 1958, I too believed that my country was defending democracy. My involvement with the region in a variety of ways since then has taught me otherwise. I have taught history in Costa Rica, run a large aid program in Honduras, and defended hundreds of Central American refugees in the INS political asylum courts. I later worked as an Immigration and Naturalization Service asylum hearing officer.

"By interviewing hundreds of Asylums from El Salvador and Guatemala, both as their legal representative and then later as their judge, I came to know much about the role of my own government in this sordid, secret mess, and I went on to conduct INS seminars on the role of the U.S. government in the activities of the 'death squads' of Central America.

"All I can say is this: We the people of the United States, by averting our eyes from our government's active support of the death squads' policies have been indirectly responsible for the deaths of 180,000 civilians in Guatemala, similar numbers in El Salvador and lesser numbers in Honduras and now Colombia and Mexico.

"So it is time for a public debate on our foreign policy. We have chosen massive repression in these Third World countries because we feared democracy. From our pinnacle of vast wealth, we have looked into tiny agricultural countries where the majority of the population is slowly dying of malnutrition, and we have been afraid of political parties whose economic plans might differ from our own.

"The U.N. commission has the power to bring some of the culprits to justice. I hope it does.

"But then I think of the United States. Our complicity in this genocide has been a dirty half-secret too long. So terrible are the crimes that they may be past forgiveness. But if Americans take real responsibility for what their country does overseas, perhaps we can make sure atrocities like this never happen again."

Look at what has happened recently in Great Britain, our ally in imperialism. The death of Princess Diana was designated 'accident.' Well consider this: Princess Diana's eyes were being opened when she visited foreign countries with land mines – countries in which children and adults were rendered limbless and handicapped. And President Clinton wanted them to remain, when we had a chance to get rid of these perilous horrors. Then there was talk of her possibly marrying Dodi Fayed, a Moslem. Well, we couldn't have that because then she'd get the OTHER side of the story. Dodi's father called the coroner's results "garbage." And I agree. Being married to a Moslem has changed my whole life. I, too, believed that President Eisenhower would never go into Iran and take out the one duly-elected secular prime minister they would have had, Mossadegh. But when Mossadegh wanted to nationalize their oil, the Shah was put in and we trained his secret police at Fort Benning, Georgia – as only we could.

In the Philadelphia Inquirer, 10/16/97, Mark Fazlollah said, "In a bizarre twist in a law enforcement scandal, state narcotics agents have filed a federal lawsuit contending that the CIA destroyed their careers because they tried to investigate politically connected Dominican drug dealers.

"The suit contends that the dismissals were part of a conspiracy to protect Jose Francisco Pena Gomez, an unsuccessful candidate in last year's presidential election in the Dominican Republic.

"It said Pena Gomez's Dominican Revolutionary Party was and is protected and sanctioned, unlawfully, by agencies of the U.S. government, to include the CIA and the State Department, enabling the Dominicans to distribute illegal drugs at will to the black and Hispanic populations of the Eastern Seaboard." (I did not quote the whole article.)

We have to look at our southern border where drugs come in every day. Without drugs, these tyrants couldn't get away with the crimes against humanity which they commit daily. George Soros, the billionaire, puts his money in drug legalization. Wonder why?

Former CIA agent, Victor Marchetti, tried to expose the workings of the CIA in a book, "The CIA and the Cult of Intelligence" (Dell), but they imposed 340 deletions.

Also, "Deadly Deceits" by Ralph McGahoe.

NAFTA AND GATT

The North American Free Trade Agreement and the General Agreement on Tariffs and Trade were signed into law by President Clinton, even though every president since Truman tried to get them through.

Ross Perot called NAFTA the "giant sucking sound" the loss of American jobs would make as they flowed down the economic drainpipes to Mexico for the benefit of big business and their slave labor forces.

In the Washington Times, December 6, 1993, Anglo-French financier Sir James Goldsmith said, "If the masses understood the truth about GATT, there would be blood in the streets of many capitals. . . ." He warned that GATT would mean social upheaval and political instability bringing far worse global consequences than the Bolshevik Revolution. In part these are his remarks:

"Global free trade will force the poor of the rich countries to subsidize the rich in the poor countries. What GATT means is that our national wealth, accumulated over centuries, will be transferred from a developed country like Britain . . . to developing countries like China, now building its first oceangoing navy in 500 years.

"China, with its 1.2 billion people, three Indochinese states with 900 million, the former Soviet republics with some 300 million, and many more can supply skilled labor for a fraction of Western costs. Five dollars in China is the equivalent of a $100 wage in Europe.

"It is quite amazing that GATT is sowing the seeds for global social upheaval and that it is not even the subject of debate in America. . . . A healthy national economy has to produce a large part of its own needs. It cannot simply import what it needs and use its labor force to provide services for other countries.

"We have to re-think from top to bottom why we have elevated global free trade to the status of sacred cow or moral dogma. It is a totally flawed concept that will impoverish and destabilize the industrialized world while cruelly ravaging the Third World."

Goldsmith summed up the case against this global fiasco in a nutshell. The World Trade Organization (WTO) gives the once-powerful U.S. one vote – the same as any of the 114 countries. And, with this treaty, any third world country has a right to sue the U.S. if we do not comply with the "rules" in this 20,000 page document. NAFTA has 11,000 pages.

We see now that George Bush is complying with NAFTA rules. No borders between Mexico, Canada and the U.S. As a matter of fact, President Bush does nothing about the border issues because he can't, and a Congress who pretends that they want to stop the flow of immigrants – after signing the documents – should be summarily tossed out! They're all complicit in deceit or stupidity.

The label "isolationist" is so insulting. The corporate powers would like Americans to think that if you are against Chrysler plants in America relocating to Saltillo, Mexico, you are against all trade. These manufacturers pay the Mexicans next to nothing for building their cars, and those Mexicans are coming across the border thinking that the pay is better here. They don't know that pensions and health care, which used to be paid for by the employers are now being lost to American workers. This is why Sen. John Edwards, the multi-millionaire ambulance chaser, can pay $400 for a haircut, and the Clintons are calling for National Health Care. They know what's in store for us – "the workers in the vineyard."

Gus Stelzer, in his book <u>The Nightmare of Camelot</u>: "The Great Masses of People . . . will more easily fall victims to a big lie than to a small one." (Adolph Hitler)

"Among the many myths and downright lies fostered by free trade globalists is that the Smoot Hawley Tariff Act 'triggered' the Great Depression of the 1930s. (Smoot Hawley raised tariffs and lowered taxes.)

"During the so-called NAFTA debate on the Larry King Show between Vice President Al Gore and Ross Perot in November of 1993, Gore invoked the red herring of Smoot-Hawley on three occasions.

"Blaming Smoot Hawley for starting the Great Depression has no more validity than blaming the writer for starting the Chicago Drake Hotel fire in July 1963 because he slept there that night.

"Almost every writer on the subject of the Great Depression who penned his work <u>before</u> 1945 leaves no doubt that it was triggered by 'the crash' of financial markets in October 1929 and the subsequent collapse of the banking system. Emphasis is placed on publications prior to 1945 because Smoot Hawley did not become the 'fall guys' for the Great Depression until some time after the formation of GATT, the one-world socialist cartel in 1947, and John F. Kennedy's dream of a 'global Camelot' in 1960.

"In 1934 the average wage for non-supervisory workers was under 50 cents an hour with virtually no fringe benefits. As a result of the 1935 Labor Relations Act and subsequent labor laws, base wages now average $11, plus numerous fringe benefits, bringing hourly wage costs above $19 an hour. This did not happen by accident. It happened because millions of people prevailed on federal, state and local politicians to pass laws designed to raise the living standards of working people. In so doing, it raised the cost of every American product. Other laws mandated safer, healthier work standards; anti-discrimination, malpractice and product liability lawsuits spawned by costly litigation; social security taxes added 5% to producer costs; public education 6%; defense 5%; price supports for farmers 2%; welfare programs 4%; health care 6%; building codes, endangered species laws, and on and on."

This is why our products are more expensive – we have protections added in. Wal-Mart offers the consumer lower prices because we subsidize the workers' health care, and their products come from China which pays slave labor wages with none of the protections we have. so that if you buy a pair of child's pajamas at an inexpensive price, it's because no liability is there if the pajamas catch on fire. It's cheaper, but at what price.

The corporations, step by step, are wiping out all of the benefits of the Labor Relations Act that millions of Americans worked hard to bring about. Don't forget – we build those pajama factories for the Chinese and Mexicans so that American corporations can sell pajamas at a bigger profit and no liability.

Corporations want tariffs on imports to be totally erased, in effect subsidizing their profits even more.

"Thanks to tariffs, at least some part (about 30%) of those industries have been retained in America, thereby adding $700 billion a year to our national

income, over 1,000,000 jobs, and over $25 billion a year in federal, state, and local tax revenue. Import tariffs run about 2% or we would have no import income. (Before GATT and NAFTA, 85% of our national income came from tariffs.)

"Most imports are like bootleg whiskey. They are cheaper, or of arguably better quality, primarily because they are made under conditions that circumvent laws. If any American corporate executive ran his company in like manner, he would be arrested, convicted, and sent to the slammer."

The author, Gus Stelzer, was a corporate executive and makes no money from this book, which is excellent. Its purpose: "to take America back." (1-800-939-9827). Peanut Butter Publishing, 226 2nd Avenue, West Seattle, WA 98119.

If it weren't for outstanding activists like this, America would have been long gone. President George W. Bush and his corps of neo-cons and impotent democrats and republicans needed your sons and daughters to defend these corporate monsters on foreign soil because poor people all over the world woke up to this game a long time ago. Americans are still in the dark. Why? No debate. No education. But wait. Poverty is coming to a place near you.

For instance, today Rush Limbaugh had Walter Williams, professor of economics, substitute for him. It was the same old lesson he comes on with every time he has an audience. The "Free Market" is wonderful. It gives Mr. Williams "and millions of Americans the opportunity to buy a suit at Wal-Mart for $150," saving perhaps $300 if that suit were bought at one of our retail stores. He's always jubilant about the money poor people and rich people can save if they want to. They have "choices." What he doesn't say – and I can't believe that he's teaching this garbage – is that no society can stay wealthy if all they do is consume. Wealth can only be acquired by production. This is what made America great. One can buy all of the Chinese pajamas he wants at $3.99. But when he loses his job because the factory at which he's working moves to China, it's goodbye any pajamas. And, if he is on welfare and the middle class loses their jobs, it's homeless time for all.

Gus Stelzer, whom I cannot praise enough, was an executive at General Motors with 35,000 employees, 1,000 dealers, and $2 billion in annual sales, until his retirement in the late seventies. He's written over 100 articles on free trade, etc. People like him should be teaching economics at our colleges and universities.

He describes very simply what has happened to America since we have allowed corporations to merge and avoid anti-trust laws, and literally get away with murder.

President Kennedy passed the Trade Expansion Act of 1962, putting us on the road to free and expanded trade, to Camelot, the world of fantasies. With the national debt at $9 trillion, we are facing a "nightmare," not a land of bliss. No one in Congress knows what is causing our national debt. Until 1970 all cars made by General Motors were made in the United States. Germany made its Opal in Germany, etc. But the 1960s and the internationalists in the State Department and the Treasury Department allowed cars like the Volkswagen to come to the U.S. at the price of $1,395. The U.S. couldn't compete. (Remember, our products include pensions, education, health care, etc.)

So Chrysler and Ford began moving offshore; consequently losing jobs, income, and tax revenues. Even the Wall Street Journal couldn't diagnose the problem.

"Our trade policies subsidize foreign industries. People think that we have Free Enterprise but the excessive mandates put on industry – millions of federal, state and local laws, regulations and monetary controls – impact on those who produce our goods and services. They have to recover those losses at the cost of their products. The rising cost of American products has increased 800% to 900% since WW II. Due to political laws, the tax burden on the average American products is 50%. From 1946 to 1971 we had a surplus of $19 billion; then from 1972 to 1994, the U.S. had a trade deficit of $1.6 trillion." (Seattle Intelligencer.)

Lee Iacocca (auto executive) warned Congress to change policies in respect to industry before Chrysler moved offshore.

For 125 years, between 1789 and 1914, when the 1913 income tax law was passed, and the Federal Reserve came into play, 50% to 85% of our tax revenues came from tariffs on imports, enabling us to run the government and protect industry. Americans had the highest living standards. When the internationalists decided to cut back on tariffs and instead, pass the unconstitutional income tax, less than 1% of our federal revenue comes from imports, so that foreigners get a free ride and we taxpayers subsidize the imports, coming from countries using slave labor, and <u>no</u> regulations. Third world countries don't have regulations on working conditions or any other safety provisions.

Congress pays no attention to the fourteenth Amendment, the Equal Protection Clause. They give aid to foreigners who send their products here at a lower price, but our companies must follow all of the regulations for products we export. We can't compete.

Stelzer: "No nation can 'consume' its way to wealth. Only production, the labor of people, creates wealth."

Our "wonderful" State Department made 55,000 concessions under the GATT treaty (according to Senator Malone). Only Congress has the right to regulate trade under Article 1, Sect. 8 of the Constitution. But Congress delegated its power to the World Trade Organization (WTO) in Geneva, Switzerland, run by appointed people we don't know and where the U.S. gets one vote. Treason. And don't tell me that any of the members of the House or the Senate read the 20,000 pages.

President Clinton, in an effort to reduce our trade deficit with Japan, threatened to put a luxury tax on imported Japanese cars like the Infinity. Australia and Japan threatened to file a complaint with the WTO, and Mickey Cantor, our trade representative under Clinton, caved. The Wall Street Journal must have called Clinton.

We don't have enough investment capital to finance our own debt. We have borrowed $800 billion from foreign countries who buy our treasury bills with money they get from sending us their imports.

Congress wants to reduce social security and Medicare benefits because they have forfeited money which would have gone to social security and Medicare through our trade deficit. If we had produced exports worth $166 billion instead of importing products made by China - $230 billion in one year – we would not have the social security crisis we now face. But Congress says nothing about the cause, because they are "free traitors."

Our deficit spending is financed by the Federal Reserve which gets about $300 billion in interest which has to be collected from somebody -- $3,500 per household. Who gets it? We pay $60 billion a year to foreign holders of our treasury bills. Foreigners hold the mortgages on our debt – remember, with our money from imports.

Robert Rubin, Treasury Secretary under Clinton, reflected on "how nice it is that Asian countries buy our debt!" When the Mexican peso collapsed, Dole, Rubin and Gingrich shored up the peso with billions of our dollars.

Ninety percent of our money (interest) goes to 10% of the wealthiest people.

The CEO of SONY: "We could never defeat the U.S. militarily, but economically we could overcome the U.S., and we'll do it with your money."

Remember this when you think about voting for the candidates already chosen by the corporations: We built up Red China to a point where they are now a threat to us.

As though "free markets" aren't enough, those we entrusted to protect us borrow money to give foreign countries so that the debt incurred is on the shoulders of our children. And we have forgiven billions of dollars in loans to foreign countries so that those debts, too, will come from you and your children.

THE CLINTONS

Before anyone rushes out to vote for another Clinton in the White House, let us review some of their past deeds. It's not bad enough that those of us who are against U.S. foreign policy have no avenue through which to speak because of the neo-con, pro-war line-up on the radio – Bill Bennett, Laura Ingraham, Glenn Beck, Dennis Prager, Michael Medved, Rush Limbaugh, Sean Hannity, O'Reilly, Smerconish, Mike Gallagher – to listen to the Air America types, one would think that "all would be well" if only there were another Democrat – any Democrat – in the White House.

They talk about President Clinton as though his biggest sin was lying under oath about Monica Lewinsky. In my opinion, the Lewinsky affair was a nice little cover-up for the real happenings under his presidency. I voted for George Bush because I thought that the lying and refusing to hand over papers to relevant people, and the secrecy in general, would stop. I was wrong. President Bush carried on the secrecy at a faster rate. People are catching on to the diabolical plot to do the same thing to us as they have been doing to third world countries. They're giving away good American jobs to slave labor. Closing more factories and giving us less critical time to assess the damage going on under our noses. Corporate greed is what it's all about, and Americans are not happy with slave labor wages when heads of corporations are making five hundred times as much as the workers. And our educational system doesn't help. The foundations would like the U.S. to follow Holland's plan – where children decide which courses they want.

Let me refresh your memories. Hillary started out with 400 health care and insurance representatives at a "secret" meeting hosted by Hillary and Dr. Magaziner. She wants universal health care, but since she has done nothing about the influx of illegals on our southern border, does this include twenty million illegals? She has also advocated that "we should fund international family planning and reproductive health care worldwide." Her husband gave away millions of American jobs when he passed NAFTA and GATT, the two trade agreements which have paralyzed the middle class. But if everyone has socialist health care, maybe they won't notice that their jobs and homes are gone, while the Hillarys and her friends get richer and richer and more untouchable, and the rest of us get poorer and poorer. I've told you. They want socialism for us and unregulated capitalism for themselves. Only problem is that fewer and fewer doctors will be willing to work for peanuts, and kill themselves taking care of endless patients when socialist doctors from abroad are coming here to get jobs which they thought paid better.

These con artists are neutralizing the masses so that there is no place to run. The only factor not thought about: who takes care of one of the rich politicians when they come to an emergency room full of illegals, who also need treatment? Wait their turn! And, since it's socialized medicine, the wait may be three weeks!

Hillary invented the nurse practitioner who gets a high salary for acting as a doctor. Only problem is that I don't want an "actor." I think that we need doctors more than we need corrupt politicians who pretend to care about the poor. And Michael Moore is a whack job! He should leave for Cuba.

Bill Moyers' investigation into money and politics revealed the painful truth – that free speech and the certainty that one will be heard is guaranteed only to those who can afford it. And corporations can afford it. Whether through purchasing massive amounts of advertising for political purposes, or by owning the companies that bring people the news, powerful corporations are able to drown out the voices that disagree with them – and today in America, it's all perfectly legal. (the Center for Public Integrity) During his term, President Clinton gave away free speech with the Telecommunications Act of 1996 – marking "the biggest corporate giveaway to an industry already dominated by a few corporate giants."

Phyllis Schlafly of Alton, Illinois, who for years has done an incomparable job in bringing out the travesties in government, has brilliantly summarized some of Clinton's wrong-doings. I shall use two:

1. "He implemented more and more unconstitutional executive orders that amass more and more power in the hands of the federal agencies." (Through the Administrative Procedures Act, a president may place an "order" in the "Federal Register." If it is not contested in 30 days, it becomes law.)

2. "Pushed hard to fulfill his global agenda by locking us into a 'web' of treaties that transfer our sovereignty to global bureaucrats (World Trade Organization –WTO), and implement invalid and unratified treaties." Although every president since Truman tried to get the North Atlantic Free Trade Agreement (NAFTA) through, it took Bill Clinton's snake charm to finalize it. It enabled George W. to erase the borders of the U.S., Mexico, and Canada so that anyone could come through. And Congress pretends that they don't know why this is happening. Well, they haven't read the 11,000 pages of the NAFTA agreement which they signed.

Other deeds:

1. The Red Chinese (and I use that term so that the reader is aware of the fact that we are not fighting communism) channeled money into the campaign funds of the Democratic National Convention. James Riady pled guilty to giving money to the DNC. Later on, shipping rights were given to China in Long Beach, California. The Chinese were accused of taking in arms for Chinese gangs, and of smuggling Chinese citizens into the U.S. Penalty? No.

2. The debts of Third World countries were forgiven, and placed on the backs of American children.

3. Clinton raised the number of H1-B-trained technicians who could enter the U.S. and take away computer jobs, etc., of American citizens. It was 100,000. At present it is over 200,000 and, remember, Congress has to give its OK.

4. Also during Clinton's presidency, he took part in the Oslo Agreements which falsely maintained that Arafat was given everything and refused to sign the agreement. The real reason was that there

were many roadblocks still there, and that the Palestinians had to sign on to a clause which stated that they would never complain about going back "home." Who would sign it?

5. Senator Jim Leach: "Susan McDougal took $300,000 from the Small Business Agency meant to help the poor." Clinton pardoned McDougal – I think for her silence. Also, he pardoned some Hasidic Jews who cheated the government out of $40 million for a non-existent religious school in New York City. Again, it is my opinion that this pardon helped Hillary become Senator from New York.

6. In President Clinton's speech to the United Nations in 1994, he said, "Nationalism is a cancer."

7. He added 87% more regulations to Health Care and Human Services.

8. Ron Brown, his Secretary of Commerce, was also under investigation for receiving money from China, involving the sale of two satellites to that country. Brown was killed in a plane crash.

9. Clinton closed 77 military bases.

10. Allowed dams in California to be breached, eliminating hydraulic power, not considering repercussions.

11. Implemented the "roadless" policy so that no fire trucks could save our forests until helicopters arrived. Hence, small fires become large ones and the environmentalists who hate trees to be cut by loggers, supported the bill. Go figure. I listened to a debate in which seasoned Park Rangers argued that fires could be extinguished much earlier if there were roads to get to them. And what about the coveted wildlife, the restocked wolves, etc.? Aren't they burned as well?

12. Started the Balkan Adventure in which NATO bombed Kosovo for 70 days. Some thought that the bombing was a way to get charges of Chinese espionage out of the press.

13. Roger Tamaraz, a Lebanese oilman, wanted by Interpol, was invited by Congress to speak about a Turkish route to get Caspian oil to western markets. Remember, Turkey and the Kurds are very pro-United States and Israel. Tamaraz was treated royally. He had given $300,000 to the DNC. When Congress couldn't decide on a route, Roger moved on to Red China who needs oil for its industrial projects, thanks to our policy of everything "made in China" – to the detriment of Americans and America. And Bill O'Reilly dares to

call anyone who points out corruption in high places "anti-American"?

14. WACO, Ruby Ridge – citizens labeled "anti-government" were shot. A young boy was shot in the back on Janet Reno's (Attorney General) clock. American citizens. This is why the Student Weekly Reader asks questions of Americans such as "Would you shoot another American?"

15. Missile codes were given to Red China from Loral Arms merchants.

16. "The Clinton administration allowed an obscure treaty to establish UN authority over Yellowstone National Park, the Statue of Liberty and other American sites. House Democrats backed the grab" (Insight, October 28, 1996).

17. Gave one million acres of Utah's coal rights to Indonesia (61 billion tons of coal).

18. Rented the Lincoln Room in the White House to anyone who could pay $100,000.

19. Al Gore, of Occidental Petro stock: Occidental gave Clinton and Gore $470,000 in campaign contributions since 1992. Since the energy crisis in 2000, the stock prices had gone through the roof, "boosted by higher oil and gas prices, and increased production during that period" (WSJ, 2000).

20. Clinton claimed "executive privilege" on a document he received from Louis Freeh, FBI Director, blasting the administration for organizational policies that contributed to the increasing supply of heroin and cocaine in the United States. Freeh personally delivered the memo which Clinton would not release.

21. A directive was issued allowing anyone in the world to come to the United States for AIDS treatment.

22. Secretary of the Interior, Bruce Babbitt, used his regulatory authority to halt mining, grazing, logging, and oil and gas exploration on public lands. All recreational uses would be banned except for walking and meditating. I might add here that only the states have the right to hold public land and designate its uses. Governor Rendell is trying to lease our turnpike – public property – to a private, foreign entity with a public "partnership." Our tolls will be out of sight if some state legislator doesn't wake up soon, as one of the brave legislators in Kentucky (Virgil Moore) stood up to Senator Mitch McConnell

when the senator said, "I'm taking 20,000 acres . . . for . . ." and the legislator replied, "Oh no, you're not, Senator."

23. In <u>Bloodsport</u>, Jim Foster, a Clinton friend, was quoted as saying, "in Washington, ruining lives is a sport." Jim Foster's death was investigated by the "Park" police.

24. In May 1994, a Presidential Decision Directive placed U.S. Forces under a foreign commander and under UN rules of engagement.

25. Hillary: "Jerusalem should be the capitol of Israel."

26. Rhodes "scholar." And we thought it was about Lewinsky!

27. Clinton's National Security adviser, Sandy Berger, stole 9/11 documents from the National Archives. Any penalty? No. Did Clinton know about 9/11? We'll never know because right wing talk shows won't allow an investigation. They would rather demonize Rosie O'Donnell for even questioning whether or not two administrations knew about it.

28. Clinton's appointee to the Supreme Court, Ruth Bader Ginsbeg, a radical feminist, would like Boy Scouts to merge with Girl Scouts. How many aspects of our lives must these unelected drones control?

29. Clinton already had the Patriot Act on the table. President Bush first signed it into law (A. Cockburn).

We thought that the Patriot Act came about after 9/11 to protect us by giving the government more power. We are never protected by giving the government too much power.

Under this law, the FBI can go to a library and get your reading list and then tell the librarian not to mention it. No lawyers allowed.

For those of you – and I'll <u>never</u> understand why – who say, "I'm not doing anything wrong, so I don't care!" – imagine that you want to learn more about a middle-eastern country and get a book about it. Should you be arrested as a non-combatant or terrorist because you seek knowledge? I don't think so! Must you and your family be permanently dumbed down? And who are these agents keeping databases on us and our children? The same ones who may have manipulated intelligence to get us into war?

Remember, it was President Clinton who said, "I would die for Israel" (New York Post). Not America, but Israel. Such patriotism!

HOME RULE CHARTER

I came to the conclusion that the Home Rule Charter should have been named "Home Ruled." I present two arguments made in the Philadelphia Inquirer, 4/21/1944.

The first, by Lance Haver, director of Consumer Education and Protective Association:

"There are some Philadelphians who say it is time to 'modernize' the Home Rule Charter. Perhaps they have forgotten that modern isn't always better. It was Congress' modernization of the banking laws that led to the S&L debacle. PECO Energy modernized its generating plants with nuclear power and now we pay the second highest rates in the nation. And modern living means living with the fear of crime.

"The question is not whether the changes make the charter newer, but will they make it better. The only way to answer that is to know what the recommendations are, something the commission that drafted the changes has made very difficult. The chances are you don't know anyone who knows what even six of the 61 changes are.

"Many of us who oppose the Charter revisions believe that it is not an accident. Unlike the charter reform in 1951 which began as a result of public outcry, this charter reform was started by a handful of politicians.

"From the beginning, the Commission chaired by City Council President John F. Street, shut the public out. They refused to examine proposals that would give the public greater control of the School District or issues like term limits. They held most of their public meetings at 7:30 in the morning and withheld

their recommendations until one week before the public hearings. Street stacked the hearings, skipping over opponents of the Charter changes so that he could limit criticism. Even now the commission is refusing to appear at League of Women Voter forums if a spokesperson for the Vote No Coalition is given equal time.

"What the Charter commissioners don't want us to know is that the recommendations transfer power from the citizens to politicians. Proposal after proposal take away the rights of the individual. The very first proposal would take away the people's right to amend the Charter. If it passes, we would no longer have the right to reject charter changes in a public vote. In the name of efficiency, the politicians will do it for us.

"Recommendation number 21 would remove the public's protection against 'sweetheart' real estate deals. As it is now, every long-term real estate lease has an escape clause that can be activated after four years. That gives the public protection against corrupt politicians who burden the taxpayers with long-term leases to their friends.

"Proposal number 55 gives City Council the right to 'affirm all bills listed on a consent agenda by a single unanimous vote of Council without debate.' Unbelievably, this gives the politicians a way to pass bills that the public didn't even know were being considered.

"Several of the proposals limit the protection the public gets from civil service. Remember, civil service was developed because the politicians were hiring their friends and selling public jobs. Now this generation of politicians, using buzzwords like 'efficiency' and 'modernizations,' is recommending we take a step backward toward the bad old days when who you knew mattered more than what you know. The recommended changes will make it easier for the politicians to hire their friends, but strangely enough, there is no provision in the Charter to make it easier to fire unqualified people.

Proposal number 37 removes the City Controller as the elected person sitting on the Pension Board, a board that is supposed to ensure that the money set aside for city workers' pensions is invested wisely. If the Charter changes are passed, the Controller will be replaced by the President of City Council or his designees.

"Proposal number 48 would give City Council and other elected and high ranking officials automatic pay hikes. Rather than hold hearings to determine what the people of Philadelphia want to pay their elected officials, this proposal places that decision in the hands of an appointed 'Compensation Board.' The board, without hearings or a public vote, would grant pay hikes.

"There are more changes, like giving the mayor control over all the boards and commissions in the city, failing to eliminate no-bid contracts, and making the Fairmount Park Commission less independent.

"Some of the proposals that sound good really aren't. The recommendation to establish a Utility Commission is an example. As someone who has fought for years to have the Water Department regulated, I know that the proposal will not keep water rates down. The Charter Commission refused to give the Utility Commission the power necessary to control the Water Department. As a result, all the Utility Commission will be able to do is force us to pay for the Water Department's mistakes.

"And nowhere in the recommendation does it say how many new people will be hired and how much it will cost the taxpayers.

"Still wondering why they met at 7:30 in the morning?

"Yes, there are a few good ideas in the 61, but the Charter Commission won't let you vote for the ones you like and against the others. They decided to force people to vote on all 61 at once, knowing full well that the overwhelming majority of the voters will not know what they are voting on. They are counting on our ignorance to take our power. That's why it's so important for you to share this with your friends and make sure everyone you know votes no on May 10.

"Who knows? If the Greeks had tried the Charter Commissioners' tactics at Troy, they might not have had to build the Trojan horse."

The second article is by Thatcher Longstreth, a member of City Council until a very late age – as a reward, in my opinion, for pushing regionalism and all the other "secretive" laws that have brought this country ruin. Imagine, we send "servants" to represent us, and they pass bills at secret times. Seems a good time to me to rescind all this secret mess, and send the politicians a-packin'.

Longstreth: "I'm old enough to remember back to 1951 when Barney Samuel was in his second term as mayor and the voters of Philadelphia revolutionized their local government by adopting the first Home Rule Charter in the Commonwealth of Pennsylvania.

"That charter was a reform document which broke cleanly with a past of entrenched corruption and mismanagement. A key provision prohibited a third mayoral term, making Samuel a lame duck. New fiscal requirements, civil service protections, and restrictions on partisan political activities were adopted to foster honest government.

"The Charter also sought to implement an innovative new principle – that most municipal power should be vested in a single elected official accountable

to the people, the mayor. However, to ensure against the return of the corrupt system they sought to break, the Charter framers shackled management into a rigorous bureaucracy at the expense of permitting honest officials the freedom to respond to government challenges.

"After 43 years, this balance needs realignment. City managers need the flexibility to run an efficient government responsive to citizens' needs by streamlining procedures, eliminating bureaucracy, and implementing new management rules. Voters can help make Philadelphia a can-do city by voting on May 10 for the new revitalized Charter developed by the Independent Charter Commission.

"The Charter affects almost every aspect of city life – from police and fire protection, to trash collection, to public health, housing and human services. Its personal provisions affect every division of city government – and some 27,000 municipal employees.

"The new Charter will authorize graduated numbers of civil service-exempt employees based on department size. This will allow city managers to administer new policies and effectively form a team of their own to design and implement those policies. Alternatives to written tests for employee selection will become available as better barometers of performance, facilitating the hiring and promotion of highly-qualified and competent workers.

"Like personnel, procurement policies are inflexible and prohibit government from operating efficiently. The new Charter will allow our Procurement Department to employ competitive, sealed proposals designed by the American Bar Association's Model Procurement Code, enabling the City to purchase sophisticated goods and services – including high technology items – if competitive bidding is impractical or detrimental to the City. This will facilitate time and cost-saving measures and save tax dollars.

"Longer-term real-estate leasing with no penalties for termination will be permitted and will benefit taxpayers by allowing the City substantial savings.

"Today, City government is expected to provide more services, such as public health, housing, and environmental protection, yet we have fewer resources to pay for them.

"The new charter will allow departments to be created to address fundamental needs which emerge in the years to come. And it will allow tasks to be rearranged within and among departments to enhance service delivery. The 1951 charter, for instance, didn't create a Department of Housing. We didn't need one. Today we do.

"New charter finance and budget provisions will require long-range planning, public accountability, and interim reporting of the state of our city so that

the public and elected officials can easily determine when fiscal problems are arising and eliminate them before they escalate.

"The new charter will create a more efficient government to better meet the needs of its citizenry.

"These are different times, challenging times, and times of historic change. They require us to move in bold directions, to revitalize the city.

"With the innovations contained in the new charter, we know that the years to come will be marked by greater governmental responsiveness, efficiency and productivity."

How insulting these changes are. No civil service exams, creating a dumbed-down force of patronage hacks to serve the city. Longstreth knew very well about educational plans like Goals 2000 and No Child Left Behind, meant to create an illiterate citizenry.

The mayor, who could hardly deal with crime, is now placed in City Manager mode.

Corruption – worse than before. "Different times" indeed, created by a group of politcal hacks whose time it is to leave.

No city controller will be there to cap taxes or account for expenditures.

Philadelphia passed many of these provisions, one by one, with 7:30 a.m. meetings, in a City Council with a member who didn't know the three branches of government.

Home Rule gave Philadelphia "two" budgets – capital and operational.

The Mayor and City Council have the right to eliminate or create departments, authorities, and commissions with a two-thirds vote of City Council. If they wish to create a Housing Department, or Transportation Department for patronage cronies, they could. Before this Charter, City Council was weak; now it could have its own attorneys to fight the Mayor – not that they would.

The PICA Authority (Pennsylvania Intergovernmental Council Authority) was created so that if the issue of over-spending arises, the Mayor and City Council could refer to the "Authority," the fall guy. The same tricks are played nationally, such as the public paying for schools which don't exist (in Philadelphia, a Black Muslim school).

If architects, doctors, attorneys, etc. must take tests in order to continue in their professions, so should politicians take tests on the constitution of both state and federal laws, and on anything else that they vote on – zoning, immigration, and the history of every country we engage in war.

I guarantee that the halls will be empty, and that these purveyors of waste will have a hard time finding another job.

Last, but not least, one of the main changes in the Charter besides no caps on taxes and spending, would be to eliminate the Sheriffs. Sheriffs are beholden to no one except we the people. The Federal Government has no jurisdiction over the sheriff.

Sheriff Mack was elected by the people of Grand City, Arizona as the protector of the Constitution. It is the responsibility of the State Legislature to stop the federal encroachment upon the Sheriff who is the leading law enforcement officer – higher than the president, because he reports directly to us. He is the ultimate protector of the Constitution. So today we can look at a corrupt Congress (Conyers) trying to stop Sheriff Arpaio of Arizona from arresting illegals.

When the Brady Bill was signed into law in November 1993, it provided that the ATF (Alcohol-Tobacco-Firearms) would be in charge of implementing the Brady Bill, and that all sheriffs and police chiefs in the country had to comply. The goal of the Charter "planners" is to take away the power of the sheriff and place it in the court system. The sheriff should not be appointed for that reason. In 1974, Sheriff Charles E. Murray of Philadelphia said that he was under attack by the courts. The bureaucrats wanted all power to be shifted to Judge Jamison who tried to deputize thirty individuals. When Sheriff Murray said that he wanted to supervise them, the court said, "The hell with you. We'll do it through the courts." And they created a "peace officer."

The sheriff is the only one who could deputize a federal officer.

The Western States Sheriffs Association included eleven western states who voted to oppose the Brady Bill. The provisions of the Brady Bill were hidden by the government and the media.

When Civil rights are violated, there needs to be:

1. Civil disobedience
2. Class action lawsuit
3. Civil protest – for taking "feds" to court.

We need more people like Sheriffs Mack and Murray who opposed the Brady Bill. Guns were meant for the protection of the people against an oppressive government. Guns were not meant for criminals to kill innocent people. Sheriffs defend that right to hold and bear arms. Anti-gun people should read the constitution or get a grip.

The Framers knew what they were doing, and that's why these dufusses we've elected want the sheriff out.

In Home Rule, the Mayor might as well be called the Czar. He controls education, the City Controller (whose duties are taken over by the City Council President), HUD, utilities. There will be automatic pay raises. There are no checks and balances because the wolves are protecting the hen house, and it's only a matter of time….

We mustn't forget Sheriff Joe Arpaio from Maricopa Cty, Arizona, or Mayor Barletta from Hazelton who took their constitutional oaths seriously and arrested illegals encroaching upon the rights of taxpayers.

If churches are to survive, they must become the citadels of liberty, where truth and free speech abound. Students who hear stories of political corruption every day, every hour, are too sophisticated to pray for "our mayor" or "our governor," and now "our president and Congress." Priests and ministers have to get real with this younger generation, jaded by an educational system which 'Simonized' their value system, making them question God, authority, values, and life.

They are the graduates of public high schools and colleges wherein less and less is said about the past and more and more about internationalism, multiculturalism, environmentalism, racism, and Martin Luther King. Jefferson and others have taken a back seat. And, if they've missed the message with "Barney," they won't miss it at school. Of course, no opposing views are allowed. University professors who dare to present both sides are tossed out. Not-so-bright-students take tape recordings for Sean Hannity.

They're told about the environment and the Green Group raking in millions for Vice President Gore, not exactly a physics major. Students are programmed into accepting CAFÉ standards for carbon emissions while Al Gore travels in private jets., And, I'm certain that his children don't travel in tin-plate cars, which will cause thousands of road deaths, while watching for F-16s, Blackhawks, and bombers overhead. No emissions there! Ca ching!

Don't insult our youth with talk about social justice when there is no social justice here. Millions of our own teens get no help from parents or teachers. They have their own injustices to deal with – alcoholic parents, drugs on the streets, bullies. No minister is there to help. No dad.

Many of the young people today are grandchildren of the Haight Ashbury "love" children of the '60s whose claim to fame was sexual promiscuity, drug abuse, and the passing out of flowers…mindless individuals who fit the maxim "when you don't stand for something, you fall for anything."

Foundations such as Ford, Rockefeller, Carnegie and others were instrumental in changing the mindset of youth from family to self. And the "self" brings no rewards, only catastrophe. When you see Carnegie (C-SPAN2, 1/28/09) or the Counsel on Foreign Relations (CFR), American Enterprise Institute (AEI), and AIPAC, the Jewish Lobby written on the background draperies sponsoring speakers like George Friedman, author of *The Next Hundred Years*, be assured that these bastards are the 'conspirators' who have funded this profound change in America. If any of these money-hungry slobs cared about America, drugs would be replaced with jobs. Tunnels from Mexico would be bombed. But no, their money is spent on funding "think tanks" who come up with 'land mines' in foreign countries. Friedman, incidentally, is the man who sees the new America with drones in war after war. Completely psychotic! And we wonder where teens have gotten the violent ideas they unhappily store in their heads because parents don't care to question school or the useless politicians.

I can only restate the words of that brilliant woman, Nesta Webster, who untangled the web of the conspirators like the Jewish illuminati, the Bilderbergers (who now publicize the fact that they are meeting, knowing that the public has no clue) and the CFR. "Their revolution is a moral and spiritual revolution, an anarchy of ideas by which the standards set up throughout nineteen centuries shall be reversed, all honored traditions trampled underfoot, and above all, the Christian ideal finally obliterated." Who can see what has happened to this great country since World War II and not see the fulfillment of her words??

Our children are inundated with homosexual rights, pro-life rights and race, from the time they reach TV with "Barney." Homosexuals are not happy with civil marriage. No, they want religious weddings, plumbing aside, children's mental well-being aside. We have pro-lifers who are 'morally' against abortion and the death penalty, even in cases of multiple rape-murders of young boys (John Wayne Gacy), and will attend, with candles yet, his execution...but who see nothing wrong with setting up landmines leaving poor people limbless or our killing of 800,000 innocent Iraqis. No wonder many pro-lifers drink! No wonder America is hated. And, by the way, looney tunes Bill Ayres was at the Gacy execution with a candle!

Enter Bernadine Dohrn and her spineless-creep husband, Bill Ayres, claiming the '60s fame of the "flower children" who really had no loyalty to anyone or anybody. Oh, yes, and they latched onto the anti-Vietnam War protestors. Their job was not about war, but about changing our culture, as you will learn. Husband and wife were interviewed on C-SPAN2, 6/13/09. Bill Ayres, in his golden earrings, and Bernadine, with a flower in her hair, reminiscent of the looney '60s, spoke about their involvement in 'education'…or is it indoctrination? Bill teaches at – where else? – Chicago University. Bernadine is employed by the Children's Family Justice Center, after having served eleven months jail time for refusing to cooperate with the FBI. She has been 'teaching' this garbage for eleven years:

1. "Families can be 2 daddys, 2 mommys, 2 children or 2 daddys and 2 mommys with 2 children.
2. "We should have 'universal' health care.
3. "We need 'universal' service groups volunteering every 10 years at 18, 28, 38 and 48 years old.
4. "Every family has drug addiction.
5. "We should pay for family leave, day care, and health care.
6. "For those with 'green' jobs, we should provide bicycles. The military is important but not the only course."

When a gentleman from the audience stated, "I feel that 911 was an inside job," he probably was laboring under the delusion that these misfits were against war.

Bernadine:"I believe that 911 was carried out by those accused. Presidents Clinton and Bush might have overlooked information. I don't agree with you." (None Dare Call It Conspiracy!) Bernadine and Bill were implicated in the Fort Dix Dance nail-bombing gone awry. Nice people!

What a travesty that this trash is teaching at Justice Center at Northwestern, getting grants for this Simonizing job. These treasonous rots are going along with the One World Scheme which is progressing along lines of changing to a One World Currency – if we let them.

If Iranians can get three million protestors on the streets, why can't we? Peaceful protesting is our constitutional right. Obviously, Congress has to be tossed out. If they can't do what we want – out! President Obama just gave the IMF untold millions for God-knows-what damages.

It's a disgrace that our last three presidents – Clinton, Bush and Obama – have abused drugs. Spineless, weak-willed men are a threat to our freedoms. President Obama is rushing bills through Congress at an alarming speed. Sorry, but I don't feel that this is transparency. Couple this with what young people are exposed to with no challenge and we are in a situation which needs to be changed, particularly if ABC intends to barrel through a health care system encompassing twenty million illegals by allowing the President to speak <u>at</u> us. Doctors will be paid less, while President Obama earned three million dollars in '08. Which doctor will stay in medicine if he can't pay malpractice insurance or his student loans and mortgage? Something is wrong when Kennedy and the Clintons and the rest of the corrupt politicians are living in grandeur. And will Bill Clinton's recent appointment as Envoy to Haiti bring in more poverty refugees and a nice money addition to his foundation? And endless votes?

Irish Catholics speak for Israel: O'Reilly, Hannity, Hugh Hewitt. The latter asked for Iranians to weigh in on the recent protest in Iran (6/16/09). First of all, anyone who pronounces Iran (Ear-rahn) as eye-ran or eye-ranians is no Persian. That said, anyone who calls in with pro-regime change, which would benefit Israel, is allowed to speak. For those callers who remember the ten year war between Iraq and Iran, provoked by the United States and Israel during which war the United States was on Iraq's side – sorry! President Bush never learned to pronounce Iran. Disgrace! Obama, on the other hand, pronounced the country's name correctly.

Nobody in Iran who remembers the United States-Israel puppet, the Shah, could honestly say "We need the help of the West." Their dreaded Savak was trained by our CIA at Fort Benning, Georgia, just like all of the other puppets – Noriega, etc. Beware. Only a turncoat could ask for Western help. Now we see the dirty hands of Germany's Merkel and Great Britain getting into the fray. Iranians are bright people; they don't need any help from intelligence groups sneaking around in their country to cause dissention. When they see fit to throw out the Ayatollah, they will do it; however, the West and Israel must stop their embargoes and sneaky attempts at making Iranians lose their energy jobs; it's despicable. As far as I'm concerned, Medved, Hewitt and the other talk show hosts who do not allow truth to be told, should be tried for treason, as Great Britain has denounced Michael Savage – rightly so.

I, who have <u>never</u> questioned the holocaust, now wonder why there is no mention of the fact that Jews, Christians (Jehovah Witnesses who believed in End Times), gypsies, and homosexuals were also killed. Why can't we hear from a priest regarding the engineering aspects of the horrible sites? Why, after 64 years, only the Diary of Anne Frank is honored. Surely the misery of a 12-year-old child's diary-portrayal of her experience is noteworthy, but how about all of the Palestinian children who had no roof to protect them when their families were bulldozed like so much garbage? No tribute for them?

I'm not so naïve as to think that no Jews were involved in the carrying out of the holocaust. Jews with money will kill Jews with no money just as President Bush and Cheney didn't mind sending off Christians to die. Religion has nothing to do with it; it's about money. And they've all made a lot. Mr. Cheney still hobbles around calling for "war, war." He could substitute war with "money, money." Now his daughter has joined the act, defending daddy with hopes of a Senate seat and more hidden torture programs. Stay home! Get the hell off of our backs!

As for someone like James Von Brunn, who unfortunately shot and killed an innocent guard at the holocaust museum, I lay the murder at the foot of the Zionists who dared to put this museum in the center of D.C. Washington belongs to America, not Zionists whose loyalty is to their Israel. I'd like to know which congressmen okayed this project. And just once, just once, I'd like to hear what Von Brunn had to say rather than hear 'stories' about how anti-Semitism and white supremacy played a part in his life. Zionists love to include race and other religions rather than take the blame for millions who hate their tactics and treachery alone. This way more people hate the perpetrator without ever knowing why – as with the Lebanese Christians whom they own. (Philangists) Zionist Supremacy and Black Supremacy – untouchable?

Americans will never hear from Lee Harvey Oswald who killed President Kennedy, because he was murdered by an angry Jew – or was it set up? Americans will never hear from Timothy McVeigh who supposedly brought down the Oklahoma Building. His execution was fast and with no public contact. When he was interviewed by some TV host, McVeigh knew that one wrong word and he would get shot right there. We, who are supposed to control Washington, have let them control us. Time to get the CIA files unredacted so that we finally get at all truths. Specter must know who killed President Kennedy. Why can't we? Who the hell is Specter, a 46-year veteran of a political dream job. Give it up already! Stay home and count your money.

Let's change the Holocaust Museum to War Museum and expose all of the barbarians – Stalin, Hitler, Churchill, Kissinger, both Bushes, Pol Pot, Cheney, the Stern Gang and Sharon, Karl Marx – everybody. And let's include "germ warfare," which Israel is now working on, bulldozers, drones, carpet bombs, torture chambers, rendition, secret meetings…Blackwater!

Radical loonies like Bernadine and Bill Ayres have been polluting the minds of young people, both here and in places like Iran, for more than 30 years. This couple had no criticism of George Bush's 'No Child Left Behind,' which was exposed as a recruitment technique (war games) for those who won't have jobs. Instead, they talked about protecting "teachers' rights, not parental rights." Think! Aren't these two supposed to be anti-war?

Isn't it about time that the public can at least ask Von Brunn why he tried to make a citizen's arrest of Paul Volcker, head of the Federal Reserve under Reagan, in 1981? I'll bet that millions of people would like to make a 'citizens' arrest of Federal Reserve members. This secrecy for the few is what breeds hatred. I'd like to know whether or not James Von Brunn is a White Supremacist or merely a scapegoat for those hijackers of our country who like to combine hatreds – "they hate Christians and Jews" or "they hate Blacks and Jews" – when the truth is that "they" hate Jews, period!

Our Pentagon asked a test question calling protesting "a low form of terrorism." (Fox tickertape 6/17/09) If this is true, those in the Pentagon spewing this anti-American, anti-constitution hatred should be thrown out, and our liberal funds going to these creeps should be stopped.

Medved on Senator McCain, when a caller criticized the Senator 6/18/09: "McCain has served this country for 28 years." (I assume he's talking about Israel, right?) "He has been a fiscal conservative, and we would be better off if he were president. So get over it!"

If McCain were president, we would have followed Netanyahu's orders and already bombed Iran – costing us trillions of dollars in addition to the Bush wars with which McCain agreed. Fiscal conservative?? Although McCain, the consummate actor, was against torture, he was totally against the release of CIA tapes exposing it. His daughter, too, is making her rounds for a political job. Well, stay home! We need brains, not seat fillers.

The rest of us would like American jobs returned so that the victims of our educational system won't be homeless. If you want to do something, try reading the Constitution and then give some hope to the jobless.

McCain and his 'de-mentor,' Senator Lieberman, introduced a resolution 6/18/09 during this protest in Iran after the recent election. You remember the cool McCain with his "ba-ba-bomb Iran?" Well, now the guy feels sorry for the protestors and feels that President Obama should step in and help. All heart. All nut job! Hopefully, the President stays his course and does not interfere. I'm certain that Israel would love to send U.S. troops in and bring back puppet Reza Pahlavi. (Shah's son)

With all of the Nazi U.S. stations covering this 'violence,' no one is showing pictures of the results of our drones which just killed several Afghans this morning (6/20/09).

And was anyone jailed during the '60s protests in the United States when two Kent State students were killed? Were the U.S. Marshals who shot Randy Weaver's 14-year-old son in the back and Randy's wife, nursing a baby, in the head, jailed – while calling her name, knowing that she was dead…Vicky…Vicky…. Oh, and they killed the dog, too. That'll teach conspiracy thinkers to go off and criticize government! Our list of treachery goes on and on, while Congress allows schemes like Acorn to go on, just as they did in the '60s with Saul Alinsky types, shades of the Soviet Union and the Bolshevik Revolution.

Acorn is where extremely wealthy blacks are making their money, and like the Christians and Jews before them, they couldn't care less about who is killed. Heh, Heh…they just want reparations – for now – Heh, Heh.

No group is without blame. It's the middle and low class that will be used for World Service – if we let them. They're all preparing for our downfall.

In the meantime, when you hear a woman on Booknotes with a Moslem-sounding name, from Iran, who wrote a book "Reading Lolita in Tehran" – know that she's a phony – particularly when she defends the West…just like the 'young' groups of protestors with signs in English.

The only true spokesman I've heard today was a Columbia University student from Iran who mentioned McCain's 'ba-ba;'bomb Iran' comment; and said "the West should stay out of our business." Anyone in Congress who wants to step into this mess, should be exposed as a traitor, just as those very phony, very wealthy Iraqi women playing poor, who testified before Congress about Big Bad Saddam's turning off respirators for babies, killing them. Later, they were exposed, but the mission of getting America into war with Iraq was accomplished.

Americans should be concentrating on the multi-trillion dollar health care plan for 300 million people, including 20 million illegals and whoever else comes across our open borders. I'm certain that Rahm Emanuel and his doctor-brother Ezekiel have plans to bring us into national health care like that of Israel's…with six million people.

Wake up before it's too late! We shouldn't have people in government, from Marxist backgrounds, helping America solve its problems. If they were so happy in Israel or other socialist countries, by all means, go back. Leave America alone.

However, where are the young men and women who have lost their 401Ks and jobs and families? What does it take for the Simonized group to start looking for answers in our schools and government? When do they stop watching dumb shows like Jon and Kate? What future lies ahead if the hijackers continue to rule without objection.

Just look at what happens whenever a so-called young congressman replaces an elderly congressman…. Immediately, he sees the grandeur of his new job – exercise rooms, restaurants, franking privileges, free passage to places all over the world, aides, photo ops, opportunities for family jobs, graft…graft. Big money ops. He turns out as bad or worse – if that's possible – than his predecessor.

When do we say – okay, that's it! Either work for eight hours a day at a <u>newly</u> <u>set</u> salary, or you're out!

UNITED NATIONS

"The Charter of the United Nations has become the 'Supreme Law of the land and the judges in every State shall be bound thereby, anything in the Constitution or laws of any State to the contrary, not withstanding.' Article VI, para. 2. The position of this country in the family of nations forbids trafficking in innocuous generalities but demands that every State in the Union accept and act upon the Charter (of the United Nations) according to its unmistakable purpose and intent." (Committee to Restore the Constitution, June 1990, Committee Bulletin #340.)

Senator John Bricker tried to introduce the Bricker Amendment which would have protected us from treaties bringing about world government. The amendment failed one vote short of the two-thirds majority in the Senate. No one in the State Department would have been able to authorize representatives of foreign countries to have a voice in our domestic affairs.

Article VI, para. 2 of the U.S. Constitution is known as the Supremacy Clause:

"This Constitution, and the laws of the United States which shall be made in pursuance thereof; and all treaties made or which shall be made under the authority of the United States, shall be the Supreme Law of the Land. And the Judges in every State shall be bound thereby, anything in the Constitution or Laws of any state to the contrary notwithstanding."

The paragraph at the top of this page illustrates how the politicians who signed this treaty misinterpreted the actual clause which followed.

Ed Norton, a brilliant and patriotic constitutional attorney, pointed out that "the Supremacy Clause does not say that the federal government can go into areas outlawed by the States. (The Federalist). The State has the power to correct powers in their respective boundaries; States can extricate themselves by creating a statute which abrogates the compact. Just the threat of a State Statute forcing the enforcement of the Constitution would be enough to abandon federal regulation."

Hence, the State can overturn regionalism, abortion, anything we the people don't want. Unfortunately, there are no Ed Nortons in the legislature. I doubt that any Congressman or aides to Congressmen read the 20,000 pages of the General Agreement on Trade and Tariffs (GATT), or the 11,000 pages of the North Atlantic Free Trade Association (NAFTA), or they would know that NAFTA requires no borders between Mexico, Canada, and the U.S.

Ed Norton: "Lincoln pointed out that the Supreme Court is unduly criticized for doing things it really isn't doing. Judicial power is not legislative power; it is merely a right to apply, not to interpret. But if others make their powers broader, as in policy, (determines cases, not questions), <u>we have resigned our authority to the Court</u>. States can intervene. Ex., no authority for Supreme Court to have anything to say about abortion. <u>States, through their legislators, may use simple but plain facts which bind courts in the States and render decisions void</u>. Civil damages may be incurred." This is the way we can overturn treaties, etc.

In Pennsylvania our State legislators are thinking about the money they're going to make with casinos. It's time for a wake-up call!

The U.N. Charter places us at the mercy of a World Court and places all decisions, not in the hands of "we the people," as the U.S. Constitution states for our republic, but in the hands of a five-member appointed Security Council (Russia, China, France, Britain, United States). How this plan is "pursuant" to our laws is a question whose answer should have been demanded from the Congress in 1945 but citizens weren't given the chance.

Blunder after blunder. The Supremacy Clause is clear; that is why Churchill and Roosevelt had to act quickly at Malta to compile this one-world scheme which they called the Atlantic Charter. The people of the U.S. rejected the first attempt at World Government – the League of Nations.

On January 1, 1942, representatives from twenty-six countries met in Washington, D.C. and signed the U.N. Declaration. Giving away our sovereignty was a done deal. No vote, debate, discussion on this charter, or it would have been rejected again. Our raw materials were pledged to the world as were our fighting men and women.

It's always about peace. Or communism. Yet, Russia and China are two of the signatories to the Charter. The Vietnam War was supposed to be about communism. After 58,000 American lives were lost, former Secretary of Defense McNamara said that he knew "it was a war we couldn't win." Unconscionable.

Since the U.S. has to get permission for war, we could not have fought the Revolutionary War!

The Charter has created a group in Washington, D.C. who runs our country like a private business. They work for the world. No borders. No laws. No domestic policy. Just a group of men and women concerned about their next election.

Alger Hiss, convicted as a spy, was the main author of the United Nations Charter. The Charter was marketed to the American people as a vehicle to "world peace." The admission ticket to membership was having declared war against Germany and Japan.

The Great United Nations War was also known as the Korean Police Action of 1950-53, a "no-win war" which could not be won with the number two U.N. official in place being one Soviet communist after another. The secret deal that a communist would always hold this position with authority over all U.N. military, political and nuclear questions had been made by Secretary of State Edward Stettinius (Hiss was his adviser) and Molotov in London in 1945, and was revealed in the <u>Course of Peace</u>, written by the second U.N. Secretary General, Trygve Lie (pps. 45-46). General Douglas MacArthur, a brilliant leader, led this U.N. war and 54,246 soldiers died.

U.N. bureaucrats lead an extravagant lifestyle with immunity from crime and, many times, cash payments. Their tax free funds and benefits are paid for with money from U.S. taxpayers.

The conniving politicians from Third World countries use the U.N. as a way to bleed American taxpayers for money sent, not to poverty-stricken populations, but to the ruling clique of cutthroats who kill off the opposition.

The U.N. spawned a group of agencies – UNESCO (United Nations Educational Scientific and Cultural Organization) which contributed much of the curricula for one-world government to U.S. schools (Weekly Reader, etc.). Although President Reagan took us out of UNESCO temporarily, President Bush, Sr. rehabilitated the reputation with the Gulf War and his statements about the NWO.

President Clinton did get us into several foreign wars as a means of turning the U.N. into an international establishment that would field its own military forces. He talked about "peace-keeping" operations, but he deployed our troops to foreign lands where there was no peace to keep, and "peace-keepers" were used to fight wars. These peace-keeping operations cost us $3 billion per year. The U.S. should not be engaged in world police actions and civil strife. U.S. forces are subordinated to foreign commanders and foreign rules of engagement. President Clinton tried to use a Women's Conference in Cairo in order to give the U.N. separate power to tax American citizens. (Congress took up this issue again in 2006.)

For three years in the Balkans, the U.S. Army had been quietly pursuing the practice of requiring American soldiers to wear U.N. uniforms with the red, white and blue U.S. flag on the left arm, and the blue U.N. insignia on the right arm, with the blue helmet or blue beret.

Only one young man had the courage to dissent: U.S. Army Specialist E-4 Michael G. New, a medic with the Third Infantry Division who had an exceptionally exemplary military record throughout his 2 1/2 years of service, receiving several commendations. He said, "I took an oath to defend the Constitution of the U.S. of America against all enemies, foreign and domestic. My army enlistment oath is to the Constitution. I cannot find any reference to the U.N. in that oath." Under the U.S. Army's rules of engagement for the U.N. peacekeeping operation, our U.S. forces are specifically defined as "United Nations personnel." New requested a full and complete legal justification for the orders he received, but received no written response from the army.

President Clinton's document PDD25 was kept secret under lock and key, but the State Department "summary" dated May 1994 contained enough information to enable patriots like Phyllis Schlafly, an attorney and publisher, to challenge its constitutionality. He was facing court martial because of his patriotism. (Phyllis Schlafly Report. Vol. 29, No. 4, Nov. 1995) P. O. Box 618, Alton, ILL 62002.

Even though President Wilson and his most trusted adviser, Colonel House, could not get the League of Nations treaty for world government through at the end of WWI, the effort for a United Nations continued.

In 1912 Colonel House had written a novel entitled <u>Philip Dru: Administrator: A Story of Tomorrow</u>. We get an interesting view of what House and President Wilson's plans for America were. Of America, House wrote:

"America is the most undemocratic of democratic countries. Our constitution and our laws served us well for the first hundred years of our existence, but under the condition of the day, they are not only obsolete, but even grotesque.

"Nowhere in the world is wealth more defiant and monopoly more insistent than in this mighty republic . . . and it is here that the next great battle for human emancipation will be fought and won."

There can be no doubt that Colonel House had the complete confidence of international bankers. In fact, according to Professor Charles Seymour, who edited <u>The Intimate Papers of Colonel House</u>, it was said of Colonel House that he was the "unseen guardian angel" of the Federal Reserve Act. "The Schiffs, the Warburgs, the Kahns, the Rockefellers, and the Morgans had faith in House. So it took another war, WWII, to get the Charter through" (Skousen, <u>The Naked Capitalist</u>, p. 21.)

On June 26, 1945, President Truman signed the United Nations Charter. On December 14, 1946, the U.N. accepted a gift of $8.6 million from John D. Rockefeller, Jr., to buy the eighteen acres of land along the East River in New York City upon which the current building sits. The next year, the U.S. Congress approved a $65 million interest-free loan to finance the construction of the U.N. buildings.

"As banker James Warburg, the son of Council on Foreign Relations (CFR) founder Paul Warburg, confidently told the U.S. Senate on February 17, 1950, 'We shall have world government whether or not we like it. The only question is whether world government will be achieved by conquest or consent'" (Griffin, <u>Descent into Slavery</u>, p. 214).

And so, we are paying for our own demise through the U.N.

The Charter provided that the five major powers – the U.S., Russia, Great Britain, France and China – would be permanent members of the Security Council. Six other members would be elected by the Assembly for two-year terms.

The U.N. is replete with corruption. Recently, U.N. peacekeepers were accused of rape in the Congo. And Boutros Ghali's son was involved in an oil-for-food scandal. Was there an investigation? Of course not – so long as the members vote the way we wish them to vote, and that's for more and more aggressive acts against Moslem countries, oil countries.

In this book I have quoted Catherine P. Baldwin (<u>And Men Wept</u>). Well, she also testified before Congress on July 28, 1945. Her testimony is in the Congressional Record, July 9, 1945. This was a period in our time when women were courageous and stood for something. They were the backbone of this country; it was the women who single-handedly raised families – and successful ones – when their husbands were killed in foreign wars.

Today, financiers have so indoctrinated the schools that we have pitiful graduates who know little or nothing about the problems ahead of them.

Essentially, Mrs. Baldwin told the Senate that the U.N. Charter was unconstitutional and that rather than being an instrument for peace, this document was an instrument for war. She spoke about the infiltration of schools and churches (United Council of Churches). She predicted the Mideast war as WWIII. The Senate was reminded that "sharing raw materials" was not a new concept but one that Andrew Carnegie declared in his book <u>Triumphant Democracy</u>, 1893.

Mrs. Baldwin brought out the fact that the Charter guaranteed nothing, and that the framers never wanted U.S. sovereignty to be vested in the hands of five appointed men whom we did not know. It sabotaged our Constitution and no president or Congress had the right to do that. Also, the debts incurred by this charter were unconstitutional.

Rep. William Langer, also in the Congressional Record, brought out the point that eleven million fighting men and women were not in the U.S., but fighting a war and should have been present for this charter signing. He believed that millions of people from Poland to India, from Korea to Java, would be enslaved.

The Charter contains 19 chapters and 110 articles, which I'm sure few Congressmen read. Chapter VII was used as our excuse to send troops to Saudi Arabia.

Please get a copy of the Charter and you will be surprised that we still deal with this unconstitutional document. We should cut this expenditure off. (Dept. of Public Information, U.N., N.Y. 10017).

Mrs. Catherine Palfrey Baldwin was the descendant of Colonel William Palfrey, a soldier and Paymaster General with General George Washington. He was the first to have given his life for the new republic.

Incidentally, many of us asked for Beverly LaHaye's help. Beverly is the wife of Tim LaHaye, that solid proponent of the "end days" racket; the "don't get involved in politics" crowd, because Jesus is coming to solve everything. Beverly had a following of 800,000 women, and when we asked her to help us get out of the U.N., she stated, "We can't get involved." So much for her "values." But I'll bet that her bank account is solvent! And Tim still talks on, rascal that he is!

IS THE CONSPIRACY JEWISH?

I will first quote an article by Henry Makow, Ph.D., "Is the Conspiracy Jewish? – The Controversy of Zion." (Montgomery County, Observer, 9/25/00).

"I was once asked this question on an American patriot talk show. The assumption was that, as a Jew, I could answer it. After reading 'A Controversy of Zion,' by Douglas Reed, I can venture a reply.

I begin by explaining my perspective. Recently I borrowed a video on Judaism from the library. I wasn't sure what Jews believe. I suspect I'm pretty typical in this respect.

The video showed how Jews were persecuted in Egypt and how God punished the Egyptians. After a few minutes I turned it off. It seemed the religion of the Jewish people was the Jewish people. No wonder so many Jews look for religious meaning elsewhere.

My parents were Poles who survived the war as Catholics. After they immigrated to Canada, they just wanted to assimilate. They gave their children anglicized names. Dad flirted with the Unitarians. Mom said prayers on the Sabbath. Except for attending synagogue twice a year, that was it.

Religion is our connection to eternity. Growing up without it was growing up in a vacuum. At first I sought my 'identity' in terms of community.

I became a Canadian nationalist; then a Zionist. In 1972, at age 22, I tried to make 'aliya' (immigrate to Israel) but this experience made me realize I could not sacrifice my individual freedom for 'community.'

For example, I was picking oranges in a tree on a kibbutz (a collective farm settlement in Israel). My radio was tuned to BBC. Someone came by, changed the station, and walked off.

I left the kibbutz and went to Jerusalem, but the attitude was the same. Israel seemed to devour its citizens. It had many endearing qualities but I couldn't find the spirit of brotherhood in everyday life. It seemed more 'dog eat dog' than Canada. I returned home but considered myself a Zionist nevertheless.

Douglas Reed's book, 'The Controversy of Zion' (completed in 1956 but published in 1978) has helped me to understand my ambivalent reaction to both Jerusalem and Israel. During the 1930s, Reed was the 'London Times' correspondent in Berlin, Vienna and Budapest. He accompanied Anthony Eden to Moscow in 1935. When his warnings of Hitler's warlike intentions were spiked, he quit the newspaper in order to search for the hidden agenda.

The title of Reed's book refers to an age-old 'controversy' between those Jews who believe in a loving God and those whose image of God is spiteful and tyrannical.

According to Reed, the 'House of Joseph' believed that the Divine Principle is love and universal brotherhood. These Jews were inclined to identify with their Gentile neighbors and devote their energies to the common betterment of humanity.

On the other hand, the 'Levites' championed a vision of a capricious vengeful God ('Moloch') that demanded his followers segregate themselves ('chosen people') and obey an arbitrary law.

Obeying the Lord and achieving hegemony over the Gentiles were synonymous. If the Levite didn't obey, they would be persecuted. If they did, they would destroy the Gentiles and rule the earth. Persecution, revenge, and destruction was an integral part of their identity.

Reed cites Deuteronomy as an example: 'This day will I begin to put the dread of thee and the fear of thee upon the nations. . . . And when the Lord thy God shall deliver them before thee, thou shalt smite them, and utterly destroy them; thou shalt make no covenant with them nor show mercy unto them; neither shall thou make marriages with them. . . . For the Lord thy God hath chosen thee to be a peculiar people unto himself above all people that are upon the face of the earth.' According to Reed: 'Thus, the iterant priests (turned) one small, captive people away from the rising idea of a God of all men, to reinstate a blood-thirsty tribal deity and racial law, and to send the followers of this creed on their way through the centuries with a destructive mission . . . . The end was to be the triumphant consummation in Jerusalem when world dominion was to be established in the ruins of the heathen and their kingdom' (3-4).

The Old Testament contains both the hateful and loving image of God, which is very confusing. Jesus championed the loving image and denounced the priests for making arbitrary laws in the name of a tyrannical God.

Flash forward 2500 years. The Jews of the House of Joseph were content to assimilate. The Levites, centered in Russia, were not. Around 1850, Reed believes the Levites took over the 'Illuminati Conspiracy' which eventually controlled Communism (and possibly Zionism).

Winston Churchill described this conspiracy in 'A Struggle for the Soul of the Jewish People' (1920). He distinguished between 'national' (House of Joseph) and 'international' (Levite) Jews: 'This movement among the (international) Jews is not new. From the days of (illuminati founder) Spartacus-Weishaupt to those of Karl Marx, and down to Trotsky (Russia), Bela Kun (Hungary), Rosa Luxembourg (Germany) and Emma Goldman (United States), this world-wide conspiracy for the overthrow of civilization and for the reconstitution of society on the basis of arrested development, of envious malevolence, and impossible equality has been growing steadily' (http://www.corax.org/revisionism/documents/200208churchill.html).

Reed describes how Zionism and the New World Order took control of England during WW I. World Zionist leader Chaim Weizmann lobbied Prime Minister Herbert Asquith and Army Chief Sir William Robertson to divert soldiers from the Western Front to conquer Palestine. When the British leaders demurred, Weizmann used money and control of the press to install Lloyd George and Sir Henry Wilson in their place.

More than a million men were then diverted to the Middle East. Palestine was conquered and promised to the Zionists in a letter to Lord Rothschild in November 1917 (the Balfour Declaration). During the same week, the Bolsheviks took power in Moscow. American soldiers replaced the British troops on the Western Front. The conspiracy was firing on all cylinders.

The other people in Lloyd George's pro-Zionist government – Lord Milner, Philip Kerr (later Lord Lothian), Robert Cecil – were all members of the 'Round Table,' Cecil Rhode's secret society dedicated to world government.

Listen to what Weizmann says (in his autobiography Trial and Error), about Robert Cecil: 'To him the re-establishment of a Jewish Homeland in Palestine and the organization of the world in a great federation were complementary features of the next step in the management of human affairs' (Reed, p. 249).

How do the Zionists make cause with British aristocrats?

The aristocrats were shareholders in the Bank of England with the Rothschilds. Central bankers wanted the New World Order to protect this monopoly that allows them to charge billions in interest for money they created out of thin air.

The bankers and their corporate allies are consolidating a global system of privilege and oppression. They hoodwinked atheistic Jews, the product of the barren primitive Levite tradition, with promises of an egalitarian 'brave new world' or 'national home.' Reed provides evidence from diaries and biographies that international bankers and their allies have used communists and Zionists (both Jews and Gentiles) to control British, American and world politics since WW I.

Flash forward to the projected attack on Iraq.

Given Douglas Reed's perspective, Israel likely has a secret role in the bankers' bizarre NWO. It will be the seat of world government and religion and will help to 'convert' the Moslems to 'modern' ways.

Americans and Israelis, indeed the whole world, are hostage to fanatics who worship Moloch and are creating an Orwellian tyranny ruled by a 'chosen' few.

Is it Jewish? Many misguided or opportunistic Jews are part of it. So are many Gentiles. The owners of the central banks and allied corporations are both Jewish and Gentile.

I agree with the preceding articles, but I would like to add Professor Carroll Quigley's comments. I mentioned the Professor in "Conspiracy" as one of President Clinton's favorite teachers at Georgetown.

"In describing the characteristics of the Rothschilds and other major international bankers, they (Zionists) remained different from ordinary bankers in several ways: they were cosmopolitan and international; they were close to governments and were particularly concerned with government debts, including foreign government debts; these bankers came to be called international bankers (Prof. Quigley, p. 52 – 'Tragedy and Hope').

"The Jewish members of this conspiracy have used an organization called the Anti-Defamation League as an instrument to try to convince everyone that any mention of the Rothschilds or their allies is an attack on the Jews. In this way they have stifled almost all honest scholarship on international banking and made the subject taboo within universities.

"Any individual or book exploring this subject is immediately attacked by hundreds of ADL committees all over the country. The ADL has never let truth or logic interfere with its highly professional smear jobs. When no evidence is apparent, the ADL which staunchly opposed so-called 'McCarthyism,' accuses people of being 'latent anti-Semites.' – Can you imagine how they would yowl and scream if someone accused them of being 'latent communists'? (Since 1971 the ADL has moderated its position dramatically and even taken hard anti-communist positions now.) ('Call It Conspiracy, Larry Abraham, p. 47)."

In my opinion, when the Simon Wiesenthal Center, the main branch of the Israeli Lobby on the West Coast, can monitor radio, television and internet – and get away with it because Simon was a holocaust survivor, it constitutes a breach of our First Amendment rights, particularly when the Anti-Defamation League places your name on a "list." (Is this another Schindler's List, or what?) This is America, not Nazi Germany. Just who are these meisters judging what can and cannot be said. And leave it to the pro- Israel ADL callers to flood the station with calls until the host feels threatened with loss of his job and proceeds to block any callers mentioning Israel.

Whenever Europe denounces Israel's behavior in the Middle East, we in America get a double dose of holocaust scenes and reminders. Or the Ku Klux Klan (infiltrated by government moles as they were during the time of Martin Luther King) suddenly swings into action on the Geraldo Show. Insulting.

I resent the fact that the "never again" group forces young school children to view holocaust videos without mentioning the fact that Israeli bulldozers mowed down Palestinian refugees in Jenin and allowed no cameras in until the land was flattened, people and all.

Almost every appointee we send to the Mideast is a person of Jewish descent – at least the "important" ones. Clinton had Jamie Rubin, Wm. Cohen, Madeleine Albright, Sandy Burger (his security advisor who stole 9/11 documents from the archives), and others. President Bush was surrounded by Jewish advisors, Cabinet members, and emissaries. Seems like a flagrant display of an "Orwellian tyranny ruled by a chosen few."

Pat Buchanan called Congress "occupied territory." President Truman, who gave away the store for Israel had uncomplimentary things to say about those whom he helped, in his diary: "Selfish." "Neither Hitler nor Stalin has anything on them."

Lt. General Ricardo Sanchez: (paraphrasing), "Congress, the press, and the State Department must bear some responsibility for this war" (CNN, 10/14/07).

Fox News host, Neil Cavuto, treats Jewish guests with reverence and awe; Moslems are treated with filibustering and disgust. As an Italian, the fact that only Italians from Stupidsville are chosen to represent the token Christians, I'm offended. Groveling Christians abound on cable and the major networks, acting as water-carriers for the super rich.

While our culture deteriorates, America is carrying on a war costing us three trillion dollars. We are allowing foreign entities to run our country. Great Britain and Israel are letting America do their fighting. British Petro could do nothing without our help, even though the Framers warned about foreign alliances. Don't forget: General Schwarzkopf received a Medal of Honor for his work in Father Bush's Gulf War on behalf of the Queen of England. It's totally unconstitutional for the U.S. military to receive this foreign honor.

Meantime, we're flooded with reality shows depicting women who act as though they have nothing to lose, throwing themselves at characters like Flava Flav. No wonder no-account men treat them like "hos." These women who should be holding good jobs, underestimate themselves when, for money, they look as though they would chew the star's toenails. What a pity that women have sunk so low, tattoos and all.

I feel that Zionists and those who go along with them, meddle in affairs which should be none of their business. For instance, the Catholic Church's document, Vatican II, which was drawn up during the years 1962-1965 by Pope John XXIII, and upon his death by Paul VI, marked the death knell for traditional Catholics.

Pope John XXIII, a good friend of Nikita Khrushchev's, decided to inflict "liberation" theology on the Catholic Church.

"From that point on, it didn't matter what religion you belonged to, all religions were included. Even non-religious groups were included. The bulwark against communism stopped. Secularism, ecumenism reigned. The de-Catholicization of the Roman Catholic hierarchy, clergy and faithful began.

"The important effect of these globalist dreamers is the weight they add to the forces already intent upon disposing the world toward the idea of an earthly utopia and away from the knowledge of the transcendent truth of a loving God who, as John Paul is convinced, had a very different design in store than any they are able to imagine" ("The Keys of This Blood," Malachi Martin).

In short, the Catholicism I grew up with, wherein Christ was crucified, died, and buried, and on the third day arose from the dead – was over. "Now, Pope Paul VI embraced the Jewish lobbyists for recognition of Israel on one hand, and avoiding any close identification with the Arab Mideast" (ibid., p. 126). Imagine a Pope taking it upon himself to selectively hate a group on the basis of pressure from lobbyists. No wonder many churches are empty. No wonder the church has become a sanctuary for illegal immigrants.

The Church I knew hated no religious group – propaganda to the contrary. It was the biggest threat to decadence. Today, the Catholic Church has become the apologist for uncommitted wrongs, the crusader for unwed mothers, and drug addicts. It's the laughing stock of those who have taken away our heritage, our glorious past.

What has this change wrought? The crutch of drugs and alcohol. Broken families. Decline in church attendance. Crisis of pedophilia. Suffering of good priests. I hope that there's a hell for dividers and agitators.

Lynn Yeakel, once a candidate for public office, lost her bid because of the fact that her Presbyterian minister commented, during the service, that "we should use an even hand in the Mideast." Apparently, someone in the audience recorded these words, and used them to defeat the candidate. Hitlerism? You bet.

Even billionaire Ross Perot, a presidential candidate, wasn't allowed to buy thirty minutes airtime.

Senator Schumer of New York and the now deceased Representative. Tom Lantos (California) were the ones who pushed for hate crimes legislation so that, in America, the land of the used-to-be-free and the brave, we can elevate calling someone a name to the height of a felony as they do in Bavaria. This is politically correct fascism. Intimidation.

Perhaps the answer for the intimidation lies in the "Gotha Programme," wherein Karl Marx says: "The man who possesses no other property than his labor power must, in all conditions of society and culture, be the slave of other men who have made themselves the owners of the material condition of labour. He can only work with their permission and, hence, only live with their permission."

Quoting from the "New Class" by Milovan Djllas, a defected communist theoretician, published by Frederick A. Praeger, 1975: "The communist revolution was carried out in Russia in the name of a purely scientific view of the world, for the purpose of creating a classless society (p. 32). It resulted in the most complete authority of any new class, everything else is a sham and illusion" (p. 36).

"He who grabs power, grabs privileges and indirectly grabs property. Consequently, <u>in communism, power or politics as a profession is the ideal of those who have the desire or the prospect of living as parasites at the expense of others</u>" (p. 46; emphasis added).

"The so-called socialist ownership is a disguise for the real ownership by the political bureaucracy (p. 47)."

"By various methods, such as nationalization, compulsory cooperation, high taxes, and price inequalities, private ownership was destroyed and transformed into collective ownership" (p. 57). We're experiencing this in America today with politicians leasing our bridges to foreign and domestic entities, and condemning private property for "Natural Habitats" or for buildings bringing in more taxes.

"A slave laborer, no matter how little you feed him, costs more than he can produce when you count the administrative apparatus needed to assess his coercion" (ibid., p. 111). Dysfunctional lunatics who think Marxist thoughts fashion themselves as rulers, elite. Absolute madmen.

Our government should be of the people, for the people, and by the people; instead, it has become a cesspool of corruption run by bureaucrats who are systematically destroying the middle class by lowering education standards and moral standards. We are hit with higher property taxes, higher prices for gasoline and utilities, outsourcing of jobs, runaway crime, and unreachable representatives. With twenty million illegals who need health care – and according to the last democratic debate, they will get it – housing, food stamps and education, it's good-bye America and hello Third World.

The goal is no cars, only public transportation, no guns and consolidated police and fire stations – an America run by World Police and a World Court. President Kennedy signed onto this plan when he signed the Disarmament Treaty.

We had former Prime Minister Olmert of Israel and his side-kick, Netanyahu, determining which country in the Mideast the U.S. should bomb next. We have American troops all over the world protecting Wendy's. These troops should be protecting our borders from convicted felons and drug and arms dealers.

We don't need WW II Memorials and propaganda films to show the bravery of the past. We all know how badly veterans are treated once their job for the corporations is through. The films are there merely to get the young in a jingoistic mood so that they join up to defend "America." Besides, we're losing jobs here.

We don't need propaganda about Madrassa schools in the Mideast teaching children to hate Americans and Jews. We have our own hate mills on talk radio 24-7: "dirtbags," "vermin," "they hate us," "they love to die." Besides, don't the Iraqi youth live with the daily air raids and killing of innocent civilians? To them, we're worse than Saddam because at least they had electricity, running water and air conditioning. Today, having doors kicked in is a daily event. The middle class has left, and those who remain live in terror and chaos. Hundreds of thousands died. Heil Democracy!

Those of us in America who assume that poverty equates with ignorance, make a wrongful assumption. I've met farmers in remote areas of Iran who had no television sets, but who knew more about world affairs than our college graduates today. And they spoke some English.

If what Michael Weinstein, author of "With God on Our Side," said is correct, that our "air force is being told that if they don't accept evangelism, Jesus won't bless their mission," and that "West Pointers now have to read a religious book," we should be concerned. "How much is the ideology of Armageddon in the military?" (C-Span 2, 8/10/07)

Are we creating a generation of youth who feel that killing fields will hasten the appearance of Christ on earth? Are we forgetting that the Christ who has been systematically ridiculed in films and cartoons said, "My kingdom is not of this world"?

Was Pat Tillman becoming aware of the injustice of this war? Has the military turned into the dreaded "industrial complex" President Eisenhower warned us about?

The only Christ we have in our future on earth is the anti-Christ as revealed in the Revelation of St. John the Divine. Everything else is a "sham and illusion."

I certainly regret the years I've spent thinking that the billions of dollars for defense would make us safer. It only played into the hands of the corporate thieves, the war profiteers who spend their time in foreign countries stirring up trouble, using their people as slaves, and backing up their mischief with U.S. troops.

Congressman Ron Paul, the candidate for president, whom the Nazi media won't allow us to hear, said "We've been bombing Iraq for ten years. . . . Right now we're building an embassy in Iraq that's bigger than the Vatican. We're building 14 permanent bases. What would we say here if China was doing this in our country, or in the Gulf of Mexico?" (Liberty, 8/07).

Laura Ingraham, the other flag waver, patriot, and advocate of free speech – for herself and those who agree with her – was commenting on a statement by Senator Kerry who called Iraq "genocide." Her guest, author Ralph, was plugging his book and said that the Senator was "comic relief." "The holocaust was genocide, the calculated extermination of a particular group. 'Ethnic cleansing' is what was done after WW II. Not that it's nice, but if we would leave Iraq, Iran would control the oil." (paraphrased, 7/19/7). So remember, ethnic cleansing is a much nicer way to go!

So is the conspiracy Jewish? While I agree with Douglas Reed's perspective that many misguided or opportunistic Jews are part of the Zionist conspiracy, I also agree with Dr. Quigley's assessment that unlike the wealthy Christians in this unholy alliance, the Zionist Jews remain close to governments on an international scale. In my opinion, he who controls what we see and hear controls the country.

I believe that the sinister "divide and conquer" technique is theirs. They've used it in Lebanon with the Phalangist Christians. They've played both sides of war and they've encouraged Black Americans and Cuban Americans, many of whom are Zionists, to use the same techniques. We have pro-Israel candidates like Vice President Biden calling for a division of Iraq into three parts – Kurds, Sunni, Shiites. Biden knows zip about Iraq. The division will never work, but who cares? The more Moslems we can kill off, the better. Unconscionable!

Somehow, the likes of a George W. Bush taking part in the destruction of America baffles me. He enjoyed a magical life of wealth and privilege, was a "cheerleader" in college and later led a carefree, alcoholic life. Apparently, he found Jesus, and stopped drinking. I think that he found the anti-Christ and decided to let a flood of illegal immigrants in so that the face of America would be changed forever. Remember, the America in which his family prospered with war games, is now up for sale or lease to any foreign bidder, including Red China. His trip to Australia for the Asia-Pacific Summit was not the final nail in the U.S. coffin. More jobs lost to the "free traitors." Next, Colombia!

Imagine. When Attorney General Gonzales resigned, former President George W. was considering placing Michael Chertoff, the head of Homeland Security, in his place. Chertoff was not the brightest bulb on the tree, and he did nothing in Katrina for two years. According to a former member of the Ethics Committee at the Department of Justice, Michael Chertoff worked there during the case of John Walker Lindt, the young American who was caught fighting with the Taliban in Afghanistan. Mr. Chertoff was advised not to question him without an attorney present. The advice was ignored and subsequently, the employee who spoke up was fired. Chertoff was a national disgrace.

Ron Paul was right when he said that, if elected president, he would do away with the IRS, CIA, Department of Education, and Homeland Security. It's a good start. Definitely the State Department and the Federal Reserve.

Even the old-time Mafia wasn't as treacherous as this group of Christian and Jewish thugs in Washington, D.C. Before drugs came on the scene in the 1960s, thanks to the Vietnam War and its aftermath, the Mafia had a code of honor which entailed a great respect for America, in spite of their personally messed up lives. It's amazing how the FBI can always locate an 82-year-old Mafia member who isn't paying taxes, but can't seem to finger that drug czar taking in carloads of heroin to destroy America's youth. And they just can't seem to zero in on the MS-13 gangs from Ecuador and Colombia, 10,000 strong, terrorizing American citizens. One of these gang members said, on national television, that in order to become a gang member, one had to murder someone. Why wasn't he picked up?

Unfortunately, we also have a lot of Black leaders using the same tactics of intimidation on a living population which had nothing to do with slavery. They, too, have their aggressive "community" groups and powerful people at the top, granting all kinds of money to their buddies. Non-profits abound!

Productive and successful Blacks who plow along like everyone else are rarely seen or heard. The poverty-industry types like Jesse Jackson and Rev. Sharpton have made a very lucrative living on "divide and conquer" and are preferred guests. We're bombarded with demands: "We want better housing (preferably mixed with expensive housing), more Head Start programs, day care centers, transportation, gun control, health care, more policemen in housing projects and schools, aid to Africa, more breakfast, lunch and dinner programs," and, and, it never stops. Those who work and are hardly able to keep afloat, have to support promiscuous women who feel no responsibility for their fatherless children. Drug-addicted, tattooed parents have created child after child, victims of the projects and Washington bureaucrats who reward them for their promiscuity and irresponsibility and votes.

Ward Connerly, a black attorney who is both compassionate and articulate, said, ". . . mindless blather about affirmative action and diversity . . . state sponsored discrimination . . . Civil rights belong to everyone, not just black people. The Constitution is color-blind."

Our fourteen bases in Iraq will serve to accommodate our future transgressions into the oil-rich countries of Nigeria, the Sudan, and Chad, now that China competes with us for oil because of her thriving industrial needs, thanks to our Wal-Mart, Mattel, clothing, food, medicine – everything made in China. Although Venezuela, Canada and Mexico provided us with oil, President George W. made another enemy – Venezuela.

A Catholic priest in Nigeria said, "It's Americans they see, and Americans they hate." Countries hate us because we won't allow them to nationalize their own oil, as Chavez of Venezuela is doing. Notice that the powers to be, counting on your ignorance, label every country who claims his own oil "communist" so that uneducated Americans who don't ask questions, rally around the U.S. flag which these corporate thugs have desecrated. While We the People paid over $4.00 a gallon for gas, the wives of the greedy corporate thugs were able to buy $6000 shower curtains.

Chevron is already in Nigeria, while we bomb, rebuild . . . bomb, rebuild, leaving children with eye damage and parentless in Iraq and other places.

At the moment, Congress is debating whether or not to sell Saudi Arabia $20 million in weapons and to grant an increase in aid to Israel over the next five years from $20 billion to $30 billion – money we borrow from China; hence we have nothing for social security and infrastructure. Trust me, this bill will sail through Congress as favors to benefactors, and the hell with America. Maybe that's why Obama won't wear an American flag. He knows that thieves are in control of our body politic.

The Taliban didn't want drugs in Afghanistan, but with U.S. occupation, poppy fields flourish. The U.S. counts on drug addiction to get its way.

Meantime, we talk about Middle Eastern treatment of women. I can tell you from personal experience, that those women under Chodors are no dummies. It is they who control the roost, and don't let anyone fool you. Orthodox Jewish women have their prohibitions as well. They walk behind their men who wear tall black hats and beards to the ground. But, shhhh. You mustn't know that. And of course, don't mention the fact that countless American women are murdered or have to seek shelters because of abusive husbands. Don't think about it. Just have another beer while our country goes to the hijackers – the super-rich hijackers of our freedoms.

The Politics of Change chapter said it all: We need strife and more strife to keep the politicians at their jobs, permanently. They want order. They want conditions to get so bad that we need Ollie North's "Martial Law." (FEMA – Federal Emergency Management Agency). Ollie – that "great American;" FEMA – that trustful agency with $85 million meant for Katrina, missing. President Reagan and North are the ones who authored FEMA with the National Security Council. Imagine North and Reagan wanting to inflict martial law on us, while our borders are open to all. No, it's an act wherein our Constitution would be terminated, and these old rots would be in power, with curfews, over the rest of us.

We're not Grenada or Colombia; Americans had the best lives of anyone in the world, until we forfeited our rights to Congress. Americans wouldn't stand for the treachery we put the Iraqis through – no medical care, no air conditioning, no safety or jobs, no electricity or running water, constant shelling, death of loved ones all over, house searches, the military rolling down our streets, limited schools, food trucks for those who could pay, and no protesters allowed.

We'll see Mexican trucks coming down our streets carrying more contaminated tomatoes, peppers and salsa, and no one will be able to say a word, because the very subsidized Department of Transportation gave Mexico its blessing. Tolls would be run by foreign entities, as they are now, but only the super-rich could use them. We said nothing when the Department of Transportation used its subsidized funds for art collections like "Pis Christ" and for political campaigns, so we shouldn't complain that we didn't insist on tolls being used for the 70,000 bridges found deficient by the Department of Transportation's army corps of engineers.

We allowed the Feds to join states so that they could take over states' rights – Delmarva, Pennjerdel. Remember the federal government was a creation of the state, not the other way around. "Join or Die" was the Regionalist theme of the '70s.

Senator Harry Reid's daughter and three other family members have lobbyist jobs. It's time for term limits. Our State Senator Vincent Fumo was given $17 million for his non-profit fund by PECO (electric company) and we wonder why our utility bills are high.

Casino owners are already bidding on Katrina property but this time the levees will be constructed properly, because we taxpayers will enter a "partnership." Remember too, that we're still supporting those Katrina victims who lost everything. Of course, Cheney's Halliburton received a no-bid contract to reconstruct Katrina – whenever!

The goal at the moment is to use bridge disasters as a means of placing interstate highways into the hands of multi-national corporations and Wall Street.

Samuel Schulman wrote an excellent article on this in Mother Jones (8/07). "Spain and Australia already leased a bridge in Indiana for $11 billion." Same thing happened in Chicago. Indiana could have refinanced the road and still have control of it. The road could have generated $11 billion for a number of years. "We will be paying foreign investors for the privilege of using our own highways. Congress is being paid by Wall Street." (paraphrased)

Politicians have already done major damage to us with electricity. Next it will be water. Both Presidents Clinton and George W. have dug up antiquated laws in order to impose land grabs and take away property rights. (Mother Jones, 8/07).

As though damage to us hasn't been bad enough, we have to deal every day with families who have lost their way because of godless people in our government, taking away the Ten Commandments from buildings, and trashing God on our sordid TV shows.

Stephen Mansfield who wrote "Ten Tortured Words" (Congress should make no law respecting an establishment of religion) brought out the fact that somehow, along the way, those words have been misinterpreted. They say nothing about separation of Church and State. Article I of the Constitution also gave us freedom of speech, the press, and the right to assemble. Too often the freedom to assemble is threatened by strong-armed men with tear gas and rubber bullets. Shades of Red China.

Mr. Mansfield spoke about an interview with Alan Dershowitz, author of "What Israel Means to Me." Mr. Dershowitz remarked that he didn't care what a bunch of men in the 1770s said (public Radio, 8/07). Too bad, because there are no men living today who could bring us a document, the Constitution, the envy of all.

Those who down the "Constitution" always bring up two reasons: women's right to vote, and slavery; yet it was this document which gave them liberty. America's past was rife with civil wrongs – wrongs which had nothing to do with those of us living today. We can only right the wrongs we see today, and I see no blacks or others who were wronged, speaking up about the wrongs today – drugs, bombing, cruelty to animals, Iraq. So it makes me wonder who deserves sympathy. Even many slave owners tried to compensate for their misdeeds by educating the slaves and leaving them property.

We all know celebrities and others who make money from foreign imports using slave labor called "work" – at Wall Street wages -- $2 a day. Do we do anything about it? No, we just buy the products and enjoy.

Although Mr. Dershowitz doesn't care about a bunch of men in the 1770s, I'll bet that he's willing to go back even further than that when the "chosen people" topic arises.

The cruelest injustice today – and there are many – is the rescinding of our right to assemble and to speak and exchange ideas. No group should be allowed to monopolize the ownership of speech by controlling the print media, television, radio, etc. No group should be allowed to monopolize the ownership of jobs – film industry, music industry, directors of hospitals, publishing, banking, college board committees, SATS, government officials, sports, defense appointees, media moguls, legal defense fund, ACLU, real estate, political science professors, education.

The U. of P. actually offered a course in "humanities" at the Annenberg Center, and disclosed the fact that classes taught in grade schools or junior high regarding Israeli-Arab issues were monitored, and this was years ago.

Today we have watch-dogs like David Horowitz monitoring college professors who dare to speak the truth about foreign policy, so that he could have them terminated. He already defamed a professor in Virginia who happened to come from the Mideast, and he did the same thing to a professor in Colorado who happened to be right on his 9/11 subject covering the Port Authority disaster. But with all of the pro-Israel group-ies around, both professors didn't stand a chance. America doesn't stand a chance under this kind of hammer-and-sickle.

David Horowitz once said, on the Paul Smith show, that "my parents were communists. I was a Marxist. We incinerated 100,000 Germans in Dresden just to break the spirit of the Germans. Abu Graib is nothing." Imagine anyone talking like this about Zionists, but this madman gets away with it because of the fact that he has backers in Congress and in high places as well as low places like the ADL and other groups living on intimidation. People are afraid to speak out because these provocateurs stop at nothing for money and power.

A group of pro-Israel protesters removed a principal from a Madrassa religious school in New York City and replaced her with a Jewish woman who didn't speak Arabic. As we all know from hearing about this Islamic school, children are supposed to be learning to hate America and Israel. But of course, nut-jobs preaching hate on our stations are exempt because of the imperialists who own the media. We're inundated with affective (feelings) education. Children don't know what to believe after holocaust indoctrination.

Just skim through the books for young teens in any major bookstore, and you'll find trashy offerings, published and authored overnight. Every other word is "my boyfriend." Romance novels for children 12 and up.

For the younger children, it's death education, divorce, two mommies, where do I come from (with graphic pictures), and just about any problem these so-called authors can think of to depress and confuse. The sad part is that children's questions can be answered in a few words.

Ayatollah Khomeini tried to stop these gutter books in Iran but we got there first. Innocence destroyed! Iran now has our problems with prosti-tution, etc.

America has to concentrate on its own problems, and not be propagan-dized into believing that criticism of injustices makes one anti-American. It's just the opposite. Again, read the Declaration of Independence. Moham-med said, "Without justice there can be no peace!" This is why the haters loathe the "ragheads." And they want us to hate them, too.

We have a right to know why there has been no investigation of 9/11, even though many families of the victims asked for one. We're allowed to hear only the non-inquisitive….the "yes men."

Where was NORAD – those jets at-the-ready to protect the White House? Were the suicide bombers really all Saudis? If so, wasn't President Bush, Sr. involved in the Carlyle investment group with a bunch of rich Saudis, including the Bin Laden family? Was Bin Laden part of the plan to get us involved in war for oil and land? Is this why we are unable to find Bin Laden? Is this tragedy reminiscent of the World War II Japanese kamikaze pilots who were told that their families would be taken care of if they would act as suicide bombers against American pilots? Is it true that some employees at the Trade Center were given "heads up" not to attend work that morning? Who has profited from this bombing tragedy? Isn't it the arms dealers, bankers selling our debt to China, and other war profiteers – like Cheney's Halliburton and the Carlyle Group whose investments are in arms? Why did Vice President Cheney make a secret visit to Iraq to discuss oil sharing? Why was Congressman Curt Weldon from Pennsylvania voted out of office after starting a 9/11 investigation entitled "Able Danger"? Congressman John Conyers also tried to investigate and was assigned a room in the basement of the Capitol. Are we to assume the role of the monkey who sees no evil, speaks no evil, and hears no evil as we lose our liberties?

These corporate meisters have given us their chosen standard bearers – Hillary, Obama, and McCain. All have baggage, and we should not trust people with baggage – it leads to treason!

When Colonel McCormick owned the Chicago Tribune many years ago, he exposed regionalism, the CFR, Rhodes Scholars – everything. When he died, so did honest reporting. Today we have reporters who are guests at the homes of those about whom they should be reporting. It's so friendly! So low-down and treasonous – "aiding and abetting the enemy." The New York Times and other newspapers have lost readership because of the fact that the "elite" really feels that we're a lot dumber than we are.

So far, we have had only "talk" about 9/11. When President George W. was told that the victims' families wanted an investigation, he chose Henry Kissinger whose record of war crimes in the Hague speaks for itself. Instead, we got the 9/11 Commission, a group of "good ole" boys and girl – masters at saying nothing.

We pay $30 billion for Homeland Security in spite of the Katrina fiasco. Since we started meddling in the Mideast, oil has gone from $25 a barrel to an ever-climbing $165 a barrel. Both Presidents Clinton and

Bush wanted us to believe that the CIA knew nothing about 9/11. So why are we paying these rascals $30 billion a year? And why did Sandy Berger, a Clinton security advisor, escape indictment for stealing 9/11 documents from the archives? Could you or I do such a thing?

Professors like Norm Finkelstein who spoke out against what is happening in this country, in spite of the fact that his father was a holocaust survivor, have had their contracts canceled, thanks to bullies like Alan Dershowitz who pressures universities. These bullies monitor everyone except themselves.

On the other extreme, we had a holocaust survivor from California, recently deceased (2/08), Tom Lantos, who couldn't seem to punish America enough with his trouble-provoking resolutions – the latest one, 10/14/07, holding Turkey responsible for the "1915" genocide of Armenians. This resolution almost caused us another enemy – the Kurds. It gave Turkey a reason for striking Kurdish settlements in northern Iraq. In my opinion, from what I've observed, he was an evil man. His little group of troublemakers and he obviously meant to get our focus away from this un-winnable war which neither party will stop, and on to another war between the Kurds and the Turks. This troubled man did things like this with Iran and other Mideast countries, endangering America and our standing in the world. This is what breeds anti-Semitism, not jealousy about one's social status and wealth. "No justice, no peace" (Mohammed).

I'd like to say here that any Mexican I've met so far – hard working, loyal to America – could replace any of the no-account-counts in Congress as far as I'm concerned. But their loyalty would have to be to America, only.

No president should appoint all Jewish people to top positions in government. We have to demand diversity. I don't know of any Christians monitoring political groups, synagogues, charity habits of citizens. Nobody checks out money given to Israel, in spite of the fact that it's actually painful to see our country complicit in atrocities in Lebanon and Palestine, by our silence.

I watched intimidated hosts like Peter Glen, noticeably taken aback, finger on the button, when a no-account count like Christopher Hitchens appeared on his show (C-SPAN2). A caller asked about the Israel Lobby, a no-no. Peter had to charge with "He's a regular caller." Hitchens answered sarcastically, "I know." Hitchens wrote, "God is Not Great," and listed Karl Marx as one of his favorite authors. This disgusting man came to this country because of money and opportunity, and then proceeds to denigrate what made us great. He lives too well in Washington, D.C., for a man whose claim to fame is that he had the privilege and time to read and read – probably for lack of friends. This man is so full of himself until he meets a real challenger, as I've witnessed, who asked, "Isn't it true that Israel is responsible for the terrorists hating us?" "Without Israel, they'd still hate us." Yes, Mr. Hitchens, and I believe in the tooth fairy. Wasn't it the Rothschilds who had a hand in building up the Rockefellers' Standard Oil Company from way back? Who made the U.S. a partner in pushing through the occupation of Palestine? The greed of the oil companies and the wanton pillage of Iraq, Lebanon, Palestine, Afghanistan, possibly Iran and Syria, plays no role in our relationship with oil rich countries. They must love the CIA with its dirty tricks. A former CIA agent said that the U.S. is spending $400 million on covert CIA activities in Iran (7/2/08). Is this provocation? Yes. Are U.S. warships in the Gulf provocation for war? Yes. They're bullies threatening little countries who just desire the same things that we do. How long are we going to make these bullies fly the American flag before they're tried for war crimes?

While American workers are losing jobs, Congress is talking about National Health Care for all, including the 20 million illegals who cost us billions a year in emergency rooms. Several hospitals couldn't handle the load and closed. Obama, McCain and Hillary all agree that the illegals are "God's children." Well, so are we, and our pockets are empty after paying $2 billion a year to educate them – in our state alone.

As I watch generals like Petraeus, with shoulder to shoulder medals signifying nothing except corporate subservience, I think of all the broken lives wars have brought us. Instead of calling in the National Guard to help find the coal miners lost in Utah, our National Guards are in foreign countries protecting corporations paying foreign slave labor $2 a day.

Imagine the Pentagon having a controversial data base on anti-war protesters – "students against war." They had to close the operation down when it became public knowledge. The military has become the mill for mercenaries and any recruits who could stand up and shoot. Our Defense Department outsources defense projects. What's next?

Unfortunately, there are many in this country who feel that the life of a Jewish person is more precious than that of a non-Jew. I hear it when

Michael Savage nightly refers to "Mooselims" as "vermin," and begs the President to bomb Iran. Even though I've listened and written about these hateful people, I've reached a point where I can no longer stand the sound of their miserable diatribes. The few calls they get must be from their friends in the Anti-Defamation League. Who else could stand it? It's downright evil – like yelling fire in a crowded theater. They're actually calling for the death of tens of thousands of people – people ten times smarter than they – and they're getting away with it.

Zionists are involved in every aspect of our lives: The Ruth Westheimers talking about sex for the past 40 years, and now playing a "grandmotherly" role on Sesame Street and doing commercials. We're supposed to think of Barbara Walters, Larry King, and the rest of the older crowd as brilliant minds when actually, it was the experience that sharpened their trade. Anyone can be trained to do the same thing; it's not a rocket science.

I don't want Rabbis threatening malls to take down Christmas trees or a manger. How dare any group take away the happiest time of year for both children and adults, and substitute our tradition with ridicule of Jesus or films like "The Nightmare Before Christmas"?

Michael Collins Piper, author of "The New Jerusalem: Zionist Power in America" (American Free Press, Wash., D.C.), quotes Elliot Richardson, former Attorney General in the Justice Department. Richardson was the new attorney for the Hamiltons who were cheated out of their software after winning a $10 million contract with the Justice Department. They won a case against the Justice Department, but that decision was overturned by a hand-picked judge: Dick Thornburgh, the new Attorney General, who tried to keep the matter under wraps. (The Inslaw Case – Promis Software, used for Intelligence).

Finally Richardson found (p. 44):

"The Nazi war criminal program is . . . a front for the Justice Department's own covert intelligence service, according to disclosures recently made to Inslaw by several senior Justice Department career officials."

The last paragraph of four:

"The Justice Department's secret intelligence agency also has its own 'proprietary' company that employs scores of agents of diverse nationalities, as well as individuals who appear to be regular employees of various departments and agencies of the U.S. government or members of the U.S. armed forces, according to several sources."

Several investigators in this case were found murdered. This sounds like Hitler's secret service organization, and these things are happening with no checks or balances. Senator McCarthy warned us.

If you read enough about our government, the same names appear over and over. Dick Thornburgh has been a good little dooby, and has been rewarded handsomely.

There is no doubt that the Zionists have influenced America socially and culturally with their offerings in films and television. Even rap artists who denigrate women serve those who pay their inflated salaries. This influence has not been good because there are no avenues left to the rest of us to challenge the merchants of war, lust, teenage-sex-exploitation, and violence. It won't be stopped unless we can regain access to the public airwaves. The FCC should be found guilty of violating anti-trust laws, and worse. How long can any civilized society last if we allow this barbaric destruction of traditional values to continue? Are drugs and alcohol and violence going to replace God whom the Marxists call a "crutch"? Well, allow me to select my own crutch, thank you. Nobody tells me who to hate or to love or to respect.

America can't continue to be about wars, secret legislation, and trillion dollar debts. We can't afford to be policemen of the world and a welfare state at the same time. This life isn't what we bargained for. People who work hard should be able to reap some of the benefits of their work. They shouldn't have to support a war costing us $343 million a day, particularly when 80% of the people don't want this war. Why aren't those neo-cons behind Bush made to pay for this invasion of a country having nothing to do with 9/11?

Ninety-five percent of our Congressmen are rotten to the core or they would speak out. Behind our backs they are extending the time guest workers may stay in the U.S. Behind our backs, they pretend to feel sorry for those people whose homes are being foreclosed, when in actuality, it's about paying back the mortgage companies like Countrywide, their benefactors, for the bad loans they made to unemployed people who really couldn't afford a home at this time. Are any of us repaid for our bad loans, or stock loss, or property damage? No, sir; only the greedy are compensated.

Michael Smerconish, the Philadelphia talk show host who's been hawking war since his morning show's inception, learned that 99% loyalty to Israel isn't enough. Even though Smerconish has done five shows from Israel and one show from a holocaust site, it wasn't enough for Anti-Defamation League President Abraham Foxman. Smerconish committed the cardinal sin of asking the authors of "Israel Lobby" to his show. Apparently, the host forgot that listeners aren't allowed to hear opposing views, or they'll be labeled anti-Semitic. It always works. It seems that the host saw an unflattering piece on his "misadventure" in a local Jewish newspaper. Then, of course, Mr. Foxman had to be invited to the show in order to diffuse any influence the guests might have had on the listeners – if there are any listeners. "Bigot" was one of the words Foxman used, true to form.

Then the final penance came when the host invited a WW II veteran on to speak about D-Day and a holocaust site. Oh, those WW II vets – "Old" doesn't matter when it serves the masters! In case a listener didn't hear the account the first time, the broken record was played again the next day. I'm certain that the audience will hear it again and again.

I was told that my great-grandfather was a Jew who came over from Spain, settled in Italy, changed his name to Italian, and married my maternal great-grandmother. The rest is history. We're all Italian Catholics except for some of my cousins who have married into the Jewish faith.

I know that my grandfather had to be a Jew of Joseph because my family was compassionate, humorous, generous and intelligent – like the Jewish people I know. As a matter of fact, it was a close Jewish friend who introduced me to my husband. Perhaps the Semite part of my background appealed to him. Ali made friends with everyone, including his Jewish doctor colleagues, but we found them to be clannish and to themselves. I've learned that, while Jews and Moslems are both Semites, Moslems are open to all races and creeds. Whenever I hear the propaganda that "Moslems want to take over the Christian and Jewish religions in America and place us under their laws," I don't know whether to laugh or cry. Just ask yourself, who's bombing innocent people all over the world? Jews of Moloch, in my opinion, feel – unjustifiably so – superior to all races and creeds. They are becoming the dictators of what we should feel and say. They are the thought police who want you to shake if you bring up anything resembling a reason for Moslem disgust with the U.S. and Israel. Could the hate be from years of CIA intervention and bombing of innocent civilians? Cluster bombs? Refugees?

Just listen to the thought police like Dennis Prager, Michael Medved, and Michael Savage who talk down to us, believing fully that the Gentiles – or goyim (cattle) – are as ignorant as the uninformed born-again Christians whom they control. The "Christians for Israel" robots.

The Koran mentions a bad punishment for those who have perverted "His Word" and for those who hurt children in any way. Certainly, a just God could never designate a group as "chosen." I'm certain that this statement has turned millions of people away from religion. A good father has no favorites.

Madonna's study of Kabbala has its origin in Judaism. Bahai (Iran), the religion of many Hollywood stars, is also of Judaic origin. Unitarians, Mormons, Christian Scientists and Jehovah's Witnesses are all part of the materialistic, non-spiritual world. All religions have been watered down. And potential candidates Romney, Huckabee and Palin are all end-times loonies. Not to worry. Israel will be safe.

Judy Blume, an author from the late '70s who's still around, started writing for pre-teens and teens, then changed the genre of her books with "Saturdays." She gained the confidence of the readers, then pulled a switch on content.

Traditional books stressing character, loyalty to God and country are gone. In Philadelphia, thousands of books were burned just prior to the new age of computers. If parents complain, it's always "they don't understand." Children are inundated with trash such as Go Ask Alice (anonymous) about drugs.

Bill Cosby talks about the return of fathers in black neighborhoods, and he's right. On the other hand, we should be talking about white girls and women whom I've found more brutal than most men. From grades 6 up to high school, the cliques, the gossip, the violence, the bullying – of which I was a victim – takes place under teachers' and parents' noses, but nothing is done until some tragedy takes place. Whitey should be watching his own out-of-control children, the children who bully classmates too reserved to fight over something foolish. What kind of parents spawn children like this? These girls don't belong to gangs either, just horrible parents, busy with nothing but the urge to hurt others. The Cage Fighter group. The Mohawk loonies.

For the last ten years and longer, over 80% of the people have not been allowed to address any of these issues because of the monopolistic ownership of the print media, television and radio. This is what causes anti-Semitism and racism, although it is the Jewish ownership I accuse of exposing children and teens to bawdy, violent, and obscene shows in the name of free speech. Again, this is license to hurt, not free speech. Bathroom humor, four-letter words – nothing is off-limits. But we're lucky if we can hear a host touch on crucial issues such as war at 2 A.M. Even then, you're cut off. "The troops are fighting for our liberty." Really?

According to Congressman Rohrbacker, President George W. made a secret deal with Mexican President Calderone on orders from the NWO's World Court – not our courts – to give social security to the 20 million or more illegals in this country, if he could get an amnesty bill through (6/19/07). Of course, we weren't told about this from our do-nothing Congress, but the bill failed because of public pressure.

Cliff May, a frequent guest on MSNBC from the "Foundation for the Defense of Democracies," thinks that no torture is enough for Iraqis, even if the person rounded up is innocent. Cliff reminds me of the past: "Der Spiegelmeister vil be vatching you – and listening too." We don't need the opinions of pro-Israel nut-jobs on our airwaves. His comments prove that all stations play the game of pro-war and anti-war, but when it comes to what is right for Israel – both Fox News and MSNBC – all stations, place what's best for America last. And we say nothing. Heil money!

The other load of horse manure being used to silence Americans is the tactic used by Michael Savage whenever anyone calls asking why the host always defends Israel no matter what, as one male caller did last evening (10/19/07). Although Michael gave the caller a little time – very unusual – I've never heard any host including Matt Drudge, give such a caller longer than ten seconds, if that long. And it's always the same doleful put-off: "Oh, I see, you're not anti-Semitic; you just hate Zionists." Or, "Get off my show, you ugly bigot!" Better yet: "Oh, you have a Jewish friend?" or "Are you a holocaust denier?"

Perhaps these con artists should read up on Zionists and how they maneuvered the acquisition of Palestine and the U.S. Congress! The callers are supposed to feel shame and fear. They're supposed to overlook the mind control of hatred coming over "public" airwaves. After all, aren't we the "workers in the vineyards"? This B.S. is comparable to my feigning hurt when someone mentions the wrongdoing of the Mafia. I'm afraid that Americans have heard the lies we're inundated with on a daily basis for such a long time that they can no longer tell truth from fiction. And this damage to our country is more dangerous than the money-driven corporate criminals who steal from us through free trade and other venues, because we would at least have the airwaves to talk about these issues. It's no better than using duct tape over our mouths. My country has deteriorated over the last ten years. Where do we pick up the loss with lackeys like O'Reilly, Beck and Hannity in charge? Three clowns! Three useful idiots.

During Clinton's reign, many Americans were shot for speaking out at Ruby Ridge and elsewhere. Janet Reno was the Attorney General and approved. This "anti-government" bogeyman is meant to instill silence and terror. "Anti-government" is spelled out in the Declaration of Independence. Read it. It's the document that gave us freedom from King George of England, and hopefully will give us freedom from the treasonous rots in Washington, D.C.

These new kings, the thought police, control the press corps at the White House. The reporters, who are supposed to be asking the tough questions about war, immigration, and corporate crime, instead laugh like a bunch of drunken turncoats whenever the president's press secretary makes a joke. They would do anything to keep their White House jobs!

On CNN, 10/16/07, Bill Gates said, "We're pursuing the vision of what software can do across the continents." Notice the "we're" pursuing. He couldn't do diddly without our troops, our CIA, our WMD, our drug availability for the dispossessed and our unconscionable presidents and Congress. People are expendable in this mission of the super rich against the rest of us.

The neo cons, posing as conservatives are nothing but the old Trotskyites who really were always about totalitarianism and the control of every aspect of our lives. Despotism: Tyranny on the middle class and the downtrodden who really believe that hope is on the way.

They've learned to throw in "values." Yes, they believe in family, good schools, our dear flag, the troops, legal immigration and religion. But behind the scenes they promote promiscuity, violence, taking God out of the pledge, drugs, illegal immigration, higher taxes for wars, while criticizing Obama's taxing for entitlement after entitlement. Either way, we lose. When the Trotskyites' boots descend on our faces, family, God and country will go out the window.

I often sit in utter disbelief and sorrow when I see what's happening to us in America. On Booknotes (C-SPAN2) 3/16/08, there was a program featuring holocaust survivors. A professor at the University of Toronto, Michael Marrus, who teaches Holocaust Studies, presented a number of survivors at the NYC Museum of Jewish Heritage – 68 years later All of the survivors looked in excellent health; none of the survivors stood up and denounced what Israel is doing to the Palestinians in the name of a Jewish Homeland, nor what they did in Sabra and Shatila and Lebanon, again and again.

One person in the audience commented on the legacy he'd like to leave to his grandchildren. "I'd like to tell them not to follow the law. We followed the law, and look what happened to us." Yes. They made millions in reparations!

No compassion from this audience about the brutal deaths and torture inflicted on others; only their people count!

Remember what these neo cons said in the "Project for a New American Century" (1995) – paraphrasing: "We will need a catalytic event . . . something like Pearl Harbor" . . . was it 9/11?

America has been done unto again and again. They lied to us about the Gulf of Tonkin (Vietnam) when they said that we were attacked, and Secretary of Defense McNamara knew that it was a lie, but said nothing.

We were lied to about Pearl Harbor, WMD in Iraq – on and on. Let's hold them accountable for these lies.

Let's stop these almighty hyphenated Americans, now including the "Hispanic Caucus." Quickly, the Hispanics are building the same lucrative structure that the Blacks now enjoy. Only the taxpayers who work hard are left out. Doctors and nurses are being cheated out of reasonable pay by Big Government. On CNN, 7/9/08, Don Lemon, the black anchor, asked, "Why is it so hard to take an 11% cut from Medicare doctors?" I'd like his job to be cut by 11%, particularly since his job doesn't require any sense – only chutzpah. Thankfully the cut was vetoed!

Faye Wattleton, once the attractive Black spokeswoman for Planned Parenthood in the late '70s, now is the attractive spokeswoman for the Center for the Advancement of Black Women. Since she was speaking at the African-American Women's Town Hall Meeting, I assume that she has moved up as the co-founder of her hyphenated organization.

Julianne Malveaux, Bennett College President, and other successful Black women were discussing the topics: "educational gap," "economic gap," and why poor folks can't get to the doctor (C-SPAN 7/13/08).

Get this for chutzpah and public money: National Council of Negro Women's Research, Public Policy, and Information Center. Also, Black Women's Health Imperative.

These are some of the questions, these oh so powerful Black women were asking: "How do our schools wind up with fewer computers? If our neighborhoods are poor, education will be poor. I'm not suggesting that White people turn over their paychecks…. We have to start community groups." Yeah, like Acorn! LOL

Sounds an awful lot like the other hyphenated groups earning big bucks for getting activists together and living high on our money, creating more division.

Fortunately, I can answer the computer question and the poor education question: teachers are afraid to teach in some of your schools where they need metal detectors – all because of no discipline at home, no fathers present, and no mothers interested enough to attend school meetings. Except for a few interested parents whose children become victims of gangs, nobody gets off their duffs enough to attend the schools and help, while waiting for their government handouts. Don't blame Whitey. Blame yourselves. And get off of those high-flying gravy trains such as Planned Parenthood and National Council of Negro Women's Research, Public Policy, etc.

The only Public Policy we need is justice for all. We had enough of hyphenated Americans and their needs. We need to stop the war in Iraq and close our borders so that no more leeches can live on our blood and sacrifice. Get honest jobs; with the influx of illegals and the loss of American jobs, the "ME" period is over. Have you heard that banks are closing and that foreclosures on homes are continuing? How could you, when you hyphenated Americans are busy with getting the unentitled more money at the expense of the middle class!

Don't even get me started on the Trade Policy Hearing in the Senate (C-SPAN 7/29/08). Senator Pat Roberts (R-Kansas) – after drooling at the feet of the panelists – Charlene Barshefsky, William Brock, Michael Cantor and Carla Hills – calling them Honorable this and Honorable that – he made this statement: : "Americans have to be warned that we are in a post-American season." How do you like that for treason? Needless to say, I called his office. I won't say anything else.

Barshefsky and Cantor were both Clinton appointees. Brock was appointed by Reagan and Carla Hills by Bush. Brock remarked that "we started with Israel," just before Senator Roberts started his drool. In my opinion, he should be drooled out of Congress or the Department of Environmental Protection ought to declare his home an endangered species site for coyotes. His pension should be given to someone who lost his job because of this "free traitor." Our "servants" are becoming Benedict Arnolds (the American Revolutionary General who became a traitor).

And, just when I thought that the "internationalists" were too smart to play us for drones, it happened again. The Heritage Foundation (conservative) whose loyalty I've always questioned, except for Phyllis Schlafly, sponsored a bunch of ungrateful pseudo-"intellects," eating at the U.S. trough but supporting wars for a Greater Israel (C-SPAN 2 1/18/09, replayed from 5/7/07).

The guest was Robert Kaufman, a professor no less, who wrote "In Defense of the Bush Doctrine." This professor hates Iran but still can't pronounce it, after all these years. Wow, are these truths "self-evident" or what?

Here are some of his quotes, and if it sounds very familiar, it's because it is ("Project for a New American Century" – the Wolfowitz group):

1. "The cost of losing in Iraq would be catastrophic."
2. "Ron Paul made some foolish statements when he was a candidate, but Giuliani jumped down his throat." (Translation: Ron Paul still believes that this is America.)
3. "Changed minds can be brought about by some catastrophe such as Pearl Harbor." (Translation: Another 9/11??)
4. "The Bush Doctrine of Preemptive Strikes is the only one which can take us down the road we are now on."
5. "Hamas has got to stop the violence against Israel; sometimes you have to lance the boil."
6. "We should partner with India to fight the Islamists and then, in the future, to fight against the Chinese." (Kaufman predicts that strife with China is inevitable.)

So, this Kauffman has America's future all laid out: war, war, bankruptcy for the U.S. and obscene profits for war profiteers. Oh, but wait!

We drones will get to see more bodies at Arlington Cemetery; if we're lucky, maybe memorials! If we're really lucky, we'll get to hear Mark Levin say, "You're a great American. Thank you for your service." Damn it, they always leave out – "to Israel and Wall Street!"

If President Obama bows to these neo-con internationalists who have no loyalty to this country, we are indeed doomed.

If, on the other hand, the President goes along with the group of affluent black men discussing "Black Politics" on MSNBC (1/18/09) during the inaugural festivities – the ones who see Obama's presidency as "a chance to help the 50 million blacks in the U.S. get more privileges," then God help us. The President did not get the message which is that We the People are sick of crooks! Nowhere in the President's oath does he pledge to be a globalist and spread our hard-earned money throughout the world, playing policeman. Bring our troops back from Germany and the other 129 places they're in. We don't need NATO or the World Bank to which President Obama will pay billions for third world countries. (Who accounts for how the money is spent?) Nor should we give $250 million to the IMF (International Monetary Fund). A bunch of "Robbin' Hoods" are running America!

I hope that I'm wrong, but whenever I see Rahm Emanuel and the other cabinet selections, I feel hopeless. I know that these men and women were chosen for this particular time to work in tandem with the neo-cons so that the lives of Americans will be spent in perpetual turmoil. Our future will be talking race – as though slavery happened yesterday. The new hyphenated Americans, the Hispanics, have moved up the political ladder and will endeavor to use their "clout" to get serious amnesty bills through – health care for illegals, social security, etc. It will be socialism – "National socialism" like the one in Hitler's Germany. (Hence, Na-zi.) In 1994, Milton Friedman, the economist, put it well: "Russia has been trying to capture what America had fifty years ago, and we're trying to capture what they had."

Already the signs are there – billionaire Oprah with tears in her eyes; Jesse Jackson with tears in his eyes; Stevie Wonder and other black multi-millionaires, so happy that they will finally get a chance in this "racist" America. Poor victims! They almost made me gag, especially when they've exposed us to 24-7 black-slavery episodes on Oprah and the Lifetime series ever since the inauguration. All black all the time. It seems to me that these hypocrites should be kissing our streets. Only in America could their success have happened, and they now expose themselves as the greedy so and sos that they really are!

We need our airwaves back from these sob-sisters and brothers imitating the holocaust industry. There are two new women hosts on talk radio WPHT, who apparently were hired to beef-up more hatred for the "Islamo-fascists" (LOL). Lynne Gold-bikin and Christine Flowers, downplaying torture, are our weapons of mass destruction being used to promote the terrorist state of Israel's latest one-sided war.

Please Note…

Milton Friedman is not related to the George Friedman or Tom Friedman of the New York Times whom I mention in a later chapter. Milton is a Libertarian with a small "l." He recommended that we end the Federal Reserve, which he blamed for the 1921 collapse of government. He is an admirer of Adam Smith (18th century) ("Wealth of Nations"). He captured the story of F. A. Hayek in his book "The Road to Serfdom."

Milton said that socialism paves the way to totalitarianism and that President Clinton is a socialist (Booknotes 3/15/09, replayed from 10/24/94).

While I don't agree that President Reagan was a good president (remember, Ronald "Region"), I do agree with Friedman's desire for small government and leaving the free enterprise system alone. "Government didn't invent washing machines; people did. Anything government does, as in education, is a failure. Get rid of all welfare programs." (But then people would have to think before having fatherless children.)

Unfortunately, we have too many in Congress who are paid off with family jobs, jets (Pelosi) and bribes. At the moment we have another representative from California whose name is Loretta Sanchez, a Democrat. Using her divide and conquer plea, she has joined the realm of the hyphenated Americans. When asked by former Governor of Arkansas, Huckabee, whether she thought that American troops should be on our border fighting the Mexican drug cartel: "No. I think that we should "help" Mexico and not send American troops there." So, the Hispanics are about Havana and Mexico; the Blacks are about Africa; the Jews are about Israel. Anyone remember America?? Where are our brave Americans? And why do so many nut-jobs come from California?

About Islam: Moslems believe that Jesus cursed the Jews and that Jesus was a Prophet of "divine" origin. They can't accept the Trinity since they believe in one God; and that God needs no help. They don't believe that Christ died for our sins; sins are forgiven through deeds. The Koran instructs Moslems to fight – only when attacked, unlike the lies we are told.

Their reasoning sounds quite logical. If Christ died for our sins, we're left with the notion that we can sin and sin – and still be forgiven. Nonsense!

How long do those of us who love the America that was hijacked from us stand aside while we pretend that nothing is happening in the Mideast in our name? How long do we take orders from the new head in Israel – "Netanyahu" – at the cost of more death and destruction to the Moslems because he pretends to see a desperate Hamas "terrorist" under every bed? He, through his New York Times buddy, Tom Friedman, threatened that he would take action against Iran's nuclear program if we didn't. Well, let him take action – without U.S. aid and arms – and then perhaps this bully will stop the slaughter when 22 Arab nations converge on the occupiers of Palestine. Brutal Nazis.

By now you know what I think about the moneychangers and what they can do with their money. I don't care how much money Joan Rivers makes – to me she's still the one who laughed at a model wearing a hat because of cancer. Even though Rivers didn't know it at the time, she's still a piece of mean to me. There isn't enough money in the world to keep her happy. Probably most of her charity goes to Israel, oh, Israel.

As for the greedy meatheads like Cheney and Bush who act as servants to these money-hungry crooks, they will hopefully be judged. Fortunately, Bush can't travel while the Hague is threatening to indict him for war crimes.

These old vultures have claimed enough young lives in Arlington Cemetery and in army hospitals and in homeless streetwalkers. We fought useless wars, killed millions of Germans in order to protect people who look at us like so much garbage. They'll have the youth watching Martin Luther King 'til the end of time, and, according to a movement in Tennessee, of all places, holocaust survivors said that they'd like to keep the "history of the holocaust alive." (WHYY 4/5/09) God help the children of the world to wake up and take their God-given freedoms back from the vultures in government, whether they be Jewish or so-called Christians, who have taken religion out of all cultures and replaced it with "end times" garbage.

President Bush killed, and now President Obama intends to kill more people in the Mideast in order to protect Israel. Even Poland's missile base will be there to protect Israel. Hundreds of billions of our hard-earned money. Trillions.

We have "Harold Koe," a nut job in the State Department, calling for "Global Initiatives." We have bank bailouts and trillions going to New Jersey Governor Corzine types in Goldman Sachs, Citi Group, and Morgan Stanley – all because the average American is too occupied with paying higher and higher taxes on property, gasoline, and through-the-roof utility bills and food – rotten imported food!

President Obama has gone along with Israel's demand that George Mitchell, our emissary to the Mideast, not listen to the duly-elected Hamas of Palestine unless they accept a roadmap which has not been accepted by Israel. Gestapo vultures are beginning to resemble the Hitler regime. Obama looks like another useful idiot like Colin Powell and Condoleeza Rice.

We have foreigners, like billionaire George Soros, calling the economic shots. He made $6.3 billion betting that the United States dollar would weaken, and he bet the same about the British pound and the currencies of other countries. He started the unregulated Hedge Funds (tried to sell the CSX Railroad to the Red Chinese). Lobbyists for derivatives and hedge funds got a turncoat in the Senate, smiling Phil Gramm, to sneak the "deregulatory" feature into an 11,000 page Omnibus Bill, and President Clinton signed it. Wonder how much the lobbyists paid these stooges who are used to not reading bills from being in state government where bills are already written and sent to our servants "for sponsorship."

Mr. Soros also pushed for drug legalization – not because he wants to save America from drug profiteers – but because he'd like to see an America like Kowloon, China. Drug legalization just makes it easier for the weak-minded individuals who can now buy drugs and roam streets, not knowing who or where they are. I feel this way about all of those who want drug legalization. That's why I can't fully accept all of the tenets of Libertarianism, which also proposes legalization. It's a shortsighted, soft-headed idea from many naïve people who trust that everyone will make intelligent decisions. Well, America has changed from the smart people who lived long ago. Decades of propaganda have dulled the faculties of the would-be American heroes like Senator McCarthy, former Congressmen like Gonzalez, Rarick, McFadden, Lindberg, on and on. There are no more stand-up women like Maureen Heaton or Catherine Palfrey Baldwin. The women I see are either committed to radical lesbianism or fighting for the unborn. Neither group gives a damn about the immorality taught in our schools or the scars children will have watching war, cage fighting, or being bullied by buffoons.

As for the derivatives we just bailed out for the banks in Europe and America, they could be bonds from a country like Argentina. These bonds are "repackaged" and given a Triple A rating by "regulatory" agencies, such as Standard and Poor or Moody's – for a price. Then, knowing that the public really doesn't understand what's going on, the unscrupulous salesmen sell it to companies, like Proctor and Gamble. According to the author of "FIASCO" (Fixed Income Annual Sporting Clays Outing), a derivative could be a "bet" that a certain team could win, "just like gambling." (This type of gambling in Hedge Funds made Soros a billionaire by betting on America's weakened dollar.) To top it off, insurance companies, like AIG, that used to have legitimate types of insurance, such as fire, flooding, etc., now insure these phony frauds. Enron was involved in this scheme.

In FIASCO, Mr. Portnoy seemed to be bragging that when he joined the team of 70 at Morgan Stanley of New York, London and Tokyo, he was in his twenties making millions of dollars. Managers could earn $15 million a year for being a part of a scheme that could make investors lose a billion dollars.

I think that two quotes from his book sum up what is happening in America today. This is NOT capitalism; it is runaway fraud by a group of unscrupulous men who have no character. The sad part is that the Security Exchange Commission, supposedly protecting us, was not watching. And Mr. Cox of the SEC was not indicted.

Quotes

1. "Behind every great fortune there lies a great crime." (Honore DeBalzac)

2. "Most of us enter the investment business for the same sanity-destroying reasons a woman becomes a prostitute: it avoids the menace of hard work, is a group activity that requires little in the way of intellect, and is a practical means of making money for those with no special talent for anything else." (Richard Ney, the Wall Street Jungle)

And get this: these merchants of fraud confide that the leader at Morgan Stanley is John Mack (where he is still known as Mack the Knife). "There's blood in the water; let's go kill someone!"

"Outside of work, they honed their killer instincts on skeet shooting clubs (like Cheney?), safaris, and dove hunts in Africa and South America. These events set the mood for the firm's barbarous approach to its clients' increasing losses." Unbelievable! (The Cheney comment is mine.)

Since the influx of these immigrants from Eastern Europe and Russia, our country is in the sewer.

Who is this Hungarian Jew, Soros, to get press coverage on CNBC and other stations directing our country into a one-world currency? Who are these chosen people who have taken over our giant supermarkets with aisles and aisles of kosher food? Who are these zealots leading us into war, killing the youth and destroying industry?

Who are these sponsors of sex for children like "Dr." Laura Berman (doctor of what) who are leading American children down a treacherous pit?

It's becoming gag time, and these vocalists for theft and debauchery should be tossed off the air and out of our schools. If it's fascism they want, let them all go back to the countries they left.

Leave America and our children alone. Take your filth back to wherever, along with your bawdy humor and the F-bomb.

On the Fox tickertape (4/7/09).... "The Black caucus would like better relations with Cuba." Well, I don't give one damn about their desires nor the desires of their partners in the chosen hyphenated Americans.

For all of my life, I've had no avenue to express free speech. There was always the threat of being escorted out, even though Thomas Jefferson said that "the highest form of patriotism is dissent." How dare anyone keep millions of Americans, who feel like me, quiet! For just one day I'd like to know what Code Pink is protesting. For just one day I'd like to see the worldwide protesters who feel like me about the Israeli occupation of Palestine. The Palestinians are treated like garbage by the chosen criminals who block all access to free speech all over the world, with their backup of force and rubber bullets and whatever it takes, and they're in every country!

I'd like to hear Cindy Sheehan instead of Laura Schlessinger or Christine Amanpour or Madeleine Albright, Andrea Mitchell, Barbara Starr, etc. – all appointed by stooge Clinton – all Israel, all the time.

It breaks my heart that Iran may be bombed by the chosen murderers, with the sanction of frauds like John Hagee and Franklin Graham – all hype and no truth. Histrionics, Inc. The pool of TV "preachers" is a joke.

We cannot allow the press to select candidates like Palin and Senator McCain's daughter for the next election. Nor should we sit by and be fooled by the Minnesota battle for the Senate seat between Norm Coleman and Al Franken, both pro Israel all of the time. Not to worry, Norm was already promised a job by the Israel Lobby. Norm and Franken are both goons like their leaders.

RELIGION

The New Testament was just that – new. All of the so-called covenants and the promises of land and temple were fulfilled in the Old Testament.

"The Scofield Bible is one of the main sources of the spreading of the Kingdom Message of Phariseeism (ancient Jewish sect), but they call it Dispensationalism, Fundamentalism, and Millenialism. There are two glaring mistakes in the book: that the Abrahamic Covenant was unconditional; that it had not been fulfilled by the Jews and is, therefore, in the future. Scofield mentions this over and over. But read passages: Gen. 18:19, Gen. 26:4, 5; Lev. 26:40, 42; Deut. 7:12; Neh. 9:23. All passages are glaring contradictions. Scofield also says that the Seventieth Week of Daniel is still in the future, but the Seventieth Week is the week in which Christ was crucified. Scofield also says that the Sermon on the Mount was for Jews only, but Matthew 7:24–28 exposes this falsehood. Christ talks about the wicked and the saved rising from their graves on Judgment Day and that the wicked shall face damnation. No rapture. No tribulation. (John 5:28, 29) (W. F. Mullin in "The Second Advent")

Scofield relies heavily on Revelation to prove his millennial errors, but they are all disproved by the historian Rev. Foy E. Wallace, Jr. in his "Book of Revelation" in which he proves that it was written before 70 A.D. (not later in 95 A.D.), and fulfilled in the siege and destruction of Jerusalem. It is therefore past and can have no future application to a materialistic Kingdom on Earth. Hundreds of other examples could be given to show that Scofield's notes do not teach the Christian Gospel, for the Christian Gospel is spiritual, not worldly, and is for mankind, not just the Jews. Scofield was a British Phari-see Jew who wanted to contribute to the idea that there will be an earthly kingdom run by Jews. Instead he perverted the Christian mind from belief in God's true Spiritual Kingdom (Helen M. Peters, Historian, "Common Sense" 9/71).

Children today don't know what to believe. Moral relativism has been forced down their throats by the humanists who believe in nothing. Parents go along with anything because they don't want to expend energy in their children's lives. Parenting has become a joke in many instances. A child is placed before a TV set and that set becomes his teacher, right or wrong. Later, the computer becomes the babysitter. Since the feminist influence, mothers, in many cases, feel that they're doing too much housework, but having children is a lot of work and both parents should help. Parents should listen more.

For most churchgoers today religion is about "Social Justice" – helping AIDS victims, the homeless, druggies, and third world countries. No more love for country or sovereignty; we are all one people now. We are to forget the past and think globally so that billionaires like Bill Gates can sell his products on several continents.

The sad part is that charity begins at home with a good grasp of the Ten Commandments and a strong value system so that we are able to extend our hands to the unfortunates in this country FIRST. Without a true perception and knowledge of history, no one can help third world countries, particularly when our military helps those tyrants in poor countries keep protest down, or suffer consequences. And, of course, tyrants cover Christians, Jews, Blacks, Whites, Asians, all.

After World War II, Father Coughlin, a Catholic priest, had a radio show during which he tried to inform the public about events that were going to happen to us and the Catholic Church. He was demonized, but the things he warned about have happened.

Today, we have uninformed so-called talk show hosts telling listeners that "if you don't like my show, turn the dial." Trouble is that all of the stations, except weather, are complicit in the economic, cultural, and intellectual downfall of America. I've tried to expose, for those of you who can't listen to talk radio, just how dangerous this propaganda weapon is – and it was used frequently during World War II. Movies and songs were created so that every American felt a need to go get 'em. Of course, after the war, these same Marxist creeps did everything to get our Pledge of Allegiance and God out of the classroom – the same classrooms that trained those loyal Americans who thought that they were dying to save our country.

"For the Evangelicals: In the Old Testament order, God dealt separately with the nation of Israel (Jews), and they were then God's chosen people. But at the Cross, God did away with that order and instituted the New Testament order, bringing individuals to Christ, not just from one nation but from all nations, through One body – the spiritual "Israel of God" (Gal. 6:16).

"After the Cross there were no more Jews and Gentiles in the sight of God – just sinners and Christians, regardless of race or nationality. God's chosen people today are those who have entered this One Body through faith in Jesus Christ.

"The true Jews (Rom. 2:28, 29) in the beginning of the Bible believed that Christ was their Messiah, and through this faith they were delivered into the Kingdom of His Dear Son (Col. 1:13) and became "Spiritual Jews." This is the only Jew that is of God since the Cross, and the "true Jews" remained among God's chosen people.

"But they were no longer called Jews for they took the name of "Christian" in fulfilling Isa. 62:2 and 65:15. "Synagogue of Satan" and "you are of your father, the devil" were terms used to describe those who did not believe in Christ (John 8:44).

"Christ did not want us to fight the unbelievers, the Pharisees, but He was concerned that we oppose their religion and not be deceived into believing it – "Beware ye of the lesson (doctrines) of the Pharisees, which is hypocrisy" (Luke 12:1). And although we do not fight the Jews as people, it is our Christian duty to oppose the Jews' religion of Kingdom on Earth – no matter who is teaching it. Upon careful observation it can be seen without a doubt that most of our churches, and nearly the whole of World Evangelism, is teaching the millennial reign of Christ. We know that the Jews are in most places of power and that many belong to our church organizations who pretend to be converted to Christianity." (Unitarian Church, in particular) "And, indeed, there are many Christians who believe that Jews won't attain salvation unless they believe in Christ."

"Remember that Christ said to Pilate: "My Kingdom is not of this world" (John 18:36). I don't know how this message could be any clearer.

"Mr. Roy E. Wallace in God's Prophetic Word says that promises concerning Israel are history – they have been fulfilled in the events and experiences

of the past. He says that there are three sections to the Old Testament promises and prophesies: the land promise to Abraham and his seed after him; the restoration promise to Israel, and the spiritual promise to all nations. The land promise to Abraham was fulfilled in Joshua 21:43, 45; 23:13, 14; the restoration promise was fulfilled in the decree of Cyrus...II Chronicles 36:11, 23 and Ezra 1:1-4; and the spiritual promise to all nations was fulfilled in Jesus Christ, as set forth in Gal. 3:26-29.

"Although the millennial preachers declare that the recent return (1948) of the Jews to Palestine is fulfillment of Bible prophecy, scripture says that the nation of Israel could never be restored again. Their nation ended forever at the destruction of Jerusalem in 70 A.D. Moses said that they would perish, Deut. 30:17, 18; Joshua said that they would lose their inheritance for lack of obedience to God, Joshua 23:12-16; and Jeremiah said that they could not be restored but were to be a broken vessel, never to be made whole again, Jer. 19:1-12.

"Moses positively declared that the nation of Israel would perish, Deut. 8:20; also, in Deut. 28, 29, 30. Moses has said that their dispersion would be permanent. In Jeremiah 5:18, Moses said that some would survive, that He would not make a full end with them, but "ye shall leave your name for a curse unto my chosen." Although the few who survived were Pharisees, they must call themselves Jews in order to fulfill the prophecy of Isaiah 65:15.

"The Pharisees had a political side as well as a religious side." Without going into the history of why the Pharisees were called the British Israel Pharisees — Andrew Carnegie and Cecil Rhodes, both from the British Empire, wanted, and left in their wills and papers, the desire for our reunification with Great Britain. Hence, people like Bill Clinton who received a Rhodes Scholarship was a one-worlder, also seeing the United States as caretaker of the world. Such compassion with our hard-earned money! And sadly, many government appointees are Rhodes scholars, educated at Oxford, "serving" our government and making the big bucks by selling us out — "step by step," as the Fabian Socialists say.

"To recapitulate: Masonry and British Israel are both controlled from the British Empire. If you remember, it was Benjamin Disraeli, a Pharisee Jew, who brokered the takeover of Palestine by the Zionists in 1948. They dreamed of a One World Superstate — the Kingdom of God on Earth, British Israel — Judeo-Christianity is the spirit of the revolution; the British Empire is its body and structure. Masonry is its servants working in every facet of political,

military, and religion – and the blueprint for world conquest is a scheme of Bible prophecy which seeks to justify mass murder in the world as it enacts its prophecies on the way to an "earthly kingdom."

"While these prophets of doom tell us that their great tribulation is to come through big, bad communist Russia, the "Great Tribulation" of Matt. 24:21, preceded by "wars and rumors of wars," is already past. Matt. 24:3-34, which includes verse 6 on "wars and rumors of wars," describes events preceding the destruction of Jerusalem and the excision of the Israel nation from the Kingdom in 70 A.D. when Christ came to judge the disobedient Jews. In conjunction with this, read Matt. 24:36; no sign will be given for the Second Coming of Christ – at Judgment Day.

"The Pharisees talk about the message of Gizeh and the Great Pyramid in their "British Israel World Federation" report, p. 13. They say that Russia will begin to crucify the Church and State in America and Britain. It was the Pharisees who went over to Russia and began the crucifixion of the "body politic" – Christianity and nationalism."

Look around you. It's already happened in America. And wasn't it the Lenin Bolsheviks who slaughtered the Christians of Russia and their leaders? Wasn't it the Zionist Pharisees who created political communism? "Russian communism was started by those Jews who wanted to create a slave country, which Russia became."

"Wars and rumors of wars" are being set up by those who don't want the word "conspiracy" to reach the masses. Who is behind these wars in Iraq, Iran, Lebanon, Syria – on and on? It's the same group about whom Professor Quigley wrote in his book, exposing the "conspiracy." It's the group which involves itself in every government in the world and which now has Americans doing its dirty work. This is precisely why the Framers did not want a standing army used at the will of the president.

"While they have provoked many well-meaning people into fighting 'communism,' their goal is spiritual communism wherein "everyone on earth shares" (except them). The whole idea of communism and their other "isms" is meant to deceive and pervert and destroy the most wonderful country in the world – America.

"World Service" is to be our role in the New Age millennium, and we are being educated for that very thing. Pyramids Prophecy circulated by the British-Israel World Federation in London (p. 37) states: "The most that we can say is that America has for the present a twofold destiny to fulfill in a falling world. It is her destiny to support the weak and supply the needy, and at the same time to uphold, by successive and temporal proppings, all that is best in a sagging and crumpling old world order, until the new world order is ready to take its place."

I have checked all of the Biblical sources mentioned above in the Bulletin Common Sense, by Helen Peters (King James Version).

Notice that our public and private schools teach Citizenship, including Volunteering. Citizenship to the elite means that you do what you are told to do. Volunteering is another aspect of citizenship wherein students are told to go out into the community and pick up trash. This latter service should be just that – volunteering, not 'forced service' which the elite have in mind.

My objective in going into depth on the preceding issue, Kingdom on Earth, was to open the eyes of just one of the forty million Americans hypnotized into believing a message created in evil, which will end in totalitarianism. From my personal experience in sitting in on some of these local bible teachings, nothing is said or done about what our children are forced to hear and see on TV, videos, print media and schools. According to these groups corruption will be taken care of by Jesus. These suppliers of myth talk about "signs" to look for – signs which they have created by sitting on their duffs. Unchecked borders, new diseases, pestilence, wars, brainwashing of children, values clarification, crime – all of these things could be solved by a determined public. But, no, this group would rather listen to the ranters and ravers of this world.

It seems that the truth is hard to handle for the average American. "Am I therefore your enemy because I tell you the truth?" (Gal. 4:16).

The popularity of the recent "Spring Break" has had a devastating influence on young children. Diving into bed with every Tom, Dick and Harry, and flashing breasts and tongues is as ugly and barbaric as it looks. It reflects the values of their permissive parents, who have been school and media-indoctrinated into believing that it's okay for girls to take drugs and romp in the grass with just about anybody. It's not a new phenomenon that depicts America today; it's the same old white trash, the bullies, cursing their way through life. It's not about youth; it's about sleaze. Their parents drink, so they drink. Their parents curse, so they curse. The only reason that television cameras are there is to play up degeneracy. In ten years, the spring breakers will regret their actions. Two sleazy meatheads jumping on each other is passionate only to the participants, degenerates, and the moneymakers.

I hope that you watched Senator Obama's minister, Reverend Jeremiah Wright, curse America. The right wing talk show hosts were more offended with what he said about Israel. Yes, the land of the Untouchables we must fear. Young people listening to Sean Hannity – a stoop if ever there was one – are propagandized with disinformation about Reverend Wright's wrongful accusation that Israel sponsors state terrorism on Palestinians. Unfortunately, Sean, from the limited sound bites I've heard from Pastor Wright, he happens to be accurate. There is slaughter and genocide on the Palestinians, but people like you won't let the truth be told. Somehow, someway, God willing, people will have to hear the truth and take positions to detach our involvement in this slaughter.

Sean would rather set up a call from a father, John, who lost his young son five years ago in Iraq. Sean and his emotional acceptance of what the father was allowed to say, unchallenged, about those "terrorists" went on for some time. Imagine a "terrorist" daring to protect himself and his family from the brutal occupation and killing of over 800,000 defenseless civilians – on their own land. What would we do if the situation were reversed?

We send marines – "America's finest" – to fight for democracy and liberation. Liberation to what – more torture and death? Our values – two laughing marines caught throwing a puppy over a cliff? I can only imagine what some of these marines do to civilians. They don't represent America. They represent the Hannitys, the O'Reillys, Limbaughs, Levins, Pragers, Medveds, Savages, Hewitts, and the Dennis Millers. Ah, yes, Dennis Miller, the hatchet man for the Trotskyites in the press who invited Vincent Bugliosi on his show (6/12/08).

Bugliosi was the prosecuting attorney in the Manson case. Everyone said that he was brilliant. Then he wrote about O.J. Simpson. His latest book, "The Prosecution of George W. Bush for Murder," was the topic on the Miller show.

Miller realized that Bugliosi was making a documented case for his hypothesis – stating that pre-911, Bush suggested that B-52s go over Iraq, under a UN flag, so that, when the Iraqis fired, the U.S. could get resolutions through to sanction Saddam as much as we could. At the same time, the United States would have a provocation for war.

Miller then started to harass the author with demeaning accusations, as only he could. "Looks to me as though you've gone around the bend. You're not the same man I once knew." These are the insults patriotic Americans have endured since the Clinton mergers took over our public airwaves. Miller is by far a scumbag of gigantic proportions, and he has a huge role on the O'Reilly show, the property of Rupert Murdoch, Fox News.

When Miller asked Bugliosi why Americans who are serving in Iraq would stay if they felt like the author: "They don't know, and they don't want to know."

That's it in a nutshell. When the Levins and Millers talk against the Fairness Doctrine, stating that "liberals" want to have local opinions on radio, it should be insulting to all of us. Our media is totally controlled.

The Nazis in the media play us for fools. We dumb crackers pay subsidies to black universities whose students get 40% of the 30,000 Pell Grants and are obliged to pay only 15% of their loans, while their poor white counterparts whose families make all of $80,000 per year are ineligible for Pell Grants. Of course, the Office of Civil Rights was recently before Congress asking for more money because of the fact that "China has become competition" (C-SPAN 2, 3-17-08). Middle class white "racists" pay for Medicaid, day care, transportation – everything – even breakfast and lunch. No wonder we're hated.

So long as the public is unaware of the games the media plays, we will live in subjugation. While we concentrate on race, the real wheeler-dealers on the air and in schools are making out like bandits with our properties, our children, and our culture. Who's going to complain when lots of people are paid off?

We don't need black supremacists and their white KKK counterparts who were always conned into these divisive groups by government agents – which I have witnessed. While the Black Panthers rant and the KKK puts on their shows, important issues are kept off the table. The uneducated masses provide the membership needed to incite the public into fighting class issues instead of focusing on what the real culprits are doing.

Think of the power that blacks could have if the NAACP, church groups, congressmen and others would get together, study the curriculums of their children's progress, and then act upon it – with us.

Instead the moneymakers, like Reverend Wright, go along and use showmanship – screaming like a bunch of madmen, instigating about

Whitey. They brag that their congregation has its own culture and songs – but no 'sacred' songs, as though not assimilating is a badge of courage.

Well, sad to say, religion, as we know it, has changed. All sins are now forgiven. Everything that was wrong is now right. And people are far worse off and unhappy with "anything goes."

When Reverend Wright talks about "liberation theology" (the religion of Trinity Church), it brings back happier times when women, young and old, black and white, dressed up in their Sunday best to attend church on Easter Sunday. It was definitely a parade of beauty. Those were the times when grandmothers and dads showed off their grand children and nurtured them.

Today, it's a different story. Father Malachai Martin described "Liberation Theology" in The Keys of This Blood: "the fundamental struggle in which the church and all Catholics were engaged was no longer in the supernatural plane at all. The personal war between Christ as Savior and Lucifer as the Cosmic Adversary of the Most High in the quest for men's souls was no longer spiritual. It was in the material circumstances of the tangible, sociopolitical here and now. It was the class struggle Marx and Lenin propounded as the only worthwhile combat zone for humans. Liberation was therefore no longer release from sin and its dire effects. It was the struggle against oppression by big capital and by the authoritarian colonialist powers of the west – particularly the United States as the arch villain of all human history." (They forgot Stalin and Red China.)

"Within five years of the end of Vatican II, the whole of Latin America was being flooded with a new theology – Liberation Theology – in which basic Marxism was decked out in traditional Christian vocabulary and retooled Christian concepts. Books written mainly by co-opted Catholic priests, together with political and revolutionary action manuals, saturated the volatile area of Latin America, where over 367 million Catholics included the lowest and poorest strata of society – that ninety percent of the population which had no concrete hope of any economic betterment for themselves or their children. Liberation Theology was a perfectly faithful exercise of Gramisci's principles. It could be launched with the corruption of a relatively few well-placed Judas Goats.

"Corruption of the best is the worst corruption. It was not long before a majority of diocesan bishops – not only in Latin America but in Europe and the United States, as well – were swept up in the new theology of this worldly liberation. The entire effort was helped along by the careful and intricate networking of Catholic dioceses by a new creation: the Base Community. Essen-

tially composed of lay Catholics, each Base Community decided how to pray, what priests to accept, what bishops – if any – would have authority, what sort of liturgy they would tolerate. All references to traditional Catholic theology and to Rome's central authority were considered secondary, if not altogether superfluous. The most powerful orders of the Roman Catholic Church – Jesuits, Dominicans, Franciscans, Maryknollers – all committed themselves to Liberation Theology.

"The Base Communities in Latin America – riddled with Liberation Theology and openly Marxist in their political philosophy – were pronounced in their hatred for America." ("The Keys of This Blood," Malachi, p. 261.)

This is the religion of Pastor Wright's church. His church, like the Catholic Church was done unto by a few "Judas Goats." Marx said, in an earlier chapter, "When you can only work with their permission, you can only live with their permission."

If what has happened in Russia and China with tens of millions of people slaughtered isn't enough of a lesson to us, then it's hopeless. And who helped finance Russia and China? We did, the wonderful country of democracy, no longer a republic, which we would like to share with other countries – at the point of a machine gun or land mines, or even constant bombings and nukings.

If those in America cared about Africa – this includes Pastor Wright – they would see that our aid goes to the poor, not to our rich puppets who enslave their own people so that those on the bottom stay uneducated, impoverished, and forever hating countries like America, instead of the Marxist creeps who hijacked America.

They've taken religion away. They've destroyed the one religion feared by all – Catholicism – because our children were well-behaved and knowledgeable, language proficient, and endowed with a love for our Creator. Incidentally, science and religion go hand in hand. When we say that God created heaven and earth in seven days, each day could stand for millions of years. Evolution and religion are compatible.

I believe that the Catholic pedophilia scandal was the work of evil forces that placed the final nail in our coffin. Let's bring back the Baltimore Catechism and throw the Marxist whackos out.

Even Earth Day is a part of this scheme of God and nature being one. Just look at what these whackos have done since the sixties. They've created a drug culture, violence through stupid videos and television shows, disrespect for parents, dumbo audiences who laugh at bathroom humor and four letter words, teens who can't speak well and who know little about American history or the Constitution but plenty about Britney Spears and her very young sister. Bad parenting has led to the troubles of these young sisters who certainly have enough money to care for a child, but it's the father at home that counts.

Shows like Mad TV (Change of Heart) wherein freakazoids called comics attempt to make people laugh with crude, unfunny skits, should be thrown off the air lest someone from a foreign country think that this is American humor. Certainly, young minds should not be subjected to this.

We have thousands of American servicemen committing suicide. Why? Because of the fact that seeing blood close up is a lot different from riding down a pretend street in Grand Theft Auto, heisting cars and killing people.

Television has become a dangerous weapon against the young if not monitored, and, of course, I've heard the lie that most children are not affected by watching these shows. Not so. Violence begets violence. Expose a child to these shows and cursing at school every day, and you have a different child on your hands.

Congress has been complicit in every problem we have. Remember what I said about the Bahai religion in Iran. Well, on C-SPAN (7-08), Representative Kirk introduced H. Resolution 1008, which would give money to Iranian Bahais who are being persecuted. AIPAC must have reached the congressman, because the Bahai religion is considered Jewish-inspired. I wonder who gets our money.

President Clinton allowed millionaires to become billionaires with all kinds of deregulation and mergers. Now, his wife, Hillary, has promised her Jewish audiences that she will dutifully "obliterate" a sovereign country, Iran, which would cost us trillions of dollars and more enemies. Wars will be the future of America, the once great land of rule of law and freedom of speech, the speech which addressed government wrongs.

Senator McCain, the war hero, pledged his loyalty to Israel almost daily during the campaign. He and his puppeteer, Senator Lieberman, looked as though they were joined at the hip.

In America today, it's the CEO making the big bucks. They're the ones telling the 50-year-olds to take their pensions and "git." They're the ones telling doctors to 'take it or leave it.' I wonder what people will do when they need neurosurgeons. Maybe they'll call Hillary at 3 a.m. and ask her to negotiate with the two neurosurgeons who will be left. Just look at your health insurance statements wherein a doctor asks for $250 and gets $25 – if he's lucky. National health care? You're kidding, right?

We have a problem with too many appointees in government from Goldman Sachs – Secretary of the Treasury, Henry Paulson, William Cohen, Governor Corzine, former Secretary of the Treasury Robert Rubin – advising President Obama while 50-year-olds are looking for jobs.

Because of the censorship on radio and in the media, we can't share our opinions. We can't share the truth, so corporate crime proliferates. We're told that if it weren't for corporations, there would be no jobs, except that jobs and the corporations left this country.

All of the signs with "World Peace," the UN, NATO, are nothing more than war machines, armed to the nines, working for the Super Rich. It's getting to a point where one million dollars won't be enough to sustain a family and a home and a car, or anything else.

Knowing the past of President Obama, I have no hope that he will be any different from McCain or any of the other politicians thrown at us, except for Ron Paul. Obama has already proven to be a regionalist when he was State Senator in Chicago. He is for federal mandates in schools – the sex ed, drug ed, and environmental programs. Environment is fine except when it's taught to indoctrinate the young into paying a global tax. We are not the keepers of the world, nor should we contaminate the environment with our missiles, bombs, and chemicals. Obama also supports the free passage of illegals across our borders. He feels that sponsorship of illegals trespassing into our country is the "heartfelt" thing to do. It's not so heartfelt when we pay billions to support the new invaders with their drugs, guns, and families. President Obama apparently doesn't feel so heartfelt about those of us supporting this out of control invasion. Same with McCain.

When President Obama first became State Senator in Chicago (1997), he went along with the public subsidies to private developers. He supported controversial developers who made fortunes from public housing and who later went into high-end housing – thanks to our generous middle class which is forced to pay for partnerships of the rich. (Example: Philadelphia stadiums, etc.) One of his recipients was involved in the nice home which the former Senator acquired, but the President claims no favors were given. (Tony Rezko)

President Obama learns fast and, consequently, he wants to expand on Clinton's and George W's Faith-Based Initiatives. Suddenly, separation of church and state doesn't matter. Just give subsidies to these con artists called ministers, and they'll bring out the vote for their benefactors. It's a con game which has to come to a halt. But Obama wants a special place for the Faith-Based.

Notice that those Afro-Americans who criticize America have done very well, like Reverend Wright, Obama's pastor. All of them have assimilated into the culture because of their language skills. No ebonics for this group.

MSNBC often invites Professor Eric Dyson, Georgetown, to tediously reflect on slavery and white culpability. The Professor speaks as fast as an Acela train, repeating the same diatribe again and again. Dyson: "We live in the land of 'AMNESIA'." He went on to say that "children have to see black policemen, firemen, and teachers, not just the genius of Oprah and Obama." Unless Professor Dyson has been in solitary confinement for many years, he would have noticed that black policemen and firemen, black doctors and nurses, judges, attorneys, actors, musicians, congressmen and mayors have been around for decades. In effect, he is telling his students that he made it but that they are too stupid.

And, ah yes, the genius of Oprah and Obama. Let's get real. Geraldine Ferraro, former congresswoman, was right and everyone knows it. Oprah and Obama reached towering heights because of affirmative action. They stay on top so long as they know what they can and cannot say.

Congresswoman Cynthia McKinney lost her job when she naively spoke out against the situation in the Mideast. Big money defeated her. When Congressman Conyers, also black, called for a 911 investigation, he was relegated to a basement room in the Capitol. So much for black power or free speech.

Reverend Wright can talk about those gosh awful rich white people and bad America, but he lives in a super-high-end home, and I'm certain that his children go to school with some of those gosh awful rich white people. His ranting and raving is show time for the downtrodden who really believe that blacks in America have no chance. The Reverend knows what to say in order to keep the division going or he wouldn't have been given $15 million in U.S. Government grants for food, low income housing, and other charity projects. His church has become a multi-million dollar enterprise. Would he have reached this height in Africa? I don't think so.

While we peasants argue about race, abortion rights, and homosexuality, the powers in the media and boardrooms are deciding our futures, and it's not good. There will be endless wars, higher gas prices, property and utility bills through the roof. If any of you believe that crime, drugs, rampant weather changes, and a failing education system are accidents, think again.

The Clintons, good little doobys, have amassed over $100 million in the last ten years. Fifteen million of that money was due to Bill's visits to places like Dubai. If you remember, Dubai is part of the United Arab Emirates. George W. wanted to lease our ports to Dubai, without any input from us. This is another giveaway of our assets with no congressional investigation because corporations and lobbyists are running America like a family business. What did Bill Clinton promise Dubai for the $15 million he received? We'll never know. I wouldn't pay this leech fifteen cents.

Meanwhile, we're allowed to call in to station WPHT and talk trivia with Dr. Mazz, a new addition to "Big Talk." His topic: "I'd like you to weigh in on why a waitress wearing a wedding ring makes more than a waitress wearing an engagement ring. Then we can talk about the Kentucky Derby." (5-4-08) Yippee!

So long as this chicken head keeps on trivia, his job will be guaranteed. Just don't mention Ron Paul.

Because of our do-nothing Congress, our food inspectors are ineffective, our form of government has been changed without the consent of the governed, and corporations and lobbyists rule.

Congress has untouchable pensions, excellent health care, exercise rooms, immunity from lawsuits, restaurants, and security guards to protect them from us. They must feel incomparable. It reminds me of the Tibetans and how protestors are treated by the Chinese. It's coming to a town near you. It already has!

They gave Governor Corzine a pass – probably because he was Chairman at Goldman Sachs – when he lately "decreed" that New Jersey's 323 towns with populations of less than 10,000 people will have to "merge" or face drastic cuts. He threatened zero funding for towns with less than 5,000 people (*Washington Post*, 3-23-08). This means loss of police and firemen jobs and loss of local government jobs. (He wants to "regionalize" or "consolidate" so that we, the people, are easier to manage.)

But he doesn't mention that Goldman Sachs (Treasury Secretary Robert Rubin) received $50 billion from us when they made poor investments in Mexico. Nor does he mention that Goldman Sachs and Jay P. Morgan took over Bear and Stearns security firm with $30 billion from our unconstitutional Federal Reserve Bank of private bankers. Fourteen thousand employees lost jobs and are living on pensions. But he wants to save us money by "consolidating." Yeah, right!

Will Congress investigate this takeover? Not if they want to keep their jobs! We are a country being run by a plutocracy – wherein only billionaires and multi-multi-millionaires have a voice. (And this doesn't include sports figures!)

How long are we going to be threatened with the future insolvency of social security and health care by our elected representatives and their lobbyists? If we can bail out Goldman Sachs, we can bail out social security and health care. If not, the "private" bankers at the Federal Reserve who print money out of thin air will have to forgive our debt as they forgave the debts of those third world countries who owed us money. No more bailing out Wall Street and placing the debt on future Americans. While we're at it, anyone who signed NAFTA and GATT with its 31,000 pages and gave away American jobs, should be charged with treason – "the free traitors." Allowing congressmen and congresswomen to retire in luxury without facing serious charges of negligence after they were complicit in changing the face of America and bankrupting us with higher taxes, higher utility bills, higher pump prices, loss of jobs, a failing educational system, and an environment of fear – not from terrorists – but from politicians on the take, would be a dereliction of our constitutional duty.

When corporate czars like Bill Gates can get a representative, Lamar Smith (Texas), to propose a bill raising the quota of H-1B visas from 250,000 to 400,000, disregarding the fact that we have 300,000 students graduating in the fields of science and math, representative Smith should be tossed out. Apparently, Mr. Gates isn't satisfied with American graduates; he prefers Pakistanis. But the American grads are free to buy his computers!

If I were not in Washington, D.C. on 4-10-08, I would never have known that there were blocks of trucks in protest to the diesel fuel price, lined up en route to the Capitol. There was no mention of this fact on the major news networks. This is censorship ala Soviet Russia by a media that has become the thought police.

We listened to Senator McCain talk about the forces fighting for "our way of life." I'd like to know what life he is referring to. During the decades Senator McCain has been in office, American life has changed drastically.

We have children, six and up, who now engage in "cage fighting," a blood sport in which the two contenders kick, punch, and dig into the faces of their opponents. Unfortunately, these children are at the mercy of their barbaric parents. Any child who kicks another child with all of his might, like the girls from Florida who kidnapped and beat a cheerleader mercilessly, needs mental help along with his or her parents. Too bad that many couples who would really love to have children are unable to, but parasites like these abusive parents seem to have no problem bearing children.

Our schools lack discipline and a dress code. No child should come to school with black fingernails and Gothic-like clothing. I feel that my taxes would be better spent on children whose parents care. Violent children should not be accepted without anger management,. They are a bad influence on other children who become desensitized to violence and cursing for no reason. Rosie O'Donnell's "America" would be a good avenue to explore – they need love and direction.

Crack-addicted parents smoking joints with young children should serve real jail time. Health and Human Services is no answer to child abuse. Some of the social workers need help themselves. We need to bring back orphanages with couples who are paid very high salaries to care for unfortunate children. The couples should be selected because of their success as parents. And their salaries should exceed $250,000 a year.

The fascist media has brainwashed us into feeling guilt when we say "you people," even though parents and families use that term all of the time. Would they prefer that we say "you who are gathered here." Just think about how low Americans have sunk when we are told what is politically correct, and we conform.

We're no longer able to praise Thomas Jefferson, a slave owner. So what; he wrote the Declaration of Independence. And Washington, the father of our country, has no celebration nor did Abraham Lincoln who abolished slavery, until Obama entered the scene.

Instead, we have our new leader, Martin Luther King, who certainly deserves praise, but days and nights of recounting what happened when he was shot 40 years ago is absurd. In my opinion, King was merely the catalyst who seized a moment in time when civilized people, both black and white and Asian, would no longer tolerate separation of rights for blacks. No one should go to the rear of the bus because of his color. It's inhumane and stupid. Lots of people were discriminated against, not only blacks.

I believe that many bright black men could have done the same thing if the motivation were there. Motivation is the asset of the successful.

Under the Fourteenth Amendment of Equal Protection, we should have no special groups. It's reverse discrimination, and it's destroying this country because it's making racism a constant problem, to the exclusion of real domestic problems. I have no desire to see Michelle Obama, with bitter undertones which she can't hide, express feelings for the oppressed. We are the ones who are oppressed – the ones she wants to avenge for past issues until we have no money for our own families. She was well educated and still has resentment towards white people. Today, no one claims responsibility for his own actions. We have rewarded promiscuous women with undeserving lifestyles for several decades. Having fatherless children is a profitable business. They have no taxes to worry about. No rent or food bills to pay. No wonder we have so many black and white rebellious children forced to accept handouts. This lifestyle is all they know. There are many black people involved in regional projects – many from Illinois – who make a nice living being subsidized by the rest of us with project after project.

Earmarks (pork projects) are added to bills having nothing to do with the bill itself, such as war funding, transportation, etc. For example, Congressman Kanjorski (D. Penna.) created a Regional Equipment Center, Cornerstone Technologies, in his district supposedly for jobs. Taxpayers gave $10 million to this project which totally served his family. (Now bankrupt.) Was there an investigation? Of course not! Speaker of the House, Dennis Hastert, a Republican, used a bill to create a trust for his wife and family. He backed the building of the Prairie Highway, over $200 million from the taxpayers and a headache for the farmers involved. One of the families had lived in this farm area for two centuries only to find a highway cutting through the front of their property. Hastert bought 137,000 acres of land knowing that the highway was coming. He then sold his share to developers for millions of dollars. Nice profit for a man whose fortune was $250,000 when entering Congress and multimillions when retiring from Congress. No wonder an 81-year-old woman farmer called him "Hastert, the bastard." We have many in Congress feeding their families on pork benefits. (Earmarks, Chris Wallace, 6/8/08, Fox News)

On the Homeland Security Bill, President Bush included liability protection for vaccine manufacturers. (I'd assume that it covers China.)We need more prisons, not foreign bases.

Most of the anchors, guests, and correspondents on TV are either black or Jewish, with trained seal Christians going along. Only Jack Cafferty ("It's Getting Ugly Out There"), CNN, manages to speak his mind as much as he can without jeopardizing his job. At least he gave Ron Paul a mention.

It beats me how anyone could say that President George W. Bush is a good Christian. How could anyone who has caused the death of 4,000 men and the wounding of over 25,000 men and women be anything? Only Stalin and warmongers can answer that question. We hear the "conservative" talk show hosts take calls from veterans who served in Iraq: "Thank you for your service to America, my friend." Knowing that these talk show hosts would never invite a guest on who was a "vet against the war," it kind of makes one gag.

When I hear that our military "storms through houses in Iraq like tornadoes, separating the men and women and children, and jailing innocent fathers," I question why God doesn't step in and smite these senseless, violent troops who don't represent America, but demagogues like George W. Iraq has checkpoints like those in Israel…. I wonder whose idea that was! "We have convoys acting like death trains going through streets at 60 mph crashing into cars and killing civilians." How would we like it??

As I see it, these brutal cowards are the same ones who probably post their senseless acts on Youtube in order to incite other senseless cowards to do the same thing…throwing soft drinks at workers on fast food lines. These men are the bullies – the 'young' bullies America is stuck with. If someone attacked these faceless nut jobs in their hometowns, they would be shaking like leaves on a tree.

Any man with a sense of history wouldn't be in Iraq, and we have to stop them before they 'volunteer' to do the same thing in Iran – killing brilliant people who are unarmed civilians. (Read all about it in "Collateral Damage" by Chris Hedges and Laila Al Arian, whose father, a doctor, has been jailed for nothing.)

Staff Sgt. T. J. Westphal (Iraq – 2004-05): "I'd be an insurgent, too, if someone did this to my family." (WYBE, 6-10-08)

Christian Zionists, I believe, have captured center stage. These are the people defending more wars, more George Bush, more McCains and Hillarys – all war hawks – the uneducated masses who are helping to destroy the futures of their children. These are the fools who are made to think that God is on their side and that Moslems actually want to die in order to see the 72 virgins.

Speaking of the "72 virgins" propaganda which filled our airwaves for years, I listened to NPR (WHYY) on 6-8-08 and heard that the Jewish religion believes in 72 names for God. One of them is Yahweh. Another is "quick to anger." I remember now that my Moslem husband remarked, "How could God, who created the entire world and all of its beauty, be 'quick to anger' or be a 'jealous God'? Makes no sense."

This country has been done unto by a treasonous Congress. Capitalism is now a monopoly with no caps or rules or regulations of antitrust. A bunch of super rich, old, white men, who should be giving money away at this point in their lives, are still looking for power – power to destroy the young.

We need diversity in foreign policy appointees and no one group should control America's destiny. Also, we should not have a cavalcade of attorneys and people in backrooms running the business of Palestine's destiny. We are hated, as Israel is, all over the world, while Americans are watching Britney Spears.

Listening to our former ally, Tony Blair, answer questions before Parliament, I realized that even the Brits have more free speech and open dialogue than we do on the Middle East. Parliament members asked compassionate questions about the Palestinians: "Should Israel be occupiers of Palestine?" Tony Blair dismissed the question but admitted that the two hour wait in the blazing sun that Palestinians must go through before reaching Jerusalem is turmoil that causes anger. Also, Blair said that the Palestinian population is mostly under 25 years of age and that, with no hope for jobs, they join Hamas.

I wonder how they feel when American tourists sail through to Bethlehem and Jerusalem without a problem. Hagee and the other Zionist preachers will one day answer for this interminable tyranny which they and our unconscionable presidents have brought to the Palestinians. (C-SPAN, 6-8-08)

Now that we are positive that we went to war in Iraq for oil – because of a slip made by Senator McCain (5-2-08), we don't have to call it "conspiracy talk" any longer.

In my chapter on Electric Power and Ken Lay, I discussed the fact that FDR, our socialist president who started the mess we're in today along with Woodrow Wilson (the League of Nations, Income Tax, Federal Reserve), did one thing right. He regulated the obscene profits of utility companies. When our Congress was looking at $4.00 a gallon for gasoline, it turned down a bid to tax 25% of oil profits and to stop tax breaks for oil companies. (C-SPAN, 6-8-08) We gave $15 billion in subsidies to Big Oil.

As you can see, corruption is systemic, and nothing will be done to keep gas prices lower until all of the "experienced" Congressmen are tossed out of their jobs and we start drilling.

The same energy czars, Exxon Mobil, etc., with subsidies from us are now investing in alternative fuels which they know are prohibitive for the average person. Ethanol, solar panels, windmills. For those who encourage windmills, go to Holland and for heaven's sake, don't forget your clogs. We'll pay your way!

The globalists want all traditions buried in the sands of time. Young people are not allowed to hear about the past. No old books. No older people. No rule of law. Only filth and trash for young, naïve minds who will regret the loss of liberty, but then it will be too late. Liberty comes with a price.

Neglectful parents, a failing educational system, together with an impotent police force by design and the Nazi press have created a group of unrepentant, young American boys who get their kicks from targeting bikers with paintballs. Let's stop giving freebees to these ingrates and put them to work!

It's obvious that the "nature of man" has been successfully changed. The mindset of those in the military has changed from World War I when it was strange to shoot another human being. By World War II things changed because of the fact that we had been "struck" by the Japanese (or did we know?). At this point, between the sexualization of the young and violent videos dreamed up by military nut jobs, our volunteer military will shoot anything moving. Our First Lady is encouraging recruits. For Afghanistan?

Today, we don't hear a word about the security of the United States;

it's always about Israel. Congressmen and presidents have to pay homage to Israel, that country committing genocide of the Palestinians, with our condonation. Palestinians live in a police state with no sewers.

Candidates are afraid to lose their jobs if they don't say the right thing. This is blackmail. We hear about the infamous Jewish vote.

Even the Pope was admonished on his last visit to the United States (4-08). He was asked to exclude the word "conversion" from a Catholic prayer. Jewish influence has been blasphemous on the Catholic religion. Out with the old and in with the new. Rabbi Arthur Schneider remarked: "Our relationship with Catholics has not been good."

Although I mentioned this in an earlier chapter, I think that it bears repeating. Two Catholic nuns, who were living during World War II in Italy, wrote a book about this very thing. "Pope Pius XII did everything humanly possible to hide and convert the Jews, short of getting executed." Zionists want blood.

I believe that America has suffered a coup. All important jobs belong to one group. It's becoming more and more evident that a tangled web has been woven. It's painful and it's treasonous. What happened to the Palestinians will soon happen to us. Weather changes, etc. are only the beginning. In 1948, 700,000 Palestinians were forced to leave their homes by the Israeli forces. Today, less than three million refugees live in Gaza. They have no water or electricity, so they have improvised with their own electric setup. More Palestinian refugees fled to Lebanon, and some of us remember the 1981 shelling and slaughter of Palestinians living in the Sabra and Shatila refugee camps at the hands of the pro-Israel "Christian" philangists. (Hence, the pro-Israel fascists say "the Moslems hate Christians 'And' Jews.") Then in 2006, another slaughter took place in Lebanon, destroying the infrastructure, etc. because of a missing Israeli soldier. And we sent the pro-Israel Condoleeza Rice out there, the woman who points to African carnage but who just can't see what's happening in Palestine. Probably too much money is blinding her view. Again, I advise young people to master the English language (and other languages, if you can) so that you can start replacing these unconscionable excuses for human beings. They are masters at saying nothing, and it is they who control your destiny.

Always, in countries run over by totalitarianism, the first group to be sacrificed is the farmers. Farmers in the United States have been taxed out of family farms so that developers can move in. Conglomerates like Archer

Daniel Midland reign. The rest of the farmers are either paid not to grow crops or they are looking for jobs. Read about the French Revolution and how it started with grain shortages. (We have an excuse: the alternative fuels.) And remember what I said about the EPA's breaching dams, which could be responsible for the farm floods, etc. (Clinton)

In the 1950s I remember my father suggesting that we should feed the whole world with our grain and, at the same time, make international friends. If he were to come back and see reptile-like men and women with tattoos, smoking pot and proud of it – with nose rings, etc., he'd probably die all over again.

My father loved America and was generous to a fault. I'm happy that he isn't around to see how America has deteriorated into a tyrannical, secretive government, operating on fear. And I know that he would have stood up and protested the movie "Reservoir Dogs" with John "Revolta." No father should be in a movie showing a man dancing around someone tied to a chair while having his ear carved off – to beautiful music. There are few real men left today. No standup men and women that "used to be." What a crisis we face. No McCarthys. No Maureen Heatons.

Few young people today have pride in their jobs. When I grew up in Little Italy (South Philly), one man with lots of energy and common sense but little formal education rose to the status of multimillionaire because of his insights and the improvements he made in sewer construction. He started out as the low man on the totem pole and rose to the top.

George W. Bush visited Israel with his wife, Laura, in order to celebrate the 60th year of Israel's independence. "Independence" from what? The Israelis took over Palestinian land, set up countless checkpoints so that mothers couldn't reach medical help for their babies, and then reduced them to a maze and no industry. No jobs, except for those no one would want. No hope. If they dare to throw a rocket into Israel, hell reigns on them for days with all kinds of retaliation. Little by little, Palestinians are dying. We're told that Israel, our ally, is a democracy. It is not; it's occupied territory. We're told that Israel has our values. Well, speak for yourself. I couldn't torture the lowest insect the way we torture people. Notice that there are few older people left in Palestine, if any. Israel wants the young, like our young in the United States, to be desperate enough to beg for jobs, any jobs – ala Karl Marx – with no memory of grandparents who could tell them what "used to be." Like me.

When the former president spoke before the Israeli Knesset (Parliament), he was teary-eyed and fraught with emotion. (5-14-08) He was given a standing ovation, which just about gagged me, as he promised to be a good little dooby and criticize anyone who was in favor of talks with Iran. Somehow JFK could talk to Khrushchev who had missiles pointed in our direction and said, "We will bury you." President Nixon could talk to the Red Chinese, and President Reagan could tell the Soviets to take down the wall, but we aren't allowed to talk to the Iranian president, Ahmadinejad. Israel forbids our speaking to Iran without preconditions. Netanyahu, who went to school in Cheltenham Township, Pennsylvania, came from Israel to "suggest" to Bush that short of bombing Iran, we should ask them to dismantle their nuclear program. Meantime, Israel, the most violent terrorists of all time, have from 100 to 500 nuclear missiles.

We're all here for a very short time. We can't allow our children to go to foreign countries and massacre innocent people, because of "no jobs." We must fight for jobs to return to this country. And not military jobs.

George Bush and the bankers he bailed out should be in jail for lending mortgage money to those who couldn't afford it. If politicians won't help, we must vote them out and do the job ourselves. So far there is no accountability for the bailout.

We built an Embassy in Iraq for $750 billion. That's billion. It has 21 buildings, a swimming pool, cafeterias and room for troops, plus offices. It's as large as the Vatican.

Tom Ricks ("The Gamble"), Senior Pentagon Correspondent for the *Washington Post*, said, "We'll be in Iraq for years to come. Iran worries me. Obama's Vietnam will be Pakistan. For "several" years, we'll have to manage it." (Meet the Press, 2-8-09)

Imagine! The Pentagon has taken over our lives with no explanation to average people. Our future is predetermined by a bunch of old cowboys and bullies, scaring innocent people all over the world. "Our chickens will come home to roost" if Americans don't wake up, but I know that the chickens are on the way. And our lives will be worth nothing.

The Pentagon budget should be cut drastically. Only weeks after President Obama was elected, the Pentagon wants new, top of the line helicopters at a cost of eleven billion dollars – made in Europe, by Aerbus, not in America, by Boeing. Have any of these thugs heard of "Buy America?" (2-16-09) Oh, I forgot. Their money is unvested in foreign countries!

As I wrote this book, I remembered the fear that whistleblowers suffered over the years. Not being able to speak is a crime against humanity. The military is no longer there to protect the rights of U.S. citizens. Just look at Ruby Ridge and the slaughter that took place with the ATF as backup. These victims were ordinary citizens. We shouldn't wonder why neighbors who witness drug killings refuse to talk. Who's there to protect them? They don't really know whether or not corrupt policemen are involved. Although there are wonderful policemen, there are those, too, who show no mercy, according to films exposing the kicking of handicapped prisoners. This is barbaric and un-American.

In the mid-seventies, I remember a Lebanese professor at Temple University, who was giving his students the other side of the story about those who believed in Islam. Today, we hear lie after lie after lie, and no one could speak out. He was respected and very popular. He and his whole family were murdered. Someone or some persons gained access to his house in Cheltenham Township, Pennsylvania, when his wife went outside to dispose of the trash. Nothing was pursued because of fear, coupled with the fact that his family was in Lebanon. Shortly after that, a rabbinical school was opened down the street from his home. The whole unsolved case gave me an eerie feeling.

I've heard people say, "I'd speak out but 'they' might recognize my voice." When I called Michael, the Zionist, Medved, I'm certain that they wanted me to shake with fear while on hold – while they traced my number, and then refused to put me on the air.

Millions of people know what's happening. As a matter of fact, a long time ago when Medved put me on the air and allowed me to speak for two minutes, a male caller remarked, "she should have your show, not you." From then on I was persona non grata.

This fear of speaking out is pervasive in colleges. Students soon learn what is not politically correct. It's tyranny, and most of the presidents brought us here.

Those of you who say nothing are considered dummies by those in control of your destinies. You will suffer anyway by one of their criminal acts – either another 911 or some horrible weather phenomenon. It doesn't matter that you're quiet. They care about nothing except money and power.

You must start connecting the dots. Isn't it odd that we bomb countries hiding "so-called terrorists" in foreign countries, but we don't dare bomb homes of Mexican drug cartels! Drugs and a corrupt government are ruining America, not the Islamic fascists. We're in their country; they are not in ours.

Look at the fiery plane crash #3407, near Buffalo (2-13-09). Beverly Eckert, a young widow who lost her husband in 911, was on that plane. All of us saw the words "911 widow in crash" – over and over, on the TV screen. O'Reilly and the other hosts like him, explained that "Beverly tried to keep the memory of 911 alive." But that was only half true. What this attractive, slender, blonde woman tried to do was get a "truth commission" to go over 911 details. She accepted no money, as most of the other families did. Instead, she tried to talk about 911 to more and more people. In one interview, this courageous widow said, "My husband has been betrayed by his government." She tried to sue for her money and the truth, but she's gone and the evil masters of our destinies are still floating around in luxury.

To his credit, only Anderson Cooper, CNN, told the whole story.

I was startled when I saw the TV headline "Politics of Change" shortly after the election of President Obama. If it were not for whistleblowers like Maureen Heaton, I would never have gotten the connections. And "they" feel that her facts died with her, and they can be bold.

Meanwhile we support 700 military bases throughout the world, protecting corporations against the protests of the common people. And, of course, we have troops in 130 countries who really don't want us there. These troops would better serve our country by annihilating the drug trafficking problem right here in America.

Diversions are consuming this country. California, against the vote of the taxpayers, succumbed to the wishes of an activist judge who decreed same-sex marriage legal. Marriage was to be protection for children of a man and woman. Anything else is a mockery of religion and the justice system, and has nothing to do with civil rights. These are civil wrongs.

Diane Feinstein hopes that her amnesty bill, providing amnesty for three million illegals plus their families, will go through during some of these diversions even though the protests of the public stopped an earlier try for amnesty of 20 million illegals. Feinstein's approach is step-by-step Fabian Socialism.

The Farm Bill, which will cover food stamps, more subsidies to farmers who don't need them and projects that have nothing to do with farming, will cost us $300 billion. The bill, 17,000 pages long, was admittedly read by no one.

Also, on the strength of a woman 911 caller, who pretended to be a 16-year-old victim of rape, the YFZ ranch in Texas was raided by our right wing loonies in the ATF, the same group who took down American citizens in Waco, Texas, under Clinton and Janet Reno. There was no evidence that a rape had taken place, and that woman caller was never cited for the damage she caused to taxpayers and the families whose children were taken away by the Child Protection Agency under firepower. More than 400 children, including babies being nursed, toddlers and older children, were placed in foster homes, miles away from other siblings. The Child Protection Agency is known for its not sensing the impending death of abused children on their watch, and I question the sanity of their placing so many children in foster homes so quickly. Again, this is big government at its worst. Fortunately, a Texas judge released the children to their parents. Another diversion?

Over the past few months we've heard callers and guests referred to as "extreme leftists" and "conservatives." Actually, conservative always meant smaller government, rule of law, and strict adherence to the Constitution, whereas leftist or liberal stood for higher taxes, big government, entitlements, regulations on small business, and a very free interpretation of the Constitution with 'activist' judges legislating laws, formerly and constitutionally the duty of the legislators. Simply put: they take money from those who work and place it in the pockets of those who don't until all the pockets are empty except those belonging to the politicians and the super rich. Some call it socialism; I call it tyranny, and tyranny hasn't ever worked, hence, the influx of immigrants escaping the tyranny of third world countries where the rich decide your future.

In America today, we have those people who emigrated from Eastern Europe decades ago trying to "enforce" the socialism they left behind on us. And they've been successful. So long as people vote for freebies, our liberties are lost. At this moment, the media is again playing us for fools. While then Senator Obama was in Berlin, CNN was playing a series on "Black America," as though affirmative action legislation just passed. While America may be getting ready for another military strike on Iran, we're talking about affirmative action laws of 44 years ago. (7-24-08) Another diversion? Also, stories about the Italian Mafia are always popular. There is no news about the Russian Mafia in the United States or the fact that Congressman Kucinich introduced a bill to impeach President Bush. Congressman Kucinich is a true patriot who puts America first. None of the neo cons on talk radio would dare mention his name; they'd rather call true patriots "America haters." At this point, mostly parents of servicemen and the servicemen themselves enjoy freedom of speech. Their contribution is always the same: "We're doing a fabulous job with the surge." It's monotonous gobbledy gook.

Whenever I hear "women for Hillary," I'm sorry that these fools feel that Any woman would be a good president, and that, with no reading, they're actually allowed to vote. IQ tests might be a good thing. It's hard for me to believe that many women voted for Bill Clinton because they thought he was handsome. They should be asking how these two ugly Americans amassed over $110 million in ten years and why they live in a lavish home, away from the freebie people they love so much. Hillary and Bill are all heart.

Both Democrats and Republicans have supported big government with their new departments, such as Homeland Security and domestic projects ordered by regionalists. Both parties voted for globalism when they passed NAFTA and GATT and placed us, a sovereign country, under the authority of the World Trade Organization wherein we get only one vote on trade, just like any other third world country. Americans are funding this global policy just as we fund Wall Street and countries that don't want us there.

Whether it's the so-called liberal station of MSNBC or the neo con station, Fox News, talk is the same. Hosts argue pro-war and antiwar, but President Bush received all of the money for war that he needed, from both parties. Hosts argue about illegal immigration, pro and con, but nothing happens in Congress so long as they need the illegal votes. Talk is cheap but it's the result that counts, and the useful idiots blocking antiwar calls should live in infamy. Notice that both so-called liberal talk shows and so-called conservative stations agree on one thing: Israel. And no one dares to question their wanting the United States to strike Iran. It's pathetic. The only reporter who dares question what we're doing is Helen Thomas, who has been there many, many years and was treated quite shabbily by White House

Press Secretary Tony Snow. I'd like to know when this damn coup took place and left Israel in charge, and why higher ups are not in jail. I'd like to know why we are still using Zbigniew Brzezinski and Kissinger behind the scenes advising Americans. They should have retired decades ago.

Because of the fact that the Nazi media censors all talk, the same type of forces responsible for China's Cultural Revolution in the 1950s are at work here in the United States. Chairman Mao Zedong wanted to liberate the people from a complex government and restore communism. The youthful Red Guard helped; it's always the youth needed to "change." Change was needed for the "common good." China started land reform and took land away from monks. With no religion, things are easier to "change."

In the United States we have our Department of Environmental Protection doing the nasty work of changing our Constitution and our freedoms by passing its own laws. For instance, colleges and universities get grant money for degrees in Environment and in Regionalism, which go hand in hand. They know that laws on property takeovers and zoning regulations would never pass public scrutiny, so they enter our lives through the back door – secret legislation. This is why we hear from corrupt government agents that we have a "living" constitution. In simplistic terms, it means that the Fifth Amendment in America today, 2009, has no relevance, so "we'll change it." Does this mean that freedom of speech, etc. will also disappear? It already has. Just look at the rare committee meetings the public used to attend, wherein policemen who used to protect us now protect the government, and citizens can be led out of the room for a "disruption." (Robert Levy and William Mellor, "The Dirty Dozen.") "Judges who should be defending separation of powers are leading the pack in unraveling our Constitution." Again, it's out with the old and in with the "new." It's comparable to what "agents of change" are doing with religion. Either the Ten Commandments are relevant or they are not, in 2009. Either Christ was crucified, died and was buried and now sits on the right hand of His Father, or not. If the Bible is "Living" and Christ was a hippy, as depicted, walking along drug-filled streets aiding druggies rather than smiting the drug dealers, then toss the "living" tome out because "anything goes."

Under the Fifth Amendment to the Constitution, it says "Nor is anyone to be deprived of his liberty or property without a fair hearing or a court trial. Furthermore, private property may not be condemned or appropriated for public use unless it is fully and fairly paid for." Under the DEP, government agents can confiscate your property, without compensation, because of an endangered fly, which they have already done. Government can set aside millions of acres for wetlands, wildlife and whatever it desires, including farmland for housing development or Section 8 housing for those families who have no jobs but who wish to live in the suburbs with people who do have jobs. This is all accomplished without public input, by behind-the-scene fools who were just given a degree in Environmental Protection.

The DEP can also stop oil drilling on land in California and Florida, and many other places in the United States, especially when the Big Oil companies like the status quo which allows them to keep prices at the pump high. Surely the Big Oil companies knew that demand would be high and supply low when we started bombing Iraq eight years ago. Bombing countries which have done nothing to us does not "make friends or influence people." We now have a retired oil man representing Big Oil hitting our television stations with "let's start drilling and stop paying the Mideast for oil costing $700 billion." Again, these men think that we're all a bunch of indoctrinated fools. They own most of the oil, if not all, bringing in the $700 billion. When a country like Iran wants to nationalize its oil, we bomb them. I would like the money to be spread around by hiring new oil men who can get the job done, and fast.

Chris Hedges ("Collateral Damage"), a reporter who has been in war zones, made these observations (C-SPAN2, 4-27-08): "The Christian Right has been a most damaging influence in America. Neo cons and the Christian Right engage in utopia and disregard reality. The messianic right wing minority has taken over our country.

"We send in reporters to war zones who have no understanding of the antecedence of the crisis. There is corruption in media and ignorance. Allowing AIPAC (Israel lobby) to decide foreign policy is dangerous. Yitzak Rabin, former Prime Minister of Israel, wanted justice for the Palestinians, and he was murdered. Rabin hated AIPAC and called them "scumbags."

"Eliot Abrams (National Security Council) knows as much about the Middle East as he knows about Nicaragua. We have destroyed Iraq. We have thiefdoms, militias, etc. There is no more Iraq. We've tortured human beings. We need the Rule of Law and respect for human rights." (Hedge's comments were paraphrased, WYBE.)

And the Nazi media continues to ask antiwar callers "Do you want us to lose in Iraq? Or, why do you hate America?" If there were any justice out there, these talk show hosts would be in jail along with their Nazi bosses.

Please understand that regionalism is part of the NWO. Communist countries had it and now we do. What China called "land reform," we call "land use." The breaking down of state borders was only the beginning of borderless countries – Mexico, Canada, and the United States. It's a government within a government, and young "graduates" in regionalism – who know nothing about the past when regionalism was designated "tyranny" in Indiana – are profiting from taking down the final pieces of America.

We have to ask ourselves where the seed money comes from. Where do individuals get the money to buy up whole neighborhoods? Where do they get the money to build wings on hospitals and buy off food companies and corporations? It takes money to make money and this question should be at the top of the list. The Federal Reserve has no accountability; it can lend money to anyone – secretly.

China is bankrolling our wars by buying our Treasury Bills, while we buy their products at Walmart and dollar stores. How long will this stupidity go on?

Let's bring all of the military back from foreign countries. We have lots of work to do in the United States. Television stations carrying Sci-fi and other sick shows should be shut down. It's not free speech; it's license to assault. Producers of these so-called shows should be in mental hospitals with 24-7 surveillance, along with the so-called writers. The sole purpose of this garbage is to nullify any regard for life. Tying up and gagging women – it's always women – and then strapping them to tables where they are gutted with surgical instruments, is normal fare on Sci-Fi. And we wonder why women in America are abused. Blood everywhere, but let's have another study. Maybe two! Let's stop the propaganda coming from the Nazi media about honor killings and abuse of women in the Mid-East. With our record in the United States we can't point fingers at anyone. The news media covered the Moslem financier who beheaded his wife here in the United States. Maybe he watched Sci-Fi!

We don't need studies to conclude that those teens, absent parental guidance, are headed for disaster if we don't call a halt to this madness.

The Columbine tragedy was only the beginning of a very dangerous turn America is taking. The cry for help from troubled teens can't be ignored. Money spent for looney wars had better be spent on taking back our country.

Parents can't allow ruthless propagandists like Michael Medved, hiding behind his mustache, to air tales about how Christmas started. According to Medved, our Christmas celebration started out as a shoot-em-up, drunken, spectacle – outlawed by the Puritans – until the Hebraic influence entered the scene and brought in "some biblical sanity" and dignity.

What would we "cattle" Christians do without the Hebraic influence on Christmas? Especially obvious, this Catholic diatribe took place on his Sunday Edition, 12-22-07. A nice welcome for our celebration, and it was aired several times in case someone missed it – at times when children could listen.

To top it off, Liane Hansen, Weekend Edition on NPR – with federal subsidies, engaged in a timely conversation about Greg Epstein's class at Harvard. Seems that the purpose of the "humanist" class was to denigrate Christmas and all things religious. "Rewrite them," said Joe Hoffman, an atheist. "It's not enough to just tear down religion; you have to replace it with something, and that something is "humanism."

As for Santa: thirty-four million children require too many gifts for Santa Claus on a sleigh. We'll have to outsource to China. Maybe instead of the sleigh, we can have cargo ships replacing the reindeer. Elves can go out in mobile units like they do in Iraq.

Special ops can help. Norad could enter…." How clever!

The preceding diatribe sounded like the ranting of thoughtless adolescents with nothing better to do on the day before Christmas. If I were the dean at Harvard, these dolts would be out on the street the next day. They made Don Imus look like a monk.

Moses anyone? Maybe Hanukkah? The menorah? Ooops! I forgot. They're not Christian. Christians are looked upon – and rightly so – as inferior, noncombatant fools who don't question the ad nauseum portrayal of Christ as a hippy and worse.

When do we stop turning the other cheek and rescue our children from the dire effects of too much exposure to sex and violence during their latency period, five to eleven. (Sean O'Reilly, M.D., "Sex Education in the Schools")

If it takes civil disobedience, so be it, but this corrupt Congress and teachers who feel that they can experiment with our children must get the message or there won't be a future for any of us. The television producers are getting bolder and bolder with their four letter words and wanton display of crudity. Young people are surrounded with unneeded stimulation at a time when they should be laughing and learning languages, science, math, and U.S. History.

If there is any doubt in your mind that we have a one-party system, I hope that you watched George Bush's State of the Union Address. He was greeted with deafening applause and kisses from both parties. This man, who didn't follow his oath to protect our borders, should be tried for war crimes, but was welcomed like a king. During his same old cry for surges and threats to Iran, the yoyos in the audience, excluding the Supreme Court, jumped up and down seventy times with standing, stupid ovations. Where were those democrats who were against the war?

They're all the same. We need a third party to clean this mess up. Ron Paul is a good start. No, he's the only start!

Meanwhile, we're given Tyra Banks, top model, probably aspiring to be another Oprah Winfrey, and if she plays her cards right, as she is, she'll be rolling in dough.

On 2-8-08, she had a "sexpert" on, answering questions about sex., Sue Johanson, who apparently has her own show similar to sexpert Ruth Westheimer's. The audience, for the most part, looked college age and beyond.

There's something vile about elderly women who are viewed as great-grandmothers talking about sex – especially when they try to act savvy and humorous. Pathetic old women who should be setting an example for the young, instead, for money, they'll corrupt the younger generation in order to sell condoms, porn, and unhealthy lifestyles. Ditto for Hugh Hefner and his ditsy broads! It's over, Hef!

The effect of these sexperts on college-age students has been profound, because the older bearer of sex information seems legitimate and worthy of respect. I sometimes wonder whether or not these women – and there are lots of them like Mary Calderone – ever had sex.

We have college students talking about "friends with benefits." These are friends, whether lesbian or straight, who have no commitment to each other but who can be counted on for sex. After two generations of this carnal knowledge, this is the result.

The audience went along with the old pervert as she answered their questions from a bed, while Tyra tried to smile sweetly as though she were sniffing money. Total sellouts of the young!

But I noticed one big difference. Fifteen or even ten years ago, the women in the audience would have shown some modicum of modesty and pride. These are the brainwashed progeny of the '60s when the Vietnam War brought the after effects of drugs, alcohol, and promiscuity.

Thank God that there are tens of thousands of college-age students who have been unplussed by this perversion – because of strict parenting and watchfulness, but we don't see these examples. We are left with the children of those parents gullible enough to swallow the propaganda that anything old is bad – the Constitution, the Republic, music, marriage, education, a drugless society, people, freedom of speech – all of the things that made America great. And look at those who want to "change" what we had – Hillary Clinton and her snake-charming husband who thinks that he's bright, and a bunch of druggies and alcoholics from Hollywood and Washington. Lord have mercy.

Between sex education, drug education, Black History Month, Holocaust studies, La Raza, the Black Caucus, the Jewish Defamation League – we have no time for science or anything. Mind control reigns.

We've had forty-four years of civil rights legislation which has brought us black cities just as corrupt as any white machines ever were. Since World War II, we have been subjected to enough Holocaust history to serve us for four lifetimes. And we have proven in elections that color doesn't matter.

When do the rest of us get our turn to speak? When do we say "enough of this divisive programming?"

To listen to these special interest aficionados, one would think that the rest of us have led grief-free, work-free lives. It's time to get rid of the black caucuses, the NAACP, Offices of Economic Opportunity, Empowerment zones, and Urban Development schemes – subsidized by us – like the rest of the injustices. HUD just imploded a high rise building used for welfare dwellers. The reason for its detonation – too old! It was built in 1960. What about buildings built in 1900? The fact is that those freeloaders living in projects don't really care about a building for which they don't pay. It belongs to the "government," so they abuse it until it practically falls apart. Besides, developers who pay off our legislators get their workers building more housing, at our expense. In another few years these projects will have to be torn down, until the public revolts and kicks these public housing leeches to the curb. The only thing freeloaders understand is the check in the mail.

Week after week, Booknotes (C-SPAN II) interviews black authors – always with that chip on their shoulders – the entitlement chip. After a while, these interviews begin to smell like three-day-old fish. Nothing about the war in Iraq nor street crime nor the expanding deficit. Forget immigration. We deserve an invasion. Forget a failing educational system – Whitey did it; it's his problem. This is the hate-America group we hear about…the pseudo intellects who have set themselves apart from the rest of us. We went through James Baldwin's works and have withstood the poetic cursing of that wondrous woman Maya Angelou. Now, I'd like to hear from their counterparts in Africa.

Next in line are the Hispanics – not the hard-working people – but those who fashion themselves intellects – taking over our center stage, demanding entitlements. What fools we are to tolerate such arrogance.

Policemen, who used to protect the people, now protect the corrupt politicians. I've witnessed mounted police at-the-ready, to disperse attendees at a public park meeting, questioning visitors from Israel and the U.S. Congressmen who were there to lend United States support. You know – our "servants" in Congress who earn six figures, receive health care and pensions – for yielding whatever it takes to anyone who "shows them the money." Even a busload of rabbis was held back from speaking because they disagreed with the guests. Looks like shades of the Gestapo, not America. Perhaps if people were allowed to speak out, there would be no need for policemen. Our policemen are protecting the very ones who plan to take away their jobs by "consolidating" communities. (Governor Corzine)

Why is it difficult for Americans to understand that we are losing our "natural" rights – forget civil rights – as spelled out in the Declaration of Independence? President Bush could have had anyone picked up – for no particular reason – and had him incarcerated indefinitely. Why is it hard for people to understand that it is wrong for then Senator Obama to meet with one hundred Jewish "leaders" in Cleveland? I'd like to hear a tape on what he pledged to the "leaders" in order to get the Jewish vote. They are entitled to nothing!

Mort Zuckerman (U.S. News World Report), the always-angry advocate for Israel, and Andrea Mitchell, the wife of Alan Greenspan, former chairman of the should-be-defunct Federal Reserve, were guest and anchor on MSNBC discussing words of Obama's minister, supposedly degrading Italians for having participated – get this – "in the lynching of Christ, 'Italian style'." What can I say? Probably an Italian woman turned the Reverend down! (Trumpet Magazine)

Pastor Joe Watkins, from Philadelphia, was a guest on a cable show and claimed that "Jesus wants us to bless those who curse us." Is this the same Jesus who threw over the tables of the moneychangers in the temple? Unlikely!

When our former president appointed scoundrels like John Bolton to be our ambassador to the UN, until recently, we should be concerned and angry. Bolton really represented the interests of Israel with all of his restrictive resolutions against Palestine and Iran. This man, with the huge, white, brush mustache under his nose, was a signatory to the document Project for a New American Century suggesting a strike on Iraq – long before 911. He and his neo con masters – Wolfowitz, Perle, Cheney and the usual suspects – are capable of anything. A member of the American Enterprise Institute which yields a lot of power in foreign policy considering the fact that they are self-appointed, Bolton worked for the State Department and is influenced by the Jewish Institute of National Affairs. Imagine! In America we have a religious group on "national affairs" and we criticize Moslems for listening to the ayatollahs. We have our own ayatollahs, except that they are Jewish. Bolton tried to reverse the Supreme Court's decision equating Zionism with racism. And Bolton works for us? Of course, he was replaced by Zalmay Khalilizad, another person of questionable descent. Israel is the tail wagging our dog.

Our State Department, which houses these useful idiots, should be abolished; they're certainly not defending the interests of the United States. Poor Senator McCarthy was right when he said that Stalin and Roosevelt planned the Korean and the Vietnam Wars at Yalta (9-23-50). He was unhappy with the American lives lost, and as a Senator, he couldn't reveal names of those people in the State Department who were guilty. Hence, the smear campaign and the tragedy we find ourselves in today. Not so hard to figure out then why Osama and Ho Chi Minh were on the United States payroll as intelligence agents. McCarthy couldn't reveal the names because they were all Jewish.

George Mondrot, author of "Bring on the Apocalypse," tried to make a citizen's arrest of Bolton at a foreign conference. Everyone in the world knows about the crimes United States presidents and both parties have inflicted on innocent people in the name of democracy. Even now, on 7/2/08, we learn that the United States has spent $600 million to train the Colombian military. Three contractors from America were released this week by Colombians against U.S. intervention – much like what we're doing in Iraq. Contractors from the United States have no business taking jobs away from Colombians. This is what causes hate. These covert activities by the CIA should be curtailed. Our "servants" are agents of war for Big Money. You and I just get wavering prices for gas because of the games these cowboys and bullies play. Again, remember what FDR said, "Nothing in politics happens by accident. If something happens, it was planned that way." And he ought to know!

Even Lou Dobbs, CNN, the champion of exposing the illegal immigration crisis and informing the public about our unfair trade agreements with China, etc., is mum on the Iraq War. In other words, those in Washington who have refused to fulfill their constitutional duty to check our borders and who have given away American jobs by the millions, are right on the issue of a war that should never have been. Go figure. I figure that he's paid by the Big Money, too, and knows what not to say!

There are 3,500 front companies for China in this country. Senator Evan Bayh accused the unregulated Hedge Funds (where Chelsea Clinton worked) of placing our railroad, the CSX, in foreign hands. It just so happens that the railroad carries nuclear and defense material and that our national security may be at risk. The Hedge Funds are under no obligation to reveal which foreign entity is involved. And, get this: the Hedge Fund is called the "Children's Investment Fund." The world is laughing at our stupidity. (Dobbs, CNN, 6-11-08) This year we've lost over 438,000 jobs as food and gas prices remain unstable. In June, 55,000 jobs were lost. Three million jobs were lost altogether.

We know that George W. has outsourced jobs just as Bill Clinton did when he gave our sovereignty away to the World Trade Organization (WTO). But not all of you know that our "intelligence" has been outsourced. (I wondered where it went whenever I see teens walking down the street with their butts exposed. I suppose that this is where they got the name butt-head.) Three former CIA agents and some defense appointees have built a global fusion organization, marketing CIA services to any bidder. "There are sixteen agencies, once the realm of sovereign governments." (Jeremy Scohill, "Blackwater") Incidentally, Blackwater changed its name to "XE."

This conspiracy to take America down started with the graduated income tax – and that tax has certainly graduated over the years, while the Foundations have thrived on the hardships placed on middle class America. Their motto must be "Keep them dumb. Keep them drugged. Keep them pregnant, and then send them off to banker wars!"

This is what happens when man thinks that he is God. This is what happens when victims feel hopeless because God is taken out of the picture. I can only tell you that there are wondrous things that sometimes happen to those who feel hopeless and helpless. Remember that young girl, left homeless by her parents, who went to the streets and still found a way to get educated. Today, she is a successful Harvard graduate. This is God's work. Without the Ten Commandments and a value system, the tyrants know that most helpless people will succumb to drugs and alcohol. Don't do it. Punishment awaits these monsters who have abused the young. Remember what the Chinese scientist said when the United States sent a man to the moon, and news reporters were so enthralled with what man could do. The scientist said that this achievement proved that there is a God, because no one could tell him that a 707 jet's components could all just come together without help or guidance from above. Together we have to reclaim God in our pledge and God in our churches. Forget social justice. Forget end times. We have to denounce those in the ACLU who fight against religion. We have to denounce corporate czars like Bill Gates, Ford, Rockefeller, anyone who wants to take over education – as they are doing – in order to train graduates for "service" and "volunteerism" while they get hefty rewards. We have to demand that our airwaves be unconsolidated and throw the rascals out.

Since the fifties, constitutional attorneys and countless citizens have been trying to alert the public about regionalism, the government within a government, a shadow government, rewriting our state laws with the consent of our state legislators. With the promise of money and programs for their districts ("community organizers"), our republic has been changed without the consent of the governed.

Regionalism was covered, but I will say that Acorn, an illegal community group started by two brothers, Wade and Dale Rathke, has been instrumental in making tons of money for the two "special" hyphenated groups – Blacks and Jews. Dale Rathke was charged with embezzlement but is still involved with this group which has hundreds of subsidiaries. Voter fraud and classes in 'social justice' reaping havoc on our school children are only two of the menaces created by these unaccountable Marxists changing our government. Like the other Chicagoan, Rahm Emanuel, President Obama's chief of staff, these no-account scoundrels are preparing our children for world service.

No one knows how far the other tentacles of this national and international regional monster reach, because there is no audit, no accounting, and no visibility. Glenn Beck is trying to expose this group and had the director, Scott Levenson, on his television show. (5/6/09) Levenson should not be running a lemonade stand. And the FBI talks about the mafia! This group of creeps should be under the jail! These criminals are the ones, in conjunction with Evangelicals, who will bring America to its knees.

Representative Michele Bachmann (R. Minn.) tried to stop a possible $8 billion from going to this nefarious group through the Stimulus Bill but was blocked by Representative Barney Frank (D. NY). Remember, Representative Frank and Chris Dodd were complicit in the fall of the insurance company AIG when the company decided to insure "derivatives" – the Wall Street "securities" scam. Acorn contributed $33 million to President Obama's campaign. LOL

Don't forget that the President has been involved in "community organizing" and has legally defended it. Americorp, Clinton's service organization, and Acorn are extremely subversive organizations, operating without any control or oversight. And people like Glenn Beck wouldn't let anyone speak about this years ago. But, readers, he just <u>discovered</u> it!

Who left Bill Gates in charge of education? Who died and left him and his wife boss man and woman? In my experience, no one makes it to the top, as Bill Gates did, without loads of help from the bottom up.

We've allowed the media to shape opinions. Now that the election is over (2-16-09), Philadelphia talk show hosts boast that "we don't need the Fairness Doctrine; we've invited Ron Paul on." True, but it's too late, and Dr. Paul was allowed to speak for a very short time, with no questions from listeners. This is unacceptable.

If we can't say that there are 80% of us who would like to stop spending trillions of dollars in foreign lands, building bases and embassies, and ensuring a permanent presence for our corporate takeovers of sovereign countries, then no doctrine will work. The military is too powerful and too interested in keeping their jobs permanently, while Americans lose good-paying jobs. It's Marxism when we the people have to beg for jobs from a corrupt government. We don't want "created" jobs by big government. We want our manufacturing jobs to be here in America. Bill Clinton is all over the dials talking "globalism," "sharing," aids, health care for the world. He wants "broadly shared prosperity." In short, a transfer of our hard-earned money – or what's left of it – to the poor of the world. Well, when he gives up his over one hundred and ten or more million dollars to "broadly shared prosperity," I'll still not ever forgive him for passing the two trade treaties giving away jobs. He's a super dolt who should be taken off the air. We have to go back to making our own refrigerators, television sets, furniture, cameras, flags, cars, etc. For these things, we need steel and wood and job training, and employers who will rebuild America.

Rockefeller said, "A crisis will bring in the NWO." Rahm Emanuel, the President's Chief of Staff, said, "Never let a serious crisis go to waste." I'd like to know what Mr. Emanuel meant.

If we're not allowed to say that during this economic downturn in America, we shouldn't be giving between twenty and thirty billion – yes, billion – to Israel over the next five years, then our biggest terrorists are in the media.

With our money, Halliburton contractors, Blackwater mercenaries (who have no mercy), and failed banks are living the life of luxury. George W. bailed out the banks which should have been allowed to fail so that more prudent, honest owners could have taken over.

Nobody should own a home that he can't pay for, anymore than young working people should pay for medical bills of illegals and those who choose not to work. It's not fair, but President Obama is moving quickly in that direction.

Millions of people had no health insurance for their children and selves when they were growing up in America. The poor had access to a hospital, Philadelphia General, and that was it. Then politicians figured that it would bring in votes if they granted entitlements, and it served them well. Bureaucracy after bureaucracy grew, until seated patronage workers earned more than doctors. That's where we are today, with insurance companies paying off congress, except now, they've brought in twenty million illegals – and growing – to add to the list. And no one watches our southern border, being raked over with dangerous drug cartels.

Add to this no job growth, plus added tension of job loss, and we have a dilemma on our hands. The super rich put their tax-free money in the Caymans or the Fijis, while we suffer.

Attorney General, Eric Holder, who will run the Justice Department, made a juvenile statement regarding the fact that Americans are "cowards" because we don't discuss race. Where has he been? Whenever an American speaks out, as I did in this book, the media brings him before the race junkies – Reverend Al Sharpton or Jesse Jackson, who have done well on preventing honest discourse. They'd rather see 3,000 showings of "Black in America."

I can play this con game, too: boo hoo, boo hoo. Until I learned that Christopher Columbus was Italian, I felt worthless. I had no incentive to look for a job. Italian doctors, judges, congressmen meant nothing. Fact is, seeing an Italian president would give me that push that I need to go on. Maybe an Italian Caucus or the National Association for the Advancement of Italians might help. Ya know, like empowerment zones and urban development projects to clean up the mess we've made. This would make me have hope, ya know, for the future, ya know. My five children would feel good, too. Don't forget that Italians, like the Japanese, were kept in internment camps in America during World War II. It really hit me bad. We'd like affirmative action, too, ya know. Health care and a flat screen TV might help make the days go by, ya know, until somebody buys me a home where I can plant some oregano. Reparations would help. Then, ya know, I'd feel proud of America, ya know.

I hope that the preceding monologue answered Mr. Holder's concern about not hearing the other side.

Remember what Ching-a-Chow said, "He who carry chip on shoulder, lead useless life."

In the beginning of this chapter, I showed how the Scofield Bible is used to pervert The Word. I also mentioned the fact that the military is using scripture to justify war.

Robert Draper, GQ Magazine, also brought this fact to light, 5/18/09, on MSNBC. I'm certain that we've heard Janet Parshall, Christian Radio, and Governor Sara Palin use the same passage – Isaias 26:2, in order to justify war: "Open ye the gates, that the righteous nation may enter in."

Reverend Welton Gaddy, a Baptist minister, explained the use of scripture: "You can go into the Bible and find anything you want. They (military) have used it for political reasons. It's a prostitution of religion. They've tried to say 'if you question me, you question God.' It's a strategy of propaganda – use of religion for politics." (paraphrased)

During the '08 election, both Governor Palin and Janet Parshall said, "This is God's war." (Iraq)

EDUCATION

In <u>The Schools We Need</u>, author C. D. Hirsch points out that for cultural literacy, children need a core curriculum using methods that emphasize hard work, learning facts, and passing tests, as probably the only way to reduce social and economic inequalities. Neither more money nor "school choice" will do the job. Children from disadvantaged families need a core curriculum with real content if they are to become successful citizens in the information-age civilization.

When Bill Bennett was head of the Department of Education, he promised to terminate that department so that the federal government would not take over the reins of the local government. Republicans and Democrats had a chance to do this.

Instead, what we have today – again thanks to people like Ted Kennedy who gave us the present immigration bill, saying no more Europeans, only Asians and others – is a public school system converted into "Workforce Preparation" centers to meet the challenges of a competitive global economy in the 21st Century. (Bill sponsored by two Republicans, Steven Gunderson and Bill Goodling of Pennsylvania) In effect, instead of abolishing the Department of Education, their bill would merge the Education Department with the Labor Department and have someone like Robert Reich (Clinton's Labor Secretary) in charge. Robert Reich is the man who said that Americans have to learn to <u>share jobs</u> in the future, and that we should get used to having four or five different kinds of jobs. Notice, that these windbags always seem to have the same job for a lifetime. And with big salaries at that. I call them "traitorous rots."

These people don't care about whether or not your children speak English, can read, or have to depend on calculators. They see us as the workers in their fields. Hacks like Kennedy were right up there with President Bush on "No child left behind." No child is left behind because ALL of the children are behind; SAT scores have been plummeting over the past few years. We now hear "Career" education, based on goals set by "Goals 2000," another hair-brained scheme of these faceless bureaucrats.

Colleges now have remedial classes, while Ted Kennedy enjoyed 44 years in office, leaving his family a nice foundation in the Fijis and a high fence around the family compound, protecting them from passersby.

"The bottom line of these bills is to give government the power over every individual's ability to earn a living. If we let the government decide what jobs are needed, what jobs young people may be trained for, what performance and 'outcome' standards may be enforced on school children, and what certificate qualifies them to be hired, and then track each individual's performance and behavior in school through the workforce on a national computer database, we will have lost freedom in America." (Schlafly Report, September 1995).

President Clinton's idea of National Testing just consolidates Federal Government control over curriculum – bypassing parents, school boards, and state legislatures. President Clinton knew that whoever writes the tests controls the curriculum.

I mentioned the fact that Congressmen such as Jim Greenwood are groomed to impose regional governance on us without a referendum. Well, in the process, phrases like "Sustainable Development" are used – not only in land use, but education. This approach calls for an increased number of curricula, material, and training opportunities. Students are to be taught "international factors which affect our transition to a sustainable society." Americans are to feel guilty because we consume 25 percent of the earth's resources, even though we are only 5 percent of the earth's population. For that foreigners come to this country to be educated because they would like to live as well as we do.

The only thing that I feel guilty about is that we have made greedy corporations cheat foreign countries out of their resources. The rest of us work hard to share a good life, and I'd like to see foreign countries get a share of corporate profits.

When we saw the turning of the tide in the '60s, toward dumbing down, we should have acted. There shouldn't have been talk about "old math" with its times-tables, etc. New Math, Whole Math, Algebra-Lite, no phonics, guessing words – all rubbish that doesn't work.

The old methods of times-tables and phonics turned out accomplished engineers and an America that was enviable. Today, America has the highest percentage of illiteracy of any industrial nation.

In my township, "government," which knows better than we, bussed in behavior problems from the city to further take down any semblance of discipline. Aside from the fact that the city should handle its own problems, herein lies federal government meddling where it does not belong. The aim is to neutralize.

Who suffers? The children. An example of just what we can look forward to is happening in Chicago with a CEO, Arne Duncan, hiring lawyers, community people, and Hispanics, to solve problems superintendents used to solve. Everyone but teachers, it seemed, was on the team, and the new Mayor is the "boss." Pathetic presentation. (NPR, 1/9/06). We have to get rid of the Home Rule Charters which gave the Mayor control of education, with the feds over his head. Regionalism – government with all chiefs and no Indians, does not work. Our framers said that regionalism leads to tyranny.

The Mayor has the power to hire and fire school board members from another administration. Too much power for the mayor!

In the meantime, "generous" Bill Gates who gives to AIDS, but mostly to organizations which benefit Microsoft, has opened a "partnership" school in Philadelphia, called "School of the Future." Microsoft and we are once again partners in the re-definition of what education should be.

Students of high school age are given breakfast, lunch and dinner. The school promotes gym and life-long care. Of course, lap tops. (Probably for indoctrination: "Why don't you like your parents?")

Sounds more like a home for assisted living, not young people. But then, who will fight our wars. Certainly not the Gates' family!

The Gates Foundation – like all other foundations – must give 5% of its profit to charity. The 95% left can be used to invest so that they regain the 5% spent for charity, thereby keeping their holdings fluid. The rest of us tax-paying dufusses subsidize the fortune Gates would have to pay in taxes. Nice? And the worst part is that after his seed money, or starting money, we peasants take over the cost of his school.

President Barack Obama thinks that sex education from K-12 is the "right thing to do" (MSNBC, 7/18/07). Children, he feels, "should know the difference between good touching and bad touching."

Tucker Carlson: "I would physically assault anyone who told that (good touching, bad touching) to my four-year-old." I think that most sane parents would agree but these federal bureaucrats dominate the curriculum from behind the scenes, training "sex experts" to force untried values on innocent children.

What will it take for parents to wake up and demand that "we won't pay taxes for anything dealing with sex education or drug education? We don't want any foundations contributing to our children's futures." Look at what almost five decades of sex-ed has done.

Isn't it enough that big money has contributed to the assault on children by sponsoring Gangsta Rap videos like "Grand Champ," championing brutal dog fights. Result: An NFL player with a $130,000,000 contract savagely victimized 66 dogs for gambling and entertainment. First, nobody should receive $130,000,000 – not even Oprah Winfrey. As far as I'm concerned, only a fantastic neurosurgeon or heart surgeon or dedicated doctor should make salaries commensurate with their talent. Kicking or catching a football – big whoops! It's pathetic, and it gives young people the wrong role models and heroes.

It's sad that this football player had a bad life, if he did, but dogs had nothing to do with it, and he should be scoffed off the field. <u>Victims become victimizers</u>. Even Senator Byrd cried before Congress.

When America was a giant power and respected, children used to have heroes like Charles Lindbergh, the aviator who made the first solo flight from New York to Paris. Bridge builders. Artisans. Farmers. Nurses. People who saved others at the cost of their own lives, like firefighters. On and on. It was always someone who made a contribution to society.

Today, we have Britney Spears showing no underwear, high school graduates who can't read, mothers with tattoos and no common sense, men with earrings who know every sports figure and his scores but can't name the Vice President of the United States.

Then we have Obama and Hillary trying to change the subject of a trillion dollar war and turn the spotlight on raising taxes higher and higher so that 45 million people (including illegals?) can be added to health care.

How magnanimous of them to tell us what to do with the few dollars we have left after taxes. <u>And</u>, to also tell us that we must discuss sex in kindergarten. Well, they can join the weirdoes I've met called "sexperts." I wouldn't trust them to teach a child how to tie his shoelaces.

And don't you love the ads that we pay for, using six year olds to demand national health care? Where are the fathers of these children? Try something new: get a job, if you can find one! The poverty industry with third and fourth generation recipients should be taken off the rolls. Handouts should be given to the deserving poor, the sick, disabled, and other worthy souls.

The result of our building project after project has resulted in crime and failure. The Democrats should not get seats based on giving away the money of those who work hard and barely make it.

SMART GROWTH VS. SPRAWL

The planners want to take our cars away and tell us where and how to live. They are already taking people's property away under laws that are unconstitutional. Public officials, many ignorant about the true motives, are going along with whichever bills are handed to them to propose and sign. We have no representatives; we have to go it alone before it's too late. And the way we do it is to get the state and federal legislators to give us a hearing; if we cannot get a hearing, we stage a protest to tell them what we want. But first, you decide after reading two presentations – one for so-called smart growth and the other for so-called sprawl.

These two views were debated in the Philadelphia Inquirer, 10/20/98, by Thomas Hylton, a Pulitzer Prize-winning journalist and a member of 10,000 Friends of Pennsylvania.

The opposing view, on Sprawl, is by W. C. Smith (<u>claney@usaor.net</u>) who lives and writes in Pittsburgh.

Thomas Hylton:

"During the last 50 years, cities and towns that took centuries to evolve have been abandoned wholesale, while suburban sprawl, a low-density lifestyle that randomly scatters houses, malls and industry across the landscape, has been touted in their places.

"Last month, the 21st Century Environment Commission, a 40-member panel appointed by Governor Ridge to recommend ways to improve Pennsylvania's environmental quality, declared that sprawling development is the state's No. 1 environmental problem.

"Sprawl, the commission said, consumes enormous quantities of farmland and open space, isolates the poor in our cities and towns, creates massive traffic congestion, worsens air and water pollution, and requires exorbitant amounts of tax dollars to build and maintain. Since 1985, the commission pointed out, Pennsylvania has lost about one million acres of farmland, woodlands and open space, while the number of miles driven on our state highways has increased six times faster than the rate of population growth.

"Even before the commission's report was delivered to Governor Ridge, the Pennsylvania Builders Association rejected its findings, saying that home-builders are merely responding to the public's desire to live at low densities. But consumer demand is strongly affected by public policies, and since WW II, all the incentives have favored sprawl. For example:

"Massive highway building, subsidized by general taxation, opened up huge areas for development while public transportation was allowed to wither.

"The Federal Housing Administration and Veterans Administration adopted mortgage policies that favored new housing in developing suburbs over existing housing in cities and town.

"The Federal Department of Housing and Urban Development adopted a policy of concentrating the poor in high-rise housing projects that were built in city neighborhoods, virtually guaranteeing their decline. We didn't build any subsidized housing in the suburbs.

"State and Federal governments financed the construction of new water and sewer lines in developing areas instead of helping cities and towns to maintain existing infrastructure.

"Environmental laws made it far less expensive for industry to develop virgin fields rather than re-use abandoned industrial sites. Despite recent reforms, it is still easier to develop greenfields than it is to re-develop brown-fields.

"In recent years, there has been a growing recognition that government has been promoting an unsustainable form of growth. The Urban Land Institute, the nation's premier developers' organization, is currently devoting its entire policy and practice agenda to 'smart growth.' Dean Schwanke, project direc-tor for the ULI, writes, 'The movement makes a lot of sense and provides a refreshingly positive and constructive approach to dealing with growth devel-opment issues.'

"The Institute of Transportation Engineers, which sets highway standards for public works agencies across the country, has revised its standards to permit

narrower streets that are characteristic of traditional towns like Narberth or Haddonfield.

"Numerous local governments, from Davidson, NC to Brookfield, CO, have adopted new zoning ordinances that permit a mixture of homes, stores and offices in the same neighborhoods, tied together with tree-lined streets and abundant sidewalks.

"Are people willing to trade huge lots for the ability to walk and enjoy a sense of community? In Florida, people are flocking to live in Disney's new town of Celebration (eventual population: 20,000), where people can walk to the grocery store and kids can walk to a K-12 public school. The largest lot size in Celebration, with a one million dollar home, is a quarter of an acre. Celebration is one of 200 traditional town-like developments being planned or constructed across America, including Eagleview in Chester County. That's up from just four in 1992.

"These are the kinds of 'smart growth' initiatives the 21ˢᵗ Century Environment Commission wants to see in Pennsylvania.

"In his inaugural address, Governor Ridge said, 'My avowed purpose is to summon every resource within me, and every resource within you, to re-instill, to re-invigorate a sense of community throughout Pennsylvania.' Nothing the Governor can do is more important to fulfilling that goal than carrying out the commission's recommendations."

Now, W. . Smith (about Sprawl):

"Forcing all to live one way is silly and unconstitutional. The sin of sprawl: this is why environmentalists are trying to take away Pennsylvanians' constitutional rights to property and the pursuit of their own happiness. They want a governor's finding, based on the 21ˢᵗ Century Environmental Commission's report, that sprawl and land use are a problem. They want to amend the Municipalities Planning Code to create regional and metropolitan zoning, to facilitate urban growth boundaries.

"I hope Gov. Ridge acts sensibly and issues no such finding. The environmental lobby isn't telling the truth: sprawl is good in many ways. And their quest to get people to live in one particular way — which they have decided is good for the rest of us — is both silly and unconstitutional.

"How do they define sprawl? As the construction of new houses and businesses outside of existing cities, and the construction of highways that facilitate the growth of new communities. Land use spreads out for residential, commer-

cial and industrial purposes, and that's called sprawl. They say that sprawl is inefficient, harms the environment, increases the cost of infrastructure, results in the abandonment of existing communities and eliminates open space and wildlife habitat.

"Let's take these evils one by one. Does sprawl impose new infrastructure costs on local governments? The truth is that development actually improves the road infrastructure at no cost to local or state government. Under the existing Municipalities Planning Code, as well as subdivision ordinances, a new development, whether residential or commercial, must, at the developers' expense, construct new roads equivalent to or exceeding State Department of Transportation specifications. The community gets new, higher-standard, longer-life roads and contributes to the improvement of existing roads.

"The law requires developers to help pay for the construction of water services, sewer systems and sewage treatment plants. These improvements are state-of-the-art and designed for future capacity. This helps both the rural communities and the cities. For years, older rural communities have depended on separate systems, rather than a sewage collection and disposal system. The major cities have depended on combined waste and storm water systems, which are over 100 years old and are expensive to maintain. Again, at no cost to the community, the newcomers are paying to improve an older, inadequate system.

"For the cities, the benefits are also extensive. Inner cities often are served by inadequate and often sub-standard systems. As new systems are built outside the cities, the load is reduced on the urban systems, making it more manageable.

"Thus are health and maintenance problems reduced, while providing new sources of supply for the suburbs, at no cost to the government or taxpayers. The truth is that an increased and improved water supply is paid for by development in rural and suburban areas without any cost to the government.

"The environmentalists contend that by moving to the rural or suburban areas, the citizen, as an element of sprawl, causes air pollution by driving back and forth from the central city, filling the highways with pollutants. What the environmentalists miss, or choose to ignore, is that as people and businesses move out to rural and suburban areas, population density in the cities decreases, which actually reduces air pollution. And as businesses follow citizens in moving out, driving time for employees decreases, further reducing emissions. This is why the rural counties have less pollution and lower emission requirements on their vehicles.

"This point brings us closer to the real issue here: how environmentalists want everybody else to live. The vision of the future that environmentalists cherish is wrong as well as wrong-headed. With the advent of the automobile, the interstate highway and the computer, business and work have been decentralized. Professionals no longer find it necessary to work in the city. Working at home with your computer, or anywhere with your laptop, has become the norm. The concept of creating an urban growth boundary and forcing people to live and work in a constricted city area where they would have to walk or bicycle to work or shopping, is not only fantasy; it's idiocy.

"The term sprawl is a fraudulent monstrosity created by elitist environmentalists to mislead the public officials into supporting these no-growth objectives. For them, it's habitat for wildlife rather than habitat for humanity.

"And if you think that this concept of getting us out of cars is new, think again. The so-called "elitists" who have never lived with the problems of the inner city, and who know better than the framers of our Constitution, decided that they should set new rules without the consent of the electorate.

The Philadelphia Inquirer, 11/3/72, carried an article by Paul Critchlow, the "Inquirer Transportation Writer."

"Mass transit will have to be upgraded and downtown auto-driving less attractive if the city hopes to reduce motor vehicles in Center City.

"The most drastic step would be the banning of all traffic from Center City — except for emergency vehicles and school buses.

"These proposals were contained in a report prepared by the Franklin Institute and presented Thursday to the Conference on Urban Environment sponsored by the American Institute of Medical Climatology.

"The study was prepared for the city's Air Management Services, and is aimed at reducing vehicular exhaust emissions which contribute to about 85 percent of the total pollution in Center City.

"Pollution control strategies that would make Center City less attractive include:

- *Increasing parking lot fees.*
- *Banning curbside parking.*
- *Alternating days when commuters could drive into Center City.*
- *Prohibiting daytime commercial deliveries."*

The authors of the report, J. Spencer Huston and Susan J. Fansmith, said 60 percent of all Center City motorists are optional drivers.

These are drivers, they said, who have a choice between their autos and mass transit. The pair concluded that motorists will have to be both lured and forced out of their autos and into mass transit.

The two scientists said the fundamental strategy – the lure – would be to upgrade mass transit.

This process, the authors said, means providing more parking spaces at outlying transit stations, increasing transfer points, providing feeder routes, cleaning up the vehicles, improving security and reducing fares.

The second set of actions would penalize drivers, making the auto less attractive.

This process could include setting up a two-color sticker system so commuters could drive into Center City only every other day.

William Reilly, acting head of Air Management Services, said the Franklin report is one of several being used to 'build on' in meeting Federal air quality standards by 1977.

Reilly said the city will soon sign a federally funded $20,000 contract to get more precise pollution measurements, especially at busy intersections.

I have presented these three papers in order for the reader to see how we are being manipulated by those people who have not been elected by us, but are behind the scenes. Only Mr. Smith spoke for the average concerns. Minus the articles, the electorate would not know what is happening or why. But the Mr. Smiths are never heard because the regionalists know, as admitted, that the public would never accept these draconian ideas. So they prefer hiding behind university courses and indoctrinating the very young before their power to analyze is developed.

Just consider what these advocates are proposing: they are worried about the poor living in high-rise housing projects. Well, who put them there in the first place? Who rewarded mothers with absentee fathers to have three and four children and get benefit after benefit? Who of these kindhearted congressmen steps forward when a four-year-old girl is raped, as the case in Cabrini Green Projects in Chicago? And who is there to protect those children who sometimes become the victims of children raised in projects? Certainly, not the congressmen. They live in protected environments.

Who outsourced jobs to foreign countries and then subsidized low-paying jobs "created" by Clinton who passed NAFTA and GATT (trade agreements). The answer is Government: they create the problems, then want to solve them.

Mass transit was in private hands and those hands were responsible for the maintenance, taxes, behavior codes of the drivers, safety, etc. Today, we subsidize almost all jobs, and no taxes from mass transit, only billions in subsidies.

Today at the ports, we hear "planners" like Paul Levy (NPR, 12/22/06) talking about how "the public will be responsible for the maintenance of the newly built casinos on the Delaware River." Public Partnership will take care of trash, police, etc., so that the Casino Meisters can empty the pockets of those who can afford it the least. Again, we subsidize the wealthy casino managers as we subsidize our sports stadiums in Philadelphia. Partnership means we pay and they play.

How did they get the casino deal through the State Legislatures? First, by telling them that added revenue is needed because of all the new projects – which they create – and then by dangling a one percent "take" of the profits for each legislator. Nice deal for a bunch of men and women who can't do anything else and who never read the bills before them.

Why do we need added revenue? Twenty million illegals are in this country, filling one-quarter of our prison space. And they get free medical care, food stamps, housing, legal representation, and education. Why? Because they can. In Pennsylvania, if you're an illegal, you can get a driver's license and register to vote at the same time. No questions asked.

Thanks to Ted Kennedy who passed the Immigration Act of 1964, Europeans who came over because of our freedoms were no longer preferred. Only those from Asia and Central America were preferred. So who pays for English courses? We do. When Italians, German, Poles and Irish came over in the past, there were no breaks. You learned English on your own.

Perhaps you can better understand why nothing is done about our borders. Drug and weapons trafficking went on under George W's nose, and he did nothing. Anyone without altered thinking would have thrown him and his cohorts out of office. Congress NEEDS the drugs coming in and the VOTES coming in or something would have been done yesterday.

As for pollution, I am certain that our planes bombing the hell out of the whole world, play no part in air quality. Also, the big question we should ask is where the money for "weather modification" goes, and for what purpose.

Vice President Gore warns us about using too many kilowatts of electricity. The average person uses a little over 10,000 kilowatts per year. Mr.

Gore uses over 200,000 at a cost of $30,000 per year for his electric and gas bills. He also warns against using heavy cars, while he uses private jets, thanks to his Occidental Petro revenues. And we listen like a bunch of fools going to the slaughter. This deceptive man is revered by fools. His friends are Armand Hammer and the Schiffs (bankers).

These men and women "serving" us have brought crime to the cities, and now to the suburbs, along with assisted care housing, drug rehabs, and Section 8 housing.

Last but not least, the only thing eating up farmland is the Corporate Farming Conglomerate; Archer Daniel Midland, who would rather import produce, radiate it for E-coli bacteria, and get subsidized for their generosity and compassion. And of course ADM-sponsored all of the Sunday talk shows for years.

Nothing was fresher than our home-grown farm products, but we allowed small farms to be taxed out of existence with unfair inheritance taxes, property taxes, and new zoning laws created by the unseen planners. Farmers were sold out to "developers."

So, you wanted vitamins? Buy them at a drug store that gets a five-year tax abatement and then can move on to another neighborhood. Or go over to China's store – Wal-Mart. I hear they're offering a discount. After all, Red China needs money, too. How else can they build up their army and navy?

ELECTRIC POWER AND KEN LAY

The following information was searched on Americanpresidency.org and cia.doc.gov.

During the 1920s and the early years of the Depression, the public became disenchanted with privately owned power plants and began to support the idea of government ownership of utilities, particularly hydroelectric power facilities. This disenchantment was chiefly the result of abuses heaped on utilities and ultimately on their customers by unregulated holding companies (corporations organized to hold bonds or stocks of other corporations which it usually controls). Government-owned hydroelectric power facilities could produce power cheaply and sell it to publicly owned utilities for distribution. This concept was a controversial political issue at the time with strong arguments on both sides. Because the states could not regulate an interstate holding company, the federal government stepped in. Many believed that private power did not employ fair operating practices and therefore, government-owned power was wholeheartedly supported. Others were opposed to the government entering the electricity business because they believed that the government was exploiting hydroelectric sites. The federal government did become heavily involved through the construction and ownership of several massive hydroelectric facilities.

During the presidency of FDR (1933-1945) a number of facilities were built, and publicly owned took a strong hold. Designed to create jobs and hope during the Depression, the government built four hydroelectric projects – the Hoover Dam, the Grand Coulee, and the U.S. Army Corps of Engineers flood control dams provided low-priced power for preferred customers.

Under the Tennessee Valley Authority Act of 1933, the federal government supplied electric power to states, counties, municipalities, and non-profit corporations, soon including those of the REA (Rural Electrification Administration).

As a matter of fact, in order to protect farmers during the years following the Depression, Congress passed the Norris-Rayburn Act. This act insured rural areas a ten-year integrated program for electrifying farms. For $410,000,000 the federal government subsidized the formation of rural electric cooperatives which were exempted from Federal and States taxes and exempted from Federal and State Power Commission regulations. Lower property taxes also played into this aid to farmers who are the backbone of any healthy, successful country.

President Roosevelt wrote Executive Order 6251, designating the Federal Power Commission, an agency of the Public Works Administration. He also passed the Public Utilities Holding Company Act which told electric companies where to stand and salute. It told them how much to deduct for repairs and still make a handsome profit.

Most important, FDR banned political contributions from utility companies – no "soft" money, no "hard" money, no money – period.

This is something that Theodore Roosevelt tried to do when he recommended the harnessing in of corporate greed involving railroads. Theodore Roosevelt was afraid of unbridled capitalism which we have today. Antitrust laws prohibited the merging of corporations.

For decades, utilities were able to meet the increasing demand for electricity at decreasing prices. This trend continued until the 1960s when the utility industry saw decreasing costs and growth give way to increasing costs and slower growth. Contributing to this state were the Northeast Blackout of 1965, the passage of the Clean Air Act of 1970, and its amendments in 1977 requiring utilities to reduce polluting emissions; the Oil Embargo of 1973-74 resulting in burdensome increases in fossil fuel prices; the accident at Three Mile Island in 1979. Congress designed legislation that would reduce dependency on foreign oil, develop renewable and alternative energy sources, and sustain economic growth.

While the industry was trying to recover from these damaging events, Congress passed the Public Utility Regulatory Policies Act of 1978

(PURPA). PURPA became the catalyst for competition in the electric industry because it allowed non-utility facilities to enter the market. A non-utility is a corporation, person, agency, authority or other legal entity that owns electric generating capacity and is not an electric utility. Non-utility power producers include qualifying small power producers and independent power producers without a designated service area, and which do not file forms listed in the Code of Federal Regulations (Title 18, Part 14).

Herein started our problems. We are back to corporate greed. Remember that for many, many years, America bought mideast oil at five dollars per barrel. All of our trouble started with corporations who thought that they owned the oil under the Caspian Sea. Henry Kissinger, the architect of Cambodia, played a part in making oil go to the heights we suffer today when he went to the Shah of Iran and told him to raise the price of oil. And he's still around today having given hawkish, nonsensical advice to former Presidents George, Sr. and George W., and probably President Obama.

Enter George Bush, Sr. and Enron, the new 'competitors.' Thanks to a wonderful article in the Montgomery County Observer, 9/20/03, P. O. Box 977, Worcester, PA 19490, by Greg Palast, Palast investigative fund, we have the story.

Greg Palast worked as an investigator of corporate racketeers before becoming a journalist.

Greg investigated the Power Outage of August 14, 2003, wherein a few tree branches out of Ohio led to one-third of the continent being left without power. It turns out that First Energy and Niagara-Mohawk had slashed staffing and maintenance. "Even when the Big Blackout ended, the power pirates kept us in the dark, fibbing, fabricating and faking their way through a series of bogus excuses for a disaster created by greed overload. The under-manning and the under-spending all occurred beneath the banner of 'deregulation.'

George Bush's Federal Regulatory Commission allowed the power companies to reach into our wallets and take out more cash to add wires to the transmission system – in effect replacing the loot these guys carted off in the last ten years of deregulation. 'But that won't keep the lights on,' says Oppenheimer, former Assistant Attorney General in New York, in charge of investigating utilities. 'It's not a lack of wires or lack of power plants that caused the blackout. The administration refused to conclude that deregulation has failed.'

Niagara-Mohawk blacked out and took down New York. Ni-Mo's claim to fame goes back to the 1980s. They built a nuclear plant, Nine Mile Point, a brutally costly piece of junk for which Ni-Mo and its partner companies charged billions to New York's electricity rate payers. To pull off this grand theft by kilowatt, the Ni-Mo-led consortium fabricated cost and schedule reports, then performed a Harry Potter job on the account books.

In 1988 Greg Palast showed a jury a memo from an executive to one partner, Long Island Lighting Co. (LILCO), giving a lesson to a Ni-Mo honcho on how to lie to government regulators. This jury ordered LILCO to pay $4.3 billion and, ultimately, put them out of business.

After LILCO was hammered by the law and government regulators slammed Ni-Mo and dozens of other book-cooking, document-doctoring utility companies with fines all over America, the industry leaders got together and swore never to break the regulations again. Their plan was not to follow the rules, but to eliminate them. They called it 'deregulation.'

But the power companies did not dare launch de-regulating in the U.S. Rather, in 1990, one devious little bunch of operators out of Texas, Houston Natural Gas, operating under the alias 'Enron,' talked an over-the-edge free market fanatic, Britain's Prime Minister Margaret Thatcher, into licensing the first completely deregulated power plant in this hemisphere. The English experiment proved the viability of Enron's new industrial formula: that the enthusiasm of politicians for deregulation was in direct proportion to the payola provided by power companies.

The power elite first moved on England because they knew Americans wouldn't swallow the deregulation snake oil easily. The U.S.A. had gotten used to cheap power available at the flick of a switch.

But George Bush, Sr., just prior to his departure from the White House in 1992, gave the power industry one long deep-through-the-teeth kiss goodbye; federal deregulation of electricity. It was a legacy he wanted to leave for his son, the gratitude of power companies who ponied up $16 million for the Republican campaign of 2000, seven times the sum given to the Democrats.

California fell first. The power companies spent $39 million to defeat a 1998 referendum pushed by Ralph Nader which would have blocked the de-reg scam. Another $39 million was spent on lobbying and lubricating the campaign coffers of the state's politicians to write a lie into law;

in the deregulation act's preamble, the legislature promised that deregulation would reduce electricity bills by 20%. In fact, in the first California city to go 'lawless,' San Diego, the 20% savings became a 300% jump in surcharges.

Enron circled California and licked its lips. As the number-one contributor to the George W. Bush campaign, it was confident about the future. With just a half dozen other companies, it controlled at times 100% of the available power capacity needed to keep the Gold State lit. Their motto: 'Your money or your lights.'

Enron and its comrades played the system like a broken ATM machine, yanking out the bills. For example, in the shamelessly fixed auctions for electricity held by the state, Enron bid, in one instance, to support 500 megawatts of electricity over a 15 megawatt line. That's like pouring a gallon of gasoline into a thimble – the lines would burn up if they attempted it. Faced with blackout because of Enron's destructive bid, the state was willing to pay anything to keep the lights on.

And the state did. According to Dr. Anjali Sheffrin, economist with the California State Independent System Operation which directs power deliveries, between May and November 2000, three power giants physically or 'economically' withheld power from the state and concocted enough false bids to cost the California customers over $6.2 billion in excess charges.

It took until December 20, 2000, with the lights going out on the Golden Gate, for President Clinton, once a deregulation booster, to find his lost democratic soul and impose price caps in California and ban Enron from the market.

But the light bulb buccaneers didn't have to wait long to put their hooks back into the treasure chest. Within seventy-two hours of moving into the White House, while he was still sweeping out the inaugural champagne bottles, George W. reversed Clinton's executive order and put the power pirates back in business in California. Enron Reliant (a/k/a Houston Industries), TXU (a/k/a Texas Utilities) and the others who had economically snipped California's wires knew they could count on 'Dubya' who, as Governor of the Lone Star State, cut them the richest deregulation deal in America."

Meanwhile the deregulation bug made it to New York where Republican Governor George Pataki and his industry-picked utility commissioners ripped the lid off electric bills and relieved Palast's old friend at Niagara-Mohawk of the expensive obligation to properly fund the maintenance of the grid system.

"The Pataki-Bush Axis of Weasels permitted something that must have former New York Governor Roosevelt spinning in his grave. They allowed a foreign company, the notoriously incompetent National Grid of England, to buy up Ni-Mo, get rid of 800 workers and pocket most of their wages – producing a bonus for Ni-Mo stockholders approaching $90 million.

"Bush's buddies have been flicking the switches across the globe. In Brazil, Houston Industries seized ownership of Rio de Janeiro's electric company. The Texans fired workers, raised prices, cut maintenance expenditures and, click! The juice went out so often the locals now call it, 'Rio Dark.'

"So too the free market British buckaroos controlling Niagara-Mohawk raised prices, slashed staff, cut maintenance, and click! – New York joined Brazil in the Dark Ages.

"Californians had found the end to the deregulation disaster: recall the only governor in the nation with the grit to stand up to the electricity price-fixer, Governor Grey Davis. And unlike Arnold Schwarzenegger, Governor Grey Davis stood alone against the bad guys without using a body double. Davis called Reliant Corp. of Houston 'a pack of parasites' and so he walked the plank for daring to stand up to the Texas marauders.

"So where's the president? Just before he landed on the deck of the Abe Lincoln, the White House was so concerned about our brave troops facing the foe that they used the cover of war for a new push in Congress for yet more electricity deregulation. This has a certain logic: there's no sense defeating Iraq if a hostile regime remains in California."

Greg Palast is the author of the New York Times bestseller, "The Best Democracy Money Can Buy" (Penguin, USA) and with Theo MacGregor and Jerrold Oppenheimer, "Democracy and Regulation," a guide to electricity deregulation published by the United Nations/Pluto Press.

Cheney and Bush are former energy company executives and the administration-backed energy bill, which passed the House but stalled in the Senate, provides $21.5 billion in tax breaks for the energy industry. And the meeting with their energy buddies was secret.

I voted for George Bush the first time because I hated the fact that

Hillary held secret meetings with her "health care" group. We vote them in and then they "practice to deceive."

The fact is that we have moved from regulated monopolies to unregulated monopolies. The unnecessary tragedy of blackouts began with regionalism. For years, a single power plant, PECO, serviced Philadelphia. But when deregulation came, "suppliers" from outside Philadelphia became involved in our local territory. Our wires now go across different states, overlooking the original transmission grid which could not be built today with all of the environmental regulations. "Our grid has become a coast-to-coast maze of interlocking power lines, towers, transmission stations and generating plants" (Alwell Parker, Philadelphia Inquirer, 8/17/03).

When Ma Bell controlled our telephone wires, we were better off; when PECO controlled our local transmission grid, we were better off. We used to be able to get in touch with our local office; now we find ourselves talking to someone in England or India. Ken Lay, the CEO of Enron made $500 million in online trading in 2000-2001.

And we wonder why the world is beginning to hate us; they can't stand our corporate crooks any longer.

It remains to be seen how much longer we Americans can take it.

WHO OWNS THE MEDIA

Corporate Information – News Networks

1. NBC.com (purchased by GE) – Bob Wright and Andrew Lach
2. ABC – Michael Eisner (Disney)

Viacom – Chairman of the Board, Sumner Redstone (a/k/a Rothstein), Mel Karizian (Redstone Executive Board of Jewish Philanthropy of Greater Boston, and former chairman of Jewish Philanthropy, nationally)

1. TNN
2. Trinity
3. Nickelodeon (always demeaning Arabs)
4. CBS TV and CBS Sports
5. Black Entertainment
6. Blockbuster
7. Simon and Schuster
8. Infinity
9. TV Guide
10. Permanent Pictures
11. Harvard law School
12. MTV
13. UPW
14. Showtime

3. CNN (AOL Time Warner, CEO Walter Isaacson)

1. AOL
2. HBO
3. News Line Concerns
4. Turner Broadcasting
    TBS
    TNT
    Cartoon Network
    Kids network
    CNN Radio, etc.
    Atlanta Braves
5. Warner Brothers

4. NPR – Kevin Clone, CEO; Ken Stern, Executive Vice President.
5. Fox News – Rupert Murdoch, half-Jewish, very pro-Israel

THE EDUCATION DEBACLE

"A book was published in 1954 'Citizens Committee' intended to 'guide public thinking' about policies in schools and how to guard the schools against 'attacks.'" (Barbara Morris, "Change Agents in the Schools")

With this in mind, consider how parents who 'question' any part of the curriculum are treated, and remember that we are paying for this education. School boards are always filled with those people who consider questions an 'attack' on the school. Their reaction is meant to intimidate any parent who questions their 'authority.' Chutzpah! And it works – especially when security guards are there to toss you out. We pay for the wages of these security guards.

If it weren't for 'old' people – patriots – like Maureen Heaton, we would never be aware of this duplicity in our educational system. Her valor and research are buried with her because we're kept from hearing about on-going corruption. My thirty or more years spent in research of educational corruption is nothing compared to that of Maureen Heaton's. Because of her knowledge, I was able to get the real picture of why our educational system has failed and who the culprits behind the scenes are, and why the Hitler media wants only thirty and forty-year-olds on the scene. Now, whenever I see the same old 'experienced' super-rich bastards like Ted Kennedy, Kissinger, Clintons, McCains, Lieberman, and the countless others involved in this conspiracy to train the youth for their unending wars – I know that hell will be a busy place.

Maureen's story went like this: "Rockefeller used the University of Chicago to launch the scheme of "restructuring of America" through its educational system. Frederick T. Gates used the Pillsbury flour fortune to seed the money and then got Rockefeller to continue funding the "vineyards of American education" in the cities and rural counties' grade schools, high schools, colleges, med schools and other advanced training." (Quote from a friendly biographer of John D. Rockefeller.)

Notice that the corporations, trying to take over education, claim that learning English or philosophy in college isn't necessary for job training. Well, put your thinking caps on – corporate leaders were served very well by learning the 'mastery' of English. This is why we're faced with bilingual classes wherein no child learns correct grammatical usage and, therefore, cannot express himself well. Remember that past immigrants were placed in English-only classes and did quite well. Learning foreign languages was always part of the curriculum as well. When you can't carry on intelligent dialogue, your job is at risk, but then the corporations will tell you what you need to know: "Stand aside, dummy!"

The General Education Board was initiated to penetrate local schools. The whole plan of incremental penetration was spelled out in "International Understanding," 1931. (I mentioned this under "Conspiracy.")

Charles Merriam was a leading member of The Political Science Association. Merriam was a social science professor chosen to head the 1313 branch of the international scheme – adapting governments to become units in the NWO. FDR's administration welcomed Merriam. Chicago University became the leading light for radical groups and the headquarters for the regional army beginning to shape the strategies for revolution – next door to the government headquarters at 1313 East 60th Street.

"When Harold Iches went from Chicago to Washington to serve in the Roosevelt Cabinet as "Director of Public Works," he brought Merriam in to help set up the National Resources Planning Board (NRPB), the agency created to bring 'social science' into the government. As 1313 penetrated the U.S. Government, it spread like the web of a spider. At first all of the groups centered at 1313, but then they moved to other places. "The Roosevelt Revolution" had begun with agents heavily stacked in the executive department.

"Dr. William Wirt, an obscure teacher in Indiana public schools, learned of a 'Rockefeller Foundation Grant' that was available to someone who could design an innovative program which would bring the schools into the twentieth century.'"

Dr. Wirt put forth the "Gary Plan" and was promoted and asked to lecture on his project. Then in September, 1933, he was invited to the home of his secretary who had four government officials from the Roosevelt Administration there. The Department of Agriculture (Economic section), Department of Interior, the Agriculture Adjustment Administration, and the National Recovery Administration sent representatives along with a propaganda agent from Russia. It didn't take Dr. Wirt long to figure out what was going on. Some of his informants had boasted that President Roosevelt would be the Kerensky of the coming revolution. There was a deliberate plan among the New Deal leftists to overthrow the Established Order and substitute a planned economy in our country. Apparently they considered Dr. Wirt one of their own, but they were wrong.

"Unfortunately Dr. Wirt went to his death being demonized by those on the investigating committee. The vote against him was that of Representative John J. O'Connor. O'Connor later apologized in the Congressional Record. (This investigation brought about the Committee of the House on Un-American Activities, 1938.)

"The first volunteer regional experiment in comprehensive planning in the United States began in 1924 as a Tri-State Planning Federation – Pennsylvania, New Jersey and Delaware. In New England a similar group was started, and New York joined Long Island and Connecticut.

"Volunteer groups without legal authority tried to insert these strategies into government. Two of these groups, plus the Public Administration Service (PAS) and the affiliate, the National Municipal League (NML), had been the vanguard for the City Manager Government. (Home Rule legislation which gets rid of the controller and the sheriff and commits other devious acts such as putting in its own spending "Authority." In Pennsylvania, we have PICA so that, if citizens decry excessive spending, the mayor can blame it on the "Authority.")

In 1940, PAS published a review of the City Manager Movement, in which they stated that the intent of the movement was to establish a New Form of Government, unhampered by such antiquities as "separation of powers" and "checks and balances." In this report they took credit for writing the 1921 Budget Act which transferred responsibility for the budget from Congress to the Executive Office. It was also PAS and NML which parented the initiative, referendum and recall (IRR) to facilitate their assault on representative government.

One of the first tasks of the NRPB was to survey the progress of the "volunteer" planning movement. One county planning board started in Wisconsin; 700 city planning boards were already at work, many volunteer-manned.

One year later, the NRPB reported that there were 39 more city planning boards, and 717 of the total were now "official." There were 61 planning boards, 23 regional boards, and 20 "municipal" boards. The NRPB reported that almost all of them were "nonpolitical" and had university professors on them. Nonpolitical means "nonofficial," or not approved by representatives – outside the law.

These volunteer boards assumed the power to begin the restructuring of America.

The NRPB stimulated interest in the planning boards by offering money and other assistance to encourage state planning boards. Assistance was conditional, resting on guarantees from the state executives, not from the representatives of the people.

The Governor had to:

1. promise to press for legislation to give the state planning board 'legal' standing;
2. appoint NRPB – approved members of the board;
3. guarantee office space and stenographic services;
4. guarantee a 10-year planning program;
5. appoint a planner to direct the boards; and
6. begin a study for a transportation plan.

New Hampshire was the first state to get money, then out of 48 states joined to start the process of eliminating representation for Americans.

The NRPB crowed – "State and interstate planning is a lusty infant, but the critical test will come when bills are pending in legislatures for the establishment of continuing planning organizations." The public had no idea so they couldn't protest. Representatives didn't know that the money scheme was a trap. If they resisted, 1313 neutralized them with a team of operators in Chicago.

The Board of Supervisors in El Dorado County, California, was the first to catch on when the Board of Supervisors was forced to look at some of the regional impositions at Tahoe. Among the shocking disclosures was the fact that the county was paying dues to more than sixty

1313 agencies set in motion by previous boards and approved by the Board. Local government also paid for the transportation of local officials to attend 1313 meetings where they were given 1313 solutions for local problems. (Local officials' salaries are paid through the county.) The local officials rubberstamped 1313 programs. This is not representation; it is "usurpation."

NRPB is actually the culprit which started this treasonous program raping Americans.

California, in the '50s, wanted to do away with loyalty oaths because the oaths encompassed the fact that the officials understood the Constitution and what would be "encroachments" upon it. Many organizations had ties to the representatives. At that time there was a 'Stalin Standard' – it didn't matter whether or not the representative was a card-carrying member of an organization, but whether or not he subscribed to the same standard. The purpose of these organizations was to set up a network of administrative, regional governance to replace representative government, guaranteed by the Constitution. A majority of the appointed officials are paid with the public purse, with the approval of our elected officials! Treason? These are the original Trotshyites who now call themselves neo-cons.

Chavez of Venezuela is setting up his regional councils as our neo-con leaches call him "communist." We create the Chavezes and the Castros and the Viet Congs and other radicals by coveting and taking their natural resources and giving them nothing but napalm in return. Imagine! It had to be Chavez who gave the poor in America a chance to buy their gasoline at a decent price. (Citgo)

Even President George Washington, in his Farewell Address, said that 'usurpation is the customary weapon by which governments are destroyed.'

The state is relieved of its planning duties and places this power in the hands of the feds who give out grant money to the states for different programs. Once the seed money is granted, the states take over the debt. A senior White House official handles this with a bunch of unelected bureaucrats.

Senator Alan Simpson recognized what the federal government was doing when he saw it in the Public Works and Economic Development Act of 1979 and called it "…a radical alteration that, if fully implemented, would replace the constitutional form of (our) government by the establishing of a new, unelected political order."

Had it not been for Senator Simpson, the goal to change our government would have been carried out in 1979. The underground network of watchdog newsletters and a very few courageous publishers of old-style newspapers helped as well.

A very reasoned report was issued in 1980 about the purpose of the NASA Space Program. What do those "weather satellites" really do? Instead of tracking the weather, could those billions of dollars be used to create situations which control population more effectively? (Tesla)

Without aggressive opposition we will become a de jure as well as a de facto reality. (law vs. absence of law)

Charles Merriam, father of 1313, chairman of the ACIR (Advisory Council on Intergovernmental Relations, 1313's federal beachhead), said in his biography by Barry Karl that "Even in President Hoover's administration (1929-33) a committee, unapproved by Congress, was created to write a report on constructive remedies for great social problems – the environmental movement, zero population growth, abortion, sex ed, immigration, miscegenation (racial intermarriage), the black revolution, the moral crisis, government childcare, ERA, civil rights, social gospel. Social scientists wrote it, Rockefeller funded it, and it was published by McGraw-Hill, not the government printing office, January 1933. (Social science emphasizes the living together of families, tribes, communities, races, etc. Civics and history are interwoven rather than studied separately.) Shades of the "Politics of Change!"

The National Resources Planning Board stocked with 1313 agents (a/k/a National Resource Committee) had as its job the extending of the 'Managerial Revolution' throughout the government.

Congress learned of this group in 1943 when it found that they were taking liberties with the Constitution and ordered it dissolved. But in 1937, this group had full approval of the White House and was requested by the National Municipal Association, National Conference of Mayors, and the Society of Planning Officials. Cities were targeted for reconstruction.

The 9th and 10th amendments made clear that states are not required to comply with federal mandates issued as rules and regulations or laws.

The social planners have tried to get us to fashion ourselves after the socially controlled European countries which they left because of the "social control." They fled to the freedom of the United States where they could make their own decisions because of the Constitution which gave us those powers. Now, after they have created a crime-ridden, welfare state in our cities, they want suburbanites to feel guilty for leaving and pay for it. They have brought subsidized living to the suburbs (Section 8) so that there is a distribution of wealth – not their wealth – but the wealth which those of us have accumulated through hard work. And it is hard work because these stagnating men and women in Congress sit there every day with nothing to do except regulate, regulate, regulate! They regulate small business until it's out of business by taxing it to death. They regulate farms, health care, and you name it. And now they want to tell 60-year-olds where they can live so that they don't stay in big homes and take up room. Corporations are deregulated.

About the 1937 National Resource Plan – Representative Frederick C. Smith (R. Ohio) made this remark: "To me it is truly alarming that such a destructive force as this should grow to its present size and power without the Congress and the country becoming more aware of its dangers than it apparently has…." (1943) He reported his findings to the Congress after the Resources Planning Board had been in progress for 10 years working its will on the people. When members of Congress realized that Roosevelt's New Deal was associated with the new programs, even dyed-in-the-wool democrats couldn't defend it. Had it not been for the fact that the executive budget of 1944 included this unit, it would never have been discovered. The Resources Unit was overlooked because it was started as a result of the Stock Market Crash of 1929 and the resulting Economic Stabilization Act of 1931. Congressman Smith uncovered the fact that legislative bodies are used to obtain public monies for undisclosed projects with undisclosed purposes. And they do this in spades today by just adding any old pork to any bill. (Earmarks)

The law creating the Economic Stabilization Act provided appropriations for "public works" to get the economy moving again. The Public Works described structures to house the bureaus needed to stave off a depression – acquiring sites, constructing buildings, etc.

Congressman Smith: "…certainly, there is nothing in that Act which gives this federal agency any authority to plan a new social and economic order, as its activities clearly indicate it is undertaking to do." "An instrumentality of Roosevelt."

The Planners used the same tactic for the Federal Advisory Commission on Intergovernmental Relations (ACIR). Roosevelt described this committee as the "planning arm of my Executive Office." The Board had already created an umbrella over state and local governments under the direction of the Department of Agriculture in 1943 – all without the sanction of Congress or the citizenry.

Also in the works was Harvard Professor Alvin Hansen, a special advisor to the NRPB, working in cooperation with Chairman Eccles of the Federal Reserve Board on problems of fiscal policy…relating to regional development. (Charles Merriam, in an article, 1941). The plan promised to include many duties which had been the responsibility of Congress and the prerogative of states or cities.

Congressman Smith remarked, the Planners planned to: "raze our cities and construct them anew."

Isn't this what our local, state, and federal legislators have done? Confiscating properties, Katrina, the "Delaware River Partnership" in Pennsylvania, leasing bridges, etc. are only some of the illegal and unconstitutional activities being practiced by this government within a government.

Maureen Heaton (*Impossible Dream*) wrote about malls and why they were simultaneously created all across the country in every city and town. In the 1943 report of the NRPB, she found: "The malls were not important in themselves. They were a means of moving existing businesses out of the way so that the planners would have free access to the central core of the cities to 'construct' them anew."

The planners found that taking over downtown development through "Urban Renewal" was not cost-effective. So in the 1970s, the planners began a process to obtain their objectives.

The Law Factory, 1313, came up with a "model law" which was placed in state statute books by compliant state legislators. It allows for the activation of the "Business Improvement Areas (BIA). Its provisions persuade the citizens to 'voluntarily' turn the inner cities over to the planners. The state laws passed to legalize these shenanigans encourage 'voluntary taxation' – businesses initiating taxes on themselves to obtain services which lawful government cannot provide because it is spending money on expanded social programs. (*Impossible Dream*, p. 165) "Fuzzyheaded decisions on land use have eroded the local tax base and pushed the lid off city and county budgets. Funds to pay for core projects are nonexistent.

"Twelve years after Congress gave its consent for the planners to build structures, it remained unaware that its consent encompassed social, economic, and political activities of the 'government' and its people. Education, with its family-life and land-use indoctrination, was part of the scheme. Legislators transferred powers to the executive, to bureaucrats, and to totally unaccountable citizens' advisory committees."

The plan was continued even after Congress revoked it. It is possible that some members of Congress knew what the NRPB was doing and that some might have known that the nature of what NRPB was doing was changed by executive fiat in 1933 – but did not blow the whistle.

When FDR created the National Industrial Recovery Act (later known as NRA) and got it approved by Congress, Harold Iches, Director of Public Works, by sleight of hand, recreated the NRPB as an adjunct of NRA but with a new mandate. Among its altered duties were preparation of comprehensive plans for regions as well as states and local governments; surveys to determine population, existing land use, industrial sites, housing, and national resources.

This revolution denies the Christian/Judeo ethic; it depends on the school to foster the moral relativism seen in social science projects such as Man, A Course of Study. And, it reduces man to a "resource." In a survey which took place in El Dorado County, California, in 1959, the planners found that the horrible possibility of proliferating housing for citizens of the United States threatened the national beauty of the county and demanded a planned program to contain the growth of the county population. They researched the habits, trends, and values of the people in order to build coordination, cooperation, and correlation of federal projects with local initiatives. (Ibid., p. 166)

The developers of the so-called NRPB became the founding fathers of the New Society. Congressman John Rankin, a 'liberal,' condemned the NRPB, saying that it "would wreck this republic, wipe out the Constitution, destroy our form of government, set up a totalitarian regime, eliminate private enterprise, regiment our people and pile on their backs a burden of expenditures that no nation on earth could bear."

Frederick Delano. The aging maternal uncle of FDR, was the dominant figure in the NRPB. All of the executive heads served at his pleasure. President Roosevelt submitted the last official report of the Board to Congress as 'his' plan for postwar America.

Congressman Noah Mason told his colleagues that, if they accepted this plan, they would be putting this socialistic scheme ahead of the war effort. It was Congressman Mason's research which disclosed that the Director of Research for the NRPB was Evelyn Burns, a British subject and activist in the radical movement in England. She and her husband had been "…the conduit for the underground railroad operating between the United States and Great Britain, through the office of Felix Frankfurter in the United States and Harold Laski of the London School of Economics in the Fabian-founded British counterpart of Chicago University. (Remember the Fabian Method – "step by step")

The Drs. Burns (sociologists) were instrumental in building the planned society for Britain, which contributed greatly to the decline and fall of the British Empire. Mrs. Burns wrote the socialist platform for Britain in 1932 and used the same proposals for the NRPB.

Many professors and tacticians were collaborators for the Tahoe, California, Regional Plan. Berkeley and Harvard were among the universities training students for jobs in local and state positions. This could not have taken place without the cooperation of state legislators, Congress, the White House, and public interest groups.

President Jimmy Carter, 1979, revoked Executive Order 11647 – President Nixon's placing elected officials under the umbrella of both state and federal regional councils manned by appointed devotees of 1313 who, in turn, were responsible to an appointed federal regional 'czar' in Washington. Our sovereign states became wards of the federal government. Carter then executed Executive Order 12149, replacing 11647, with "…an order to provide a structure for interagency and intergovernmental cooperation…."

Senator Alan Simpson and Senator George Ray Hudson started an investigation. Citizens were angry. Several states began to look into the situation but only Illinois carried out a full investigation. Jimmy Carter had intended his 'change' to be in response to the Public Works and Economic Development Act of 1979.

The report carried the same warnings – "intrusion by federal government into duties of states and local governments. This is an increase of federal power at the expense of local and state governments, using public money, laws, programs, requirements, and regulations to alter the structure of local and state governments. Federal councils are a threat to the sovereignty of the 50 states."

Along came Ronald Reagan who pretended to do the same thing as Carter – eliminate the federal councils. Reagan passed a new Executive Order, 12407, in which he changed "federal councils" to Councils of Government (COGs). Although the Illinois report suggested elimination of the federal councils, nothing was done. The rest is history.

There are always whistleblowers, but we don't hear about their bravery. In 1974, El Dorado Supervisor, Bill Johnson, testified against "sub-state redistricting to ACIR in San Francisco." He startled the crowd with these words: "Would you believe it if I told you that I live under a government that has taxing, police, and legislative powers, but I do not elect the governing board? Nor do I have recall rights against my governors, nor initiative and referendum rights against the 'laws' they pass. Yes, I do have that distinction, and I do live in the United States – at Lake Tahoe." They called it TRAP, the Tahoe Regional Area Plan.

I've mentioned, under regionalism, the shenanigans that go on during town meetings where there are plants (facilitators) in the audience who lead the conversation in the direction of the planner's goals.

For instance, in sex education meetings, focus is taken away from the content of the program itself and shifted to the limited planned goal of "should we use the same program which has been successful in grades K-12 for the past years." No one can ask "Why K-12?" The crowd leaves thinking that they were part of the decision-making process.

Business Improvement Areas (BIAs), like sex ed, will come to haunt us with the evil effects of each. We already see the results of sex ed over three decades. And we can now see the result of BIAs in the community of Greenberg – the Green Zone. A planner tells you which nail to use and which siding. He also tells you to get rid of anyone over 60 living in a house alone. Planners have multifamily units waiting for that house.

An administrative body is not bound by the same laws and regulations which hold for elected bodies so that elected commissioners use a COG (Council of Government) to solve problems of eminent domain, etc. Politicians acceding to this plan should serve jail time. Centralized planning by government was first practiced by the Soviets.

Don Bell, in 1959, reported on an AP dispatch that 9 state governors – 5 republicans and 4 democrats – went to the Soviet Union "to see how regional government handles regionalism." The trip was paid for by the Rockefeller Brothers Fund and the Alfred P. Sloan Foundation.

When Harvard graduates, like Senator Obama, enter "community service" organizations, rest assured that it's for money. "Public Allies" was founded by the Senator and directed by his wife, Michclle. Again, like all 'community' groups, they are funded by us, another nonprofit scheme paying $1,800 per month to organized protestors who take up causes such as aids and food stamps for illegals. In other words, we are paying for unconstitutional causes. Nurses and other professionals don't even enjoy these salaries. What's the incentive for freeloaders to get off the freebie line? Bill Clinton's Americorp, comparable to Obama's group, may cost us $500 billion. (Investors Daily, 9/5/08)

And the "elite" want us to vote for Obama or McCain. Both are pro war and pro amnesty for "20 million illegals and social security for these poor souls who shouldn't be here. Bighearted guys with our hard-earned money while they live in luxurious homes as our 'servants'." Community Groups must go! I thought that slavery was gone, but the new slaves in middle class are here to stay, unless we take action.

In 1963, the Department of Agriculture, instead of its own report, issued an update on NRPB (National Resource Planning Board).

In 1964, the ACIR issued its first major policy paper: "federal urban development policy."

In 1965, Lyndon Johnson railroaded the PWEDA through Congress – the executive could deal directly with local government, bypassing the states. Regional Councils provided the channel for federal directives to reach local districts and to obtain acceptance. PWEDA was sold as a means of breaking up the power in Washington. The carrot: federal funds; the stick, withholding federal funds.

So when the Congress thought that they had dissolved the NRPB, a group in the Senate moved the Act forward, step by step, until today we are under the Administrative Governance proposed by the NRPB. Congress then called the NRPB the Advisory Commission on Intergovernmental Relations.

State Senators, who dutifully go along with this program, find it easy to move to Washington as a reward.

Dean Clarence Manion was the first appointee to the ACIR. A former democrat, he became an Eisenhower republican who really believed in the Constitutional Republic. He was a professor of Constitutional Law. When he tried to unscramble what the "New Dealers" had been doing for 20 years, he was fired. He was replaced by Meyer Kestanbaum, clothing manufacturer from Chicago and Fellow of the Council on Foreign

Relations. Kestanbaum carried out the details of the original report and Clarence Manion was labeled a "right wing extremist." (Of course, today, he'd be labeled "antigovernment.")

With the election of a new Congress who knew nothing about the pitfalls of the last 20 years, the deal was a cinch to carry off.

In 1959, "Goals for Americans" was produced and a permanent federal Advisory Commission on Intergovernmental Relations, a new, improved version of the old NRPB.

Secrecy was no longer required, and 1313 began its program in full view of the public. Congress created ACIR without mandating oversight. No oversight was mandated for the NRPB. Was it coincidence? (Congressman John Rarick and Jo Hindman, a renowned researcher, tried to reverse the oversight part, but were stonewalled.) Manned by a group of elected federal, state and local officials and appointed federal officials and planners, the ACIR issues reports which are available to all who ask. Philadelphia has its office on 5th Street, near center city.

Governors, Congressmen, legislators, and appointees who preside over meetings, are treated to a team of "experts" who tell them how to filter the information back into the communities and begin implementing the directives, armed with knowledge about how to fend off citizen opposition.

The Senate is no longer the guardian of the 10th amendment (States Rights). Control of the Senate was passed from the state to the public, thereby making it okay for foundations to sponsor campaigns. Governors now fill vacant Senate seats with temporary appointees.

"Family Life" education entered California by way of Chicago State College in 1946, but parents were so irate that the case went to a Grand Jury which found that the program was "…not educational…but, rather, in many respects, immoral." They declared it was: "…inconceivable that any modern educator would even contemplate the use of the books…for children of high school age." The state Senate agreed.

Fast forward to the '60s and that same material is being used in kindergarten.

In the late '50s another attempt to insert sex ed in California started with a "comic book" which used two dogs, Whitey and Blacky, to demonstrate the sex act. The California Department of Education refused to disclose the names of those who prepared sex guides for teachers. We have dysfunctional oddballs controlling the young lives of "human resources."

"Degradation – of person and country – is held by the enemy to be the best and foremost weapon of conquest."

I mentioned earlier, "Goals for Americans, The Report of the President's Commission on National Goals." The President was Eisenhower. Copies can be found online.

Briefly, the goals (12) covered everything that has already happened and which I have covered. The major strategy involved two principles:

1.election of representatives – 'purging' of elected officials who do not follow 'the party line.'

2."constitutional limitation of power of those elected."

Goal 4 is for the total involvement of education in building a "new world." Global 2000: "new techniques and strategies in education."

Goal 6 is transfer of business to other countries (NAFTA).

Other goals: society change from "productive" to "service," land use planning, urban redevelopment, urban sprawl (Reagan's dream), specific programs for health and welfare, intervention in agriculture (two farmers were killed trying to resist).

This commission was appointed in1958. Permission for the system was approved in 1958, and the bill creating a 1313 cell was introduced in 1958.

Recently, we've heard John McCain accuse Senator Obama of supporting "sex ed" for kindergarten. Where has Senator McCain been for over four decades when he could have done something about it? Sex ed was piloted into poor areas first, in every city in the '60s. Then, private, public and parochial schools followed suit by government mandate with seed money from foundations. And the message wasn't about trying to inform 5-year-olds about "bad touching" – a parent's job. It was about introducing sex to all five-year-olds in order to neutralize innocence and values. Probably Governor Sarah Palin realized it too late to save her pregnant teenage daughter.

Today, any child can turn on TV in Philadelphia's Channel 3 and hear two doctors, Dr. Lisa and Dr. Travis, explain oral sex to three eleven-year-old girls who were duly shocked. I can't elaborate on the frivolity with which the subject was treated by Dr. Lisa, followed by profuse praise by Dr. Travis. This program shown at 3 p.m. is produced by Dr. Phil McGraw's family, doing quite well on the strength of sleaze, thanks to the great Oprah who certainly does her part. (9/25/08, also on The Doctors TV.COM)

After four decades of this junk, children can get a degree in sex but zip in grammar and math and science. Soft-headed judges, who get directions from "community" sources, often let pedophiles off the hook. "They had a bad childhood." This gives them the right to abuse strangers? Soft-headed thinking.

A dominant figure in re-educating the public was John Dewey. From his position at Columbia University, he was able to teach "normal" school teachers social science instead of history. "Normal" school was the name given to those education majors from 1909-1940s. Some teachers went into publishing, others sat on the underground regional railroad – school boards, city councils, state legislatures. With the help of Rockefeller's General Education Board, they were able to accomplish a lot.

In 1909, the Bishop of Emory Methodist University in Georgia, Warren Candler, wrote: "An educational trust has been formed, and it is operating to control the institution of higher education in the United States.... It proposes to change (America's) political thinking, religious beliefs, and social organization, by a scheme to dominate colleges and universities." He described his effort to bring awareness to the public as "… an unheeded voice in the wilderness." And it was; for even though his testimony was presented to the Senate, the Senate approved Rockefeller's incorporation of the General Education Board.

So, for decades, Rockefeller has controlled the forces of education which led to the obvious decline we see today. The Charter, which GEB signed, involved the right of other corporations to get involved in promoting their objectives. The "Charter" also included "matching funds" under the control of the corporations! This is the "revenue sharing" taxpayers are expected to give for the benefit of the corporate czars. Sex ed, drug ed, sensitivity training, multiculturalism, environment, outreach education – whatever those globalists deem necessary to exploit children and adults.

Brave senators, like George Chamberlain (R. Oregon), spoke out against the Charter and its effect on the ideals of America.

Authors, like Mary Follett, wrote a book, "The New State," which became the bible of the revolutionaries. (1918) Her attack was on representative government. Her goal: "A common purpose and a collective will."

In 1905, Georgia led the way into what is known today as a public education system "with the first state constitutional amendment to permit taxation for public high schools."

Augustin Rudd, head of the Sons of the American Revolution, protested the "Building America" (Rugg) series of textbooks, which were placed in American schools in the 1930s. According to Rudd, after the Soviet coup in Russia, the Soviets took over the education system, destroying traditional education and replacing it with progressive education spawned by John Dewey with his socialist friends at Columbia. The result was a generation of Soviet youth who, when they left school, could not read, write or cipher. Juvenile delinquency became a major problem in the Soviet Union, and there were bands of non-productive young people robbing, looting, and using violence against anyone.

Sound familiar? After that generation of Russian children were thoroughly perverted, the Soviet schools returned to "traditional education" except that now they were controlled by the state. And the state didn't want individuals who could think for themselves, but production-line citizens. American educators, some of them trained in the Soviet Union, began to direct American schools into the system known for destroying culture and heritage.

After Reagan told Gorbachev to "take down the wall," he began exchanging American students with Russian students and American teachers with Russian teachers. Computers were now ready to change American children into compliant citizens of the 21st century.

"Because of our diverse population, the change could not take place overnight." It wasn't possible to turn America into a police state overnight, as was done in Russia. It wasn't possible to murder millions of people, and, in so doing, 'eradicate' the poisonous influence of the older generation. It wasn't possible to destroy those with leadership qualities – their capabilities had to be destroyed in other ways.

"Our one-party economic planning system is underway, designed by the agents of 1313 known as "Councils of Government."

"The machinery for the centrally controlled police state is in place, and America's once proud 'thin blue line' – our local police – has been conditioned to control the citizens they were hired to protect should any be so bold as to speak out when they learn the truth about their 'government.' (Branch Davidians and the ATF siege in Waco, Texas) (Maureen Heaton, "The Impossible Dream")

Chesly Manly, in 1954, reported on how this revolution will take place: "The revolutionary program…calls for unbearable taxes and expenditures to create a crisis, which would provide a pretext for the government to take over the whole system at one stroke."

Michigan University and many others, along with Chicago, have agents trained in social science and group dynamics, ready, willing and able to create willing collaborators. Centers for research, gathering information on citizens is an outgrowth of this plan. This is why we should be leery of the Patriot Act which allows government to search our homes without warrants. Just who are these Hitlers ruling the lives of the rest of us? God has given us rights – not corrupt government, and we should read again the Declaration of Independence.

I can't emphasize enough: question everything, even the drastic weather changes hitting our shores.

Weather is certainly overtaking the news about war, crime, bank closings, the economy, and drugs coming in "legitimately" in Mexican trucks.

When Senator Obama and George Bush talk about "volunteerism," look out! They select what you may volunteer to do.

Cicero: "The one who looks neat, speaks softly, and turns government into tyranny – is the one who is more dangerous than a murderer." (42 B.C.) (paraphrased)

Ask yourselves why the so-called "end times" preachers are all over the dials, and in foreign countries, spreading this stupidity. They have infected the masses with this lethal virus which manifests itself even in the Pentecostal Church of Governor Sarah Palin who said, before her congregation, that the "Iraq War is a task from God. There is a plan, and it is God's plan." (Charles Gibson Interview, 9/11/08) The Governor tried to explain her church remarks by blaming them on President Lincoln. Of course Lincoln never made such a heinous statement. Once again, I remind you that these dopes who jump around and fall, speaking in tongues, don't mind the over 200,000 deaths of innocent Iraqis or the 4,000 deaths of troops sent to a faraway land to kill. They don't mind the rape of innocents, but they will defend "life." That goes for Pat Buchanan, whom I used to respect, too. He and his uninformed sister have made enough money supporting Bush.

By the way, Pentecost is named after a Jewish holiday. These mindless Christian fools can't even make up a name for their church. Pathetic! And this fraudulent religion didn't blossom until World War II when wounded troops and the boxes carrying the dead who thought that they were dying to save American values came home. Mothers, like Mrs. Sullivan, had five stars in her window, denoting the fact that she sacrificed five wonderful sons to a bloody war.

Today, America suffers from the remnants of that planned war with the patriotic songs and movies from the Hollywood moguls, relishing the money coming in from their propaganda films. Bankers and war profiteers must have been dancing all over the world as their greedy tongues thirsted for more and more of the same. Their sins are with us today whenever I hear dumbed-down men call a station and say "Let's nuke 'em all." Bloodthirsty no-account men, bullies, who don't have the brains to make a decent living for the family they shouldn't have had – sending their sons off to fight a banker's war.

On Rush's show, today (9-16-08), a caller, claiming to be leaving for Iraq as an infantryman, said that his purpose in going was "to level houses." And Rush, like all of the other rats on radio, said, "Our prayers will be with you." Rush is the man who has no children and who doesn't care about anything but money.

SINCE OBAMA WAS ELECTED...

Our corporate terrorists are the old white men, and now the old black men and other ethnic groups who never seem to have enough money. They are the tightwads who won't make a poor lottery or slot player win a dime, even at Christmas time. Usually their faces project "the evil interred in their bones."

They're the ones who have decided that our children should be dumbed down and which courses will make them the needed subjects for their New World Order. Young children are programmed in sex ed and more sex ed, environmental studies, multiculturalism, social justice, global history before American history, and deprecation of our framers, those "meanies" who gave us the Declaration of Independence.

There are no absolutes, only moral relativism. If it feels good, do it. After all, "religion is a crutch;" drugs and alcohol are the new replacements. And for those of us who still believe in God, they'll give us an updated form – "end times" or maybe motivational speakers such as Joel Osteen, the new sensation attracting overwhelming crowds. For Catholics there will be guitars, lots of laymen walking up and down the aisles while folksy tunes are played, and if we're lucky, maybe one or two traditional songs at Christmas time. But church services must "fit the times." Social justice throughout the world must prevail; bombs don't count.

Our impotent Judases in Congress gave the corporate lobbyists all of the deregulation legislation they needed in order to betray hardworking Americans by taking their jobs offshore, along with workers' pensions.

Any notion of a free-market capitalist society is long gone. We taxpayers now subsidize failing banks, and trade deficits caused by corporate pressure on Congress to eradicate tariffs on imported goods – tariffs which used to be used to repair roads, bridges, etc.

Corporate money buys votes for our congressional traitors; corporate money selects our presidential candidates. No one arrives in Washington, D.C. who wasn't chosen by "pay to play" schemes. We the People did not select McCain or Obama or Hillary.

True to form, sadly, the new President filled his cabinet with Clinton retreads: good old Robert Rubin, Treasury Secretary under Clinton, was a Goldman-Sachs man who made us bail out his group when they made bad investments in Mexico. Cost to us: $50 billion. Rubin worked with Larry Summers, former president at Harvard, who said that "women were not so competent as men in math." Needless to say, Summers was "canned" and will now serve as an advisor to Obama.

Rahm Emanuel, another war hawk who served in the Israeli – not American – military, will be Chief of Staff. Emanuel is known to curse profusely and has sent a dead fish to a pollster. He sounds like a class act from the Mayor Daley political machine in Illinois. Emanuel has already suggested that Americans 18-25 years old do compulsory service for jobs such as nuclear waste cleanups. He also called for a "national" civilian police force. And, he wants "educational involvement." Sounds like the beginning of a Hitlerian youth group. Who gave Emanuel charge of American youth? Sounds like a continuation of the Bush-Cheney dynasty, not change.

Philadelphia talk show hosts, like Dominic Giordano, have been repeating the mantra of "I can't understand the Bush haters" for six years. Perhaps if Mr. Giordano read a book or a newspaper, he would understand – not why people hate Bush – but why the world hates us <u>because</u> of Bush and the atrocities committed in his name. In Somalia, the political factions were getting along under Moslem rule until the Bush Administration engaged Ethiopia and bombed Somalia – no input from us. No wonder Somalians are pirating ships at sea; we've driven them to it. Americans are taught to believe, by cowardly yes men, that all the world is our oyster to be bullied and brutalized because we have the air, sea, and gun power to make them submit. We're learning the hard way that no country will take it any longer. Too bad that the characters in our government were able to convince citizens that to go along with governmental usurpation of foreign wealth is "pro-American" and to be against it is "anti-American."

George Bush granted no pardons to the two Mexican border guards who shot at a known drug dealer. Evidently he has no mercy on young Americans who get hooked on drugs; remember, he was an alcoholic and misery loves company. Upon leaving office, President Bush "commuted" the sentences of the border guards, who will continue to have this stain on their records.

Mr. Bush, during this economic crisis, made a deal with Colombia so that more Americans lose their jobs, and he may have used the carrot and stick approach with the bailout of General Motors.

The Patriot Act, written long before 911, serves to take away most of our civil rights, if we have any left. Government officials can now search our homes without a judge's warrant, and they can listen in on our conversations. Remember that these "officials" are the same ones who allow drugs, guns and dealers to penetrate our borders and shoot at our border guards. These "officials" make deals with their puppet nasties all over the world and use our military when needed.

In just ten years, the nature of calls coming into radio stations has degenerated greatly. Sports and trivia have clearly taken over. Male callers are pathetic with their "I'm afraid that an Islamic terrorist will strike us with another 911. President Bush has kept us safe." Perhaps the saying "what you don't use, you lose" is applicable to this group. Seems that male brains are on hold, and I'm beginning to wonder what these callers talk about at the dinner table – if someone were dumb enough to marry them.

President Bush tried to get the support of Europeans during the Iraqi occupation but was unsuccessful. Mysteriously, we now have a new leader in France, Nicolas Sarkozy, an Hungarian Jew whose family was involved in the Holocaust. The new leader in Germany is Angelina Merkel, who won by a very narrow margin and who is a committed terrorist-hunter. Great Britain had a new leader, Gordon Brown. All pro-Israel no matter what. Meanwhile Tony Blair, the former prime minister, went to Israel lending "support" while the Palestinian massacre goes on, killing as many civilians as they can. Mayor Bloomberg of New York also went to Israel, lending support to the holocaust of the Palestinians. Bloomberg made his money here in the United States, but his heart is in Israel with his "super race" comrades. Even the United States Supreme Court labeled the

Zionists "racist." When Charles DeGaulle was President of France (1959-69), he favored the Arabs and he refused to support Israel's 1967 war and placed an embargo on Israel.

Children's book sections are replete with holocaust stories so that young readers will be programmed early. Nothing in the book section talks about the plight of Palestinians at the hands of their Israeli tyrants for the past 61 years. Meanwhile in Philadelphia Mayor Nutter is closing libraries. Bookstores, too, are closing. Wonder why!

In the recent bombing of the Taj Hotel in India only the child of the Jewish rabbi and his wife, both of whom died, was sensationalized. Little, if anything, was reported about other murder victims. Fortunately, the Indian nanny of the rabbi's son was able to save the child's life by escaping unharmed. Again, only the deaths of the Chosen People are reported – the rest of us don't matter. What a joke it is for this segment of the Jewish population to invoke what Jesus said about Chosen People 2000 years ago when they've done everything possible to poke fun at the man we call Jesus. Although the Jewish Star and the United States flag were burned in effigy throughout the Middle East, we still don't get it. Our cluster bombs are gentle; our nepalm is sweet. Middle Easterners want our oil mafia and troops protecting them, out. We're fed the nonsense by military leaders that the deaths of three million Vietnamese or millions of "Islamic terrorists" are not worth the life of one American. God help us. What kind of fool believes this tripe? Americans have long lost their value compasses. It's sickening to hear "our way of life." We've allowed dufusses in Congress to pass laws taking away our basic rights. Remember that the Constitution and the Bill of Rights must go, before the Globalists take over the world and divide us into "regions." At that time, we'll all suffer what the Palestinians are suffering at this time, and there will be no document to protect us. Socialism: "little by little." Even the Hate Crime legislation is trying to make the "felony" list. As people catch on, look out – the new Nazis "vil be vatching you."

As I listened to Fox and MSNBC, nobody, but nobody, had compassion for Palestinian life. It was all about the Hamas rockets that I doubt ever reached a target. Israel and its American benefactors know that in America Israel can do no wrong. Thanks to CNN and Rick Sanchez who showed both sides. Thanks to Larry King who had Zogby debate Dershowitz and the latter lost soundly with his bad memory of Israel's history. To

Dershowitz, Palestinians are guilty of defending themselves – with rocks and homemade tin rockets.

Religion, as I've pointed out, has been destroyed; I should say "Christian religion," with its deprecation of Christ and the watering down of all Christian faiths. When Senator McCarthy called it "Godless Communism," he was right. Little did he know that these Marxists would hide behind "Globalism" and "Internationalists." And the best part is that Globalism is not working.

The same Pentagon, which can't account for two trillion dollars, is now training 20,000 troops for active duty in the United States in case of an attack (by some tiny third world country). So much for hundreds of billions going into Pentagon coffers. It seems to me that no one should be trusted with "classified" or "black budgets," especially when the public is concerned that the 20,000 troops on our streets smack of martial law. The citizens should be able to scrutinize everything – no "national security" documents with blacked out sections. George Bush, before leaving office, tried to sell nuclear technology to a nation friendly to Iran. So much for bogeymen threats from Iran where money is to be made.

When President Obama talks about helping the poor, he includes the poor of the world – "nation building in Afghanistan and grants to the USDA (U.S. Development Abroad)." He arrogantly feels that he is a "global" president.

The United States Justice Department should abandon the "Hunt for Nazis Department" started 30 years ago to show what happens to those who kill Jews. Again, nothing happens to Jews who kill non-Jews. This sentiment was best expressed by the media's comedy central channel when the Colbert Christmas comedy was aired, showing Willy Nelson bringing marijuana to Baby Jesus. It's immunity from injustice, killing our children's belief in religion. With no values or guidelines there is no meaningful life. But go to a synagogue and there are no jokes there. They pray for their land, Israel, Israel.

Mr. Gates, in the midst of our economic crisis (CNN, 12-4-08), suggested that we give to countries that have less than we. Amazing how billionaires talk down to us. The rest of us are lucky if our savings accounts earn 1% or 2% interest. Millions from the Gates foundation went to the Clinton foundation and the Saudis. I'd like to know what the payback will be. National and European banks made out like bandits, thanks to our bailouts, and these characters are all friends working together for their own interests.

Recently, I had the privilege of attending a funeral service for an outstanding career military man who gave many years to the service of his country. People came from everywhere to honor him, and honor him they did at Arlington National Cemetery.

The service was one of the most beautifully staged and memorable declarations of love that I, in my late years, have ever witnessed. One would have to be a robot not to be deeply touched by the scene just before arriving at the site. One witnesses fields – never ending fields with tombstones – of those who died in the service of their country.

And then, the inimitable stoic demeanors of the young military officers standing at attention, with faces I will never forget – faces denoting honor and duty to the America all of us want returned to us. Accompanying this grandeur was a most beautiful black multiple horse-driven carriage with two capped drivers at the fore carrying the flag-draped coffin.

Even the foreign cab driver, who took us to the gate, was shaken. "It's a terrible sight," he said. "I'm finished for the day."

One of the attendees commented that "they [military] have this service down to a tee. It's a religion." It made perfect sense. Most of you are too young to remember the funeral of John F. Kennedy with the President's three-year-old son, John, saluting his father's casket – forever burned into everyone's memory.

As someone who lived and absorbed happenings of that time and had a dad, brothers, uncles, nephews and cousins touched by war after war, I can say that these tombstones at Arlington represent lives stolen and cut short by government officials who sold the victims a bill of goods about God and country while at the same time advancing legislation to remove the Pledge of Allegiance from schools and to take any mention of God out. It was in preparation for godless tyranny. All of the presidents in my lifetime took us one step closer to the NWO.

Schools don't mention the fact that the Declaration of Independence acknowledged God four times. James Wilson, a signer of the Constitution said, "Religion and law go together." (Also in the Koran) Daniel Webster, a United States Senator and Secretary of State, 1827-1852, said, "History is God's providence."

Whenever war defenders ask "how can you say that those in the military died for nothing," it should be answered by another question: "When did the framers suggest that we involve ourselves in foreign wars over resources (oil, etc.) belonging to sovereign countries. And are we to shed the blood of the young in war after war benefiting no one until there are no young people left – so that we can say "he was a great American?" Please! A great American sees that his child protects our Constitution and liberties – not the liberties of Exxon Mobil and other war profiteers. Troops should be on our borders only. The tombstones should cry out "No more wars; no more bloodshed. Enough! <u>Don't tread on me.</u>" No, they did not die in vain if you've gotten the message.

Ask yourselves why Bill Ayers, that awful weatherman member, wasn't jailed after being cited for the bombing of the Pentagon and other public buildings. Why, of all things, is Mr. Ayers involved in early childhood education? Funny, but President Obama suggested that kindergartners be taught sex education. It's nothing new; it's the idea of the planners who have taken over education. And it seems that Ayers will be a zealous advocate for dumbing down the children, just as the new president will if he goes along with this travesty.

Translation: Ayers and Obama were selected a long time ago to be part of the water carriers for the principles of the Globalists. Racism and "radicalism" helped to downplay America's real problems of illegal immigration, crime, loss of jobs, and a growing hatred for war.

Let's hope that Obama decides to do what's right, even though it will take the courage of a real American – an American grounded in constitutional law, with no chip on his shoulder.

On C-SPAN2 (1-7-09) I watched a group of politicians, professors and CEOs decide our destinies, and it really angered me – a bunch of frauds deciding what's best for Americans now that they've taken us into desperate times with their bad judgments.

Mr. Feldstein, a Harvard Economics Professor, suggested that "recruiting for the military" might be helpful to those with no jobs. And Mr. Norman Augustine, a former Chairman and CEO at Lockheed Martin, thought that "our ability to compete is diminishing in science and engineering in this "global" marketplace for jobs. One can get five Chinese scientists for the price of one in America." Mark Zandi (Moody Economics) thought that "we should continue with unemployment insurance and food stamps."

Robert Reich, former labor secretary under Clinton, is now one of the "economic" advisors to President Obama. If you recall, he suggested that Americans get used to "sharing" jobs or training for several other jobs. Fortunately for him, this socialist dufuss has held the same job forever. His suggestion? "If government doesn't act, it won't be good."

I say that it's time to get rid of these deadbeats and tell them to train for some kind of volunteer job which will pay us back for their overblown salaries and disinformation. As for the CEOs who make millions of dollars even when their judgment is useless or they have taken investors down a hopeless path, some jail time might satisfy the rest of us. Notice that CEOs never mention our giving CEO jobs to the Chinese. I'm certain that we could get "five CEOs for the price of one in America."

These facts are why globalism isn't working. How long will Americans sit back and tolerate the arrogance of these "advisors" who clearly have no common sense? What they're saying is: hand over education to us; let your children fight for us; subsidize our companies which are relocating to China and wherever cheap labor takes us; we have no loyalty to this country; we will come and go as we please; we hope that there is strife between illegals and those looking for jobs; so long as we have our private jets and homes here and there, we can limit our involvement in your problems. C'est la vie!

Obama's economic speech (1-9-09) left much to be desired. I thought that he would mention dropping the trade laws (with no tariffs) or should I say 'traitor' laws. And this "antiwar" man is changing his tune on troops which he wants to surge in Afghanistan. Perhaps that's what he meant by Change! He's another George W.

He talked about wind turbines and solar panels but no mention of oil on our own land. He must have made the corporate czars, like T. Boone Pickens, very happy with his "alternative" energy plans. Ca-ching, ca-ching! Nothing about the effect of F-16s going over to the Mideast to bomb children and adults, but he's a 'green' advocate! He's going to do away with old light bulbs, etc.

Some facts from the United Nations Security Council meetings held on Israel's bombing of Gaza (C-SPAN2, 1-6-09):

Again, these truths are not heard from radio talk show hosts, one of whom remarked on his show – after Israel's killing of children in Palestine: "What kind of mother would send out her child as a suicide martyr?" (I must shamefully admit that this host is Dom Giordano, an Italo-American. Unless someone in his background is Jewish, I can't understand how he keeps his job at WPHT – all pro-Israel, all the time. Like Medved and others, he's a fountain of disinformation.)

Comments at the Security Council:

1. Mahmoud Abbas (Palestinian Authority President)
   "Enough suffering. There are 11,000 Palestinians jailed in Israel. There is food, medicine and water deprivation. Hundreds of checkpoints.
2. Gabriela Shalev (Israeli Ambassador to United States)
   "Rockets are coming over. One hit a kindergarten." (Fortunately, the children had off that day.) Interesting.
3. Ali Babacan (Turkish Foreign Minister)
   "This is the 11th day of this situation. Infrastructure is damaged; thousands lost homes; tragedy is severe."
4. Condoleeza Rice (Secretary of State)
   "Stopping the incursion won't help. The Hamas must stop firing rockets."
5. Abdurrahman Mohamed Shalgham (Libyan Foreign Minister)

"What the Palestinians have done is in reaction to what they have endured. The cease fire was not carried out, because of Israeli provocation – killing Palestinians. Bakeries were shut down. No sanitation; water once a week; money has not gotten through. There are air raids with cutting edge weapons; blockades of food and medicine. Israeli war machines continue to perpetrate the most heinous crimes against people without any attention to United Nations resolutions. Any delay sends a wrong message."

Only the United States defended Israel. Condoleeza Rice is Exhibit One that evil exists in all colors and groups. No savagery is enough for her so long as she gets that check and the glory of secret service men around.

For those people like Dom Giordano and others, THIS is why Americans are hated all over the world. His callers are afraid of an attack. How do you think the defenseless Lebanese, Syrians and other Arab nations (22) feel about daily bombings of their families? We bombed Iraq for ten years before occupying it. But people like Giordano spend their days over at Geno's Steaks, getting publicity for illegal immigration after doing all he could to help the illegals in the '90s when callers like me tried to warn people. At least Geno is a stand-up guy! (Joey Vento)

The Big Lie is that Clinton made a deal with Arafat (Oslo) giving the store away to the Palestinians. I covered this earlier. It was a disaster. The fact that Israel would concede any territory back to the Palestinians is a sad joke after all of the Russian settlements for which Americans – future Americans – paid, and will pay.

This segment of the Jewish population cannot assimilate. They have taken away every aspect of American culture. Our airwaves, job ownership, banking, foreign policy, religion – there are more Jewish pastors now than Christian pastors – Congress, the Presidency, State Department, Defense – all controlled by this growing cancer that deems itself the super race. Our children are being brainwashed with lies and disinformation. We have become accustomed to hearing only one side of a story. Unless we drastically change our foreign policy and send unbiased emissaries to the Mideast – not the neo-con gang under Hillary, their surrogate – I fear for young and old Americans.

We must call the Israeli Jews and American Jews who support them – and, of course, a lot do not – what they are: brutally intransigent murderers of anyone who disagrees with their goal of domination throughout the world. I might add here that we lived next to a Zionist whose property was 500 feet away from us but who planted trees – towering trees – right next to our fence and gagged us everyday with sprays for the trees. He had us in court every Christmastime for some trumped up reason such as fence height or fence placement. Needless to say, he was a lawyer and began to look more and more like Adolf Eichmann. This helped me understand what Palestinians go through.

God did have a plan for me. I met my husband, a Moslem, Mexicans, Iraqis, Iranians, a young Russian who went to Israel, and said that he joined their army. The Russian youth had a nervous tick and attributed it to an experience he had in Israel. An Arab was hiding in a trash can, begging him not to shoot; however, the young Russian said that if he didn't shoot, two Israeli soldiers on a roof would have shot them both. He never forgot it and came to America – our occupied territory because of the ingrates and greedy characters in Congress. Both groups are evil.

We're not even allowed to say "get those so-called 'allies' off of our backs; we are doing their godless killing."

We fools give millions in grants to universities, such as George Washington, so that exchange students at the George Washington Homeland Security Institute for Terrorism can trade "tactics" with Israelis and Americans training here and in Israel. Pathetic that they have us murdering people as unfortunate as we. But when 34% of Americans can't read, this is the result.

Not everyone is stupid and programmed. A student, who attended a conference dealing with the Palestinian question, asked Sallai Meridor, the Israeli Ambassador to the United States, "Why don't you disband your propaganda unit in Great Britain? Isn't the greater threat to Israel, peace?"

Hopefully, I have given you the other side of the story before it's too late. Jon Stewart, Jewish, on Comedy Central, tried to give the true side as well. Shepherd Smith, too, gave both sides. They deserve praise.

With courage and prayer, we can reach millions of people who will understand that the Palestinians, Afghans, Syrians, Egyptians, etc., etc. want what we want – peace, not war; liberty, not serfdom.

Michael McConnell, Director of National Intelligence, was interviewed by Charlie Rose (WHYY, 1-8-09). The fact that this man is the head of anything is scary. He was talking about the fact that "global communication can now be made in a minute." So what? Does this mean that those of us in the United States have to abandon our own needs and take care of the world? He talked about the things I've mentioned earlier – the fact that China and India will become major economic leaders, above the United States, in the near future. Why? Because duds like this see nothing wrong with having everything made in China, completely selling out our national interests and building up China, India and Russia. These duds are TRAITORS - CITIZENS of the WORLD. They should be in jail! As usual, Charlie Rose asked whether or not Iran would be a nuclear threat in the future? "Yes." As though McConnell knows anything. In my opinion, these traitors are worse than Charles Manson. People like McConnell see themselves as power czars…Global Power Czars. People mean nothing, except as workers in their fields. He admitted that immigration in the United States would be a problem. As a matter of fact, we can blame this kind of traitor for not protecting our borders and for not allowing immigrants to enter the legal way. This corrupt government counts on immigration becoming a problem so that it can institute martial law, and then it's God help us all. (Politics of Change)

I implore young people to learn English well so that you can speak with authority when you need to throw the two-party system out and get America working again. I hope that Ron Paul is on board to help

America should not have to borrow money and put the future generations in debt so that we can be "magnanimous" with the money of the unborn. The three billion dollars and two billion dollars we give to Israel and Egypt should be stopped immediately. Only charity money and food should be sent to those countries in need – with oversight.

Of course, Charlie Rose can't hide his loyalty to Israel so he expressed his "concern" about "terrorists" from the Mideast. "Sissy-pants McConnell" said that "we're safe here in the United States because the U.S. has a presence in that part of the world." Translation: constant wars, a draft if necessary, more money for Lockheed and the arms companies, while America "services" the needs of the Chinese, Russians and Indians and becomes an impoverished land.

Things I'm disappointed about in the Obama Presidency:

1. The President rushed the Stimulus Bill (1049 pages) through Congress before they had a chance to read it. Transparency? Constitutional?

2. Rahm Emanuel, Chief of Staff, has a nameplate in his office, from his two brothers: "Undersecretary for Go ___ yourself." This stupidity we don't need when his office is so close to the President's. (The New Yorker, 3-2-09) The White House belongs to the People. Have respect for Us.

3. Pell Grants (college) could be switched from discretionary to mandatory. It is not my duty to pay for college access when I had to cosign for my own children, and they had jobs. They paid for their loans. Besides, where are the jobs or are they training for regionalism, urban development, environment, sex ed, and global warming?

4. More troops to Afghanistan is not my idea of ending military occupation. How long can we afford to pay $365 million a day for war?

5. Throwing more money at education is NOT the problem. The NEA should be tossed out; bad teachers can't be fired.

6. Nobody is addressing drug wars on our southern border. "Refugees" will be heading to the U.S. in addition to the twenty million illegals. I do not agree with Governor Napolitano that "we must confer with

President Calderone." It is Our problem. She took an oath to the United States Constitution, not the world.

7. After all of the "diplomacy" pre-election talk about Iran, President Obama wants to reset our relationship with Russia – another communist country – against a nuclear program in Iran. Iran would have been the only democracy in the Mideast had it not been for Eisenhower's installing the Shah instead of leaving Mossadegh, the elected leader, in office.

K.T. McFarland (female, former aide to "Kissinger") (Fox, 3-4-09) "Even though Americans are hurting economically, the Russians are hurting more. If we can help Russia, they may stop Iran from building a missile. Then we wouldn't need the base in Poland to stop Iran from nuking Israel." (paraphrased) (The base is already there.)

So…all of this deterrent billions – hundreds of billions – spent in Poland is, again, for Israel. Hillary, speaking from Jerusalem, pledged $900 million to Gaza, from our money, to help restructure what the murderers in Israel did. All of our billions go to Israel. Something is wrong here.

Andrea Mitchell (wife of Alan Greenspan, Federal Reserve) speaking from Jerusalem – emphasized only Gazan "rockets." Sending a Christian to Jerusalem wouldn't help, either!

8. With Prime Minister of England, Gordon Brown's last visit here to see President Obama (3-3-09), it was clear to me that the President did not present the truth to us before the election. President Obama called Brown, "Our greatest ally" – true to form for the NWO. The money left behind by Rhodes and Carnegie for propagandizing our unification with Great Britain certainly worked on what was thought to be a "bright" Obama. He may be articulate, but, unfortunately, anyone who sees hardworking Americans wiping out "World Poverty" is on a delusionary track. No one in America who has been used to the best will settle for such an injustice.

9. Bankers are now "World Bankers;" we are told to invest in other countries, as though America died.

Most Americans just want a well-paying job to pay off their mortgages and help their families. We cannot afford to let these brainwashed politicians destroy a country which God – not they – has blessed with our own resources – oil, coal, steel, everything – because these "Fools" are selling out the Best Country in the World. I wish that they'd leave before Americans react to the horrors planned for us. It won't be pretty or easy. It's the Revolution all over again: Taxation without Representation.

MILITARY ROBOTS

Lawrence Rockwood wrote an article (Montgomery County Observer, 7/29/96) entitled "When Robots Take Over the Military." Lawrence was an intelligence officer who was court-martialed for conducting an unauthorized inspection of the National Penitentiary in Port-au-Prince, Haiti. Dismissed from the military, Rockwood's sentence was stayed, pending an investigation of the unit's conduct by the Army Inspector General.

"Friedrich Nietzsche observed in "Thus Spoke Zarathustra:""I see many soldiers, would that I saw many warriors." Both a soldier and a warrior are of course participants in the use of force. However, technology has dehumanized modern war to the point where primordial warriors, with their spiritual commitment to personal sacrifice and individual aggressiveness, have become secluded and self-serving killers.

"Personal firearms drove the first wedge between "soldier" and "warrior." Soon the advent of aviation and weapons of mass destruction increased the distance between the warring sides, but soldiers still needed to be on battlefields, risking their lives.

"Recently, the Pentagon decided to contribute Unmanned Aerial Vehicles (UAVs) called Predators to the support of our U.N./NATO allies in Bosnia. As with the airlift to former Yugoslavia, the United States performed military tasks while keeping its troops comfortably far from the war theater. Indeed, those Predators can observe the battlefields in Bosnia while the men and women operating them are safe and secure in Albania."

Rockwood goes on to explain "force protection," as military commanders who want low casualties as the standard set in the Gulf War, and prefer to be overseeing remote control operators. If the Bosnians, let's say, mistakingly believe that "force protection" is synonymous with "forces-that-protect," it would be a huge error.

The Pentagon has recently initiated "Pentagon Speak," a $200 million project used in conjunction with President George W. Bush's "No child left behind" fiasco. This initiative is used to influence children to sign up for the military, even though parents may disagree. Knowing what I know, it is unlikely that parents realize that behavior modification is going on under their noses.

It used to be that it was an honor to graduate from West Point or Annapolis. Today, I feel that it takes more courage to stand against corruption in government and to speak out, as officer Darby did in the case of the Abu Graib prison scandal. Because he was a hero, we don't hear about him. Instead, we are made to watch films of American soldiers with AK-47s kicking down doors of suspected terrorists. Of course, our troops can zero in on just the criminals who dare to want the United States corporations out of their country and lives. We should use our perceptive generals to hunt down some U.S. pedophiles, murderers and drug dealers. They seem to locate our enemies abroad so quickly!

Pentagon videos which thrive on violence ("kill the Arabs," Mortal Kombat, etc.) are shown to impressionable young people as model-type warfare. American servicemen, who have spent four and one half years in Iraq, still can't pronounce Iraq – significant to me for it means that these young people are told what their commanders want them to believe, not what truly is. The arms merchants see money and are always there with more violent videos, if needed. This is a vicious assault on our youth, who should be looking forward to a safe America, not an America hated by every country in the world. This violent mindset lends justification to those few soldiers who think that it's okay to rape, kill and torture innocent civilian Iraqis.

Thank God for the servicemen like Officer Darby who reported the atrocities at Abu Graib and supported his findings with photographs.

Anderson Cooper, CNN, asked Darby, "Are you sorry you reported what happened at Abu Graib? A lot of people would say 'so what, Saddam did it.'" Darby: "I couldn't see something like this and not report it. There were 250 men in our unit, and seven ruined the whole unit."

This speaks volumes about the home training of Darby, who was raised in a poor family, and about the host, Anderson Cooper, who was raised in the richest of families, the Vanderbilts. Character is character and we find it in any class, rich or poor. I'm certain that Cooper saw a lot that he didn't report when he was in Iraq.

I had four brothers in the infantry and medical corps in World War II. Cousins, nephews and friends were in subsequent wars. After their respective duties, they were never the same. That's what war does and that's why I have no respect for fathers who say "the service will make a man out of him." The question is 'what kind of man'? Manhood is a father's job, not that of a staff sergeant yelling in boot camp. By then, it's too late. A good father teaches his son discipline, courage, honor and compassion.

At Penn, I saw the happenings at frat houses. On weekends, it was one big beer-a-thon. If you weren't a drinker before, you certainly were one now. Today, many young men and women associate freedom with drinking and acting like the fraternity brothers at Duke, falsely accused of raping a prostitute. Careers delayed, names smeared, and why? Because mom and dad never taught these young people that freedom has limits and that excessive drinking is the luxury of cowards too scared to face life. It's rugged individualism vs. group dynamics. It's knowing when to say "no."

Nobody said that it was easy to be a parent, particularly when we have legislators with time on their hands, who want to lower the drinking age and legalize drugs. In a short time, we would look like Kowloon, China, with bodies in the street. No wonder our framers wanted the legislators to meet only twice a year.

Another method of playing down alcohol might be that of my father's. At dinnertime, he would force all of us to test-taste the red wine he made for the holidays when friends would stop in for a toast and hors d'oeuvres. None of us liked the taste and so we stayed away from alcohol altogether. Of course, he never allowed us to join fraternities or sororities either, with the hazing and other shenanigans, but I won't go there, because I agree.

According to the Center for Constitutional Rights, U.S. corporations conspired with U.S. officials in Iraq to torture, humiliate, and abuse persons detained by U.S. authorities. A class action suit was filed in this regard on June 9, 2004, by the Center for Constitutional Rights and the Philadelphia law firm of Montgomery, McCracken, Walker and Rhoads. The suit, filed in San Diego, named as defendants the Titan Corporation of San Diego,

California and CACI International of Arlington, Virginia and its subsidiaries who work for these companies. It charges them with violating the Racketeer Influenced and Corrupt Organizations Act (RICO) and alleges that the companies engaged in a wide range of heinous and illegal acts in order to demonstrate their abilities to obtain intelligence from detainees and thereby obtain more government contracts. These corporations created a joint enterprise known as Team Titan to provide interrogation services in Iraq.

Anything goes, with no oversight. We now outsource to contractors – not American – the job of fighting our wars, interrogating and torturing, without accountability. Mercenaries, who show no mercy, armed to the hilt, kicking tied-up victims and leaving their bodies turned upside down, as they did in Afghanistan, are armed cowards. And the Special Forces, they're 'special' alright. They act at the bidding of the corporate meisters who will one day butt kick these mindless robots into a trash heap. For those 'moms' who ask, what kind of mother would send her child out to die with a bomb strapped to his chest? A mother who knows that any day a U.S. or U.N. 'peacekeeper' may blow her child's head off, because our educational institutions are indoctrinating the youth to hate, to kill, without challenge. And if a teacher dares to speak out, he is threatened with the loss of his job by the likes of the raging lunatic David Horowitz, who sees a holocaust under every rug…or pretends to.

Worse yet, the servicemen feel that they are fighting for "freedom of speech" and American 'values.' They haven't noticed that America has audiences who praise Michael Vick, a dreg of society. Standing ovations yet, by a bunch of knuckleheads who could never withstand the torture meted out to dogs by this sociopath.

In the United States we have barbaric men and women who now take their children to see 'cock fights' with razor blades attached to the claws of the birds. We have families who attend "ultimate fighting" bouts in which the boxers kick, claw, punch and gorge opponents while the senseless audience screams with delight.

Bullies are brave so long as they have weapons and backup. Groups against one victim. But when a Columbine happens, bullies run just like everybody else. We don't need any studies to examine the motivation of teens messed up enough to go to school carrying weapons, killing many innocent bystanders. Kids are telling adults, parents – who don't listen and who don't get involved at school – "it's too much too soon, and I can't handle it."

Zbigniew Brzezinski, a former national security advisor, told Charlie Rose about Iraq: "We could win if we were to put in 500,000 troops, willing to take casualties, and be brutal in Iraq." And this man with a thick accent cares about America and American values? I think not. He and Kissinger are vile. And we still ask them what they "think"!

I'd like to see the old guys leading the young guys into war: President George W. and his dad, Henry Kissinger, Brzezinski, Cheney, John McCain, Donald Rumsfeld, Richard Perle, Paul Wolfowitz, Karl Rove, Bill Clinton, Bill Kristol, Michael Medved, Olmert of Israel, Netanyahu – and all of the other warmongers. I'll bet that the enemy would be scared out of their pants! LOL

So, what Joe McCarthy, my hero, said is true (at the Army McCarthy Hearings). The military is 'infiltrated.' Again he called them 'communists.' He should have called them internationalists or globalists because the result for those of us who love America is the same – tyranny, loss of jobs, imported food, crime, drugs, pestilence. We have accumulated a bunch of military jackasses saluting each other until vomit time. We have accumulated a bunch of rotten seat-warmers in Congress who are not going to jail because no one can point a finger. Charlie Rangel, Dodd, Frank, those supporting agencies like Acorn, ripping taxpayers off to the tune of $8.5 billion in the Stimulus Bill. We have a president who wants to 'change' America because he feels sorry for the poor, while he made $3 million in '08, surrounding himself with a bunch of tax cheats and lobbyists. He has forced Congress to sign bills which they haven't read. And we taxpayers are not allowed to protest because the real hijackers placed this stooge in office <u>because</u> of his color so that the charge of racism could stop us from speaking out. When Obama's job is done, he'll see who the real power brokers are – when he's kicked to the curb. Ingrates like Bill Cosby joining the crew, calling protestors 'racist' after his big thrust in the past to get young black men to fill the roles of father. Cosby is another gutless stooge, after all. He refuses to believe that both whites and blacks with character – and who work – are sick of paying for absentee fathers who spawn the Michael Vicks, because it's so easy to get handouts. Welfare is a curse with the projects yielding nothing but gangs, druggies, and ingrates. Only the disabled should get welfare, not slobs popping out uncared-for babies with dummy absentee dufusses calling themselves men. Halfwits. Criminals.

We're left with the Glenn Becks who supposedly outted the inner workings of the Acorn Community Group, which people like me exposed 15 years ago. But notice that Beck and his Fox crew won't <u>allow</u> any talk on 911, George Bush, or the exposure of CIA torture. This is their game, and we taxpayers are the victims. No one in the controlled media would dare expose the proponents of the war costing us <u>trillions</u>, just as healthcare will bankrupt us with trillions spent on bureaucrats in D.C. – with Americans out of work. We're just racists.

Yes, the armed service is fighting for freedom of speech with the likes of the turncoat Lt. Col. Ralph Peters – always angry – always defending Israel and their Iraq War. He agrees that Iran is the enemy of Israel and, therefore, we should nuke it so that Israel can take control of the oil in the Caspian Sea, take it through Afghanistan and into Turkey, our 'ally,' so that Iran is excluded. And we wonder why Ahmadinajad curses Israel. They know; we're the dopes who are clueless!

This military dufuss, Lt. Col. Peters, writes at the Jewish Institute for National Security Affairs. I wonder if he even knows that this is <u>America</u>, not Amerika!

Meanwhile, the United States inherits dummies like so-called comedian Russell Brand, a young Englishman here in America <u>because</u> of capitalism, using the forum of the 2009 MTV Video Music Awards to tell Americans to adopt President Obama's health care plan. If England's plan is so great, what's the jerk doing here? Oh, yes, he's here to further pollute our culture by posing nude – much to the enjoyment of his fellow knuckleheads who take and take from America but give nothing in return.

I pity the children. I pity the children of the world at the mercy of senseless, useless sleazeballs, changing the BEST country in the world with no challenge. If left without protest, in ten years America will be the saddest country in the world, because we had it all.

ZIONISM

Zionism is understood to mean the official ideology and practice of Israeli ruling circles, linked with the financial and industrial oligarchy of other countries. In 1975, the U.N. qualified Zionism as a form of racism.

The definition of Zionism in the Webster's New World Dictionary: "A movement formerly for re-establishing, now for advancing, the Jewish national state in Palestine."

Rabbi Yisroel David Weiss was a guest on Glenn Beck's talk show, CNN Headline News (8/4/06). The rabbi said, "Judaism has been given to us for thousands of years; Zionism is a philosophy of one hundred or more years, and it has created a rift between Jews and Moslems. Jews and Moslems always got along together. The Torah forbids the establishment of a Jewish state. Do not transfer Judaism to a Jewish nationalism. Zionists oppressed Moslems and that is why they are angry. Jews lived under the protection of the Moslems."

I just gave you a small snippet of the much-interrupted conversation between the host, Beck, and the Rabbi. Of course the Rabbi got practically no chance to speak once Glenn Beck realized that it wasn't what he wanted his audience to hear.

The prohibition of free speech never stops. For instance, Hannity and Colmes interviewed a guest, Walid Shoebat, who wrote <u>Why I Left Jihad</u> (struggle). The guest started out with a Mideastern accent and later slipped into a British accent, talking about the "72 virgins" and how "Moslems like to die." All nonsense fabricated by a network of propagandists who are totally clueless about Islam.

In August 1897, Theodore Herzl, a Viennese journalist, started the first Zionist Congress. Attending were 197 delegates from 17 other countries. According to Nadav Safran, a Zionist historian, Herzl preferred Palestine as a Jewish state. Palestine was part of the Ottoman Empire.

Colonization of Palestine had begun in 1882. The Palestine-Jewish Colonization Association which was part of the Rothschild's banking empire, sent the first settlements to the Holy Land, thanks to Great Britain whose ruling circles established close ties to Zionist leaders. Great Britain had long desired to establish control over the Mideast. During WW I England had become the center of international Zionism. Chaim Weizmann, the president of the British Zionist Federation and later the first president of Israel, had his headquarters in Britain. Having won the confidence of such politicians as Prime Minister Lloyd George, Balfour, Churchill and others, Herzel recognized that Britain understood colonial expansion.

The ruling class of Great Britain felt that the Zionists would detach the Russian Jews who belonged to the Communist party (Bolsheviks) away from the workers' revolutionary struggle.

Foreign minister James Balfour wrote a letter to Lord Rothschild in 1917:

"His Majesty's Govt. views with favor the establishment in Palestine of a national home for the Jewish people . . . it being understood clearly that nothing shall be done which may prejudice the civil and religious rights of existing non-Jewish communities in Palestine." (Brevity is mine.)

Before the Balfour Declaration was published, it was handed to the U.S. President, Woodrow Wilson, who gave us the income tax and the Federal Reserve. Italy and France also received a copy of the Declaration. In 1922, the League of Nations accepted the British Mandate.

A Zionist commission appeared in Palestine with the authority of the British government to make preparation for a home. This commission became independent of British military authority and wanted to participate in the Military Administration and have the right to train Jewish military defense forces. This provoked the Arabs' resentment. In March 1920, armed conflict broke out between the settlers and the local inhabitants of Northern Palestine. Bloodshed spread to Jerusalem which the Zionists had originally said would belong to all religions.

For several centuries the Moslem majority and the small Christian and Jewish minorities lived in peace, and had long accepted and tolerated their differences. (Rabbi Weiss agreed.)

The Zionists bought good land, leaving many Palestinians homeless. They formed an army (Haganah), in the name of defense. The primary role of Haganah was secrecy. During the day, in case of a British raid, the trainees portrayed themselves as studious schoolboys or card-playing workers. At night, they would train in the basements of Jewish institutions – protected by guards – to practice Judo, jump from moving cars, burst into houses, climb ropes, etc. They even practiced rifle shooting in the desert where they hoped the wastes of the desert might muffle the sound. (Larry Collins and Dominique Lapierre, "O Jerusalem," pp. 62-63.)

As early as 1924 Vladimir Jabotinsky, an idealist of the militarist concept of Zionism: "The programme is not complicated. The aim of Zionism is a Jewish state. The territory – both sides of the Jordan. The system – mass colonization. The solution of the financial problem – a national loan ... Hence, the commandment of the hour – a new political campaign and the militarization of Jewish youth in Ersatz Israel and the Diaspora." (Walter Laguer, "A History of Zionism," Weidenfeld and Nicolson, London, 1972, p. 353.)

"Jabotinsky's argument that the Zionists have a moral right to use force against the Arab population of Palestine on whose land they proposed to create their Jewish state hardly differs from the argument of the Nazi ideologists for the mass extermination of the Jews.

"In 1935, those who were in favor of violence, formed an underground terrorist organization, Irgun, which committed severe atrocities against the Palestinian Arabs (village of Deir Yassan).

"From 1944-1948 when Zionist terrorism in Palestine reached its height, Irgun was headed by the prime minister of Israel, Menachim Begin. Another group, the Stern Gang was also started. Begin was wanted by the British Mandate Authority as a 'dangerous criminal'." (Jewish Affairs, Sept.-Oct. 1979, p. 13.)

The Stern Gang, on July 22, 1946, blew up the King David Hotel, the British High Commissioner's headquarters, killing 94 people. Most of them were British, but there were a few Jews and Arabs. In 1946, this gang also threw a bomb at a crowd of Arab traders near Damascus, Syria. The Zionists didn't want the Brits watching over them in Palestine. Now their headquarters was in Washington, D.C. We loaned them enough to make their wishes come true over the years.

In 1948, the British troops left Palestine because their mandate had expired. At this time there were to be two states as developed by the U.N. There were to be two constitutions, elections, etc. But the Zionists wanted no part of this. Chaim Weizmann received a note from President Truman, delivered by their mutual friend, Judge Samuel Rosenman, stating that if the Zionist leadership considered it necessary to proclaim the State of Israel, the U.S. would recognize it.

Shortly before this mandate by President Truman, an undeclared war for the whole of Palestine had been launched, hoping to force out the Arabs. A series of military operations took place by the Zionist leadership hoping to gain all of Palestine and this would have happened had it not been for Arab intervention and U.N. peace-keeping forces (John H. Davis, "The Evasive Peace").

The first Arab-Israeli War began shortly after the proclamation of the State of Israel. In a bid to stop the atrocities against the Palestinians, the Arab population of Jordan, Egypt, Syria, Iraq, Lebanon, and Saudi Arabia sent troops into Palestine.

Hostilities continued and the expulsion of 740,000 Arab refugees took place, as well as 340,000 native Palestinians.

The 1967 war was the same old, same old. Israel said that the Arabs provoked them into war, when in actuality Israel attacked Egypt, Syria, and Jordan. As they did in Lebanon recently, propaganda hit the U.S. about the kidnapping of two Israeli soldiers. What the U.S. press mentioned, but then hoped we would forget, was the fact that a Palestinian family on the beach was wiped out just prior to the kidnapping of the two Israeli soldiers. This action gave Israel the right to take down Lebanon's bridges, roads, buildings, power – everything, so that no one could possibly stop the violence. Over two soldiers?

No, it has always been about a Greater Israel. Israel has brought over tens of thousands of Jewish settlers to resettle on Palestinian land.

The U.S. has been complicit in these horrific dealings by sending to Israel a continuous stream of the latest Phantom Jets, etc.

"Israel's answer to the U.N. Resolution 242 which called for the withdrawal of Israeli troops from occupied territories: The river Jordan would now be Israel's security zone; Israel would remain in the Golan Heights, control the Gaza Strip which had formerly been controlled by Egypt, and the port of Sharm el Sheik on the south of the Sinai would also remain under Israeli control. Five times the area given to the Israelis by the U.N." (Igor Yaroslavtsev, "Zionism.")

"The current map of the West Bank shows unmistakenly how the idea of a two-state solution on which the agreement was premised has been undermined systematically through modern architecture and planning" (Lay of the Land, Stephen Zacks, Metropolis Magazine 2/03. (www. metropolismag.com) Architectural Magazine.)

All of this pretense by U.S. presidents about the two-state solution is so much bull.

PALESTINE AND ISRAEL

Palestine is a country the size of Vermont, ten thousand square miles. There are false claims that Jordan is part of Palestine simply because tens of thousands of Palestinian refugees have been packed into neighboring Jordan.

Joan Mulholland gave a good account of the facts: "You falsify history by insisting that Palestine actually included Jordan, a desert land much larger than Israel, so how could people be so disobliging as to resent Israel's taking a small but fertile chunk of the newly defined Palestine?

"Fact is, Palestine never included the area Transjordan, east of the River Jordan. Palestine, west of the river, was more settled and urbanized, while Transjordan was a desert and tribal economy. Palestinians are fighting for the land they owned and inhabited.

"The argument is a false rationalization for the expansion of Israel and control of the West Bank. Israel wants to push the Palestinians into the desert." (Phila. Inquirer, 9/30/82).

In a nutshell, Charley Reese summed up the occupation (Montgomery Cty. Observer, 1/26/05):

"In 1948, the state of Israel was established, and it created more than 500,000 Palestinian refugees in the process; their lands and assets were eventually confiscated. In 1967, Israel's blitzkrieg war took the rest of Palestine, including the West Bank, Gaza and East Jerusalem. The United Nations Security Council ordered Israel to return these lands, but it refused, and the U.S. has prevented any enforcement. Under the Geneva convention, Jewish settlements in the occupied territories are illegal. The U.S., by completely siding with Israel, has made itself the enemy of most of the Arab population."

In an article in the New York Times entitled "Israel Has a Unique Deal for U.S. Aid," (9/23/90), Clyde Farnsworth shows how millions of dollars bypass the appropriation policy.

This article was written in 1990, but it certainly casts a light on the modus operandi of those we have entrusted to protect us – the presidents and the congress.

"The money, almost $1.2 billion, half of the $3 billion we give Israel every year in military and economic aid, is quietly deposited in the Federal Reserve Bank of New York to immediately start earning interest at about 8%.

"The remaining $1.8 billion goes to the Pentagon, and a trust fund that pays for McDonnell Douglas F-15s, General Dynamics' Stinger missiles, FMC Bradley fighting vehicles and other goods that Israel buys from American military contractors.

"This system, used only for Israel, opens the spigots for millions of dollars of interest, in effect, added aid that does not go through the appropriations process. But this only one-way military assistance to Jerusalem is different from arms transactions with Saudi Arabia, Egypt or any of the other countries playing a central role in the Persian Gulf crisis.

"The arrangements with Israel had attracted attention during the Gulf crisis. Israel has asked the Administration (Bush, Sr.) for additional military aid this year to help it maintain its traditional military edge in the Middle East, especially with the planned sales at $21 billion in American arms to Saudi Arabia.

"The Saudis will pay cash for any arms they buy. But when Israel buys F-15s, McDonnell Douglas bills the Israeli trust fund, financed by American tax dollars, at the Pentagon.

"Egypt receives somewhat less American aid than Israel -- $815 million in economic support and $1.3 billion in military assistance – but Egypt, a developing country with a far lower living standard than Israel, gets much less in actual cash and none of it up front. So Cairo has less freedom to maneuver than Jerusalem.

"It was as a reward for its cooperation in the Gulf Crisis that President Bush, Sr. announced new aid for Egypt with his proposal to forgive $6.7 billion of Egyptian debt. (Passed on to us, I might add). The interest that Israel can now earn on its $1.2 billion Economic Support Fund from the U.S. grows under an initiative in the mid-1980s by Senator Daniel K. Inouye, Democrat of Hawaii, and Senator Bob Kasten, Jr., Republican of Wisconsin. (Earned $76.7 million last year) The bulk of the Fund – nearly $1 billion – went to payments of interest and principal on military debts to the U.S. The money was also used for grain purchases and transport debt repayments to the World Bank, procurements by Israel's Ministry of Health, and loan repayments to the Agency for International Development, the foreign aid branch of the State Department.

"Only Israel is insured against aid cut-off that confronts other countries, thanks to Senator Alan Cranston of California and Joe Biden of Delaware. Countries in arrears more than a year on military and economic loans lose all American aid except food assistance. Cranston and Biden, in 1984, stated as a matter of policy that Israel's economic assistance every year should be at least as much as its annual payments to the U.S.

"About $500 million of the Egyptian aid goes into specific development projects like sewer construction, improvement of water supplies, and expansion of education. Congress has also stipulated that Egypt buy at least $200 million of American commodities like feed grains, soybeans, and coking coal. Egypt is a poor country with 50 million people and per-capita output of $670. Israel is far richer. Its population is only 4.3 million and its per capita output is $6,810.

"Both countries need State Department approval before military contractors submit bills to each of the Pentagon funds."

"Congressional friends of Israel have tucked provisions that could be worth hundreds of millions of dollars into last-minute money bills, with little or no public discussion. The benefits range from gifts of unneeded Pentagon equipment to a $15 million refurbishing of Israel's port in Haifa." (Alexandria Journal 10/17/90).

About the viability of there being peace between the Palestinians and Israelis, Rabbi Michael Lerner wrote in Tikkun (Sept.-Oct. 2001), referring to the much-heralded Oslo Agreements made by President Clinton: "What was offered was not a contiguous state, but a set of cantons (districts) divided by Israeli settlements and roads criss-crossing Palestinian land and guarded by the Israeli army. . . . To understand the picture, imagine that someone takes over your house, lives there for 34 years running your life, and then offers to give you back 90% of it. Sounds generous? But then you find that the 10% this person wants are the hallways – which means that you can't go from one room to another without getting their permission. And how about if they asked you to sign an agreement saying that you would never raise any other issues after this. Would you sign that final agreement?"

Well, Arafat didn't sign Clinton's Oslo Agreement, and the media, knowing that most Americans didn't know the content of that agreement, still talks about "the chance of a lifetime" turned down by the Palestinians. I'll bet that the Clintons had the favor returned many times. Clinton also pardoned some New York rabbis before he left office, and Hillary became the Senator from New York. Amazing how it works: you scratch my back and I'll scratch yours. The public be damned!

If you write to a Senator, as I did to Senator Santorum, he'll send you a thirteen page report – really talking points put out by the Congressional Research Service, from the Library of Congress. It's frustrating to read a one-sided report. I'm happy that this war hawk was defeated in the last election.

President Jimmy Carter (1978) met with Sadat of Egypt and Begin of Israel. (The head of the old Irgun Gang). President Carter, too, gave away the store in the form of arms, bases, aid grants to Israel. The result of the meeting was Israel's holding onto the Arab territories in the West Bank of the Jordan (6 cities), the Syrian Golan Heights which Israel used as a security zone, and the Gaza Strip in return for a promise to return the Sinai to Egypt. As a result, we in the U.S. pay $2 billion per year to Egypt for rental of the Sinai so that Israel can be secure.

Sadat was subsequently murdered by his own armed forces who considered him a traitor. Now we have our puppet in Egypt, Hosni Mubarack.

Under Carter, Palestinian "self-rule" would be under Israeli control. And there would never be a Palestinian State in either Judea or Sumaria (The West Bank and Gaza Strip).

The day of "Judea and Sumaria" are long gone, and things have changed, but when occupiers invoke the Bible at a cost of human life – it's not about religion, it's about imperialism.

Now, President Carter must want to clear his conscience by writing this new book <u>Palestine: Peace, not Apartheid</u>, wherein he speaks out (on CNN 12/8/06): "there is tremendous intimidation of our people if you speak about Israel." On Meet the Press (12/3/06): "Arabs living in the

West Bank and Jerusalem, in occupied territory, is apartheid, if anyone sees how they are living. There are circumstances in this country intimidating people from speaking out on Israel even when circumstances are horrible. Most Americans are unaware. There should be unity government so that Mahmoud Abbas can speak for the Palestinians. The U.S. should be a major player. There should be a stop to persecuting Palestinians for voting for Hamas. American Jews and the Israeli Lobby are keeping Israel from doing the right thing."

Carter is taking so much heat from outright bullies. It's despicable.

All of the presidents sided with Israel. President Nixon sent over so many tanks that the skies over Texas were black for days.

We can't allow ourselves to be hated because of our one-sided justice. Prime Minister David Ben Gurion wanted to split Lebanon into two parts, Christian and Arab. Consequently, Palestinian refugees were slaughtered with the help of Phalangist Christians in 1983.

There are too many loyalists to Israel in our Congress and White House. On April 7, 2004 Senator George Voinovich of Ohio introduced Bill S.2272, which would require a report on acts of anti-Semitism around the world, including countries with strong democracies.

The Rep. Tom Lantos group in the House was constantly looking after Israel. The Global Anti-Semitism Review Act was signed into federal law by President George W. Bush (P.L. 108-332) on October 16. 2004.

What constitutes anti-Semitism? Shades of Adolph Hitler!!

We lost the best and the brightest in WW II because Americans were horrified by death camps. This wasn't enough. Now, we have Americanized the holocaust and have Congressmen working on holocaust museums, etc. We have Sen. Patrick Leahy talking about reparations.

When do Palestinians get reparations? When do Gold Star mothers get reparations?

Or are they the "workers in the field?"

CONCLUSION

Nowhere in the United States Constitution does it say that we owe anyone an education. And nowhere in the Constitution does it give the federal government the right to get involved in education, health care, local road building, etc. The federal government had specific powers given to it by the states, such as the building of national highways and security.

Therefore, the federal mandates coming down to us from Washington such as environmental studies, multiculturalism, sex education, and drug education can be sent back to Washington with our "no thanks." Those of us who feel strongly that, over the last two decades, these mandates have encouraged the use of drugs and promiscuous sex, should simply refuse to pay taxes. For those parents who believe that their children need sex and drug information from kindergarten through grade twelve, I implore you to get outside tutors and pay for the instruction yourselves. Usually, if not always, these parents have no clue about what their children are learning through videos and "guests," nor do they care. They just want to "go along."

Our state legislators used to meet twice a year, before all of our state constitutions were changed during the late '60s and '70s. At the same time, regionalism was given legal status, without the consent of the governed.

"People have to stop acting powerless, as they were trained in public schools – 'you can't fight City Hall.' We have a corporate crime wave going on and Congress won't address the problem. Global corporations have no allegiance to this country, and Clinton and Gore consolidated corporate power even further. Fifty-eight million people died from pollution. Giant corporations are preventing constitutional rights and obstructing justice. Ballot access is impossible with our state laws." (Ralph Nader, WYBE)

Obviously, we have to remove the incentives of money and favors from the lobbyists in order to restore our state and federal constitutions. There should be no more middle of the night, secret legislation from our public 'servants.'

After World War II, the so-called 'elite' realized that they couldn't have brave senators, like Joe McCarthy or George Malone, or representatives, like John Conlan, Thorkelson, or McFadden, speaking out in the Congressional Record, so they came up with the 'single issue' or 'special interest' phenomenon wherein we were divided into groups: pro choice vs. pro life; gay vs. straight; pro gun vs. anti gun; black vs. white and vice versa, and feminism – a misnomer if ever there was one. Actually, it should be called girl vs. man. Feminists see women leaving their children behind while going to war. Feminists see themselves as boxers, wrestlers, marines, and bar flies. On the other hand, there are those women who definitely want equal pay, but once in awhile would like a door or two opened for them, especially when carrying packages. But we tolerate in order to be politically correct.

While a bunch of the brainwashed vote for single-issue candidates, the corporations solve the real problems: wars, immigration, drugs, education, jobs, taxation, and culture.

Meanwhile, five-year-olds are being trained to hate "Andy, the Polluter," that security guard and park ranger driving through the park, checking on people's safety and storm debris, in his "gas guzzling, polluting jeep." Subsequently, a lot of Andys lost their jobs and are probably receiving unemployment compensation. As a result, parks are much less safe – and dirty.

Nothing is told to children about the last twenty years when presidents and Congress did nothing about illegal immigration. Thanks to dufusses like Ted Kennedy, the "chap of quiddick," twenty million illegals now roam our country. And presidential candidates tell us what they are going to do. Well, they had twenty years to get rid of the illegals starting forest fires, polluting our lands, threatening Arizona ranchers and mutilating cattle, using our hospitals for baby deliveries and other problems, collecting SSI, getting voting rights when applying for drivers' licenses, filling our jails, forming gangs, earning money and sending it back home, and digging tunnels for bringing through more illegals, drugs, and arms.

We reward them with subsidized attorneys and advocacy groups such as La Raza and the Hispanic Caucus, available only to the special hyphenated Americans, not the rest of us.

There are 240 million cars traveling over our bridges and roads, which were never expected to handle such traffic. No country, including Mexico, has this open door policy. Mexico arrests and deports as soon as possible.

We have President Reagan to thank for granting amnesty to millions of illegals thereby inviting more. And we have George W. to thank for allowing Mexican trucks to travel in our country, without inspections. Now illegals can come here, as well as drug dealers and arms carriers, without digging tunnels.

Just when I think that things can't get worse, C-SPAN2 (7/6/08) is airing Professor Stephen Cohen who teaches Russian Studies at NYU. The professor used to spend six or seven months in Russia, and these were his observations: "Neo cons want to end the UN and militarize NATO in a League of Democracies. The United States is planning a missile base in Poland, but Poland doesn't want it."

Also, the first President Bush promised Russia that we would not move NATO east, but Clinton and George W. broke that promise.

On 20/20, 8/24/07, several billionaires were interviewed by John Stossel about "charity giving." One of them laughingly told the host that "there is a difference, you know, between charity and philanthropy. We're philanthropists because we try to change." I'll say! Remember what Eleanor Roosevelt said in her book, that we need to "change the nature of man"?

The dead-wood patronage gang over at the Department of Education plans to pilot in a new program in Delaware called "Virtual Schools." Funny, but I thought that we already have virtual schools. We certainly have enough functional illiterates graduating who can prove it! We spend hundreds of billions on education and what do we have to show for it? We have children in the second grade who can't read or write and need special teachers. We have graduates from high school who can't relay two sentences without saying, "like, ya know, like."

Children in Philadelphia, instead of being deluged with information about sex and drugs, should be asked, "What should we do…Governor Rendell has just granted a billionaire $200 million for a hockey field? Should we have to subsidize it? Shouldn't the public have meetings on matters such as this?"

The less input we have the bolder these con artists in public "service" are getting. For instance, the Department of Health and Human Services now pays for public service announcements – with taxpayer money. Using children, the announcement has a child telling his parents: "Talk to me about sex. My friends do." The whole ad deprecates the role of parent-child. Suddenly, children have become smarter and more experienced than adults. Sadly we have replaced business advertisements with public service announcements. Good subsidies for these radio stations!

Congressmen should have to pass a test on the Constitution, just as they require every other professional to do in his field of expertise. We need to recapture the essence of America – God, family, country – and we need to remind our public servants that this country is still America.

Of course, special interest groups are paralyzing this country. When I see a man carrying a sign "abortion is murder," I'm certain that he feels like a productive activist. I'd like him to study his child's curriculum and have the courage to get involved with the feminist agenda: "Abortion is a 'contraceptive' alternative." Perhaps then I can have some respect for this dolt who thinks that he's the only one who respects the sanctity of life. All life is sacred, even the lives of 25,000 Iraqi children whose faces or bodies were burned or wounded and who were separated from their deceased parents – thanks to our smart bombs and illegal warfare used to bring in 'democracy.'

Abortion is never an easy decision to make. I've seen whole families suffer whenever a brain-damaged, helpless child is brought into their midst, confined to a life in a wheelchair. Who are you or I to decree which course a person should take? Try walking in their shoes!

On the other hand, partial birth abortions and cavalier abortions are another matter, which should be resolved by state senators, not McCain nor the Clintons nor anyone else in Washington. My experience has been that the feminist agenda over the last two and a half decades is responsible for the devaluation of life's sanctity. Remember MACHOS where children decide who gets thrown from the boat. Look at our commercials trying to give small children adult status. No wonder the young have no respect for their parents. No wonder they need anger management!

As for the homosexuals and lesbians, I don't know of anyone who wouldn't want a monogamous couple to share in each other's life savings upon one or the other's death. None of the monogamous couples I know indulge in flamboyant parades nor in in-your-face tactics. The gays I know are industrious, witty, and charming. And they're not spawning fatherless children!

But then there is that radical group – and it's always the divide and conquer culture which exists outside the norm – demanding that children of five read about two mommies, aids, etc., etc. And that is where I say enough is enough. Their rights stop where mine begin. Nobody has special rights here. I don't particularly care to see any two adults making out in public. It was never appropriate, and it's still not appropriate.

The Boy Scouts is another example of injustice. In order to please one eighteen-year-old scout who wanted the whole troop of younger boys to know that he was gay, Boy Scouts have lost their right to meet in public places. This organization has trained so many thousands of boys over the years, and I'm certain that no one ever brought up one's sexual proclivity while trying to start a fire with two sticks. No, this frivolous case was brought into court to cause trouble and to assert "special rights." We should ask "who paid for these attorneys?" Who profits? Those who want to "change the nature of man." (I talked about this under 'conspiracy.') The elite want to neutralize everyone so that no one stands out. No one has character. We're told that it's "political correctness." No, it's the shedding of any vestige of individualism and courage from the masses. The dehumanizing of mankind for an easy takeover requires raising taxes, abandoning religion, breaking up of families, dumbing down of the masses, and no communication. So far we have all of them. "Step by step."

While we are engaged in this bankrupting war in Iraq, commissioners in a suburban county decided that there will be no comments during public meetings. Also, there will be no tax meetings televised. How do you like that for chutzpah?

They know that we're angry. They also know that millions of Americans are unaware of the magnitude of their treachery and deceit.

Three policemen were shot within four days in Philadelphia. While the talk of a manhunt went on, there was also the cry to "remove all guns." The second amendment guaranteed the citizens the right to protect themselves from a corrupt government and property loss – not to wreak havoc on a community. The Constitution went so far as to suggest a well-regulated militia of able-bodied men to challenge a corrupt government. We know how the media savages loyal Americans who bother to read the Constitution. We know what the Clinton administration did to the people at Ruby Ridge and others who dared to fight "government" corruption. But our watchful politicians can look the other way when gangsters enter our country with guns for gangs, drugs, and prostitutes; and we say nothing lest we be considered "antigovernment." One word is left out – corruption. We see young teens beating homeless people to death. We see schools being targeted for killings; but we say nothing. Pedophilia is rampant. We are told by halfwit talk show hosts: "You dare to criticize the president or a general!" Americans are fast becoming illiterate, indoctrinated robots who never suffered the bombings and treachery we have inflicted on foreigners around the world. Rock bands dress in black and look angry in order to convey the message that there are things in America which are wrong, but they lack the backbones to do anything about it except pander to the druggies and other cowards in the audience. It's all about money and indoctrination. When the rockers get old, they get their own reality shows and mellow out, leaving victims of brainwashing behind.

Just be angry and forget everything with drugs. Don't attempt to change anything. Wait until it's too late.

Bloodthirsty neo-cons are now urging Americans to bomb Iran. Kill and torture more innocents. The new video Manhunt 2 was designed to encourage violence and to desensitize our youth – the youth who will be needed for the rich, old, white men's wars.

The University of Delaware dropped a mandated program, "Thought Reform," meant to "change behavior." One test question: "When did you first learn your sexual identity?" As you can see, they continue this garbage started in kindergarten right through colleges turning out students who don't know who the vice president is – nor do they care.

These programs are piloted into schools for which we pay optimum dollars at the expense of the students whose parents don't care a wit. It's the feminists' special agenda – sex and more sex from a bunch of unhappy women who should not have any part in the school curriculums. Special interest groups have become "special" and affluent, receiving grants and contributions for their part in destroying the education which served us well for more than one hundred years. "Non-profits."

The fourteenth amendment grants us "equal protection." I don't force my values on other people, and I don't want a group of women, who usually, if not always, have no children, to force untried values on my family. We are all witness to what the values of these "special interest" groups have done to innocent children over the years – "girls gone wild," etc.,. etc. These fools are now equal to men! Big whoops.

This con game, which forces us to yield to pressure from unknown sources working behind the scenes to destroy innocence and wonder, has been played in Sweden and Holland where the suicide rate is high. Drugs are rampant. I hate to see America repeat the horrible happenings in other countries which never offered the hope of America with its strict values. The infamous Mary Calderone, who introduced the outrageous program, Sex Information and Education in the U.S. (SIECUS), was from Sweden. Her program went to the Soviet Union as well as England. It has not been successful in Soviet Russia, in Sweden nor in England. Roland Huntford wrote about the failure of sex education in Sweden in "The New Totalitarians." (Stein and Day, NY, 1971) As Dr. O'Reilly has pointed out, the vested interest groups such as contraceptive manufacturers, pornographers and organizations such as Planned Parenthood and SIECUS, have done well.

Don't be fooled by the friendly "you can always opt your child out." Why should any child have to leave a classroom for which all of us pay taxes, simply to appease those planners and those parents who have no clue about the secrecy shrouding this invasion of a child's privacy?

While George W. Bush and his cronies can't account for billions missing in this interminable war, there are those people who still care about America enough to investigate his abuse of power. According to Marjorie Cohen (president of the National Lawyers' Guild), Khalid Sheik Mohammed, alleged mastermind of 911, was water-boarded so ruthlessly that his faculties were compromised.

An army sergeant, Sam Provance, was told by higher ups not to say anything about the happenings at Abu Graib. (1/25/08) Dogs, nudity of the detainees treated as sub-humans, laughter by interrogators, etc. were only some of the abuses taking place. "Some of the interrogators could have been spies from other countries," absent any signs of conscience. Provance was surprised that none of his division reported the abuse. I'm not surprised. Practically two dond one-half generations have been brain-washed with this cavalier attitude toward life. The violence is showing up in Iraq and in ordinary homes and schools.

We subsidize the corporations fleeing to Mexico, China and elsewhere, where there are no regulations regarding the environment, worker safety, fair play, decent working hours, or health care. With our zippo tariffs, these corporations can re-enter the United States with their foreign-made merchandise at no cost, while foreign countries charge us for United States exports made in America. Previously, high tariffs paid for our road repair and reconstruction, but now our roads and bridges – "our assets" – are under the control of foreign and domestic entities. Meanwhile, corporations dump here on land and sea. Some landowners have paid for corporate misdeeds with their lives. But Nazi radio keeps information censored.

Monica Crowley, substituting for Laura Ingraham on talk radio, is another devout mouthpiece for the neo-con Nazis in the media. Her threshold for free speech is zero. When I think that this super dolt is getting paid for brainwashing those young and naïve people who may be listening, it's frightening. The same suspects – David Frum, speechwriter for Bush, and other warhawks – are her only guests. Now that she's a permanent fixture on the McLaughlin Report, I have lost respect for what used to be an unbiased news analysis.

Although not one Moslem from the Mideast is ever heard on any show, whether cable or radio, lots of lies are told, particularly about Moslems wanting to take over all religions. In my case, my husband left religion to me. His exact words: "There are no mosques here, so let the children attend a church or a synagogue. It doesn't matter." I chose Catholicism because I knew it best.

These "interfaith" groups are a joke. It isn't Moslems taking over religion but "Hebrew Catholics," flooding churches with "end times" mythology and phrases such as "he who curses Jews will be cursed." It's gag time, especially when the moneychangers were thrown out of the temple. Even then, Christ couldn't stand the sight of greed.

Talk show hosts now pollute the airwaves with propaganda about "Islamo-facists." But let's talk about the "Zionist fascists" who have remade America, incrementally, into their "promised land" – the land where American "yes men" at the Pentagon and Congress are allowing the neo-con Trotskyites of old to change every tried and true tradition America ever had. Senator McCain and President Bush went along with their treasonous objective:

> "The final goal of world revolution is not Socialism or even Communism; it is the destruction of civilization in a material sense. The revolution desired by the leaders is a moral and spiritual revolution,

an anarchy of ideas by which all standards set up throughout nineteen centuries shall be reversed, all honored traditions trampled under foot, and above all, the Christian ideal finally obliterated." (Nesta H. Webster, Historian who exposed the Illuminati. 1876-1960)

We now have neo-cons in every high place of authority in this country – advising the military, sharing "intelligence," and getting us involved in preemptive wars. Dimitri, a Russian Jew, was a guest on Book Review (2/9/08). He said, "If these Bolsheviks and Trotskyites are advising presidents, it's something to think about."

As a matter of fact, I don't know why college students are even required to study the history of these revolutionary lunatics. The end result of their "isms" always ended with the killing of 45 or 50 million people or whatever it took to satisfy their mental demons. China killed tens of millions. Study should be limited to what these nut jobs ended up doing to masses of people. They should not be treated as anything but purveyors of greed and madness.

Douglas Feith (Defense Department), Peter Rodman (Defense), Paul Wolfowitz (Defense Department and later head of the World Bank), Elliot Abrams (National Security Council), Richard Armitage (State Department), John Bolton (State Department), Richard Perle and Congressman Stephen Solarz – originators of the Open Letter to the President "demanding a regime change in Baghdad," Fred Icle (Defense Policy Board), Zalmay Khalilizad (White House), Donald Rumsfeld (Secretary of Defense), David Wurmzer (State Department), and Dov Zakheim (Defense) – all unelected appointees. (Jim Marrs, "The Terror Conspiracy")

This event of 'regime change' was suggested in 1996 – long before 911. According to Jim Marrs, "Richard Perle goes on to explain that Israel can shape the strategic environment in cooperation with Turkey and Jordon, by weakening, containing and even rolling back Syria." (Ibid., p. 129)

Of course, U.S. money and aid to Jordon and Turkey will help. So, America's future children will pay – who cares? They have sex and violence to release their woes. And booze and drugs – we mustn't forget.

These neo cons are the ones who advised President George W., wrapping themselves in the American flag and crying out "Support the Troops" – or you'll be considered anti-American. They want us to believe that every serviceman or woman is as pure as the driven snow, when, in actuality, thousands of negligent parents can't wait for their out-of-control and incorrigible teens to get the hell out of the house. Their hope is that the military will straighten them out. Yeah, right! Convicted rapists and felons are recruited. No problemó.

In watching Booknotes today (4-20-08, C-ASPAN2), I listened to a bunch of guests praise the book of Aaron David Miller at the Woodrow Wilson Center – "The Much Too Promised Land." He was an Arab-Israeli advisor from 1978-2003. Since he claimed to be nine-years-old when JFK died, that means that a 24-year-old young man was advising the State Department about Arab-Israeli issues. Twenty-four-years-old! Other guests: Marvin Kalb, Samuel Lewis, Haleh Esfandiari (an Iranian Jew) – not one Christian or Arab advising the United States Government. But Miller did use Christians to promote his cause – Israel. He mentioned Falwell, Robertson, Hagee, Ralph Reed (who was involved in the Abramoff case), and Gary Bauer. Marvin Kalb remarked about the wonderment of a "German" Jew, Henry Kissinger, becoming head of the State Department. No wonder President Carter feels remorse about what he did to the Palestinians. Miller said, "Israel has so worked itself into the fabric of America, with values and all, that there is no turning back." (paraphrased) Of course, Marvin Kalb brought up "Israel Lobby," the book I mentioned earlier. Kalb was astonished that anyone would bring up a discussion on the Israel Lobby which Miller said was very effective "on aid and resolutions in favor of Israel."

"What a tangled web they weave when first they practice to deceive." Israel and Zionists in America have asserted themselves in every aspect of American life, and we do nothing to terminate the jobs of all of those politicians who sold us out in order to get job insurance. I had to turn the "chosen people" off – the people who talk down to us without a challenge, simply because they've learned to put two sentences together without saying "ya know what ahm sayin." Language is their one skill, like millions of other Americans, but the content of what they say is garbage and propaganda, and we need a debate on aid and everything else concerning Israel and Zionists.

George W. Bush, according to Matthew Rothschild (no relation to the Illuminati Rothschilds!) had the FBI forming, along with the Fortune 500 gang, a group called Infra Guard. This group was given the right to shoot to kill anyone trying to threaten the 25,000 businesses under their control, with impunity. Homeland Security is also involved. "It is a secret organization (Infra Guard) with astonishing powers." Recently this group met at Hunter College. It has local and state chapters, 86 in all. Yet none of us would know anything about it if it were not for a whistleblower who researched this secret organization. We have covert outsourcing to Blackwater, the organization providing us with 170,000 mercenaries who get paid $1,000 a day and are immune from prosecution if criminally charged. I'm certain that al qaeda wears redcaps so that these forces can identify them before shooting. Yeah, right. But we have "liberated" the Iraqis by killing at least 800,000 civilians and displacing 200,000 others. We've bombed their infrastructure and built fourteen American bases there for future pentagon misadventures, serving the oil meisters. (Read Rothschild's book, "You Have No Rights." He is the editor of the Progressive) WYBE.

If you want to hear 24-7 controlled radio, it's station 990, WNCP. The Christian and Jewish Zionists, absent any input from an Arab or American against the war, will sanction torture, the Patriot Act, and bombing Iran: Bill Bennett, who promised to get rid of the Department of Education, Laura Ingraham, Monica Crowley, Dennis Prager, Hugh Hewitt, Mark Levin, Dennis Miller, Michael Medved, Michael Gallagher and Michael Savage reign. The stench is devastating. Nobody is given a chance to speak, and these hosts are the ones playing Ray Charles' version of "America" and closing with "the greatest country on God's green earth."

Unfortunately, America was the greatest country on God's green earth until these flunkies sabotaged it by not allowing dissent.

John McCain went to Canada to assure the Canadians that he would support free trade. "I'm the biggest free trader you'll ever meet." (I'd spell that free "traitor.") His campaign advisor was Carly Fiorina, the CEO who laid off the Packard employees and was then fired herself.

The meeting in Canada was before a business group, probably their Chamber of Commerce, the globalists who have had a big role in regionalism. Then the Senator went to a closed meeting in Chicago to assure Hispanic advocates that he would back amnesty (for 20 million illegals) if he were elected. McCain tried to appeal to the hyphenated-unAmericans by saying that, in his state, Arizona, Spanish was the first language spoken. Lou Dobbs corrected his false statement by reminding his audience that "American Indian dialects were spoken for hundreds of years." (6/20/08, CNN)

McCain, considering the fact that he was running for president of these United States, was a very busy man those last couple of days. Obviously, like George W. Bush, he fancied himself president of the world – a global president. Both men should be happy that they could remember their names, without worrying about the borderless highway joining Canada, Mexico, and the United States ala the NAFTA Agreement of the NWO. But then, what do we expect from a great hero who sings "ba-ba-ba-ba bomb Iran," to the tune of the Beach Boys' song. What a horrible sneak.

The 650 billion dollars headed to the Pentagon should be spent on deterrents only, not on pilotless planes dropping bombs on innocent people in the middle of the night. These sad excuses for men who want to play cowboys and Indians with our money should be stopped. The only winners are the arms merchants in the Carlyle Group (Bush and Osama), the oil barons (Bush included), and the other war profiteers. Taxpayers get only broken families and higher taxes.

"The military uses gangster rappers, like 50 Cent, Young Blood, Pitbull, and Juvenile to encourage the soldiers to kill, with lyrics about twisting guns and mad dogs." (paraphrased)

"This is a far cry from Bob Hope," said the former police officer, Rafael Turner, who just completed a book on this subject. Since Turner is black and was a police officer, he got to see firsthand what was affecting the youth. "These rappers talk about killing Whitey, etc." It's just what the bankers ordered.

It used to be that heroes were General MacArthur, scientists and outstanding professionals, great musicians, and ordinary citizens who saved someone's life. Yes, we had great sports figures as well. Today, however, every sport is filled with violence – ice hockey, football, ultra fighting, etc. Who needs to see fistfights on a night out to enjoy yourself? It's all hype and stupidity.

There was music of all kinds – jazz with greats like Coltrain and Billie Holiday, country music, classical. A person could sit back, reflect and relax after the day's hardships and grind. There was freedom of choice.

Today, we have dancers either grinding into each other or doing flips and other acrobatic moves called dancing. Dancers had class. Then came the Vietnam era with its protestors, and the protesting was commendable. Students knew that war is hell. But along with this movement came a relaxation of moral standards and the introduction to drugs and alcohol, the weapons of choice in condemning the young to a state of numbness and irresponsibility. Many of these young people, not all, wound up with drug-addicted, homeless children. And today we are seeing the scars that this era caused.

This is what happens to a country when God is abandoned for moral relativism. (Whom do we throw off the boat?) This is what happens to the young when they're brainwashed into believing that the Motley Crue is about 'music." Guests on the Larry King Show, 6/20/08, the Motley Crue's sound bites and lyrics expressed the group's view on life very well: "We were always into everything that was rebellious." Lyrics: "We are. We are. We signed our life away; no matter what you say."

Unfortunately, isn't this the attitude of many young people today? And haven't the politicians aided and abetted this downturn by allowing the drug industry to flourish? What kind of parents allow their children to attend these loud, blasting concerts with drugs everywhere? Two and one-half generations of this trash, and no wonder this generation feels rebellious.

Today, there is little classical music, if any, reaching the young. One disc jockey confessed that he's only allowed to play certain types of songs.

Larry King replayed this particular show in order to advertise the fact that the Motley Crue is on a world tour, with the next stop Japan. I'll bet that the Japanese love this cancer invading their society. And we've invaded them all.

One thing is certain. Larry King's children will attend the best schools available, even though all schools have been affected to a greater or lesser degree. His children won't have tattoos on their forearms or rings in their noses, eyebrows, or tongues. They'll be exposed to all kinds of music before reaching their teen years. The rest of us can't afford the luxury of $30,000-a-year schools; we're stuck with all kinds of victims, plus the mandates on sex education which brought about the 70 teenage pregnancies at Gloucester High in Massachusetts. Isn't it about time that we start showing up at school and demanding town meetings, too, so that we can jail some of these crooks who have stolen our constitutional and God-given rights?

The latest bit of news, and an excuse for not drilling for oil in the United States, is that gas prices would still be high considering the fact that teachers' pensions, etc. are invested in big oil. The other excuse is that our oil prices would have to conform to whatever the World Trade Organization says. If America drills, it would still have to let the Red Chinese and other countries building industries – thanks to us – get first dibs at the oil – our oil.

To that I say the hell with investors and the hell with the World Trade Organization. Let's get rid of the WTO, the globalists and their 3,500 Red Chinese front companies, and start building America for Americans and legal immigrants. Let's start drilling, and if the big oil companies can't do it, then we'll get men and women who can! Let's take our America back.

In all of my thirty years of research and information gathering, I have Never Never received any support about the sex agenda being forced on our children in schools and other venues, from either of the two hyphenated Americans. Jews and blacks (like Faye Wattleton, former head of Planned Parenthood) are apparently not concerned at all, or they would have made their concerns known.

So – when Americans talk about our values, eliminate the hyphenated Americans; they're living in a world I'd rather innocent children escaped.

Poor children today are being forced to talk about sex earlier and earlier. Clothing is disgracefully revealing. Ads are geared to involve children in romance, with ten-year-olds holding hands. Abercrombie and Fitch represents the money-hungry pornographers waiting for children to grow up in order to use and abuse.

Educators, like Dr. Wendy Mogel, Ph.D. "The Blessings of a Skinned Knee" (Smerconish Show), are typical of the brash no-accounts children face every day. They are not being motivated to be their best, despite home conditions. The wrong people are behind the scenes, and we need a light shone on them. We had Madonna with the crucifix between her legs crying, "I'm a virgin;" we don't need Hanna Montana to expose her love life to sub-teens. If Dr. Mogel represents teachings from the Talmud, it's not American.

These are NOT American values of the past; they are New Values from greedy moneymakers. It's a crime!

About the Author

Born and raised in Philadelphia, Pennsylvania, the author was one of six children born to Italian immigrants. Her four brothers all served in the military. She had an Ivy League education, and for many years taught in the public school system. She married an Iranian surgeon and raised three children, serving an active role in their education. The former teacher, talk show host, and chef, is now a grandmother who worries about the future of her grandchildren. During her more than three decades of political activism covering education, as well as local and state politics, the author observed a pattern of corruption and secrecy originating in the state legislatures and moving on through Congress and the White House, all servants of their corporate benefactors who spend our hard-earned money in every country but America. The legacy we leave to our grandchildren is one of joblessness, open borders with drugs and violence, and servitude to the masters of the New World Order. <u>Don't Tread on Me</u> was written for everyone who has witnessed the decline of our culture, loss of jobs, failure of the educational system and the arrogance of our elected officials. <u>Don't Tread on Me</u> exposes the con games of the government and the media, and offers solutions to this takeover of our liberties and Republic.